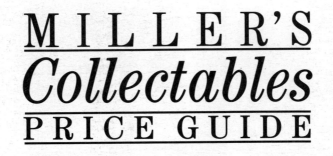

MILLER'S
Collectables
PRICE GUIDE

Don't Throw Away A Fortune!
Invest In
Miller's Price Guides

Please send me the following editions

❏ **Miller's Antiques Price Guide 1997** - £21.99
❏ **Miller's Classic Motorcycles Price Guide 1997/98** - £12.99
❏ **Miller's Collectors Cars Price Guide 1997/98** - £19.99
❏ **Miller's Pine & Country Furniture Buyer's Guide** - £18.99
❏ **Miller's Art Nouveau & Art Deco Buyer's Guide** - £18.99

If you do not wish your name to be used by Miller's or other carefully selected organisations for promotional purposes, please tick this box ❏

I enclose my cheque/postal order for £.................post free (UK only)
Please make cheques payable to *'Reed Books'*
or please debit my Access/Visa/Amex/Diners Club account number

Expiry Date............/............

NAME *Title   Initial   Surname*

ADDRESS

Postcode

SIGNATURE

MILLER'S
Collectables
PRICE GUIDE

Consultant
Judith Miller

General Editor
Madeleine Marsh

1997–98
(Volume IX)

MILLER'S COLLECTABLES PRICE GUIDE 1997–98

Compiled, edited and designed by
Miller's Publications Ltd
The Cellars, High Street
Tenterden, Kent TN30 6BN
Telephone: 01580 766411

Consultant: Judith Miller

General Editor: Madeleine Marsh
Editorial & Production Co-ordinator: Sue Boyd
Editorial Assistants: Gillian Judd, Marion Rickman, Melinda Williams, Jo Wood
Production Assistants: Gillian Charles, Karen Taylor
Design: Kari Reeves, Shirley Reeves, Matthew Leppard
Photographic Co-ordinator and Advertising Executive: Elizabeth Smith
Index compiled by: Hilary Bird, Goudhurst, Kent
Additional photography: Ian Booth, Roy Farthing, Robin Saker

First published in Great Britain in 1997 by Miller's
an imprint of Reed Consumer Books Limited

This edition published in 1998 by Chancellor Press
an imprint of Reed Consumer Books Limited
Michelin House, 81 Fulham Road
London SW3 6RB

© 1997 Reed Consumer Books Limited
Reprinted 1997

A CIP catalogue record for this book is
available from the British Library

ISBN 0 753700 514

Bromide output: Perfect Image, Hurst Green, E. Sussex
Illustrations: G. H. Graphics, St Leonard's-on-Sea, E. Sussex
Colour origination: Scantrans, Singapore
Printed and bound in England by William Clowes Ltd,
Beccles and London

Miller's is a registered trademark of
Reed Consumer Books Ltd

HOW TO USE THIS BOOK

I t is our aim to make this guide easy to use. In order to find a particular item, consult the contents list on page 7 to find the main heading, for example, Ceramics. Having located your area of interest, you will find that larger sections have been sub-divided. If you are looking for a particular maker, designer or craftsman, consult the index which starts on page 487.

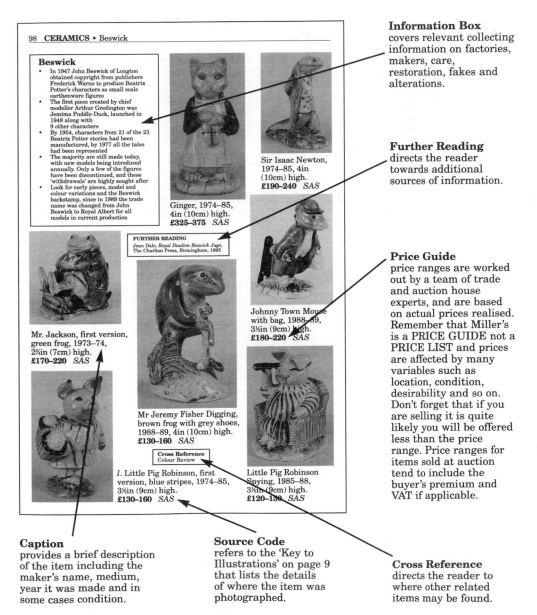

98 CERAMICS • Beswick

Beswick
- In 1947 John Beswick of Longton obtained copyright from publishers Frederick Warne to produce Beatrix Potter's characters as small scale earthenware figures
- The first piece created by chief modeller Arthur Gredington was Jemima Puddle-Duck, launched in 1948 along with 9 other characters
- By 1954, characters from 21 of the 23 Beatrix Potter stories had been manufactured, by 1977 all the tales had been represented
- The majority are still made today, with new models being introduced annually. Only a few of the figures have been discontinued, and these 'withdrawals' are highly sought after
- Look for early pieces, model and colour variations and the Beswick backstamp, since in 1989 the trade name was changed from John Beswick to Royal Albert for all models in current production

Sir Isaac Newton, 1974–85, 4in (10cm) high. **£190–240** *SAS*

Ginger, 1974–85, 4in (10cm) high. **£325–375** *SAS*

FURTHER READING
Jean Dale, *Royal Doulton Beswick Jugs*, The Charlton Press, Birmingham, 1995

Mr. Jackson, first version, green frog, 1973–74, 2¾in (7cm) high. **£170–220** *SAS*

Johnny Town Mouse with bag, 1988–89, 3½in (9cm) high. **£180–220** *SAS*

Mr Jeremy Fisher Digging, brown frog with grey shoes, 1988–89, 4in (10cm) high. **£130–160** *SAS*

Cross Reference
Colour Review

l. Little Pig Robinson, first version, blue stripes, 1974–85, 3½in (9cm) high. **£130–160** *SAS*

Little Pig Robinson Spying, 1985–88, 3½in (9cm) high. **£120–150** *SAS*

Information Box covers relevant collecting information on factories, makers, care, restoration, fakes and alterations.

Further Reading directs the reader towards additional sources of information.

Price Guide price ranges are worked out by a team of trade and auction house experts, and are based on actual prices realised. Remember that Miller's is a PRICE GUIDE not a PRICE LIST and prices are affected by many variables such as location, condition, desirability and so on. Don't forget that if you are selling it is quite likely you will be offered less than the price range. Price ranges for items sold at auction tend to include the buyer's premium and VAT if applicable.

Caption provides a brief description of the item including the maker's name, medium, year it was made and in some cases condition.

Source Code refers to the 'Key to Illustrations' on page 9 that lists the details of where the item was photographed.

Cross Reference directs the reader to where other related items may be found.

CONTENTS

ACKNOWLEDGEMENTS

We would like to acknowledge the great assistance given by our consultants who are listed below. We would also like to extend our thanks to all the auction houses, their press offices, dealers and collectors who have assisted us in the production of this book.

DAVID BARRINGTON, Yesterday Child, Angel Arcade, 128 Islington High St, London N1 8EG (**Dolls**)

BRIAN BATES, Tel: 01782 680667 (**Amusement & Slot Machines**)

BEVERLEY, 30 Church St, Marylebone, London NW8 8EP (**Chintz Ware**)

ALAN BLAKEMAN, BBR, Elsecar Heritage Centre, Wath Rd, Elsecar, Barnsley, S. Yorks S74 8HF (**Advertising, Packaging & Bottles**)

ROY BUTLER, Wallis & Wallis, West St Auction Rooms, Lewes, Sussex BN7 2NJ (**Militaria**)

RICHARD DOWSON, PO Box 55, Cranbrook, Kent TN17 3ZU (**Fishing**)

JULIETTE EDWARDS, PO Box 131, Woking, Surrey GU24 9YR (**Compacts**)

CHRISTOPHER EIMER, PO Box 352, London NW11 7RF (**Medals**)

CLIFFORD ELMER, 8 Balmoral Avenue, Cheadle Hulme, Cheadle, Cheshire SK8 5EQ (**Crime Books**)

MICHAEL GERMAN, 38B Kensington Church Street, London W8 4BX (**Walking Sticks**)

STUART HEGGIE, 14 The Borough, Canterbury, Kent CT1 2DR (**Photographs/Cameras**)

ANDREW HILTON, Special Auction Services, The Coach House, Midgham Park, Reading RG7 5UG (**Commemorative**)

KEITH HOLLENDER, Scripophily Shop, Herzog Hollender Phillips & Co, Britannia Hotel, Grosvenor Square, London W1A 3AN (**Scripophily**)

STEVE HUNT, Antique Amusement Co, Mill Lane, Swaffham Bulbeck, Cambs CB5 0NF (**Amusement Machines**)

JOHN JENKINS, Vintage Cameras Ltd, 254–256 Kirkdale, Sydenham, London SE26 4NL (**Cameras**)

THELMA JOHNS, The Old Button Shop, Lychett Minster, Dorset BH16 6JF (**Dorset Buttons**)

GRAHAM & ALVA KEY, PO Box 387, Stafford ST16 3RX (**Denby**)

PHILIP KNIGHTON, The Gramophone Man, North Street, Wellington, Somerset TA21 8LT (**Radios & TVs**)

JULIE LOUGHNAM, 18 Beauchamp Place, London SW3 1NP (**Julip Toys**)

HARRY LYON, New Century Antiques, 69 Kensington Church Street, London W8 4DB (**Rye Pottery and Christopher Dresser**)

JOSIE MARSDEN, Magic Lanterns, By George Antiques Centre, 23 George Street, St Albans, Herts AL3 4ES (**Lighting**)

BOB MOORE, USSR Collectors' Club, PO Box 6, Virginia Water, Surrey GU25 4YU (**Russian Ceramics**)

JACQUELINE OOSTHUIZEN, 23 Cale Street, London SW3 3QR (**Staffordshire Pottery**)

GAVIN PAYNE, The Old Granary, Battlesbridge Antique Centre, Nr Wickford, Essex SS11 7RF (**Telephones**)

PATRICIA PENROSE, c/o Rokit Tel: 0171 267 3046 (**Denim**)

MALCOLM PHILLIPS, Comic Book Postal Auctions, 40–42 Osnaburgh Street, London NW1 3ND (**Comics**)

TOM & ANNETTE POWER, The Collector, 9 Church Street, Marylebone, London NW8 8EE (**Royal Doulton, Cottages and Pendelfins**)

MAUREEN STANFORD, Childhood Memories, Farnham Antique Centre, 27 South Street, Farnham, Surrey GU9 7QU (**Toys**)

ALAN TONKS, Solent Railwayana Auctions, Tel: 01489 578093/584633 (**Railwayana**)

TREVOR VENNETT-SMITH, 11 Nottingham Road, Gotham, Nottingham NG11 0HE (**Ephemera**)

DAVID WELLS, 7 Monmouth Court, Ringwood, Hants BH24 1H8 (**Dinky Toys**)

NIGEL WILLIAMS, 22 & 25 Cecil Court, London WC2N 4EZ (**Books**)

TONY WOOLVEN, The British Watch & Clock Collectors Association, 5 Cathedral Lane, Truro, Cornwall TR1 2QS (**Watches**)

JOHN WOOSTER, Albert's Cigarette Cards, 113 London Road, Twickenham, Middx TW1 1EE (**Cigarette Cards**)

DEREK WYNDHAM-PARSONS, West Midlands (**Bagley Glass**)

KEY TO ILLUSTRATIONS

Each illustration and descriptive caption is accompanied by a letter code. By referring to the following list of Auctioneers (denoted by *), Dealers (•) and Clubs (§), the source of any item may be immediately determined. Please note that the inclusion of a collectable in this book does not guarantee that the item, or any similar item, is available for sale from the contributor. Advertisers in this year's directory are denoted by (†).

If you require a valuation for an item, it is advisable to check whether the dealer or specialist will carry out this service and if there is a charge. Please mention Miller's when making an enquiry. Having found a specialist who will carry out your valuation it is best to send a photograph and description of the item to the specialist together with a stamped addressed envelope for the reply. A valuation by telephone is not possible.

Most dealers are only too happy to help you with your enquiry, however, they are very busy people and consideration of the above points would be welcomed.

AAV * Academy Auctioneers & Valuers, Northcote House, Northcote Avenue, Ealing, London W5 3UR Tel: 0181 579 7466

ABr • Avril Brown, Great Western Antique Centre, Stand 25, Bartlett Street, Bath, Avon BA1 2QZ Tel: 01225 428731

ACA • Acorn Antiques, Sheep Street, Stow-on-the-Wold, Glos GL54 1AA Tel: 01451 831519

ACC • † Albert's Cigarette Card Specialists, 113 London Road, Twickenham, Middlesex TW1 1EE Tel: 0181 891 3067

Ada • Dale Adams, Fountain Antiques Market, 6 Bladud Buildings, Bath, Avon BA1 5LS Tel: 01225 339104

ADT * ADT Auctions Ltd, Classic & Historic Automobile Division, Blackbushe Airport, Blackwater, Camberley, Surrey GU17 9LG Tel: 01252 878555

AEF • A & E Foster, Little Heysham, Naphill, Bucks HP14 4SU Tel: 01494 562024

AGA * † Angling Auctions, PO Box 2095, London W12 8RU Tel: 0181 749 4175

AH * Andrew Hartley, Victoria Hall Salerooms, Little Lane, Ilkley, Yorkshire LS29 8EA Tel: 01943 816363

AL • † Ann Lingard, Ropewalk Antiques, Ropewalk, Rye, Sussex TN31 7NA Tel: 01797 223486

ALI • Alien Enterprises, Stratford Model Centre, The Minories, Stratford-upon-Avon, Warwickshire CV37 6QW Tel: 01789 299701

AMc • † Antique Amusement Co, Mill Lane, Swaffham Bulbeck, Cambs CB5 0NF Tel: 01223 813041/0802 666755

AmD • † Amelia Dolls, Pantiles Spa Antiques, The Pantiles, Tunbridge Wells, Kent TN4 8HE Tel: 01892 541377/01342 713223

AnA • Animal Antiques. Fairs only Tel: 01733 203224

AND • Joan & Bob Anderson, Middlesex Tel: 0181 572 4328

ANP • Annette Power, The Collector, 9 Church Street, Marylebone, London NW8 8EE Tel: 0171 706 4586

AnS • The Antique Shop, 30 Henley Street, Stratford-upon-Avon, Warwicks CV37 6QW Tel: 01789 292485

APO • Apollo Antiques Ltd, The Saltisford, Birmingham Road, Warwick, CV34 4TD Tel: 01926 494746

ARo • Alvin Ross, Alfies Antique Market, Stand G9-11, 13-25 Church Street, Marylebone, London NW8 8DT Tel: 0171 723 1513

ASA • A. S. Antiques, 26 Broad Street, Pendleton, Salford, Manchester M6 5BY Tel: 0161 737 5938

ASB • Andrew Spencer Bottomley, The Coach House, Thongsbridge, Holmfirth, Yorkshire HD7 2TT Tel: 01484 685234

ASP • John Aspley Antiques

ATF A. T. Fletcher, (Enthusiast & Private Collector), Lancashire

ATI • Antigo, Alfies Antique Market, Unit S012, 13-25 Church Street, Marylebone, London NW8 8DT Tel: 0958 28 36 23

AUC * Auction Centres Bristol, Michael Shorthall, Prewett Street, Redcliffe, Bristol, Avon BS1 6TB Tel: 0117 926 5996

AXT Alexis F. J. Turner, The Workshop Gallery, 144a Bridge Road, East Moseley, Surrey KT8 9HW Tel: 0181 542 5926

B * Boardman Fine Art Auctioneers, Station Road Corner, Haverhill, Suffolk CB9 0EY Tel: 01440 730414

B&F • Bears & Friends, 41 Meeting House Lane, The Lanes, Brighton, Sussex BN1 1HB Tel: 01273 202940

BaH Calamus, The Shambles, Sevenoaks, Kent TN13 1AL Tel: 01732 740603

BAL • † A. H. Baldwin & Sons Ltd, Numismatists, 11 Adelphi Terrace, London WC2N 6BJ Tel: 0171 930 6879

Bar • Chris Barge Antiques, 5 Southside Place, Inverness, Scotland IV2 3JF Tel: 01463 230128

BAS • Brighton Architectural Salvage, 33 Gloucester Road, Brighton, Sussex BN1 4AQ Tel: 01273 681656

BB • † Brian Bates, Staffordshire Tel: 01782 680667

BBR * BBR, Elsecar Heritage Centre, Wath Road, Elsecar, Barnsley, Yorkshire S74 8HJ Tel: 01226 745156

BCO • British Collectables, 1st Floor, 9 Georgian Village, Camden Passage, Islington, London N1 8DU Tel: 0171 359 4560

Bea * Bearnes, Rainbow, Avenue Road, Torquay, Devon TQ2 5TG Tel: 01803 296277

Bea(E) * Bearnes, St Edmund's Court, Okehampton Street, Exeter, Devon EX4 1DU Tel: 01392 422800

Ber • Berry Antiques, Kay Parkin, The Old Butcher's Shop, Goudhurst, Kent TN17 1AE Tel: 01580 212115

BET • Beth, GO43-44, Alfies Antique Market, 13-25 Church Street, Marylebone, London NW8 8DT Tel: 0171 723 5613

BEV • † Beverley, 30 Church Street, Marylebone, London NW8 8EP Tel: 0171 262 1576

BGA • By George Antique Centre, 23 George Street, St Albans, Herts AL3 4ES Tel: 01727 853032

BGA(K) • Kohlberg Antiques, By George Antique Centre, 23 George Street, St Albans, Herts AL3 4ES Tel: 01727 853032

BGA(R)• Robby's Antiques, 23 George Street,
St Albans, Hertfordshire AL3 4ES
Tel: 01727 853032

BKK • Bona Arts Decorative, 19 Princes Mead
Shopping Centre, Farnborough, Hampshire
GU14 7TJ Tel: 01252 372188

BKS * Robert Brooks (Auctioneers) Ltd,
81 Westside, London SW4 9AY
Tel: 0171 228 8000

Bon * Bonhams, Montpelier Street, Knightsbridge,
London SW7 1HH Tel: 0171 393 3900

BRA • Billiard Room Antiques, The Old School,
Church Lane, Chilcompton, Bath, Somerset
BA3 4HP Tel: 01761 232839

Bri * Bristol Auction Rooms, St John's Place,
Apsley Road, Clifton, Bristol,
Avon BS8 2ST Tel: 0117 973 7201

BS • Below Stairs, 103 High Street, Hungerford,
Berkshire RG17 0NB Tel: 01488 682317

BSA • Bartlett Street Antiques, 5/10 Bartlett
Street, Bath, Avon BA1 2QZ
Tel: 01225 446322/310457

BTA • Brian Taylor Antiques, 24 Molesworth Road,
Plymouth, Devon PL1 5LZ
Tel: 01752 569061

BWC § British Watch & Clock Collectors
Association, 5 Cathedral Lane, Truro,
Cornwall TR1 2QS Tel: 01872 41953

BWe * Biddle and Webb Ltd, Ladywood Middleway,
Birmingham, West Midlands B16 0PP
Tel: 0121 455 8042

ByI • Bygones of Ireland, Westport Antiques
Centre, Lodge Road, Westport, County
Mayo, Ireland Tel: 00 353 98 26132

CARS • C.A.R.S. (Classic Automobilia & Regalia
Specialists), 4-4a Chapel Terrace Mews,
Kemp Town, Brighton, Sussex BN2 1HU
Tel: 01273 60 1960

CaL • Chris & Liz, No 6 First Floor, Georgian
Village, Camden Passage, London N1 8DU
Tel: 01206 212183

CB • Christine Bridge Antiques, 78 Castelnau,
London SW13 9EX Tel: 0181 741 5501

CBP * † Comic Book Postal Auctions Ltd, 40-42
Osnaburgh Street, London NW1 3ND
Tel: 0171 586 3007

CBu • Christopher Buck Antiques,
56-60 Sandgate High Street, Folkestone,
Kent CT20 3AP Tel: 01303 221229

CCC • † Crested China Co, The Station House,
Driffield, Yorkshire YO25 7PY
Tel: 01377 257042

CCO • Collectable Costume, The Great Western
Antique Centre, Bartlett Street, Bath, Avon
BA1 2QZ Tel: 01225 428731

CEB • † Clifford Elmer Books, 8 Balmoral Avenue,
Cheadle Hulme, Cheadle, Cheshire SK8 5EQ
Tel: 0161 485 7064

CFA • Cambridge Fine Art, Priesthouse,
33 Church Street, Little Shelford, Cambridge,
Cambs CB2 5HG Tel: 01223 842866

CLW • Collectors World, Alfies Antique Market,
Stand G143, 13-25 Church Street,
London NW8 8DT Tel: 0171 286 1255

CMF • † Childhood Memories, The Farnham Antique
Centre, 27 South Street, Farnham, Surrey
GU9 7QU Tel: 01252 724475

CMO • Brian Cargin & Chris Morley, Ginnell
Antiques Gallery, 18-22 Lloyd Street,
Manchester M2 5WA Tel: 0161 833 9037

CNY * Christie Manson & Woods International Inc,
502 Park Avenue, (including Christie's East),
New York, NY 10022 USA Tel: (212) 546 1000

COB • † Cobwebs, 78 Northam Road, Southampton,
Hampshire SO2 0PB Tel: 01703 227458

COT • Cottage Antiques, Bakewell & Woburn
Antiques Centres, Bucks Tel: 01283 562670

CP • Cat Pottery, 1 Grammar School Road,
North Walsham, Norfolk NR28 9JH
Tel: 01692 402962

CS • † Christopher Sykes, The Old Parsonage,
Woburn, Milton Keynes, Beds MK17 9QM
Tel: 01525 290259

CSA • † Church Street Antiques, 10 Church Street,
Godalming, Surrey GU7 1EH
Tel: 01483 860894

CSK * † Christie's South Kensington Ltd,
85 Old Brompton Road, London SW7 3LD
Tel: 0171 581 7611

CtC • Clinton Cards, 8 High Street, Tenterden,
Kent TN30 6AP Tel: 01580 762090

CTO • † Collector's Corner, Tudor House,
29-31 Lower Bridge Street, Chester,
Cheshire CH1 1RS Tel: 01260 270429

CWA • Catherine Wallis, F058, Alfies Antique
Market, 13-25 Church Street, Marylebone,
London NW8 8DT

DA * Dee, Atkinson & Harrison, The Exchange
Saleroom, Driffield, Yorkshire YO25 7LD
Tel: 01377 253151

DAF • Arts Decoratifs, 18-20 Suffolk Parade,
Cheltenham, Glos GL50 2AE
Tel: 01242 512774

DBr • David Brown, 23 Claude Street, Larkhall,
Lanarkshire, Scotland ML9 2BU
Tel: 01555 880333

DgC • Dragonlee Collectables, Maidstone, Kent
Tel: 01622 202879

DGP • Design Goes Pop, 34-36 Oldham Street,
Manchester M1 1JN Tel: 0161 237 9688

DN * Dreweatt Neate, Donnington Priory,
Donnington, Newbury, Berkshire RG13 2JE
Tel: 01635 31234

Do • Dodo, Liz Farrow, Stand F037,
Alfies Antique Market, 13-25 Church Street,
London NW8 8DT Tel: 0171 706 1545

DW * † Dominic Winter Book Auctions,
The Old School, Maxwell Street, Swindon,
Wiltshire SN1 5DR Tel: 01793 611340

E * Ewbank, Burnt Common Auction Room,
London Road, Send, Woking,
Surrey GU23 7LN Tel: 01483 223101

ED • Elite Designs, Sussex Tel: 01424 434856

EIM • † Christopher Eimer, PO Box 352,
London NW11 7RF Tel: 0181 458 9933

ELG • † Enid Lawson Gallery, 36a Kensington Church
Street, London W8 4BX Tel: 0171 937 8444

EP * Evans & Partridge, John Partridge,
Agriculture House, High Street, Stockbridge,
Hampshire SO20 6HF Tel: 01264 810702

ET • Early Technology, 84 West Bow, Edinburgh,
Scotland EH1 2HH Tel: 0131 226 1132

EUR • Eureka Antiques, (appointment only),
Cheshire Tel: 0161 941 5453

FAL • Falstaff Antiques (Motor Museum),
63-67 High Street, Rolvenden,
Kent TN17 4LP Tel: 01580 241234

FAM • Fountain Antiques Market, 6 Bladud
Buildings, The Paragon, Bath,
Avon BA1 5LS Tel: 01225 339104

FD • Frank Dux Antiques, 33 Belvedere, Bath,
Avon BA1 5HR Tel: 01225 312367

FLD • Flying Duck, 320/322 Creek Road, Greenwich,
London SE10 9SW Tel: 0181 858 1964

FMN • † Forget Me Knot, Over the Moon,
27 High Street, St Albans, Hertfordshire
Tel: 01727 848907/01923 261172

FOX • Foxhole Antiques, Swan & Foxhole, Albert
House, Stone Street, Cranbrook, Kent
Tel: 01580 712720

G&CC • † Goss & Crested China Ltd, 62 Murray Road, Horndean, Hampshire PO8 9JL Tel: 01705 597440

GAK * G. A. Key, 8 Market Place, Aylsham, Norfolk NR11 6EH Tel: 01263 733195

Gam * Clarke & Gammon, The Guildford Auction Rooms, Bedford Road, Guildford, Surrey GU1 4SJ Tel: 01483 66458

GAS • Gasson Antiques, PO Box 11, Cranleigh, Surrey GU6 8YY Tel: 01483 277476

GEM • Gem Antiques, 28 London Road, Sevenoaks, Kent TN13 1AP Tel: 01732 743540

GKR • † GKR Bonds Ltd, PO Box 1, Kelvedon, Essex CO5 9EH Tel: 01376 571711

GL • Gordon Litherland, 25 Stapenhill Road, Burton-on-Trent, Staffordshire DE15 9AE Tel: 01283 567213

GLA • Glasform Ltd, 123 Talbot Road, Blackpool, Lancashire FY1 3QY Tel: 01253 695849

GLN • Glenville Antiques, 120 High Street, Yatton, Avon BS19 4DH Tel: 01934 832284

GM • † The Gramophone Man, North Street, Wellington, Somerset TA21 8LT Tel: 01823 661618

GN • Gillian Neale Antiques, PO Box 247, Aylesbury, Bucks HP20 1JZ Tel: 01296 23754

GOO • Gooday Gallery, 20 Richmond Hill, Richmond, Surrey TW10 6QX Tel: 0181 940 8652

GPL • Grand Prix Legends, London W10 6BR Tel: 0171 229 7399

Gre • † Tony Greenwood, Warwick Antique Centre, 20-22 High Street, Warwick CV34 4AX Tel: 01926 495704

GRo • Geoffrey Robinson, Alfies Antique Market, 13-25 Church Street, Marylebone, London NW8 8DT Tel: 0171 723 0449

GWA • † Great Western Antiques, Torre Station, Newton Road, Torquay, Devon TQ5 2DD Tel: 01803 200551

HAK • Paul Haskell, Kent Tel: 01634 669362

HAN • Hannah, Bucks Tel: 01844 237899 Mobile 0831 800774

HB • † Harrington Bros, The Chelsea Antique Market, 253 Kings Road, London SW3 5EL Tel: 0171 352 5689/1720

HCH * Hobbs & Chambers, Market Place, Cirencester, Glos GL7 1QQ Tel: 01285 654736

HEA • Peter Hearnden, Kent (appointment only) Tel: 01634 374132

HEG • † Stuart Heggie, 14 The Borough, Northgate, Canterbury, Kent CT1 2DR Tel: 01227 470422

HEI • Heirloom Antiques, 68 High Street, Tenterden, Kent TN30 6AU Tel: 01580 765535

HEM • The Hemswell Antiques Centre, Caenby Corner Estate, Hemswell Cliff, Gainsborough, Lincolnshire DN21 5TJ Tel: 01427 668389

HHa • Henry Hay, Alfies Antique Market, Stand S54, 13-25 Church Street, Marylebone, London NW8 8DT Tel: 0171 723 6105

HIK • Noel Hickey, Stand F054, Alfies Antique Market, 13-25 Church Street, Marylebone, London NW8 8DT Tel: 0171 723 0678

HnT • Heads n' Tails, Bourne House, 41 Church Street, Wiveliscombe, Taunton, Somerset TA4 2LT Tel: 01984 623097

HO • Angela Hone, The Garth, Mill Road, Marlow, Bucks SL7 1QB Tel: 01628 484170

HOA • Bob Hoare, Pine Antiques, Unit Q, Phoenix Place, North Street, Lewes, Sussex BN7 2DQ Tel: 01273 480557

HOB • † Hobday Toys, 44 High Street, Northwood, Middlesex HA6 2XY Tel: 01923 820115

HOLL * Dreweatt Neate Holloways, 49 Parsons Street, Banbury, Oxfordshire OX16 8PF Tel: 01295 253197

Hs • Hamiltons, 2 The Cellars, High Street, Tenterden, Kent TN30 6BN Tel: 01580 762010

HUX • David Huxtable, Alfies Antique Market, Stand S03/05 (Top Floor), 13-25 Church Street, Marylebone, London NW8 8DT Tel: 0171 724 2200

IW • † Islwyn Watkins, 1 High Street, Knighton, Powys, Wales LD7 1AT Tel: 01547 520145

JAd * James Adam & Sons, 26 St Stephen's Green, Dublin 2, Ireland Tel: 00 3531 676 0261/661 3655

JAK • Clive & Lynne Jackson, Glos Tel: 01242 254375 Mobile 0589 715275

JBB • Jessie's Button Box, Great Western Antique Centre, Bartlett Street, Bath, Avon BA1 2QZ Tel: 01225 310388

JBL • Judi Bland, Durham House Antique Centre, Sheep Street, Stow-on-the-Wold, Glos GL54 1AA Tel: 01451 870404/01295 811292

JDC • J & D Collectables, Kent Tel: 01227 452873

JEN • Jenies, Stand S57, Alfies Antique Market, 13-25 Church Street, London NW8 8DT Tel: 0171 723 2548

JES • John Jesse, 160 Kensington Church Street, London W8 4BN Tel: 0171 229 0312

JFG • Jafar Gallery, 24H Grays in the Mews, Davis Mews, London W1Y 1AR Tel: 0171 409 7919/0181 300 2727

JLo • Julie Loghnan, 18 Beauchamp Place, Knightsbridge, London SW3 1NP Tel: 0171 589 0867

JMC • J & M Collectables, Kent Tel: 01580 891657

JO • † Jacqueline Oosthuizen, 23 Cale Street, London SW3 3QR Tel: 0171 352 6071

JON • Jon Bird, Kent Tel: 01227 273952

JPr • Joanna Proops Antiques and Textiles, Belvedere, Bath, Avon BA1 2QP

JR • John Rastall, Stall GO47/8, Alfies Antique Market, 13-25 Church Street, London NW8 8DT Tel: 0171 723 0449

KES • † Keystones, PO Box 387, Stafford, ST16 3RX Tel: 01785 256648

KNG • Kenneth Norton-Grant, Alfies Antique Market, 13-25 Church Street, Marylebone, London NW8 8DT Tel: 0171 723 1370

L * Lawrence Fine Art Auctioneers, South Street, Crewkerne, Somerset TA18 8AB Tel: 01460 73041

L&E * Locke & England, Black Horse Agencies, 18 Guy Street, Leamington Spa, Warwickshire CV32 4RT Tel: 01926 889100

LA • Lane Antiques, 40 Pittshanger Lane, Ealing, London W5 1QY Tel: 0181 810 8090

LB • Lace Basket, 116 High Street, Tenterden, Kent TN30 6HT Tel: 01580 763923/763664

LBr • † Lynda Brine, Great Western Antique Centre, Bartlett Street, Bath, Avon BA1 2QZ Tel: 01225 837932

LEG • † Legend Lane, Albion Mill, London Road, Macclesfield, Cheshire SK11 7SQ Tel: 01625 424661

LHB • Gallery 'Les Hommes Bleus', Bartlett Street Antique Centre, 5/10 Bartlett Street, Bath, Avon BA1 2QZ Tel: 01225 316606

LIB • Libra Antiques, 81 London Road, Hurst Green, Etchingham, Sussex TN19 7PN Tel: 01580 860569

LM • † The London Mint, c/o Klaus Kobec Int Ltd, 108 Manchester Road, Chorlton-cum-Hardy, M21 9TX Tel: 0161 881 1659

MAP • † Marine Art Posters, 71 Harbour Way, Merchants Landing, Victoria Dock, Port of Hull, Humberside HU9 1PL Tel: 01482 321173

MAT * Christopher Matthews, 23 Mount Street, Harrogate, Yorkshire HG2 8DQ Tel: 01423 871756

MB • † Mostly Boxes, 92 High Street, Eton, Berkshire SL4 6AF Tel: 01753 858470

MCA * Mervyn Carey, Twysden Cottage, Benenden, Cranbrook, Kent TN17 4LD Tel: 01580 240283

MGC • † Midlands Commemoratives, The Old Cornmarket Antique Centre, 70 Market Place, Warwick, CV34 4SO Tel: 01926 419119

MGe • Michael C. German, 38B Kensington Church Street, London W8 8EP Tel: 0171 937 2771

MJW • Mark J. West, Cobb Antiques Ltd, 39a High Street, Wimbledon Village, London SW19 5YX Tel: 0181 946 2811

ML • † Magic Lantern (Josie Marsden), By George Antique Centre, 23 George Street, St Albans, Herts AL3 4ES Tel: 01727 853032

MLa • Marion Langham, London Tel: 0171 730 1002

MR * † Martyn Rowe, Truro Auction Centre, Calenick Street, Truro, Cornwall TR1 2SG Tel: 01872 260020

MRo • † Mike Roberts, 4416 Foxfire Way, Fort Worth, Texas, 76133, USA Tel: 001 817 294 2133

MRT • Mark Rees Tools, Avon Tel: 01225 837031

MRW • Malcolm Russ-Welch, 59 Lime Avenue, Leamington Spa, Warwickshire CV32 7DE Tel: 01926 882026

MSA • M. S. Antiques, 25a Holland Street, Kensington, London W8 4NA Tel: 0171 937 0793

MSB • Marilyn and Sheila Brass, PO Box 380503, Cambridge, MA 02238-0503, USA Tel: 617 491 6064 Photos: Dennis O'Reilly

MSh • Manfred Schotten, The Crypt Antiques, 109 High Street, Burford, Oxfordshire OX18 4RG Tel: 01993 822302

MUR • † Murray Cards (International) Ltd, 51 Watford Way, Hendon Central, London NW4 3JH Tel: 0181 202 5688

NAR • † Colin Narbeth & Son Ltd, 20 Cecil Court, Leicester Square, London WC2N 4HE Tel: 0171 379 6975

NB • Nicolaus Boston, Kensington Church Street Antiques Centre, 58-60 Kensington Church Street, London W8 4DB Tel: 0171 376 0425

NCA • † New Century, 69 Kensington Church Street, London W8 4DB Tel: 0171 937 2410

ND * Nock Deighton, Livestock & Auction Centre, Tasley, Bridgnorth, Shropshire WV16 4DB Tel: 01746 762666

No7 • No. 7 Antiques, 7 Nantwich Road, Woore, Shropshire CW3 9SA Tel: 01630 647118

NOS • Nostalgia Comics, 14-16 Smallbrook Queensway, City Centre, Birmingham, B5 4EN Tel: 0121 643 0143

NTM † Nostalgia Toy Museum, High Street, Godshill, Isle of Wight PO38 3HZ Tel: 01983 730055

NuP • Nubern Products, PO Box 79, Beckenham, Kent BR3 2HJ

NW • Nigel Williams Rare Books, 22 & 25 Cecil Court, London WC2N 4HE Tel: 0171 836 7757

NWi • Neil Wilcox, 113 Strawberry Vale, Twickenham, Middlesex TW1 4SJ Tel: 0181 892 5858

OBS • The Old Button Shop, Lytchett Minster, Dorset BH16 6JF Tel: 01202 622169

OD • † Offa's Dyke Antique Centre, 4 High Street, Knighton, Powys, Wales LD7 1AT Tel: 01547 528635

Oli/ WHB * Olivers, Olivers Rooms, Burkitts Lane, Sudbury, Suffolk CO10 6HB Tel: 01787 880305

OLM/ WLM • The Old Mill, High Street, Lamberhurst, Kent TN3 8EQ Tel: 01892 891196

ONS * Onslows, Metrostore, Townmead Road, London SW6 2RZ Tel: 0171 793 0240

OPH • Old Pine House, 16 Warwick Street, Leamington Spa, Warwickshire CV32 5LL Tel: 01926 470477

ORI • † Oriental Gallery, Glos Tel: 01451 830944

OTB • † Old Tackle Box, PO Box 55, Cranbrook, Kent TN17 3ZU Tel & Fax: 01580 713979

OTC • Old Telephone Company, The Old Granary, Battlesbridge Antiques Centre, Nr Wickford, Essex SS11 7RF Tel: 01245 400601

OTS • † The Old Toy Shop, 7 Monmouth Court, Ringwood, Hampshire BH24 1H8 Tel: 01425 476899

P * Phillips, Blenstock House, 101 New Bond Street, London W1Y 0AS Tel: 0171 629 6602

P(B) * Phillips, 1 Old King Street, Bath, Avon BA1 2JT Tel: 01225 310609

P(Ba) * Phillips Bayswater, 10 Salem Road, Bayswater, London W2 4DL Tel: 0171 229 9090

P(HSS)* Phillips (see **HSS**)

P(O) * Phillips, 39 Park End Street, Oxford, Oxfordshire OX1 1JD Tel: 01865 723524

PaM • † Puppets & Masks, 3 Kensington Mall, London W8 4EB Tel: 0171 221 8629

PBi • Peter Bird, 811 Christchurch Road, Boscombe, Dorset BH21 ITZ Tel: 01202 429111

PBr • Pamela Brooks, Leicestershire Tel: 0116 230 2625

PC Private Collection

PGH • Paris, 42A High Street, Tenterden, Kent TN30 6AR Tel: 01580 765328

PIA • † The Pianola Shop, 134 Islingword Road, Brighton, Sussex BN2 2SH Tel: 01273 608999

PP • † Poole Pottery, The Quay, Poole, Dorset BH15 1RF Tel: 01202 666200

PSA • Pantiles Spa Antiques, 4, 5, 6 Union House, The Pantiles, Tunbridge Wells, Kent TN4 8HE Tel: 01892 541377

QSA • Quiet Street Antiques, 3 Quiet Street, Bath, Avon BA1 2JG Tel: 01225 315727

RA • Roberts Antiques, Lancashire Tel: 01253 827798

RAR * Romsey Auction Rooms, 86 The Hundred, Romsey, Hampshire SO51 8BX Tel: 01794 513331

RAS • Royal Academy Shop, Royal Academy of Arts, Piccadilly, London W1V 0DS Tel: 0171 439 7438

RBA • † Roger Bradbury Antiques, Church Street, Coltishall, Norfolk NR12 7DJ Tel: 01603 737444

RBB * Russell, Baldwin & Bright, Fine Art Salerooms, Ryelands Road, Leominster, Hereford HR6 8NZ Tel: 01568 611166

REN • Paul & Karen Rennie, 13 Rugby Street, London WC1N 3QT Tel: 0171 405 0220

RIC • Rich Designs, 1 Shakespeare Street, Stratford-upon-Avon, Warwickshire CV37 6RN Tel: 01789 261612

RIS • Risky Business, 44 Church Street, Marylebone, London NW8 Tel: 0171 724 2194

ROK • Rokit Ltd, 225 Camden High Street, London NW1
Tel: 0171 267 3046/01273 672053

RUM • † Rumours, 10 The Mall, Upper Street, Camden Passage, Islington, London N1 0PD
Tel: 01582 873561

RUS • Trevor Russell, Staffordshire.
Tel: 01889 562009

RWB • Roy W. Bunn Antiques, 34-36 Church Street, Barnoldswick, Colne, Lancashire BB8 5UT
Tel: 01282 813703

S * Sotheby's, 34-35 New Bond Street, London W1A 2AA Tel: 0171 493 8080

S(NY) * Sotheby's, 1334 York Avenue, New York, NY 10021, USA Tel: 001 212 606 7000

S(S) * Sotheby's Sussex, Summers Place, Billingshurst, Sussex RH14 9AB
Tel: 01403 783933

SAS * † Special Auction Services, The Coach House, Midgham Park, Reading, Berks RG7 5UG
Tel: 0118 971 2949
Ronson photos: Courtesy of Douglas Howden

SBT • Steinberg & Tolkien Vintage & Designer Clothing, 193 Kings Road, London SW3 5EB
Tel: 0171 376 3660

SCA • Susie Cooper Ceramics (Art Deco), GO70-4 Alfies Antique Market, 13-25 Church Street, London NW8 8DT Tel: 0171 723 0449

SCR • † Scripophily Shop, Britannia Hotel, Grosvenor Square, London W1A 3AN
Tel: 0171 495 0580

SER • Serendipity, 168 High Street, Deal, Kent CT14 6BQ Tel: 01304 369165/366536

SHa • Shapiro & Co, Stand 380, Grays Antique Market, 58 Davies Street, London W1Y 1LB
Tel: 0171 491 2710

SnA • Snape Maltings Antique & Collectors Centre, Saxmundham, Suffolk IP17 1SR
Tel: 01728 688038

SOL • † Solent Railwayana Auctions, Community Centre, Mill Lane, Wickham, Fareham, Hampshire PO17 5AL Tel: 01489 578093

Som • Somervale Antiques, 6 Radstock Road, Midsomer Norton, Bath, Avon BA3 2AJ
Tel: 01761 412686

SPS • Sparkle at the Stables, Long Stables, Stables Market, Chalk Farm Road, Camden, London NW1 8AH Tel: 0181 809 3923
Only open Sat & Sun 10.30am–6.30pm

SPU • † Spurrier-Smith Antiques, 28, 39, 41 Church Street, Ashbourne, Derbyshire DE6 1AJ
Tel: 01335 343669/342198

SRA * † Sheffield Railwayana Auctions, 43 Little Norton Lane, Sheffield, Yorkshire S8 8GA
Tel: 0114 274 5085

SRC • Soviet Russia Collectables, PO Box 6, Virginia Water, Surrey GU25 4YU
Tel: 01344 843091

STE • † Stevenson Brothers, The Workshop, Ashford Road, Bethersden, Ashford, Kent TN26 3AP
Tel: 01233 820363

SUC • Succession, 18 Richmond Hill, Richmond, Surrey TW10 6QX Tel: 0181 940 6774

SUS • Susannah, 142/144 Walcot Street, Bath, Avon BA1 5BL Tel: 01225 445069

SW • Spinning Wheel Garage, Sheffield Road, Sheepbridge, Chesterfield, Derbyshire S41 9EH Tel: 01246 451772

SWB • † Sweetbriar Gallery, Robin Hood Lane, Helsby, Cheshire WA6 9NH Tel: 01928 723851

SWO * G. E. Sworder & Sons, 14 Cambridge Road, Stansted Mountfitchet, Essex CM24 8BZ
Tel: 01279 817778

TaB • The Tartan Bow, Suffolk.
Tel: 01379 783057

TAC • Tenterden Antiques Centre, 66-66a High Street, Tenterden, Kent, TN30 6AU
Tel: 01580 765655/765885

TAN • Tanglewood Antiques, Tanglewood Mills, Coke Street, Derby, Derbyshire DE1 1NE
Tel: 01332 346005

TAR • Lorraine Tarrant Antiques, 23 Market Place, Ringwood, Hampshire BH24 1AN
Tel: 01425 461123

TCF • 20th Century Frocks, 65 Steep Hill, Lincoln N1 1YN Tel: 01522 545916

TCR • 20th Century Retro, 166 Stoke Newington Church Street, London N16 OJL

TED • † Teddy Bears, 99 High Street, Witney, Oxfordshire OX8 6LY Tel: 01993 702616

TH • Tony Horsley, Sussex Tel: 01273 732163

TMA * Brown & Merry, Tring Market Auctions, Brook Street, Tring, Herts HP23 5EF
Tel: 01442 826446

TMi • Tim Millard Antiques, Stand 31-32, Bartlett Street Antique Centre, Bath, Avon BA1 2QZ
Tel: 01225 469785

TOT • † Totem, 168 Stoke Newington Church Street, London N16 OJL Tel: 0171 275 0234

TOY • † The Toy Store, 7 Thomas Street, Manchester City Centre, M4 IEU
Tel: 0161 839 6882

TP • † The Collector, Tom Power, 9 Church Street, Marylebone, London NW8 8EE
Tel: 0171 706 4586

TVA • Teme Valley Antiques, 1 The Bull Ring, Ludlow, Shropshire SY8 1AD
Tel: 01584 874686

TVM • Teresa Vanneck-Murray, Vanneck House, 22 Richmond Hill, Richmond, Surrey TW10 6QX Tel: 0181 940 2035

VCL • † Vintage Cameras Ltd, 256 Kirkdale, Sydenham, London SE26 4NL
Tel: 0181 778 5416

VS * † T. Vennett-Smith, 11 Nottingham Road, Gotham, Notts NG11 0HE
Tel: 0115 983 0541

VSt • Vera Strange Antiques, 811 Christchurch Rd, Boscombe, Bournemouth, Dorset BH7 6HP
Tel: 01202 429111

WAB • † Warboys Antiques, Old Church School, High Street, Warboys, Cambs PE17 1NR
Tel: 01487 823686

WAC • Worcester Antiques Centre, Reindeer Court, Mealcheapen Street, Worcester WR1 4DF
Tel: 01905 610680

WAL * † Wallis & Wallis, West Street Auction Galleries, Lewes, Sussex BN7 2NJ
Tel: 01273 480208

WCA • Wooden Chair Antiques Centre, Waterloo Road, Cranbrook, Kent TN12 0QG
Tel: 01580 713671

WeH • Westerham House Antiques, The Green, Westerham, Kent TN16 1AY
Tel: 01959 561622/562200

WL * Wintertons Ltd, Lichfield Auction Centre, Wood End Lane, Fradley, Lichfield, Staffordshire WS13 8NF Tel: 01543 263256
Photos: Courtesy of Crown Photos
Tel: 01283 762813

WLD • See **OLM**

WOO • Woolworths, Tenterden, Kent TN30 6BN

WP • † West Promotions, PO Box 257, Sutton, Surrey SM3 9WW Tel: 0181 641 3224

WTA • Witney and Airault, Prinny's Gallery, 3 Meeting House Lane, The Lanes, Brighton, Sussex BN1 1HB Tel: 01273 204554

YC • † Yesterday Child, Angel Arcade, 118 Islington High Street, London N1 8EG
Tel: 0171 354 1601

INTRODUCTION

From advertising tins to TV toys, this edition of *Miller's Collectables Price Guide* provides an unmatched survey of the marketplace and the latest collecting trends.

Many new features are included this year. While few of us are likely to have an original Arthur Conan Doyle manuscript lurking in the attic, most people have a detective novel on the bookshelf, and first editions of comparatively recent thrillers can now make high prices.

It is not just stories of murder that are attracting high-spending readers. As our feature on comics shows, nostalgia is a major spur and British comics have been steadily rising in value. Collectors are prepared to spend hundreds of pounds on children's papers that first sold for pocket money and if the original free gift has been preserved prices can double.

It is often the most unlikely and ordinary items that become collectable, because once they served their purpose they were simply thrown away. A case in point is denim, featured in our section on Textiles and Costume. Denim was invented for miners, worn by labourers and it was not until the 1950s that it became a fashion item. Most early jeans and jackets were literally worn out. Vintage examples are rare today and fetch exceptionally high prices. Another surprising first in our Costume section is trainers. Every parent knows that these can be frighteningly expensive, but few realise perhaps that there is now a market for 1970s trainers, the prototypes of today's fashionable footwear.

As well as exposing the cutting edge of contemporary fashions, the guide also focuses on more traditional areas. Our section on Ceramics includes an extensive feature on Parian ware, a favourite with the Victorians. Alongside the Art Deco creations of Susie Cooper and the ever-popular Clarice Cliff, we also look at some of the prettiest ceramics of the 1920s and '30s: Cottage Ware and Royal Winton Chintz ware, hugely sought-after today, both in Britain and America. We also go further afield to cover Noritake and Russian and Soviet ceramics and return to England in our Kitchenware section with a feature on Cornish blue and white kitchen ware.

Food and drink has inspired many of the objects illustrated in this guide, from drinking glasses to cutlery. This year we turn the spotlight on bottles and breweriana, and our section on Guinness collectables shows that it is not only the drink itself that can be good for you. For those more concerned with the healthier pursuits of life, we have a major section on sporting collectables. Recent auction prices have included a world record price of £17,000 paid for a Hardy fishing reel and, like golf, fishing is a sport that attracts both active participants and collectors across the world.

In last year's edition of the guide, our feature on gnomes created a massive amount of interest. This year we cast a glance at the decorative history of fairies, and more prosaically we focus on the collectable pig. Material related to comic characters and to film and television continues to increase in value. As well as illustrating traditional toys such as puppets and rocking horses, we boldly go where no man has gone before and explore the rocketing demand for science fiction merchandise and memorabilia. By contrast the oldest object featured in this edition of the guide is a Roman coin (see Collectables Under £5 – page 431).

Last year we asked you to send us your suggestions for a Collectable of the Future. One subject received so many nominations that we picked the winning entry out of a hat. Our congratulations to Nicola Bradley of the West Midlands who suggested Wallace and Gromit, the Oscar-winning characters created by Nick Park, given pride of place on page 432. Thank you to everyone who wrote in and please send us your tips for next year's hottest collectable. Our winning entrant will receive a free copy of *Miller's Collectables Price Guide* each year until the year 2000.

Future planned features range from Disneyana to Suffragette memorabilia. If there are any other subjects that you would like to see covered, please let us know. It is suggestions from enthusiasts in every field that help to make *Miller's Collectables Price Guide* so comprehensive and an essential read for every collector.

As ever, happy hunting!

ADVERTISING & PACKAGING

The fact that today's rubbish can become tomorrow's collectable is proved conclusively with advertising and packaging. Included in the following section is a WWII toilet roll. Not only is it understandably unusual to find 'antique' lavatory paper, but the historical interest of the item is enhanced by the copy on the paper packaging which attributes the absence of the firm's usual cardboard carton to wartime restrictions.

Much of the more traditional and most sought-after advertising and packaging material dates from the pre-war period. Featured in this year's guide is a particularly fine selection of cut-out show cards. These free-standing, often three-dimensional, shop displays date from the 1930s and were part of a unique private collection formed by the late Leslie Harris, a freelance artist working in the advertising industry during the same period. As well as being highly decorative, the show cards were in particularly good condition and when sold by Phillips in Bath many exceeded their auction estimates. Generally speaking with such material, the prettier the image (preferably attractive girls or winsome children), the higher the price.

Three glass paperweights advertising William Wilson & Sons, Glasgow, boilers, c1900, 4in (10cm) wide.
£40–48 *WAB*

r. A giant metal Yale key, for use outside a shop, with The Yale & Towne Mfg Co/Yale in raised letters and Yale Keys Cut Here printed down the side, paint worn, c1940, 31in (79cm) long.
£140–160 *BBR*

l. A giant Christmas cracker, in original box, complete with gifts, 1950s, 26in (66cm) long.
£15–20 *WAB*

A glass flask advertising Churchman's Isabella Cigars, c1890, 8½in (21.5cm) high.
£200–245 *MJW*

A Miss Muffet WWII toilet roll, 1940s, 5in (12.5cm) high.
£10–15 *WAB*

Enamel Signs

A Raglan Cycles enamel sign, c1914,
18 x 24in (45.5 x 61cm).
£120–140 *MR*

A Brasso Liquid Metal Polish enamel sign, with white
lettering on a brown background, chipped, 1920s,
19½ x 48in (49.5 x 122cm).
£140–160 *BBR*

A Songster Gramophone Needles stand-up tin sign,
c1930, 2¾ x 6¾in (7 x 17cm).
£100–120 *BBR*

A Waverley Mixture double-sided enamel
sign, with wall mounting plate, c1935,
12 x 18¼in (30.5 x 46.5cm).
£20–25 *SOL*

A Hall's Mineral Waters double-sided enamel
sign, chipped, c1930, 9 x 18in (23 x 45.5cm).
£50–60 *BBR*

A Two Steeples Pure Wool Underwear enamel
sign, c1940, 41 x 60in (104 x 152.5cm).
£100–120 *MR*

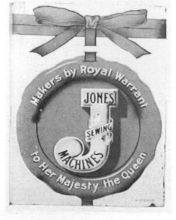

l. A Jones Sewing Machines
double-sided enamel sign,
rusting, 1930s, 20 x 15in
(51 x 38cm).
£130–150 *BBR*

r. A Michelin man double-sided
enamel sign, yellow, white and
black on a blue background,
chipped, 1950s, 31½ x 26½in
(80 x 67cm).
£55–65 *BBR*

Show Cards
& Posters

A Clarnico Chocolates calendar for 1927, by Guy Lipscombe, 14 x 10in (35.5 x 25.5cm).
£40–50 *Do*

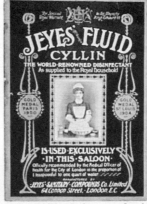

A Jeyes' Fluid show card, with white lettering on a green background, slightly worn, c1900, 10¼ x 7½in (26 x 19cm).
£40–50 *BBR*

r. The Blackstone Oil Engines show card, showing 4 different engines, worn, c1940, 14 x 19in (35.5 x 48cm).
£60–70 *BBR*

A late Victorian Snow Queen Flour show card, the snowman depicted as a bag of flour, 18½in (47cm) square, framed.
£120–150 *BBR*

Three multi-coloured hanging cards for Golden Bough, Chivers' and Smedley's and a counter card for Smedley's Fruits, 1930s, largest 19¼ x 13¼in (49 x 34cm).
£240–280 *P(B)*

A Peek, Frean's Biscuits hanging show card, depicting an African scene, by Lawson Wood, 1930s, 18¼ x 24¼in (46.5 x 61.5cm).
£120–150 *P(B)*

A Bovril multi-coloured
hanging show card, 1930s,
19 x 14in (48 x 35.5cm).
£175–200 *P(B)*

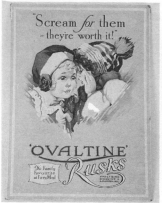

An Ovaltine Rusks multi
coloured stand-up show card,
1930s, 22½ x 14⅜in
(57 x 36.5cm).
£100–120 *P(B)*

A CWS Tea multi-coloured cut-
out stand-up show card,
mounted on a curved gold
background, 1930s, 28in
(71cm) high.
£80–100 *P(B)*

Three Kolynos Dental Cream
multi-coloured cut-out stand-
up show cards, 1930s,
highest 22⅞in (58cm).
£160–200 *P(B)*

A Symington's Granulated
Gravy poster, 1920s, 15 x 10in
(38 x 25.5cm).
£80–100 *Do*

A Drink Ovaltine for Health
multi-coloured card, 1930s,
19¾ x 13¾in (50 x 35cm).
£100–120 *BBR*

Three Crawford's Shortbread multi-coloured
cut-out stand-up show cards, with sporting
themes, 1930s, 27½in (70cm) high.
£450–550 *P(B)*

A two-part Colman's Mustard multi-
coloured cut-out stand-up show card,
1930s, total length 40½in (103cm).
£200–240 *P(B)*

An Eat More Fruit poster, by
an unknown designer, 1930s,
20 x 14in (51 x 35.5cm).
£55–65 *Do*

A Wills's Gold Flake multi-
coloured cut-out stand-up
show card, 1930s, 25 x 19¾in
(63.5 x 50cm).
£110–140 *P(B)*

A Secto Cattle Louse Powder stand-
up show card, showing a cow and
milk churns, c1950,
12 x 8in (30.5 x 20cm).
£12–15 *BBR*

A Wills's Capstan
Cigarettes multi-coloured
cut-out stand-up show
card, 1930s, 22¾ x 15in
(58 x 38cm).
£60–70 *P(B)*

l. A Player's
Navy Cut
multi-coloured
cut-out stand-
up show card,
1930s, 21in
(53cm) high.
£80–100 *P(B)*

Miller's is a price GUIDE
not a price LIST

Two Ogden's Robin Cigarettes multi-
coloured hanging show cards, 1930s,
largest 16½in (41.5cm) high.
£120–140 *P(B)*

A Wills's Gold Flake Cigarettes multi-coloured show card, the cut-out section featuring a girl, 1930s, 27¼ x 19in (69 x 48cm).
£80–100 *P(B)*

A Wills's Gold Flake multi-coloured embossed cut-out show card, 1930s, 24½ x 13½in (62 x 34cm).
£55–65 *P(B)*

A Wills's Capstan Cigarettes multi-coloured stand-up show card, the front with cut-out section of an ocean liner, 1930s, 30 x 19¼in (76 x 49cm).
£120–140 *P(B)*

An HMV poster, coloured blue, green, orange, yellow, black and white, 1940s, 41 x 60in (104 x 152.5cm).
£16–20 *BBR*

A Virolax multi-coloured cut-out stand-up show card, 1930s, 21in (53cm) square.
£130–150 *P(B)*

A Wills's Gold Flake Cigarettes multi-coloured cut-out stand-up show card, 1930s, 17 x 15¾in (43.5 x 39cm).
£60–70 *P(B)*

A *Cycling and Mopeds* magazine poster, 1950s, 30 x 20in (76 x 51cm).
£75–95 *Do*

A Raleigh Bicycle cardboard sign, 1950s, 9in (23cm) square.
£25–40 *COB*

An HMV poster, coloured orange, green, black and white depicting a period radio, 1940s, 40 x 30in (101.5 x 76cm).
£14–16 *BBR*

Tins

Tins remain highly popular with today's collectors. One of the leading names in the field is Huntley & Palmers. Founded in 1822 by Joseph Huntley, the world-famous biscuit manufacturers issued their first transfer-printed tins in 1868 in celebration of being granted a royal warrant as biscuit suppliers to Her Majesty Queen Victoria. This initial process was gradually replaced by the more economical lithographic printing and by the end of the century, as well as decorated rectangular boxes, the firm was producing some of the most adventurous novelty tins, many designed for the profitable Christmas market.

Huntley & Palmers continued to manufacture shaped tins up until WWII. Popular forms were often reissued and the most successful examples were produced in great numbers. Nevertheless, this does not mean that they are commonly found today. Though tins were designed to be saved, many were used for storing 'bits and bobs' and came to a rusty end in cellars and garden sheds. Toy tins in the shape of boats, cars, etc, often ended up being played with by children, hence their rarity and high price in today's market. As the following selection shows, early and unusually shaped tins in good condition can fetch three- and even four-figure sums. At the other end of the scale, pre-war box tins and more contemporary shaped tins can still be obtained for prices beginning at under £10, providing an attractive starting point for the collector.

A Taylor's mustard tin, c1880, 4¾in (12cm) high.
£28–32 *WAB*

A Huntley & Palmers biscuit tin, featuring a collection of books, 1900, 6in (15cm) high.
£155–185 *WAB*

A Ridgways Her Majesty's Blend Tea tin, c1902, 6in (15cm) long.
£20–35 *COB*

Two miners' tobacco tins:
Top William Owens, 1908, 5in (12.5cm) wide. **£50–60**
Bottom C. Mason, 1905, 7½in (19cm) wide.
£90–100 *MB*

A Huntley & Palmers tin, in the form of a case for binoculars, good condition, c1907, 7in (18cm) high.
£330–360 *CSK*

l. A Tabloid Tea tin, tea in tablet form from Burroughs Wellcome & Co, c1910, 3in (7.5cm) long.
£15–18 *WAB*

A Harrods Ltd, Pure China Tea tin, c1910, 6½in (16.5cm) long.
£24–28 *WAB*

A selection of miniature tins,
c1910: Clock, 3¼in (8cm) high.
£40–48
Rowntree's bellows,
3½in (9cm) long.
£55–65
Globe, 1½in (4cm) diam.
£24–28
Clarnico golf club,
5½in (14cm) long.
£115–135 *WAB*

Three miniature tins, 1920s:
Rowntree's coal scuttle, 1½in (4cm) high.
£55–65
Rowntree's lantern, 2in (5cm) high.
£85–95
Clarnico horn, 4in (10cm) high.
£115–135 *WAB*

r. A Lyons Assorted Toffees soldier
tin, c1910, 11in (28cm) high.
£125–155 *WAB*

An unbranded tin, depicting
Noah's Ark, 1920s,
6in (15cm) diam.
£10–15 *WAB*

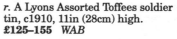

A Lovell's Black Pete Toffee
tin, c1920, 9½in (24cm) high.
£40–48 *WAB*

A Huntley & Palmers tin, in
the form of a cannon, 1924,
5in (13cm) wide.
£435–485 *WAB*

> **Cross Reference:**
> Colour Review

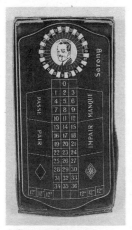

A Sarong Cigarettes
roulette game tin, in
original outer box, c1920,
12½in (32cm) long.
£55–65 *WAB*

A Crawford's biscuit tin, c1920,
10½in (27cm) long.
£18–22 *WAB*

A Belgian sentry
box tin, good
condition, c1914,
2¾in (7cm) high.
£230–275 *CSK*

A tin decorated with a hunting scene, c1930, 9½in (24cm) long.
£8–10 *AL*

A Huntley & Palmers biscuit tin, entitled 'Full Sail', c1930, 8in (20.5cm) long.
£5–7 *AL*

A Huntley & Palmers tin, in the form of a delivery van, in very good condition, 1923, 9¾in (25cm) long.
£1,400–1,700 *CSK*

One of the most desirable tins produced by Huntley & Palmers, this van bears the company's monogram and the numberplate HP 1923, providing useful evidence of its date.

r. A Huntley & Palmers biscuit tin, 1926, 6½in (16.5cm) long.
£65–75 *WAB*

These biscuits were only sold at the Wembley Exhibition of 1926.

A Rowntree's Toffee tin, 1930s, 4½in (11.5cm) high.
£15–18 *WAB*

l. A drum-shaped tin, 1930s, 2in (5cm) diam.
£10–12 *WAB*

A tin entitled 'The Optimist', c1930, 8in (20.5cm) long.
£8–10 *AL*

A Dunlop French Chalk tin, 1930s, 7½in (19cm) high.
£5–6 *WAB*

A cake tin decorated with King George VI and Queen Elizabeth's Coronation in 1937, 10in (25.5cm) diam.
£24–28 *WAB*

A tin decorated with birds, c1930, 5½in (14cm) long.
£8–10 *AL*

A Panda Cottage tin, 1930s, 6¼in (16cm) long.
£40–48 *WAB*

A tin decorated with fishing boats, c1930, 9in (23cm) long.
£8–10 *AL*

A Huntley & Palmers Tribrek Breakfast Biscuits tin, in the form of a lorry, poor condition, together with 4 pieces of related ephemera, 1937, 8¼in (21cm) long.
£300–350 *CSK*

A Vim Kolorscope tin, in the form of a miniature kaleidoscope, c1950, 2¼in (6cm) high.
£20–25 *BBR*

A tin, in the form of a lunch box, 1930s, 8in (20.5cm) long.
£7–8 *LIB*

A McVitie & Price free sample biscuit tin, 1930s, 3¼in (8.5cm) diam.
£7–8 *WAB*

l. Two tins decorated with puppies, c1950, largest 10in (25.5cm) long.
£6–9 each *AL*

A Paterson's Griddle Oatcakes container with tin lid and base, 1960s, 6¼in (16cm) high.
£3–4 *WAB*

A Player's Gold Leaf cigarettes tin, 1950s, 6in (15cm) long.
£5–6 *WAB*

A Huntley & Palmers miniature biscuit tin, 1950s, 1¾in (4.5cm) high.
£22–26 *WAB*

A Kleen-e-ze Silicone Car Polish tin, 1960, 4¼in (11cm) diam.
£10–12 *WAB*

A Cadbury's Smarties tin, in the form of a truck, 1980s, 4in (10cm) high.
£5–6 *WAB*

A George W. Horner nougat tin, decorated with a duck, 1960s, 6in (15cm) long.
£8–10 *WAB*

A Sharps Toffee tin, depicting horses and a small boy, c1950, 10 x 7in (25.5 x 18cm).
£6–8 *AL*

l. A Sharps Plain Super-Kreem Toffee tin, 1950s, 4½ x 3¾in (11.5 x 9.5cm).
£6–8 *WAB*

Don't Forget!
If in doubt please refer to the 'How to Use' section at the beginning of this book.

An O.K. Biscuits tin, in the form of a lorry, with clockwork mechanism, by Mettoy, 1950s, 9½in (24cm) long.
£320–360 *BBR*

A tin depicting huntsmen, hounds and a carriage, c1960, 7½ x 9½in (19 x 24cm).
£6–8 *AL*

AERONAUTICA

A chromium Vickers Viscount advertising model, 1950s, 8in (20.5cm) wide.
£50–80 *COB*

A leather flying coat and matching helmet, c1920.
£100–120 *COB*

A WWII Lancaster bomber drift recorder, 10½in (27cm) long.
£65–75 *SW*

A Saunders-Roe flying boat brochure, c1950, 17 x 22in (43 x 56cm).
£30–40 *COB*

An aviator teddy bear by Merry-thought Ltd, c1990, 16½in (42cm) high.
£22–25 *COB*

A Schneider Trophy souvenir print, glass cracked, 1927, 15 x 10½in (38 x 27cm).
£65–85 *COB*

l. A selection of airline labels, c1960, largest 7in (18cm) wide.
£2–5 each *COB*

r. A selection of airline key rings, c1970.
£4–5 each *COB*

Three plastic airline souvenirs, 1970–90, largest 19½in (50cm) long.
£8–12 each *OTS*

Two Ranco models wooden construction kits, for an Auto Giro and a Super Fortress, c1944, boxes 12in (30.5cm) long.
£10–20 each *COB*

AMUSEMENT & SLOT MACHINES

The most collectable amusement machines date from the late nineteenth century to the advent of decimalisation in 1971. Though there are only a few serious collectors in Britain (between 50–100 according to recent estimates), many individuals will buy a single machine. 'They remember playing with a one-arm bandit in a café in their youth, and want one when they are grown-up just for fun,' explains dealer and auctioneer Steve Hunt, 'so today there is a growing demand for 1950s/60s items.' Collectors are predominantly male, and are inspired not just by nostalgia and the historical charm of the objects, but also by a love of mechanics. 'Most enthusiasts are mechanically minded,' admits dealer and collector Brian Bates. 'Part of the fun is

doing-up machines, and unlike other antiques they can fetch more if they have been restored. No one wants a game that doesn't work.'

As dealers stress, old amusement machines are becoming increasingly hard to find. Many were simply junked when they were superseded by electronic models, whilst in America a great number of early machines were destroyed during Prohibition. In the USA vintage examples can fetch extremely high prices, though collectors tend to concentrate purely on home-grown models. 'Everyone wants a little bit of Las Vegas,' concludes Hunt, 'the British buy everything – European and US material – and British machines also appeal to the Continental market.'

A Victorian penny till, by J. C. Cox, Queen Victoria Street, London, with patented brass coin collection mechanism, shelves for counted change, coin dishes and locking cash drawer, 19in (48.5cm) wide.
£350–450 *BTA*

A grip tester, by Percival Everitt, London, c1889, 11in (28cm) high.
£1,700–1,800 *HAK*

An Anthony Harris fortune teller, by Automatic Amusement Co, London, c1889, 20in (51cm) high.
£1,600–2,000 *HAK*

Cross Reference
Colour Review

r. The Treadmill, by John Dennison, Leeds, a working model, 1898, 27½in (70cm) high.
£5,000–6,000 *HAK*

l. The Haunted Bedroom, by John Dennison, Leeds, 1896, 27½in (70cm) high.
£7,500–8,500 *HAK*

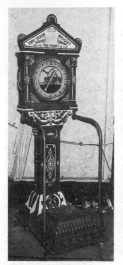

r. A game of skill, by Fortuna Automatic Skill Machines Co, London, c1901, 35½in (90cm) high. **£1,000–1,200** *BB*

Various methods were used to avoid breaking gambling laws so instead of coins this game dispensed tokens that could be exchanged at the bar for a good cigar.

Cast iron weighing scales, by Salter Scales Co, c1900, 84in (213cm) high. **£2,500–3,500** *HAK*

A cast iron mutoscope, c1900, 54in (137cm) high. **£1,000–1,250** *AMc*

r. A game of skill, by Price & Castell, London, c1899, 23in (58.5cm) high. **£1,700–1,800** *HAK*

r. A muscle tester, a revamp by Bollands, London, of the machine originally produced by Rosenfield Manufacturing Co, c1903, 60in (152cm) high. **£5,000–6,000** *HAK*

A bottle shooter, by W. H. Ell & Co, London, c1904, 23½in (60cm) wide. **£7,000–7,500** *HAK*

l. An Electricity is Life electric shock machine, c1905, 49in (124cm) high. **£1,200–1,500** *BB*

l. The Football Game, by Automatic Sports Co, London, c1904, 66in (167cm) high. **£6,500–7,500** *HAK*

l. A Shocking Jack polyphon, The Electric Sailor, electric shock machine, by Musik-Werke, Leipzig, c1910, 24½in (62cm) high. **£6,000–7,000** *HAK*

An Electricity is Life, 'Greatest remedy for Rheumatism, Gout, etc', by United Automatic Machine Co, London, c1905, 19in (48cm) high. **£1,800–2,200** *HAK*

l. Paris Courses, a horse race betting game, by Bussoz-Cons, Paris, c1910, 27¼in (69cm) high. **£3,500–4,000** *BB*

l. The Village Blacksmith game, c1910, 25in (63.5cm) high.
£2,500–3,000 *HAK*

A penny-operated football game, by Cooper, c1914, 25½in (65cm) high.
£700–800 *BB*

l. A penny-operated All Win machine, c1935, 26in (66cm) high.
£350–425 *BB*

A six-drawer fortune telling machine, by Argyle Auto Co, London, c1927, 30in (76cm) high.
£500–600 *BB*

This machine dispenses cards and promises $100 if not true.

l. A Mills Hi-Top one-arm bandit, c1950, 27in (68.5cm) high.
£225–275 *AMc*

An Oliver Whales All Win wall machine, c1955, 32in (81.5cm) high.
£275–325 *AMc*

l. A Bryans Payramid machine, c1960, 32in (81.5cm) high.
£550–650 *AMc*

ART DECO

A Czechoslovakian Art Deco liqueur set, carafe stopper damaged, 1925, carafe 8¼in (21cm) high.
£220–250 *PC*

An Ekco AD65 Bakelite table radio, 1930s, 15½in (39.5cm) diam.
£375–425 *BWe*

A pair of Art Deco plaster parrot flower vases, c1930, 27in (68.5cm) high.
£30–40 *SUS*

A harlequin set of 4 Kensington ware sundae dishes, in colours of green, mauve, blue and pink, c1922, 3½in (9cm) high.
£45–55 *PSA*

A Windsor china trio, 1930s, cup 2¾in (7cm) high.
£22–26 *PSA*

Cross Reference
Ceramics
For reference to other major factories and makers from the Art Deco Period, consult the Ceramics section and refer to the index

l. A Wade Heath galleon flower jug, c1934, 10in (25.5cm) high.
£60–70 *BKK*

An Art Deco six-sided parchment work box, decorated both internally and externally, c1930, 11in (28cm) wide.
£24–28 *BKK*

An Art Deco diamanté and Bakelite brooch, 1930s, 2½in (6.5cm) long.
£10–12 *PSA*

A pair of Art Deco amber glass bowls, with butterfly knops, 1930s, 3in (7.5cm) diam.
£13–16 *PSA*

Figures

A Plaue porcelain group, 1920s, 9½in (24cm) high.
£325–375 *BGA(K)*

A Lorenzl bronze figure of a female nude, 1925, 8in (20.5cm) high.
£100–150 *PC*

An Art Deco plaster figure, by G. Lionardi, London, 1920s, 24in (61cm) high.
£175–200 *DAF*

A Czechoslovakian Art Deco ceramic figure of a male skier, c1930, 10in (25.5cm) high.
£200–250 *WTA*

l. A Royal Dux ceramic figure of a Mexican dancer, c1930, 8in (20.5cm) high.
£400–450 *WTA*

An Art Deco silver-plated and cold-painted spelter figure, c1930, 15in (38cm) high.
£350–400 *DAF*

An Art Deco spelter figure, on a marble base, 1930s, 15in (38cm) high.
£200–240 *ML*

l. A Goldscheider ceramic figure, c1930, 15¼in (39cm) high.
£500–600 *PC*

An Art Deco lamp, in the form of a bronze spelter figure of an athlete, c1930, 15in (38cm) high.
£300–350 *DAF*

r. An Austrian Art Deco ceramic group of a dancing couple, c1935, 13in (33cm) high.
£450–500 *WTA*

Metalware

An Art Deco Sheffield plate fish knife and fork, with bone handles, 1930s, 8in (20.5cm) high.
£35–40 *BET*

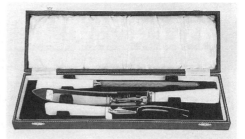

An Art Deco Sheffield plate carving set, 1930s, box 5 x 15¼in (13 x 39cm).
£80–90 *BET*

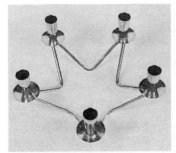

An Art Deco silver-plated candelabrum, 1930s, 10in (25.5cm) diam.
£45–50 *BET*

An Art Deco silver-plated hors d'oeuvre dish, 1930s, 12in (30.5cm) diam.
£75–85 *BET*

An Art Deco silver-plated fruit bowl, with Bakelite handles, 1930s, 11in (28cm) diam.
£85–95 *BET*

An Art Deco silver-plated cruet set, with blue glass liners, 1930s, pepper pot 3¼in (8.5cm) high.
£80–90 *BET*

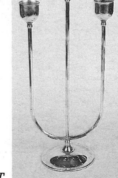

r. A pair of Art Deco silver-plated candelabra, 1930s, 12¼in (31cm) high.
£85–95 *BET*

An Art Deco silver-plated cocktail shaker, with internal lemon squeezer, 1930s, 10in (20.5cm) high.
£85–95 *BET*

A Brittania metal four-piece tea and coffee service, in Art Deco style, by James Dixon & Sons, 1930s, coffee pot 8in (20.5cm) high.
£150–180 *DN*

An Art Deco chrome plated three-piece tea set, 1930s, teapot 5in (12.5cm) high.
£25–30 *BSA*

l. An Art Deco chrome plated three-piece tea set, 1930s, teapot 5in (12.5cm) high.
£25–30 *BSA*

Photograph Frames

An Art Deco photograph frame, on a marble stand, c1930, 8in (20.5cm) wide.
£80–90 BKK

An Art Deco mahogany swing mirror and photograph frame, c1928, 10in (25.5cm) high.
£80–90 BKK

Wall Masks & Decorations

A Czechoslovakian Art Deco ceramic wall mask, c1930, 6¼in (16cm) high.
£130–150 CSA

An Art Deco plaster wall mask, 1930s, 9in (23cm) high.
£60–70 DAF

An Art Deco plaster wall mask, by G. Leonardi & Co, London, 1930s, 14¼in (36cm) high.
£60–70 DAF

A pair of Art Deco plaster posy wall plaques, 1930s, 9in (23cm) wide.
£35–40 SUS

A Goldscheider terracotta wall face mask, 1930s, 10in (25cm) high.
£180–220 DAF

A Czechoslovakian wall mask, c1930, 5in (12.5cm) high.
£200–225 WTA

ART NOUVEAU

A Royal Doulton chamber pot,
with Art Nouveau decoration,
c1917, 10½in (26.5cm) diam.
£60–70 *PSA*

An Art Nouveau ceramic tile,
c1900, 6in (15cm) square.
£30–40 *OD*

Cross Reference
Colour Review

A French high fired vase
by Müller, sculptor C. Vibert,
c1900, 5¼in (13.5cm) high.
£500–600 *SUC*

A pair of Royal Stanley Jacobean
ware vases, c1915, 7in (18cm) high.
£50–60 *PC*

Four chromolithographic menu
cards, by Alphonse Mucha, for
Moët & Chandon, c1900,
9½ x 6in (24 x 15cm).
£100–120 each *DW*

l. A French cameo
glass vase, by
Arsall, c1890,
5in (12.5cm) high.
£750–900 *ASA*

r. A Gallé glass vase,
with red ground and
brown cameo
decoration, c1900,
5¾in (14.5cm) high.
£250–350 *PC*

A Gallé glass vase, the
with lemon ground and
brown cameo
decoration, c1900,
4½ (11.5cm) high.
£250–350 *PC*

l. A cameo glass landscape
vase, by Légras, c1900,
5in (12.5cm) high.
£800–1,000 *ASA*

A French Art Nouveau carved horn
brooch, c1910, 5in (12.5cm) high.
£70–80 *GOO*

A silver and enamel brooch, by Charles
Horner, c1908, 1¼in (30mm) wide.
£70–80 *GOO*

An Art Nouveau silver
brooch, with turquoise,
matrix and pearls, c1900,
1in (25mm) wide.
£100–120 *GOO*

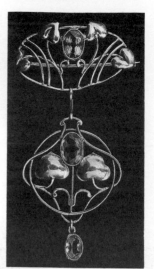

An Art Nouveau 9ct gold
brooch, with detachable
pendant, set with
peridots, by Murrle
Bennet & Co, 1884–1914.
£450–550 *WL*

An Art Nouveau WMF
gilt-metal two-branch
table lamp, in the form
of a girl in flowing robes
standing on a tree
stump, impressed mark,
early 20thC, 13¼in
(33.5cm) high.
£240–280 *DN*

A French aluminium repoussé box, made
by Alfred Daguet for S. Bing, c1898,
13½in (34cm) long.
£650–800 *SUC*

A pewter tobacco
barrel, designed by
Archibald Knox for
Liberty & Co, c1905,
4½in (11.5cm) high.
£200–250 *GOO*

A pewter dish, designed by
Archibald Knox for Liberty & Co,
c1905, 9in (23cm) long.
£100–120 *GOO*

*Arthur Lasenby Liberty founded his
famous London store in 1875. As
well as retailing Oriental arts and
crafts Liberty's commissioned
contemporary works from British
designers and their name became
synonymous with the Art Nouveau
style. Archibald Knox (1864–1933)
was one of the leading figures to
produce metalware for the company,
designing both for the 'Cymric'
silverware range and the 'Tudric'
pewter collection. His work is
distinguished by Celtic inspired
motifs, the organic decoration
reflecting the influence of
early jewellery.*

A Newlyn copper wall
plaque, Glasgow School,
possibly by Gilmore,
signed, c1890,
14in (35.5cm) high.
£400–500 *SHa*

A pewter cake tray, designed by
Archibald Knox for Liberty & Co,
c1905, 12in (30.5cm) long.
£100–120 *GOO*

A pair of Art Nouveau
terracotta plaques,
signed Otto, Austria,
c1890, 15in (38cm) high.
£800–1,000 *VSt*

AUTOMOBILIA

l. A complete set of 12 French transfer-printed 'Automobiles' plates, each with blue floral border and monochrome central design, individually numbered 1–12, c1902, 8in (20.5cm) diam.
£600–700 *S*

A pair of kerosene car headlamps, by Camelinal, Birmingham and London, c1900, 13in (33cm) high.
£200–250 *ET*

A Michelin clock, in mock tortoise-shell case, 1930s, 3in (7.5cm) high.
£40–50 *FAL*

l. A French dashboard clock, with 8-day movement, in gilt-brass case, marked 'Deposé, France', 1920s, 2in (5cm) diam.
£70–80 *CARS*

An Art Deco poster, advertising Panhard, c1937, 14 x 11in (35.5 x 28cm).
£20–35 *COB*

> **Miller's is a price GUIDE not a price LIST**

r. An American oil spout, 1930s, 8½in (21.5cm) long.
£50–60 *MRW*

l. An Esso Ethyl oil can, c1938, 5in (13cm) high.
£15–20 *FAL*

Travelling with an oil can was essential in a period when garages were few and far between. The cans are often date coded on the base plate, eg:
935 = manufactured in September 1935
1038 = manufactured in October 1938.

A tinplate cover for a car headlight, used during the blackout in WWII, 1940s, 8in (20.5cm) diam.
£10–15 *WAB*

l. Two British Racing Drivers Club arm bands, 1952–53, 3½in (9cm) wide.
£15–20 each *COB*

A German pottery model of a petrol can for a jeep, 1950s, 6½in (16.5cm) high.
£6–10 *PC*

A drinks flask, in the form of a Jaguar radiator, with glass inner liner, leaping cat mascot on cup top and miniature car badges applied, c1966, 5½in (14cm) wide.
£50–60 *CARS*

> **Miller's is a price GUIDE not a price LIST**

l. A nickel-plated brass AA Light Car Member's badge, No. 156114, with later wings and bird mascot, c1917, 5½in (14cm) high.
£60–80 *S*

Badges

A Morgan 4/4 Car Club badge, chromed-steel and coloured enamel, for badge bar fitment, 1990s, 2¼in (6cm) wide.
£20–25 *CARS*

r. Three Brighton Car Club badges, chromed-steel and plastic based enamels with clear Perspex covers, c1988, 3¾in (9.5cm) diam.
£8–15 each *CARS*

A Ferrari car badge, chrome-plated aluminium with applied plastic enamel, 1990s, 3¼in (8.5cm) wide.
£8–10 *CARS*

l. Two RAC nickel-plated brass Associate Member's badges, each 6½in (16.5cm) high:
Top with glass and enamel central flag, c1920.   **£125–150**
Bottom c1912.   **£150–180** *CARS*

The Automobile Club was founded in 1897 by F. R. Simms and became the Royal Automobile Club (RAC) ten years later when King Edward VII, a keen motor enthusiast, became its patron. The Automobile Association (AA) was founded in 1906. Both societies produced badges to be attached to members' cars and early examples are particularly prized.

Key Rings

Three Ferrari brass and multi-coloured enamel key rings, c1990.
£8–15 each *CARS*

A selection of car key rings, 1960–70s.
£2–3 each *COB*

Mascots

Many drivers decorate their cars with personal mascots, but the first car manufacturer to produce their own mascot was the Vulcan Motor Company, choosing as their symbol Vulcan the Blacksmith, which appeared on their vehicles from 1903. Seven years later Rolls-Royce, disapproving of the various emblems being applied to their cars, commissioned British sculptor Charles Sykes to design a suitably exclusive mascot. 'The Spirit of Ecstasy' first appeared on Rolls-Royces in 1910 and, still in use today, is one of the most famous mascots in the world. Original condition of mascots is important, and replating, alterations or damage will lower their value.

A French cheeky fireman mascot, mounted on a radiator cap, 1920s, 4½in (11.5cm) high.
£120–150 *S*

A nickel-plated Vulcan mascot, in the form of a farrier holding a wheel on an anvil, mounted as a radiator cap, 1920s, 5¾in (14.5cm) high.
£100–120 *HOLL*

A chrome on brass fish mascot, 1920s, 5½in (14cm) high.
£85–95 *BGA*

A chrome Jaguar mascot, c1967, 7½in (19cm) long.
£70–80 *TAC*

A cast bronze boxer dog mascot, 1920s, 4in (10cm) high.
£75–85 *WAB*

A cast bronze horse's head mascot, 1920s, 4¼in (11cm) high.
£75–85 *WAB*

A Bentley cast bronze chrome-
plated mascot, inscribed
'H. R. Owen Ltd, London',
c1936, 4in (10cm) high.
£550–600 *CARS*

A Bentley cast brass
chrome-plated mascot,
c1966, 4in (10cm) high.
£150–200 *CARS*

Model Cars

A Rolls-Royce cast-bronze
nickel-plated Spirit of Ecstasy
mascot, signed C. Sykes, 1911,
3½in (9cm) high.
£380–450 *CARS*

*Produced for the Silver Dawn
to Silver Wraith series and
pre-WWII cars.*

A 1962 BRM P56 model car, as
driven by G. Hill, produced
1980–95, 3½in (8.5cm) long.
£200–250 *PC*

*Winner of the 1962
World Championship.*

A 1903 Ford Model
A car, 1:16 scale.
£120–140 *BKS*

r. A 1907 Rolls-
Royce 40/50
Silver Ghost
model car,
1:24 scale.
£80–100 *BKS*

A 1924 Hispano-Suiza
hand-built wooden boat-
tail model car, with a
copper-plated under
chassis, 1:24 scale.
£260–300 *BKS*

r. A 1965 Green
Monster model
car, as driven by
A. Arfons, 6¼in
(16cm) long.
£420–500 *PC*

Model Cars

These cars are not toys but hand-
built precision models of great race
winners, produced in extremely
limited numbers. Since cars can
change, literally from race to race,
with technical alterations or the
addition of a new sponsor's logo,
precise attention to detail is all-
important to collectors. As interest
in motor racing expands, so values
of such models continues to rise.

A 1991 McLaren MP4/6 model car, as driven
by A. Senna, 4¼in (11cm) long.
£125–150 *PC*

Le Mans Winners

A 1923 Chenard Walcker model car, produced 1980–95, 3½in (8cm) long.
£125–150 *PC*

First car to win the Le Mans 24-hour race.

A 1983 Porsche 956 model car, produced 1980–95, 4¼in (11cm) long.
£220–250 *PC*

A 1995 McLaren F1 GTR model car, 1995, 4in (10cm) long.
£250–300 *PC*

A winner in their first year of competition at Le Mans.

A 1930 Bentley 6.5 litre model car, 4¼in (11cm) long.
£125–150 *PC*

A 1963 Ferrari 250P model car, produced 1980–95, 3¾in (9.5cm) long.
£175–200 *PC*

A 1973 Matra 670B model car, produced 1980–95, 4in (10cm) long.
£175–200 *PC*

Games & Toys

A German tinplate Porsche 356 two-seater Speedster, battery-operated, c1958, 10in (25.5cm) long.
£350–400 *BKS*

l. A collection of Shell and Esso tinplate toys, by various makers including Dinky Toys, Gama and St Nicolas, 1950s.
£120–140 *BKS*

Cross Reference
Toys

r. A Ford GT40 Computacar set, by Merit Ltd, c1960, complete and contained in original box.
£100–120 *BKS*

BICYCLES & CYCLING

The bicycle was a 19th century invention. The first two-wheeled machine was devised by Baron Karl de Drais de Sauerbrun and exhibited in Paris in 1818. Commonly known as the 'Hobby Horse', this wooden vehicle had no pedals and was propelled by paddling the feet on the ground. In 1861 Parisian coach-builders, Ernest and Pierre Michaux, created the 'Velocipede', driven by two pedal cranks attached to the front wheel. Though these soon gained the sobriquet 'Boneshakers', on account of their wooden and iron frames and painful susceptibility to every bump in the road, Velocipedes were a great success, and the craze for cycling was launched. In Britain, the 1870s saw the development of the 'Ordinary', better known as the 'Penny Farthing'. Capable of high speeds and very popular for racing, the Penny Farthing was nevertheless a perilous means of transport and by the end of the decade it had been almost entirely superseded by the 'Safety'

bicycle. With its equal sized wheels, rear-wheel chain drive, pneumatic tyres, diamond pattern frame and centrally placed saddle, the Safety machine established the standard format for the bicycle.

Pre-WWI machines in good condition are hard to find and expensive. Penny Farthings can fetch four figure sums and highlights in the following section include a remarkable collection of early tricycles sold at auction by veteran cycle enthusiast Roger Street (founder of the world's first museum devoted solely to multi-wheeled cycles). An auction record of £22,000 for a cycle was set by a machine dating from c1882 and known as the Coventry Sociable: a quadricycle (four wheels) that could seat rider and a passenger, or could be converted into a tricycle for a single user. Other tricycles from the collection also made high prices, reflecting the great rarity of such early material.

An American silver-plated tricycling trophy, The Springfield Cup, bearing an engraved inscription, the lid surmounted by a scale model of a Salvo style tricycle with statuette of its rider, 1885, 19in (48cm) high.
£2,800–3,200 *P(HSS)*

First Prize for 5 miles tricycle race, awarded to Percy Furnivall, a leading British tricyclist of his day, on a Humber tricycle.

r. A nickel-silver cylindrical police style whistle, stamped on one side 'The Cyclist's Road Clearer' and on the other 'H.A.K. & Co, London', 19thC, 3¼in (8cm) long.
£120–140 *P(HSS)*

A brass bicycle bell, 1920s, 2½in (6.5cm) diam.
£15–18 *WAB*

A Bacon's map of London, for tourists and cyclists, c1898, 7¼ x 4¼in (18.5 x 11cm).
£12–15 *COB*

l. A pair of gilt-brass button cuff links, advertising New Departure Coaster Hubs, c1900, 1½in (4cm) long, together with a gilt-brass medal advertising the same, c1900, 1½in (3.5cm) diam, and an advertising postcard, from Brown Brothers Ltd, c1905.
£140–160 *P(HSS)*

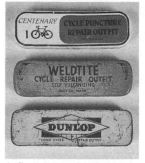

A Centenary plastic repair box, 1970s, together with Weldtite and Dunlop tin repair boxes, 1930s, 4½in (11.5cm) long.
£3–4 each *WAB*

A collection of bicycle badges, 1930s, largest 3in (7.5cm) high.
£5–10 each *FAL*

The price depends largely on quality and rarity of image. Many badges have suffered from rust over time making them less attractive as a collectable.

r. A Liberty lubricating oil can, 1920s, 7½in (19cm) high.
£10–12 *WAB*

Bicycle Lamps

A Lucas metal bicycle lamp, c1880, 6¼in (16cm) high.
£200–240 *PC*

A Parker's Silver Crown bicycle candle lamp, c1910, 7½in (19cm) high.
£125–150 *FAL*

r. A Lucas King of the Road penny farthing metal hub lamp, c1880, 9½in (24cm) high.
£520–650 *PC*

l. A brass bicycle candle lamp, c1910, 7in (18cm) high.
£140–150 *PC*

A Lucas Silver King bicycle petroleum lamp, c1914, 5½in (14cm) high.
£45–55 *FAL*

r. A Lucas nickel-plated brass bicycle candle lamp, c1920, 9in (23cm) high.
£130–160 *PC*

A Lucas metal bicycle rear light, c1920, 5in (13cm) high.
£24–28 *FAL*

Ephemera

An advertising lithograph poster, A Few Riders of Humber Cycles, by G. Moore, restored, c1905, 25 x 33in (63.5 x 84cm), framed and glazed.
£280–330 *P(HSS)*

A full-colour chromolithograph show card, advertising Imperial Rover Cycles, good condition, c1897, 20½ x 18in (52 x 45.5cm), framed and glazed.
£240–280 *P(HSS)*

A full-colour chromolithograph poster, advertising Premier Cycles, restored, c1901, 37 x 25½in (94 x 65cm), framed and glazed.
£380–450 *P(HSS)*

A French colour lithographed linen-backed poster, advertising Terrot cycles, some damage, c1900.
£100–120 *BKS*

An embossed and glazed chromolithograph fold-out cut-out Christmas card, 1890s, 6¾in (17cm) high.
£130–160 *P(HSS)*

A Japanese paper fan, with lacquered wooden blades, depicting a watercolour scene of a girl, boy and a tricycle, late 1920s, 8 x 16in (20.5 x 40.5cm), framed and glazed.
£100–120 *P(HSS)*

Bicycles

An Ordinary bicycle, fitted with 'The Eolus' patented hub bearings, saddle, handlebars and simple lever brake, good condition, 1877, leading wheel 56in (142cm) diam.
£1,800–2,000 *S*

An Ordinary bicycle, frame No. 4834/48, with cow horn handlebars and turned wooden grips, fitted with North Pole patent 4xA solid white tyres, some wear, leading wheel 48in (122cm) diam.
£1,800–2,000 *S*

A Farringdon Ordinary pneumatic-tyred racing bicycle, with oval backbone, dropped handlebars with T-handles, no step or brake, some restoration, painted grey, c1892, leading wheel 54in (137cm) diam.
£2,800–3,200 *P(HSS)*

A gentleman's light roadster bicycle, the wheels with rims for tubular pneumatics but fitted with cushion tyres, no brake, good original condition, c1893, wheels 28in (71cm) diam.
£1,300–1,500 *P(HSS)*

A Rudge gentleman's bicycle, good original condition, c1907.
£220–260 *BKS*

r. A Hercules lady's bicycle, with leather Lycett saddle, bell and pump, good unrestored condition, c1920.
£12–15 *BKS*

A Royal Sunbeam lady's bicycle, fitted with acetylene lamps to front and rear, chainguard and saddle bag, c1925.
£120–140 *BKS*

An Armstrong Moth Magnificient tandem, with Trivolex three-speed gearing, internal expanding hub brakes front and rear, c1938.
£500–600 *ADT*

Trivolex gears have a fixed chain line and sprockets that move on the hub splines, as made by the Triumph Motorcycle Company. Until recently this machine was in regular use, competing in international tandem rallies.

A Claud Butler (London) lightweight touring bicycle, No. 3123, fitted with Heuret five-speed derailleur, Mafag centre-pull calipers, saddle and mudguards, excellent green paintwork with yellow banding, good condition, c1946, 23in (58.5cm) frame.
£180–220 *P(HSS)*

r. A working model of a bicycle, c1960, 5in (13cm) high.
£25–30 *BGA*

Tricycles

A Rantoone tricycle, with lever drive to cranked rear axle, steerer in lyre-shaped fork with patent parallel lever linkage, operated from turning handle and chains, good original brown paint with red lining, c1865, 29in (74cm) track.
£15,000–18,000 *P(HSS)*

The Rantoone was patented in England by Joseph Goodman in 1863, probably acquiring its North American Indian name Flying Wagon after being patented and advertised in the USA in 1864.

This tricycle is driven by both foot treadles and hand levers, all operating on the rear axle. As all four limbs were employed at the same time the machine was sometimes referred to as a 'gymnasium in miniature'.

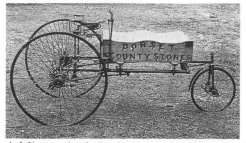

A delivery tricycle, in the livery of the Dorset County Stores, direct driving cranked axle to 2 front wheels each fitted with free-wheel mechanism and external contracting band brake, sprung rear steerer on rack-and-pinion, Arab sprung saddle forward of spring-mounted open wooden carrying box, in sound condition, the frame painted black, c1880, 34½in (87.5cm) track.
£7,000–8,200 *P(HSS)*

This machine was acquired by the Dorset County Stores of Knightsbridge, Wimborne and Broadstone in 1904 and remained in service until 1943.

r. A Harding dual front wheel tricycle, with Westwood steerers, Sturmey AB three-speed gears, with hub brake, centre-pull Phillips pattern caliper brakes to steerers, in good condition, re-enamelled in black, c1957.
£500–600 *P(HSS)*

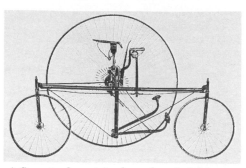

A Coventry lever tricycle, rack and pinion steering to 2 right hand wheels, lever drive to left hand wheel with external contracting band brake, Otto type seat with leaf spring, in sound condition, repainted black with gold lining, c1879, 24in (61cm) track.
£15,000–18,000 *P(HSS)*

A Coventry convertible sociable quadricycle/tricycle, with rack and pinion steering to male side, each wheel independently driven from cranks and chains, the male side fitted with Arab spring saddle and luggage carrier, the detachable female side fitted with chain cover and pan seat on leaf spring, in sound condition, repainted green, c1882, track as sociable 51in (129.5cm).
£22,000+ *P(HSS)*

BOOKS

This year Miller's devotes a special feature to crime, featuring both non-fiction crime books and mystery novels. According to bookseller Clifford Elmer, who has specialised in true life crime books for fifteen years, collectors tend to concentrate on either truth or fiction, only rarely crossing over between the two. His own clients range from 'the little old lady who likes a grizzly story' to American universities, where crime is becoming an increasingly important academic subject, to TV companies looking for famous Victorian trials and classic murder cases to dramatise.

In the non-fiction field, murders tend to be the most popular subject matter, rather than the more mundane, less violent crimes, and current strong sellers include books on serial killers. Jack the Ripper remains a perennial favourite. Over the years, this mysterious multiple murderer has inspired a host of publications (to say nothing of films, TV programmes and songs), and Ripper enthusiasts tend to be specialists, only collecting Ripper-related crime books.

The 1880s, when Jack the Ripper haunted the streets of London, also saw the birth of the greatest literary detective of them all, Sherlock Holmes, creation of Arthur Conan Doyle (1859–1930). Holmes made his first appearance in *A Study in Scarlet*, 1887, and by the turn of the century the character had seized public imagination on both sides of the Atlantic, establishing the classic format for the detective story. Today there is an enormous market for collectable crime novels, both in Britain and the USA. According to book dealer Nigel Williams, *Beeton's Christmas Annual*, 1887, in which the first Holmes story appears, can now fetch in the region of £20,000. Also popular are writers from the 1930s, such as Ngaio Marsh, Agatha Christie and Margery Allingham, the so-called golden age of crime fiction where the detective was very definitely a lady or gentleman, the setting was a country house, and even if the butler did not do it, he was certainly there to clean up afterwards.

'A lot of the appeal and value lies in the dust jacket,' explains Williams. 'Since jackets are obviously quite ephemeral, very few survive in good condition.' More recent detective stories might be less glamorous, but can still fetch high prices. As Williams notes, first editions of the very first crime novels by contemporary greats such as Ruth Rendell and P.D. James can today fetch in the region of £1,500, and newer writers in the genre, such as Minette Walters, are also inspiring collectors and escalating prices. 'However, you've got to be careful,' he concludes. 'Fashions in literature change like everything else, and what one generation prizes could be worth very little to collectors of the future. Buy a book because you like it, not just for investment.'

Crime Books – Fiction

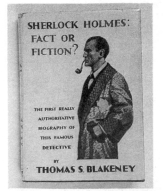

Thomas S. Blakeney, *Sherlock Holmes: Fact or Fiction?*, published by John Murray, Albemarle Street, London, 1932, 6¾ x 5in (17 x 12.5cm).
£100–125 *NW*

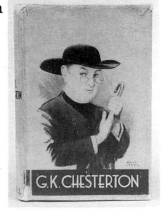

G. K. Chesterton, *The Scandal of Father Brown*, published by Cassell, fourth printing, 1936, 7½in x 5¼in (19 x 13cm).
£15–20 *NW*

Agatha Christie, *Evil Under The Sun*, published by The Crime Club, Pall Mall, London, first edition, 1941, 7½in x 5in (19 x 12.5cm).
£700–800 *NW*

Agatha Christie, *Sparkling Cyanide*, published by The Crime Club, Pall Mall, London, first edition, 1945, 7½in x 5in (19 x 12.5cm).
£65–75 *NW*

Arthur Conan Doyle, *The Hound of the Baskervilles*, published by George Newnes Ltd, first edition, 1902, 7½in x 5in (19 x 12.5cm).
£800–900 *NW*

r. Arthur Conan Doyle, *The Adventures of Sherlock Holmes*, with watercolour painting on fore-edge, published by George Newnes Ltd, 1905, 7¼ x 5in (18.5 x 12.5cm).
£190–225 *HB*

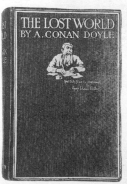

l. Arthur Conan Doyle, *The Lost World*, published by Hodder & Stoughton, London, first edition, 1912, 7½in x 5in (19 x 12.5cm).
£120–140 *HB*

Here Conan Doyle experiments with adventure rather than crime, the book introducing his other enduring literary hero, the great, Professor Challenger.

Lindsey Davis, *Poseidon's Gold*, published by Century, London, signed first edition, 1992, 9½ x 6½in (24 x 16.5cm).
£25–30 *NW*

Dick Francis, *Dead Cert*, published by Michael Joseph, first edition, 1962, in second impression jacket, 7½ x 5in (19 x 12.5cm).
£300–350 *NW*

If this book was in its original first impression jacket, its price range would be £1,000–1,200.

Jonathan Gash, *Gold from Gemini*, published by Collins Crime Club, first edition, 1978, 8 x 5¼in (20 x 13cm).
£150–175 *NW*

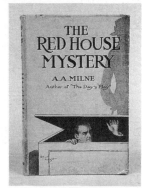

A. A. Milne, *The Red House Mystery*, published by Methuen, early re-reprint 1924, first edition 1922, 7¾ x 5½in (19.5 x 14cm).
£35–45 *NW*

Reginald Hill, *A Fairly Dangerous Thing*, published by Collins Crime Club, signed, first edition, 1972, 8 x 5in (20 x 12.5cm).
£75–85 *NW*

Peter Lovesey, *A Case of Spirits*, published by Macmillan, signed, first edition, 1975, 8 x 5in (20 x 12.5cm).
£40–50 *NW*

Miller's is a price GUIDE not a price LIST

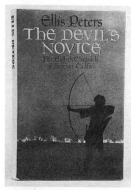

l. Ellis Peters, *The Devil's Novice*, published by Macmillan, first edition, 1983, 8 x 5¼in (20 x 13cm).
£55–65 *NW*

r. Ellis Peters, *A Morbid Taste for Bones*, published by Macmillan, first edition, 1977, 8 x 5in (20 x 12.5cm).
£250–300 *NW*

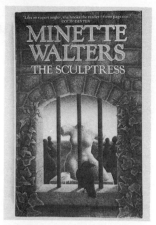

Minette Walters, *The Sculptress*, published by Macmillan, first edition, 1993, 8¾ x 5½in (22 x 14cm).
£30–35 *NW*

Super Detective Library, No.2 *The Armchair Detective* and No.3 *Bulldog Drummond*, and *Harry Lime*, some tape to spines, 1953, 5¼ x 7in (13.5 x 18cm).
£80–100 *CBP*

Crime Books – Non-Fiction

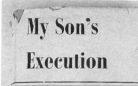

l. William George Bentley, *My Son's Execution*, published by W. H. Allen, 1957, 8¾ x 5¾in (22 x 14.5cm).
£35–45 *CEB*

The father of Derek Bentley examines the evidence and challenges the verdict against his son, which resulted in his execution. The Craig-Bentley case caused a public outcry and the controversy still continues.

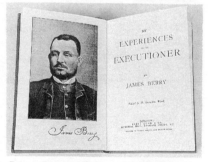

James Berry, *My Experiences as an Executioner*, published by Percy Lund & Co, 1891, 8 x 5¼in (20.5 x 13.5cm).
£130–150 *CEB*

Glaister & Brash, *Medico-Legal Aspects of the Ruxton Case*, published by S. Livingstone, Edinburgh, 1937, and Francis E. Camps, *Medical and Scientific Investigations in the Christie Case*, published by Macmillan, 1953, 10 x 8in (25 x 20cm).
l. **£60–70**
r. **£85–95** *CEB*

Karl Berg, *The Sadist*, published by William Heinemann Medical Books, 1945 re-issue, 9 x 6¼in (22.5 x 16cm).
£160–190 *CEB*

Margaret Cheney, *The Co-Ed Killer*, published by Walker, 1976, 9¼ x 6¼in (23.5 x 16cm).
£35–45 *CEB*

Dr John F. Condon, *Jafsie Tells All!*, the inside story of the Lindberg-Hauptmann case, published by Jonathan Lee, 1936, 8½ x 6in (21.5 x 15cm).
£65–75 *CEB*

l. J. Curtis, *Maria Martin, The Red Barn*, published by Thomas Kelly, Paternoster Row, London, 1828, 8¾ x 6in (22 x 15cm).
£75–85 *CEB*

r. Alexander Dumas, *Celebrated Crimes*, 8 volumes, with illustrations, published by H.S. Nichols, London, 1880, 9 x 6in (23 x 15cm).
£180–225 *HB*

Robert Elman, *Fired in Anger*, published by Doubleday, 1968, 10½ x 7½in (26.5 x 19cm).
£30–40 *CEB*

George Godwin, *Peter Kürten – A Study in Sadism,* published by William Heinemann Medical Books, 1945, 9 x 6in (23 x 15cm).
£150–175 *CEB*

Arthur Griffiths, *Mysteries of Police and Crime*, 3 volumes, published by Cassell & Co, London, 1904, 9 x 6¾in (23 x 17cm).
£85–95 *CEB*

Cross Reference
Colour Review

l. John Howard, *State of the Prisons*, published by William Eyres, Warrington, third edition, 1784. 12½ x 10in. (32 x 25cm)
£250–295 *CEB*

r. Mrs Eleanor Mason, *The Secret to the Maybrick Poisoning Case*, published by D'Vauz Press, Rangoon, 1890, 9½ x 6in (24 x 15cm).
£800–1,000 *CEB*

Four Jack the Ripper publications, 8¼ x 5⅝in (21x 14.5cm):
Elwyn Jones and John Lloyd, *The Ripper File*, published by Arthur Barker, London, 1975.
£80–100
Robin Odell, *Metropolitan Police*, published by George Harrap, London, first edition, 1965.
£30–40
Frank Spiering, *Prince Jack*, published by Doubleday & Co, New York, 1978.
£35–45
Allan Barnard, *The Harlot Killer*, published by Dodd, Mead & Co, New York, 1953.
£80–100 *CEB*

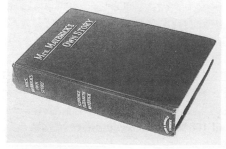

l. Florence Elizabeth Maybrick, *Mrs Maybrick's Own Story*, published by Funk & Wagnalls Co, 1905, 8¼ x 5½in (21 x 14cm).
£70–80 *CEB*

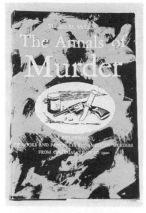

E. H. Porter, *History of the Borden Murders,* illustrated, published by George R. H. Buffington, 1893, 9½ x 6¼in (24 x 16cm). **£500–550** *CEB*

Margaret Seaton Wagner, *The Monster of Düsseldorf, The Life and Trial of Peter Kürten,* published by Faber & Faber, 1932, 8 x 5½in (20.5 x 14cm). **£85–95** *CEB*

Described by judges at his trial as 'the king of sexual delinquents', Kürten's crimes have been likened to those of Jack the Ripper and he himself expressed admiration for the 1888 killer. He committed rape, arson, murder and mutilation on a massive scale and claimed association with the werewolf and vampire tradition, striking terror into the local population.

Thomas M. McDade, *The Annals of Murder,* a bibliography of books and pamphlets on American murders from Colonial times to 1900, published by University of Oklahoma Press, 1961, 9½ x 6½in (24 x 16.5cm). **£40–45** *CEB*

Josiah Thompson, *Six Seconds in Dallas,* illustrated, published by Bernard Geis Associates, New York, 1967, 9¾ x 6¾in (24.5 x 17cm). **£55–65** *CEB*

One of the rarest volumes on the assassination of President John F. Kennedy. A micro-study of the events claiming that three gunmen murdered the President.

Crime Books – Trials

l. A Collection of the Most Remarkable and Interesting Trials, Volumes I and II, published by R. Snagg, 129 Fleet Street, London, 1775–76, 10½ x 8¾in (27 x 22cm). **£350–400** *CEB*

FURTHER READING

Catherine Porter, *Collecting Books,* Miller's Publications, 1995

l. Criminal Trials in Scotland, 4 volumes, published by William Tait, Princes Street, Edinburgh, 1833, 10¾ x 8¾in (27.5 x 22cm). **£250–300** *CEB*

r. Three volumes of Notable British Trials, by various authors, published by William Hodge & Co, dated from *l.* to *r.* 1952, 1929 and 1935, 8¾ x 6in (22 x 15cm). **£30–35 each** *CEB*

Illustrated & Children's Books

Richard Adams, *Watership Down*, published by Rex Collins, first edition, 1972, 8¾ x 5¼in (22 x 13cm).
£525–575 *NW*

Hans Andersen, *Fairy Tales and Legends,* illustrated by Rex Whistler, 10 full-page prints and numerous black and white illustrations, published by Cobden-Sanderson Ltd, 1935, 8vo.
£200–250 *DW*

One of 200 copies, signed by Whistler on half title.

Enid Blyton, *Look out Secret Seven,* published by Brockhampton Press, fourth impression, 1967, 7¾ x 5¼in (20 x 13cm).
£4–5 *NW*

Roald Dahl, *Matilda,* illustrated by Quentin Blake, published by Jonathan Cape, 1988, 9½ x 6¼in (24 x 16cm).
£10–15 *NW*

Cross Reference
Colour Review

l. Walt Disney's *Brave Little Tailor,* published by Collins, Australia, 12 page colour illustrated booklet, 1930s, 7½ x 6½in (19 x 16.5cm).
£12–15 *CBP*

l. Rev W. Awdry, *Very Old Engines,* published by Kaye & Ward, 1981, first published 1961, 4¼ x 5½in (11 x 14cm).
£3–4 *NW*

Elisabeth Beresford, *The Wombles,* published by Ernest Benn Ltd, 1968, 8½ x 5¼in (21.5 x 13cm).
£15–20 *NW*

Collectors of children's books are often inspired by nostalgia. Today's thirty-somethings grew up with television and there is a growing market for books relating to such favourites as The Wombles, The Magic Roundabout, The Clangers *and other TV characters from the 1960s–70s.*

Alexander Dumas, *The Dumas Fairy Tale Book,* edited and translated by Harry A. Spurr, illustrated by Harry Rountree, published by Frederick Warne & Co, 1924, 8 x 6in (20.5 x 15cm).
£35–45 *HB*

Lewis Carroll, *Alice's Adventures in Wonderland,* published by Macmillan, first edition, 1898, 7¾ x 5in (19.5 x 12.5cm).
£80–100 *NW*

Lewis Carroll inspires specialist collectors; some enthusiasts collect illustrated editions of Alice *throughout the decades. Sir John Tenniel and Arthur Rackham have been succeeded by such notable artists as Salvador Dali and Ralph Steadman as illustrators.* Alice's Adventures in Wonderland *was first published in 1865, but was almost immediately withdrawn because Carroll was unhappy with the illustrations. According to dealer Nigel Williams, only 27 copies of this first edition are known to exist, and only one is on the market.*

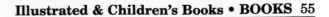

Hollywood, published by
Fawcett, 1938, and *Walt
Disney's Snow White and the
Seven Dwarfs*, published by
Dean & Son, 1938,
11¼ x 8½in (28.5 x 22cm).
£35–40 *CBP*

Giles Annual, No. 2, 1947,
7¾ x 10in (20 x 25.5cm).
£175–200 *NW*

First published in 1946, over
the following decades the Giles
annual was a popular
Christmas stocking filler. Prices
depend on age and rarity. The
first 5 annuals can fetch
around £200, 1950s volumes
range in price from £8–50,
whilst most volumes
from the sixties onwards tend to
be worth under £5 each.

Giles Annual, No.11, 1957,
7¾ x 10in (20 x 25.5cm).
£8–10 *NW*

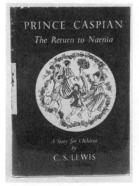

r. Hugh Lofting, *Doctor Dolittle's Post
Office*, published by Jonathan Cape, 20th
impression, 1964, 8 x 5¼in (20 x 13cm).
£10–12 *NW*

The first edition was published in 1924.

C. S. Lewis, *Prince
Caspian, The Return
to Narnia*, illustrated
by Pauline Baynes,
published by Geoffrey
& Bles, first edition,
1951, 8 x 5½in
(20 x 14cm).
£250–300 *NW*

**Miller's is a
price GUIDE
not a price LIST**

Dominic Winter
Book Auctions

*We hold regular monthly sales of
Antiquarian and General Printed
Books & Maps, plus twice-yearly
sales of Sports Books & Memorabilia,
Art Reference & Pictures,
Photography & Ephemera (including
toys, games and other collectables).*

Please contact us for advice and
information regarding the sale valuation
of any of the above categories.

A free sample catalogue will be sent on request.

The Old School, Maxwell Street,
Swindon SN1 5DR

Tel 01793 611340 Fax 01793 491727

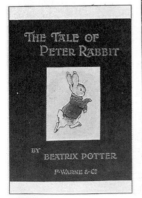

Beatrix Potter, *The
Tale of Peter Rabbit*,
published by F. Warne
& Co, first trade
edition, 1902, 12mo.
£1,600–1,800 *DW*

A. A. Milne, *The
House at Pooh
Corner*, illustrated by
E. H. Shepard,
published by
Methuen, signed first
edition, 1928, 7½ x
5in (19 x 12.5cm).
£1,000–1,250 *NW*

S. R. Praeger, *How They Went to School*, 1904, 8¼ x 10½in (21 x 26.5cm).
£30–50 *MRW*

Margarete Steiff, *Teddy und Verwandte reisen durch die Lande*, published in Munich, 1928, 9 x 11in (23 x 28cm).
£500–600 *TED*

A rare publication.

J. R. R. Tolkien, *The Hobbit*, published by G. Allen & Unwin Ltd, fourth impression 1963, first published 1937, 7½ x 5¼in (19 x 13cm).
£20–25 *NW*

l. In Nurseryland, with Louis Wain, Father Tuck's Golden Gift Series, 1920, 10¾ x 8in (27 x 20cm).
£80–90 *TAR*

l. Geoffrey Willans and Ronald Searle, *How to be Topp*, published by Max Parrish & Co Ltd, first edition, 1954, 8 x 5½in (20 x 14cm).
£20–25 *NW*

Rupert

More Rupert Adventures, Daily Express annual, 1943, 12 x 10in (30 x 25cm).
£110–130 *P(B)*

Rupert, Daily Express annual, 1968, 10 x 7in (25 x 18cm).
£15–20 *NW*

If the 'magic' pages have not been painted, annuals (even from this comparatively late period) can be worth in the region of £100.

The New Adventures of Rupert, Daily Express annual, 1936, 12 x 10in (30 x 25cm).
£520–550 *DW*

The first Daily Express Rupert Bear annual.

Rupert's Adventure Book, Daily Express annual, 1940, 12 x 10in (30 x 25cm).
£100–120 *P(B)*

This was the fifth Rupert annual and was the first one to be produced in colour.

l. Rupert, Daily Express annual, 1970s, 10 x 7in (25 x 18cm).
£4–6 each *CMF*

r. Three *Rupert* annuals, 1944–46, 12 x 10in (30 x 25cm).
£30–40 each *OTS*

BOTTLES

A shaft and globe shaped bottle, with evenly pitted surface, c1660, 9¼in (23.5cm) high.
£800–1,000 *NWi*

In the mid-17thC, glass bottles were expensive luxuries. Owners would have their own bottles, often marked with their coat-of-arms, which they would send to the wine merchant to be filled. The long neck and spherical body show this rare example to be amongst the earliest of wine bottles, hence its high price.

An early onion-shaped bottle, c1680, 7in (18cm) high.
£200–250 *NWi*

A north German mould-blown flat-sided bottle, c1720, 8in (20.5cm) high.
£200–250 *NWi*

A half-size mallet-shaped bottle, with excavated character, c1740, 6½in (16.5cm) high.
£125–150 *NWi*

A glass cylinder bottle, c1760, 14in (35.5cm) high.
£125–150 *NWi*

A double magnum bottle, with seal for Edmd. Whiteway, c1776, 44in (112cm) high.
£420–500 *NWi*

A globular olive green glass serving bottle, with opaque white decoration in the Nailsea style, c1780, 12in (30.5cm) high.
£650–750 *NWi*

Cross Reference
Breweriana

l. A Continental mallet-shaped olive/amber glass bottle, c1740, 7½in (19cm) high.
£170–200 *NWi*

A Dutch square-tapered olive green gin bottle, c1800, 9½in (24cm) high.
£80–90 *NWi*

Two embossed glass bottles, c1885, tallest 9½in (24cm) high.
l. **£60–70** *r.* **£10–15** *BBR*

A late Victorian amber glass bottle, c1885, 10¼in (26cm) high.
£50–60 *BBR*

A glass wine bottle, the applied seal with 'C' beneath a baronet's coronet, c1800, 10¾in (27cm) high.
£120–140 *NWi*

A French translucent green olive oil bottle, with applied seal and pontilled base, c1840, 11in (28cm) high.
£100–125 *NWi*

A Belgian 'cheat' bottle, with exaggerated 'kick-up' to base, c1850, 10in (25.5cm) high.
£80–100 *NWi*

An olive green gin bottle, with embossed trademark, c1870, 10½in (27cm) high.
£80–100 *NWi*

l. An Ally Sloper's Relish bottle, c1910, 11¾in (30cm) high.
£12–20 *OD*

This bottle was dug out of the old Potts Railway tip at the Welshpool / Shreswbury Railway. The Relish was very popular during WWI but went out of production around 1930. The bottles were factory produced from 1900.

r. A rehoboam champagne bottle, 1950s, 23½in (60cm) high.
£18–22 *WAB*

A rehoboam contains the equivalent of 6 bottles.

Ceramic

An off-white glazed disinfectant bottle, with black transfer Maw's Lavatory Disinfector, chipped, c1900, 4in (10cm) high.
£36–40 *BBR*

Two white ceramic bottles, with black transfer The Plynine Coy Limited, Hawick, Household Ammonia, Warranted Pure, c1900, tallest 11in (28cm) high.
£30–35 *BBR*

l. A Doulton commemorative gin bottle, 1910, 8in (20.5cm) high.
£70–80 *PC*

Cross Reference
Advertising & Packaging
Doulton

Two stoneware bottles, both manufactured by George Okey, Wilnecote, Tamworth, 16½in (42cm) high:
l. with internal screw stopper, inscribed '1d will be charged for screws if not returned in bottle', c1910.
r. embossed Lawrance & Sons, Yarmouth, Beccles & Saxmundham, c1900.
£25–30 each *PC*

A ceramic bottle, with pink lip, printed G. & C. Moore, Stone Ginger Beer, Springfield Bottling Stores, Bridgeton, Glasgow, chipped and repaired, c1910, 8½in (21.5cm) high.
£100–120 *BBR*

A ceramic bottle, with blue lip and swing stopper, printed Bailey, Clark & Co Ltd, Celebrated Stone Ginger Beer, Glasgow, c1910, 8½in (21.5cm) high.
£100–120 *BBR*

A ceramic bottle, with swing stopper, blue transfer Forrest & Co, Ginger Beer, Inverness, restored lip, c1910, 8¾in (22cm) high.
£42–50 *BBR*

A ceramic bottle, with blue top and blue transfer The Licensed Victuallers Pure Mineral Water Co, Quench Your Thirst With Our Ginger Beer, minor chip, c1910, 8½in (21.5cm) high.
£250–300 *BBR*

A ceramic bottle, with blue/black transfer Morecambe Aerated & Mineral Water Compy, c1910, 7in (18cm) high.
£8–10 *BBR*

A stoneware wine bottle, with transfer Matthew Gloag, Bideford, Wine & Spirit Merchants, Established 1839, c1915, 6¾in (17cm) high.
£20–25 PC

A stoneware bottle, manufactured by Bourne Denby, with transfer and embossed Schweppes Purveyors To The King, 1920s, 6¾in (17cm) high.
£8–10 PC

A pottery brush bottle, c1950, 7in (18cm) high.
£10–15 GL

Cross Reference
Guinness

A stoneware bottle, manufactured by Price Powell & Co, Bristol, with transfer for C. C. Dornat & Co, Barnstaple, Bideford & Ilfracombe, 1920s, 6¾in (17cm) high.
£8–10 PC

A brown and cream stoneware bottle, with transfer Wilson & Co, Ginger Beer, 1930s, 7½in (19cm) high.
£8–10 PC

Drug Rounds & Medicine

A Dutch heavy olive green glass medicine bottle, c1760, 4½in (11.5cm) high.
£100–125 NWi

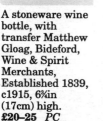

A clear lead glass medicine bottle for Dr Sibly's Solar Tincture, c1810, 6¼in (16cm) high.
£250–300 NWi

A green glass flat medicine flask, with seal inscribed Riga Balsam, c1800, 4½in (11.5cm) high.
£100–125 NWi

A clear glass drug round, with gilt, white, red and black octagonal label, 19thC, 15in (38cm) high.
£15–20 AXT

A clear glass drug round, with gilt, white, red and black label, late 19thC, 25in (63.5cm) high.
£20–25 AXT

Cross Reference
Scientific Instruments

l. A French apothecary jar, late 19thC, 11in (28cm) high.
£30–40 AXT

l. A pair of clear glass drug rounds, with painted black and gilt labels, 19thC, 19in (48cm) high.
£15–20 each AXT

Milk Bottles

In the Victorian era, milk was delivered first by milkmaids and later by horse-drawn floats. The container customers used was a hand-can into which the milk would be decanted. After WWI cheaper production methods enabled bottles to come into widespread use. Since it became illegal to sell milk in open containers these were sealed with a cardboard disk which was used to carry advertising messages.

The aluminium foil milk bottle top was first devised in Sweden in 1914 and introduced to Britain in 1929. Though cardboard caps were still being used up to the 1950s, they were gradually ousted by their aluminium rivals. Advertisers then found a new source in decorating the bottle itself.

The advertising bottles featured below date from the 1980s. Value depends on the advert and the way it was presented on the bottle. If placed across the 'seam', printing is uneven and images could also become rubbed if the bottle made too many journeys in the milk crate. Bottles were often printed both front and back with advertising slogans or recipes.

A one-pint milk bottle with a selection of cardboard caps, one inscribed 'Long Live the Queen, Coronation June 1953', 1950s.
Bottle £4–5
Caps 50p–£1 each *REN*

Three one-pint milk bottles advertising Knorr sauce mix, with recipes on the reverse, 1986.
50p–£2 each *JMC*

Three one-pint milk bottles, with advertisements for Bowyers meats and Ready Brek, c1986.
50p–£2 each *JMC*

Three one-pint milk bottles, with advertisements for Brooke Bond and Ty-Phoo tea and PG Tips tea bags, c1986.
50p–£2 each *JMC*

Three one-pint milk bottles, with advertisements for eggs, c1986.
50p–£2 each *JMC*

Three one-pint milk bottles, with advertisements for the Dairy Diary 1987, Hermesetas and Farmer's Wife Bread, c1987.
50p–£2 *JMC*

r. A one-pint milk bottle advertising LBC News Radio, c1986.
50p–£2 *JMC*

r. Two one-pint milk bottles, with advertisements for The Mirror and Sunday Mirror and on reverse a Bingo game, c1986.
50p–£2 each *JMC*

BOXES

A lacquered tortoiseshell patch box, 18thC, 2½in (6.5cm) wide.
£220–260 *MB*

A miniature heart-shaped box, mounted in silver, c1810, 2in (5cm) wide.
£100–120 *MB*

A black sealing wax card case, c1820, 4in (10cm) wide.
£80–90 *MB*

> **Cross Reference**
> Sewing

A penwork box, with brass handles and ball feet, c1820, 8in (20cm) wide.
£235–285 *MB*

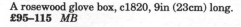

A rosewood glove box, c1820, 9in (23cm) long.
£95–115 *MB*

A mahogany brass-banded campaign box, c1820, 11in (28cm) wide.
£235–285 *MB*

> **Cross Reference**
> Writing

An early Victorian tortoiseshell trinket box, 3in (7.5cm) wide.
£70–80 *MRW*

A rosewood brass-inlaid vanity box, c1835, 9in (23cm) wide.
£400–460 *MB*

l. A miniature tortoiseshell casket, c1825, 2½in (6.5cm) wide.
£70–80 *MB*

Four Victorian turned ebony and ivory boxes, largest 3in (7.5cm) diam.
£30–60 each *MRT*

An oak brass-banded glove box, c1850,
10in (25.5cm) long.
£130–150 *MB*

l. A walnut
jewellery box,
inlaid with
tulipwood,
c1860, 10⅞in
(27.5cm) wide.
£150–175 *MB*

A palmwood glove box, c1880,
15¼in (39cm) long.
£235–285 *MB*

A burr-amboyna mini chest, inlaid with
brass and mother-of-pearl, c1880,
6¼in (16cm) wide.
£175–200 *MB*

*Amboyna wood takes its name from the
island of Ambon, in the Maluku province
of Indonesia. Hard and with a richly
figured grain, it was popular for veneers
and decorative woodwork.*

An Edwardian lady's morocco dressing case, with outer canvas cover, the green silk-lined interior fitted with silver-mounted bright cut engraved accoutrements, glove stretchers, manicure set, morocco jewellery box and writing sachet, the silver-mounted items London 1912.
£300–350 *HOLL*

A papier mâché hand-painted box, 1920s, 7in (18cm) wide.
£30–40 *SUS*

Cross Reference
Colour Review

An ivory box carved with elephants, 1930s, 10in (25.5cm) diam.
£130–150 *TAR*

l. A crossbanded flame mahogany tea caddy, c1800, 8in (20.5cm) wide.
£200–235 *MB*

Tea Caddies

A Georgian inlaid tea caddy and silver caddy spoon, c1790, caddy 4in (10cm) high, spoon 2¾in (7cm) long.
£210–250 *PC*

A George III mahogany single tea caddy, c1790, 4¼in (11cm) high.
£220–260 *MB*

A mahogany tea caddy, with original glass liner, brass handles and claw-and-ball feet, c1820, 11¾in (30cm) wide.
£325–385 *MB*

A rosewood tea caddy, inlaid with mother-of-pearl, c1835, 8in (20.5cm) wide.
£170–200 *MB*

A boxwood bound mahogany tea caddy, c1815, 7½in (19cm) wide.
£160–200 *MB*

A Wills's Star Cigarettes cut-out stand-up show card, 1930s, 30in (76cm) high.
£100–120 *P(B)*

A Potter's Catarrh Pastilles 3-D cut-out counter card, with slogan 'Conquer Your Catarrh', 1930s, 15 x 10in (38 x 25.5cm).
£40–50 *P(B)*

A Bile Beans cut-out show card, with slogan 'Bile Beans for Biliousness', 1930s, 14½ x 13⅓in (37 x 34cm).
£45–55 *P(B)*

A Player's Cigarettes 3-D cut-out stand-up show card, 1930s, 26¾ x 20½in (68 x 52.5cm).
£150–180 *P(B)*

A Beatrix Potter composition advertising figure, Peter Rabbit, 1950s, 16in (40.5cm) high.
£150–200 *TOY*

A Redgate fruit drinks tinplate advertising sign, c1960, 27½ x 19in (70 x 48cm).
£20–25 *SOL*

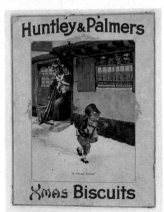

A Huntley & Palmers show card, 1930s, 18 x 12in (45.5 x 30.5cm).
£350–400 *P(B)*

A set of 4 McDonalds' Batman Forever glasses, American, issued 1995.
£20–30 *TOY*

A Liberty plaster model, c1935, 21in (53.5cm) high.
£100–120 *COB*

A Huntley & Palmers biscuit
tin, in the form of a post box,
1908, 6½in (16.5cm) high.
£160–185 *WAB*

A Huntley & Palmers biscuit
tin, in the form of a windmill,
1920s, 12in (30.5cm) high.
£650–750 *WAB*

A biscuit tin, depicting the
Trooping of the Colour, c1960,
8in (20.5cm) wide.
£7–9 *AL*

Three Cadbury's biscuit tins, in the form of an
animal circus, 1980s, each tin 4¾in (12cm) long.
£5–6 each *WAB*

W. & R. Jacob & Co biscuit tin, in the form of
Edward VIII's Coronation carriage, produced
prior to the abdication, 1935, 8¾in (22cm) wide.
£225–265 *WAB*
This is a rare item.

A Maison Lyons Turkish Delight tin,
1930–50s, 8in (20.5cm) wide.
£18–22 *WAB*

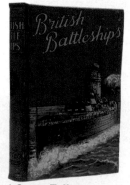

A Lyons Toffee tin, in the
form of the book c1930,
5½ x 3½in (14 x 9cm).
£65–75 *WAB*

A tin, decorated with the
painting *Good Companions*,
after Arthur William Devis,
c1930, 6in (15cm) wide.
£8–10 *AL*

r. A sweet tin, in the form
of a suitcase, 1950s,
8in (20.5cm) wide.
£20–30 *COB*

A Try Your Grip 1d machine, by Mechanical Trading Co, c1895, 10in (25.5cm) wide.
£5,000–6,000 *HAK*

A French Roulette Serpent betting game, 1912, 30in (75cm) high.
£1,200–1,500 *HAK*

A La Comète one-armed bandit betting game, by Caille, USA, 1907, 20½in (52cm) high.
£900–1,200 *BB*

A French All Win style *Le Dragon* machine, 1914, 30in (76cm) high.
£750–950 *BB*

The New Improved Pickwick game, No. 436B, made in Belgium, 1914, 35in (89cm) high.
£1,200–1,500 *BB*

An Oliver Whales All Win machine, 1955, 32in (82cm) high.
£275–325 *AMc*

A Bryan's U-Win 1d slot machine, 1960, 25in (64cm) high.
£300–350 *BB*

A Bryan's 12-win clock slot machine, 1950s, 24in (61cm) high.
£175–225 *AMc*

r. A Mills Hi-Top 6d one-armed bandit, 1955, 25in (64cm) high.
£250–350 *BB*

A hand-painted plastic crinoline lady brush and crumb tray, c1933, 6½in (16.5cm) wide.
£25–30 *BKK*

A ceramic trio jazz band cruet set, 1920–30s, 2½in (6.5cm) high.
£60–80 *PC*

A Continental ceramic model of a sailing boat, c1930, 18in (45.5cm) high.
£100–120 *DAF*

An Art Deco plaster wall mask, 1930s, 9½in (24cm) high.
£30–50 *PC*

A set of playing cards, with score cards, in original box, 1930s, 8in (20.5cm) wide.
£30–35 *BEV*

r. An Art Deco ceramic vase, by James Kent, 1930s, 9½in (24cm) high.
£70–80 *HCH*

An Art Deco female plaster figure, c1920, 22½in (57cm) high.
£165–195 *TCF*

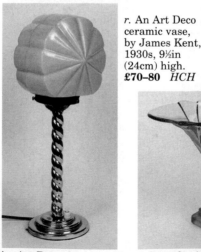

An Art Deco chrome table lamp, with glass shade, 1930s, 17in (43cm) high.
£100–120 *ML*

A Sowerby Art Deco pressed glass vase, c1932, 6½in (16.5cm) high.
£32–40 *BKK*

A 1949 Ferrari 166 resin model car, limited edition, 3½in (8.5cm) long.
£125–150 *PC*

A 1995 Benetton B195 metal model car, as driven by Michael Schumacher, limited edition, 4½in (14cm) long.
£150–175 *PC*

A Gamages Motor Oil tin, 1920s, 21in (53.5cm) high.
£65–75 *WAB*

A 1983 Thrust 2 metal model car, as driven by Richard Noble, limited edition, 7½in (19cm) long.
£200–250 *PC*

A Köhler dashboard clock, 1930s, 2⅛in (5.5cm) diam.
£65–75 *ATF*

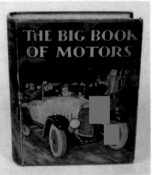

The Big Book of Motors, edited by Herbet Strang, 1927, 8½in (21.5cm) high.
£25–30 *OD*

A copper ashtray or pin tray advertising Pratt's Motor Spirit, marked JS & SB, 1930, 4½in (11.5cm) diam.
£10–15 *PC*

A Smiths Bluecol anti-freeze tin, excellent condition, 1930s, 9in (23cm) high.
£20–30 *SW*

A Coracle picnic hamper, 1930s, 16¾in (42.5cm) wide.
£110–120 *SW*

A grease set, in original tin, 1920s, 6¼in (16cm) long.
£25–30 *SW*

A nozzle and gauge, 1950s, 11½in (29cm) high.
£45–55 *SW*

Cecil Aldin, *The White Kitten Book*, published by Hodder & Stoughton, mint copy, c1920, 9¼ x 8½in (23.5 x 21.5cm). **£200–250** *NW*

Enid Blyton, *Noddy and His Car*, published by Samson Low, No.3, first edition, 1951, 7½ x 5½in (19 x 14cm). **£12–15** *NW*

Animals Tame & Wild, published by S.W. Partridge & Co, late 19thC, 12½in (32cm) wide. **£190–230** *HB*

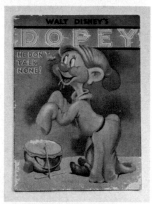

A miniature leather-bound bible, c1780, 1¾ x 1½in (4.5 x 4cm). **£250–300** *PC*

l. Bookano Stories, with pictures that spring-up in model form, 1930s. **£60–100** *MRW*

Walt Disney, *Dopey*, published by Whitman, US, some wear, 1938, 12 x 8¾in (30.5 x 22.5cm). **£45–55** *CBP*

The New Rupert Book, Daily Express annual, 1946, 10in (25.5cm) high. **£40–50** *P(B)*

Walt Disney, *Donald Duck Days*, published by Birn Bros, 1930s, 7in (18cm) high. **£50–60** *CBP*

Hans Andersen, *Fairy Tales*, illustrated, Oxford University Press, 1936, 9¼ x 7in (23.5 x 18cm). **£80–90** *HB*

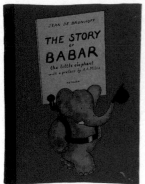

Jean De Brunhoff, *The Story of Babar*, first edition, 1934.
£70–90 *NW*

Giles Annual, published by Daily Express, 1975, 7¾ x 10in (20 x 25.5cm).
£4–5 *NW*

The Boys' Book of Heroes, published by Birn Bros, 1950, 11 x 8¼in (28 x 21cm).
£30–35 *CBP*

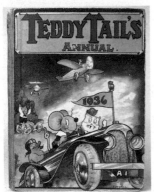

Teddy Tail's, Daily Mail annual, 1936, 11in (28cm) high.
£18–22 *CMF*

Geoffrey Willans and Ronald Searle, *Whizz for Atomms*, first edition, 1956, 8in (20.5cm) high.
£20–25 *NW*

Richmal Crompton, *William The Gangster*, 3rd reprint 1935, 7½ x 5 (19 x 12.5cm).
£40–50 *NW*

Kathleen Hale, *Orlando's Magic Carpet*, 1958, 7½ x 9in (19 x 23cm).
£50–66 *NW*

Dougal, a Purnell shape book, printed in Italy, 1973, 8in (20.5cm) square.
£4–5 *NW*

l. A selection of miniature pocket books, c1940, 2¾in (7cm) square.
£1–2 each *OD*

Roald Dahl, *James and The Giant Peach*, published by Allen & Unwin, first edition 1967, 9½ x 6¼in (24 x 16cm).
£100–125 *NW*

Black Bess, 2 volumes, published by E. Harrison, Salisbury Court, Fleet Street, London, c1868, 10¼ x 7in (26 x 18cm).
£250–275 *CEB*

Charles Stoddart, *Bible John – Search for a Sadist*, published by Paul Harris, c1980, 8¾ x 5¾in (22 x 14.5cm).
£25–30 *CEB*

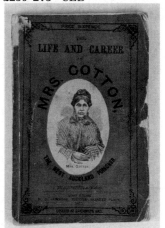

The Life and Career of Mrs Cotton, published by W. J. Cummins, Bishop Auckland, 1873, 7½ x 5in (19 x 12.5cm).
£100–120 *CEB*

Arthur Conan Doyle, *The Starkmunro Letters,* published by Longmans, reprint 1927, 7 x 4¾in (18 x 12cm).
£30–35 *NW*

Margery Allingham, *The Fashion in Shrouds*, published by W. Heinemann Ltd, first edition, 1938, 8 x 5⅛in (20.5 x 13cm).
£175–200 *NW*

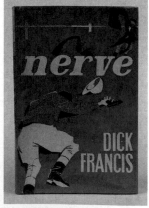

Paul H. Gantt, *The Case of Alfred Packer*, published by University of Denver Press, 1952, 8¾ x 6in (22 x 15cm).
£40–50 *CEB*

Four photo panel crime stories, *Picture Crimes*, 1937, *Rip Kirby, Crime Detective, The Perfect Crime*, 1950s, 10¼ x 7¼in (26 x 18.5cm).
£90–100 *CBP*

Dick Francis, *Nerve*, published by Michael Joseph, first edition, 1964, 7½ x 5in (19 x 12.5cm).
£475–525 *NW*

A case bottle, with
straight sides, c1750,
10½in (26.5cm) high.
£250–300 *NWi*

A bottle with
gilt label, c1790,
9in (23cm) high.
£150–175 *NWi*

A Dutch gin bottle,
c1920, 10in
(25.5cm) high.
£15–20 *GL*

A Scotch
whisky bottle,
c1920, 12in
(30.5cm) high.
£20–30 *GL*

A Mackinlay's
whisky display
bottle, c1940,
18½in (47cm) high.
£30–40 *GL*

Two Victorian Aldridge & Co,
Cod bottles, with original
labels, 9in (23cm) high.
£10–12 *TAR*

A bisque porcelain spirit
flask, modelled as Charles
Lindbergh, c1980,
12½in (32cm) high.
£80–100 *SAS*

A V-J full gin
bottle, c1920,
9¾in (25cm) high.
£75–85 *GL*

A Firth's stoneware
ginger beer bottle,
1920s, 7in (18cm) high.
£30–35 *PC*

A ribbed glass drug
round, with label, 19thC,
10¼in (26cm) high.
£30–35 *AXT*

Three one-pint milk bottles, advertising
Crusha Milk Shake and Fruit Juice, c1986.
50p–£2 each *JMC*

Two one-pint milk bottles,
advertising Mars, c1986.
50p–£2 each *JMC*

A French satinwood trinket box,
with brass feet, early 19thC,
8in (20.5cm) wide.
£200–240 *COT*

A rosewood writing box, decorated with mother-of-pearl
inlaid into ebony, with secret drawers, c1815,
15¾in (40cm) wide.
£400–460 *MB*

A sewing box, painted with a scene of
Tonbridge, together with thread holders,
c1820, 8½in (21.5cm) wide.
£150–180 *COT*

A boxwood novelty pencil case, in the form of a
trunk, mid-19thC, 7⅞in (20cm) wide.
£250–300 *PC*

A papier mâché two-division tea caddy,
c1860, 8½in (21.5cm) wide.
£250–300 *PC*

A rosewood sewing box, inlaid with abalone,
mother-of-pearl and brass, c1840,
11¾in (30cm) wide.
£500–575 *MB*

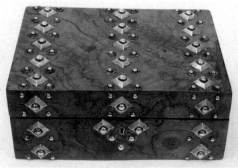

A figured walnut box, with brass bands,
c1870, 10¾in (27cm) wide.
£150–200 *MB*

A hand-painted papier mâché travelling desk,
c1845, 13½in (34cm) wide.
£350–400 *MB*

A copper ale muller, 19thC,
15in (38cm) long.
£150–175 *BSA*

Two Scottish pottery ale jugs, modelled as Johnny
Soutter and Tammy Shanter, c1870,
11in (28cm) high.
£350–385 *WAB*

A Whitbread match holder and
striker, 1930s, 4in (10cm) high.
£65–75 *BSA*

A green glass jug, advertising
Braemar Scotch Whisky,
c1890, 6¼in (16cm) high.
£190–225 *MJW*

An Associated Pottery jug,
advertising Mitchell's whisky,
c1910, 6in (15.5cm) high.
£135–155 *GL*

l. Two lamps, one with a
ceramic barrel base by
Wade, the other an ale
glass, both with labels on
the shades, 1960s,
11¾in (30cm) high.
£15–20 each *GL*

Two whisky labels, c1900, 5in (13cm) high:
l. Albion Blend Highland. **£5–8**
r. The Goblin Scotch. **£2–3** *GL*

A flat-backed rubberoid
sign, advertising Old
Angus Scotch Whisky,
c1950, 15in (38cm) high.
£75–100 *GL*

A Carlton Ware
Beefeater Gin
figure, 1960s,
17in (43cm) high.
£140–150 *DBr*

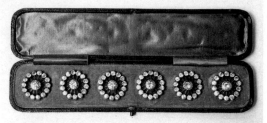

A set of 6 silver and paste buttons, 18thC,
¾in (20mm) diam, contained in original box.
£150–175 *JBB*

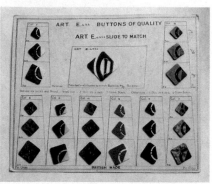

An Art Deco complete sample card
of buttons, late 1930s, 9½ x 11½in
(24 x 29cm).
£25–40 *MRW*

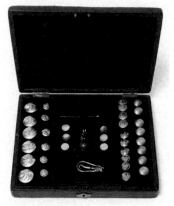

A set of Victorian gentleman's
buttons, Scottish, contained in
original box, 8¼in (21cm) wide.
£150–180 *OBS*

A Perspex button, with
floral decoration, c1945,
1½in (35mm) diam.
£4–5 *OBS*

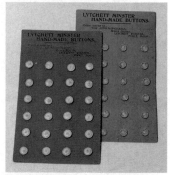

Two cards of Dorset hand-made
buttons, recarded in Lychett
Minster in 1903, 7 x 4¼in
(18 x 11cm).
£4–15 each card *OBS*

A pair of Victorian metal pansy
buttons, ¾in (20mm) diam.
£10–12 *OBS*

A copper button, with
porcelain inset centre,
1¼in (35mm) diam.
£18–22 *JBB*

An Oriental silver-gilt two-piece
clasp, with enamel centre and
turquoise stones, c1900,
4in (10cm) wide.
£75–85 *JBB*

An Oriental *cloisonné*
two-piece clasp, c1910,
2½in (60mm) wide.
£65–75 *JBB*

A set of 5 jade buttons and
jade belt buckle, 19thC,
2¾in (70mm) wide.
Buttons **£70–80**
Buckle **£85–95** *JBB*

A Leica Leicina 8mm camera, c1960, 8in (20.5cm) long.
£70–80 *HEG*

A mahogany and brass copy camera with red bellows, c1900, 12in (30.5cm) long.
£75–100 *HEG*
Used for copying negatives onto 2¼in (5.5cm) magic lantern slides.

A Box Ensign camera, 1920s, 7in (18cm) long.
£60–70 *SW*

A cardboard Stereoscope, with transparencies, 1940s, with original box, 5in (13cm) wide.
£10–15 *HEG*

An Eagle black Bakelite projector, transformer, instructions and 2 films, with catalogue, by Martin Lucas Ltd, in original box, c1953, 10in (25cm) long.
£350–400 *CBP*

A Finetta 35mm camera, with interchangeable lenses, c1952, 5in (12.5cm) wide.
£25–30 *Gre*

A Kiku 16 sub-miniature camera, c1956, 2¼in (6cm) wide, with carrying case and box.
£120–140 *Gre*

A Father Christmas camera, made in Taiwan, the lens hidden beneath the nose, c1990, 4in (10cm) wide.
£10–15 *HEG*

A Lancaster & Son quarter plate Instantograph, 1902, 5½in (14cm) wide.
£160–200 *VCL*

A novelty ornamental press camera, c1990, 3½in (9cm) wide.
£4–5 *HEG*

Three Beswick finches, with flower-decorated bases, now discontinued, 1970s–80s, 3in (7.5cm) high.
£14–20 each *TAC*

An Austrian pottery dog, c1930, 5in (13cm) high.
£30–40 *WAB*

A Beatrix Potter story book figure of Fierce Bad Rabbit, by Beswick, 1st version, 1974–85, 4¾in (12cm) high.
£90–110 *SAS*

Three Limoges hand-painted pill boxes, in the form of cats, with gilt-metal mounts, 1990s, 4in (10cm) high.
£100–150 *JPr*

A Beatrix Potter story book figure of Anna Maria, by Beswick, 1974–85, 3¼in (8cm) high.
£140–170 *SAS*

A Midwinter deer, c1950, 7in (18cm) high.
£28–32 *AND*

A Beatrix Potter story book figure of Mr Tod, by Beswick, 1988–89, 5in (12.5cm) high.
£160–200 *SAS*

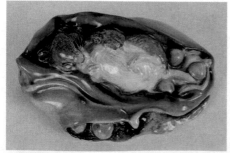

A Beatrix Potter story book figure of Timmie Willie Sleeping, by Beswick, 1985–88, 4¼in (11cm) wide.
£70–90 *SAS*

A set of four green Denby rabbits, 1930s, 1½–6½in (4–16.5cm) high.
£80–110 *TAC*

A Grainger's Worcester dish, c1860, 5¾in (14.5cm) diam.
£18–22 *HEI*

A Victorian soup plate, Wild Rose pattern, Barker & Son, 10in (25.5cm) diam.
£38–42 *PSA*

A Copeland Spode Italian pattern tureen, c1925, 10in (25.5cm) wide.
£90–110 *TAC*

A Copeland Spode Italian pattern cheese dish, 1930s, 7in (18cm) wide.
£100–125 *TAC*

A Royal Crown Derby teapot, Wilmot pattern, with gilt decoration, c1883, 5¾in (14.5cm) high.
£85–95 *PSA*

A Burmantofts bottle vase, 1881–1904, 10in (25.5cm) high.
£150–180 *NCA*

A Burmantofts double gourd vase, 1881–1904, 8½in (21.5cm) high.
£150–200 *NCA*

A Copeland Spode Italian pattern blue and white breakfast cup and saucer, c1954, saucer 6in (15cm) diam.
£10–15 *PBi*

A Copeland Spode Italian pattern sandwich plate, c1920, 8½in (21.5cm) wide.
£18–22 *TAC*

A Davenport blue and white plate, c1870, 9¾in (25cm) diam.
£60–70 *PBi*

A Brannam plate, with sgraffito fish decoration, by James Dewdney, c1896, 12in (30.5cm) diam.
£350–400 *NCA*

A Burmantofts vase, 1881–1904, 5in (12.5cm) high.
£80–90 *NCA*

A pair of Clarice Cliff early Banded candle holders, factory marks, c1930, 2¼in (6cm) high. **£200–250** *WTA*

A Clarice Cliff Crocus pattern plate, 1930s, 7in (18cm) diam. **£30–35** *BEV*

A Clarice Cliff Blue Autumn vase, c1930, 8¼in (21cm) high. **£500–600** *PC*

A Clarice Cliff Diamonds pattern coffee cup and saucer, 1930s, saucer 4in (10cm) diam. **£200–250** *RIC*

A Clarice Cliff Melons pattern tray, from a Lemonade set, Bizarre mark, c1933, 14in (35.5cm) wide. **£600–700** *WTA*

A Susie Cooper Paris shape jug, Moon and Mountain pattern, c1930, 5in (12.5cm) high. **£200–225** *WTA*

BREWERIANA

The market for Breweriana has flourished in the last five years. As auctioneer Alan Blakeman explains, demand for British material was initially fuelled by Australian collectors: 'Living in the middle of nowhere, Australians were creating their own personal pubs inside their houses and coming over here to buy the traditional fixtures and fittings.' Antipodean interest inspired British collectors and today the field has expanded enormously.

High on the list of Breweriana collectables are pub jugs, enthusiasts being divided between those who collect lower-priced modern jugs, who often tend to go for quantity, and more specialist collectors, looking for unusual, more valuable pieces. Jugs can be desirable both for the identity of the maker (Doulton, Shelley, Wade) and the brewery. Popular names in the current market including Dewars, Greenlees, McCallum, and Buchanans (the last a favourite with Australian collectors).

Also in demand are advertising show cards, bar-top figures, ashtrays, match strikers and trays. As well as beer-related material, an increasing number of collectors are focusing on whisky, a subject with an international appeal – particularly objects associated with the rarer brands.

Most collectors tend to be male, perhaps unsurprisingly, and though they might focus their collection on their favourite tipple, as Blakeman concludes: 'if you are going to collect seriously, you can't afford to spend too much money on the alcohol itself!'

r. Two packs of playing cards, advertising King's Liqueur and Ambassador Old Scotch, c1950, 3½in (9cm) high.
£10–15 each *GL*

> **Cross Reference**
> Advertising & Packaging
> Guinness

l. A Red Seal Whisky dispenser, by James Buchanan & Co Ltd, the domed cover with octagonal finial, 19thC, 24½in (62cm) high.
£280–320 *Gam*

A Yates Bros pine beer crate, c1950, 22in (56cm) wide.
£15–20 *TAN*

Two packs of Black and White Whisky playing cards, 4in (10cm) high:
l. 1950. **£10–15** *r.* 1960. **£8–10** *GL*

A Britvic pineapple
lamp, c1960, 11in
(28cm) high.
£30–35 GL

A Double Diamond lamp,
c1965, 12¼in (31cm) high.
£30–35 GL

A Hedges & Butler
porcelain bottle
top pourer, c1960,
6¼in (16cm) high.
£10–12 GL

A Courage brass
menu holder, 1960s,
3¼in (8cm) high.
£3–4 TAR

Two Babycham plastic bambi
advertising stickers, 1960s,
10in (25.5cm) high.
£25–30 DBr

A Watneys Red Barrel beer
rubber advertising counter
display, 1960s, 6in (15cm) high.
£25–30 DBr

A whistle mug, inscribed
'Whistle for your Beer' and
'Wet your Whistle' on
reverse, unmarked, 1970s,
4¼in (11cm) high.
£15–18 WAB

l. A Titanic Brewery Traditional Ales
jar, 1980s, 8in (20.5cm) high.
£5–6 COB

Advertising Signs

r. A Black and White
Scotch Whisky tin
advertising sign, 1960,
30 x 20in (76 x 51cm).
£80–100 GL

A Bos Whisky
plastic-covered tin
multi-coloured
advertising sign,
1930s, 7 x 5½in
(18 x 14cm).
£45–55 BBR

A Dewar's Whisky
enamel advertising
sign, chipped, good
overall condition,
c1900, 40 x 36in
(101.5 x 91.5cm).
£280–300 BBR

An Emu Brand
Burgundy advertising
sign, c1900, 22½ x 17¾in
(57 x 45cm).
£80–90 *BBR*

A James Buchanan & Co Ltd, advertising sign,
depicting 3 black Scottie dogs, c1920,
20½ x 27¼in (52 x 69cm), in original frame.
£150–175 *GL*

Cross Reference
Advertising & Packaging

A Sandeman Port
multi-coloured cut-out
stand-up show card,
1930s, 33 x 18½in
(84 x 47cm).
£80–100 *P(B)*

Ashtrays &
Match Strikers

A Bailie Nicol Jarvie Whisky
advertising ashtray, c1910,
4in (10cm) diam.
£9–12 *COB*

A Haig Whisky
advertising ashtray, c1920,
4 x 5¼in (10 x 13cm).
£60–70 *GL*

r. A Black and White Whisky
advertising ashtray, by Shelley,
c1938, 5¼in (13cm) square.
£20–30 *GL*

A Jamie Stuart Willow
pattern ashtray, by Shelley,
c1930, 4in (10cm) wide.
£30–40 *GL*

A Hanson's Ales match striker,
with EPNS top, 1930s,
2in (5cm) high.
£15–18 *WAB*

A Lang Bros Ltd Whisky
advertising ashtray, c1940,
5¾in (14.5cm) diam.
£20–25 *GL*

A B. L. Scotch Whisky
advertising ashtray, c1960,
5in (12.5cm) diam.
£10–15 *GL*

Bar-Top Figures

An Auld Shepp Scotch Whisky composition advertising figure, 1950s, 10in (25.5cm) high.
£90–100 *DBr*

r. A Currie's No. 10 Perth Whisky rubberoid advertising figure, c1950, 13½in (34cm) high.
£75–85 *GL*

l. A Captain Morgan Rum plastic advertising figure, 1940s, 4¾in (12cm) high.
£18–22 *BBR*

l. A Flowers Keg Bitter rubberoid advertising figure, in the form of Shakespeare's bust, 1940s, 10in (25.5cm) high.
£120–140 *BBR*

l. A King George IV Old Scotch Whisky rubberoid advertising figure, c1940, 14½in (37cm) high.
£90–100 *GL*

l. A Drambuie pottery advertising figure, 1960s, 14in (35.5cm) high.
£40–50 *DBr*

r. A Long John Scotch Whisky composition advertising figure, 1950s, 7in (18cm) high.
£90–100 *DBr*

Jugs

A quart measure ale jug, with Mochaware decoration, late 19thC, 6in (15cm) high.
£100–130 *BS*

A pint measure ale jug, with Mochaware decoration, late 19thC, 6in (15cm) high.
£100–125 *BS*

A Crawford's Liqueur Scotch Whisky ashtray and jug, decorated in Willow pattern, c1935, jug 2½in (6.5cm) high.
Jug £65–75
Ashtray £25–30 *GL*

Two Lang's Scotch Whisky water jugs:
l. Wade jug, c1965, 3½in (9cm) high.
£40–50
r. Barbour, Belgium, c1960, 2in (5cm) high.
£50–60 *GL*

Three water jugs:
l. King George IV Old Scotch Whisky, c1935, 4½in (11cm) high.
£40–50
c. Watson's No. 10 Scotch Whisky, c1930, 5½in (14cm) high.
£70–80
r. King William IV VOP Scotch Whisky, c1950, 3½in (9cm) high.
£50–60 *GL*

A Royal Doulton display set, all limited editions of 100, 6¼in (16cm) high:
l. Jim Beam Whiskey water jug, c1983.
c. Pickwick Deluxe Whisky water jug, c1984
r. Dewar's Scotch Whisky water jug, c1984.
£155–175 each
Stand, limited edition of 500, 1986.
£95–105 *GL*

Three Royal Doulton water jugs, advertising whisky, limited editions of 2,000:
l. Kwik Whisky jug, depicting Mr. Pickwick with a green hat, c1981, 3¾in (9.5cm) high.
c. Dewar's Whisky jug, depicting Sergeant Buzfuz, c1982, 3¾in (9.5cm) high.
r. Jim Beam Whiskey jug, depicting Mr. Pickwick, c1983, 3¾in (9.5cm) high.
£75–85 each *GL*

r. A Royal Doulton Uncle Sam with eagle water jug, advertising Beam Whiskey, limited edition of 500, c1985, 5½in (14cm) high.
£110–125 *GL*

Two commemorative Captain James Cook water jugs, advertising Pickwick Scotch Whisky, c1984, 4¾in (12cm) high.
£15–20 each *GL*

Three Pickwick Scotch Whisky, advertising water jugs, commemorating the marriage of Sarah Ferguson and Prince Andrew, 1986, 4¾in (12cm) high.
£15–20 each *GL*

Labels

A selection of wine and spirit brand labels, 1900–1930, 12¼ x 17¼in (31 x 44cm), framed.
£30–40 GL

A Fordham's Brewery Stout label, c1940, 3 x 2in (7.5 x 5cm).
£7–8 ED

A Mitchells & Butlers Export Pale Ale label, c1930, 4 x 2½in (10 x 6.5cm).
£5–6 ED

Pub Mirrors

l. A Dewar's Whisky pub mirror, c1880, 15¾ x 11¾in (40 x 30cm).
£80–100 GL

Cross Reference
Guinness

r. Four beer labels, advertising Guinness Worthington's and Bass, c1930, 3¼ x 2¼in (8 x 6cm).
£1–2 each GL

r. A Haig Whisky pub mirror, c1930, 12¼ x 17¼in (31 x 44cm).
£50–60 GL

Trays

A Bulloch Lade Scotch Whisky tin tray, c1935, 12½in (32cm) diam.
£80–100 GL

A Teacher's Highland Cream Whisky copper tray, c1930, 8½in (21.5cm) wide.
£15–20 OD

A Lochside Ales enamel tray, c1920, 10in (25.5cm) diam.
£40–50 BBR

BUCKLES

A pair of polished steel buckles, c1880, 2¾in (7cm) wide.
£40–60 *MRW*

A Burmese low grade silver three-piece clasp, c1890, 6in (15cm) wide.
£75–85 *JBB*

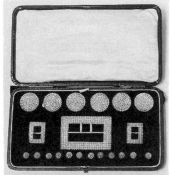

A Chinese silver-plated two-piece clasp, c1900, 3¼in (8cm) wide.
£40–50 *JBB*

A silver two-piece clasp, Birmingham 1898, 3½in (9cm) wide.
£85–95 *JBB*

A silver-plated and enamel two-piece clasp, c1900, 3½in (9cm) wide.
£38–48 *JBB*

A silver button and buckle set, by Charles Horner, Chester 1900, boxed, 9½in (24cm) wide.
£400–450 *JBB*

A silver and enamel button and buckle set, Birmingham 1910, buckle 2½in (6.5cm) wide.
£120–140 *JBB*

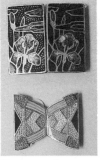

Two enamel clasps, 1920s, 1½in (4cm) wide.
£40–50 each *JBB*

An Art Deco Bakelite buckle, 1930s, 2½in (6.5cm) wide, on original card.
£10–12 *MRW*

A celluloid buckle, 1930s, 2in (5cm) wide.
£15–20 *MRW*

l. An enamel buckle, 1930s, 2½in (6.5cm) wide.
£25–35 *MRW*

BUTTONS

Even as small an object as a button can conceal a wealth of history. Featured this year is a selection of hand-stitched Dorset buttons (see page 91). As button historian Thelma Johns explains, Dorset was home to the first button industry in the world, started in 1650 by farmer's son Abraham Case. 'It was the tail end of the plague, farmers had died or escaped the county leaving an unemployed workforce and tremendous poverty. Case had an interest in wool and textiles, flax was widely grown in the area, and he set up a factory employing local people to make buttons. It was the first time that button-making had ever been established on an industrial scale.'

Though the factory closed down after Case's death, it was opened up again by Yorkshireman John Clayton in the mid-1700s. Piecework labourers were employed – men, women and children – who were paid one shilling a gross. 'It might not sound much,' adds Thelma Johns, 'but compared to an average wage of 7/6d a week for a farm labourer it wasn't bad and it was something the whole family could do.' As she notes proudly, the Dorset 'buttony' employed more people than any other industry in the county, either before or since, other than agriculture. Button-making continued in Dorset unabated until the mid-19th century. 'Ashton's button-making machine was exhibited at the Great Exhibition of 1851 and mechanisation killed the Dorset industry stone dead,' says Thelma Johns. 'Once again people were put out of work and the Government actually subsidised former button workers to emigrate to Australia.'

Humble as they might seem, the buttons concluding this section represent a great local craft, a brave new enterprise and part of the history of Britain.

A set of 6 silver and paste buttons, 18thC, 1¼in (30mm) diam.
£60–70 *JBB*

r. A Napoleon enamel and brass button, c1800, 1¼in (30mm) diam.
£30–35 *JBB*

FURTHER READING
Hughes, Elizabeth & Lester, Marion, *The Big Book of Buttons*, New Leaf Publishers, 1996

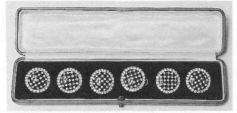

A set of 6 silver and paste over enamel men's jacket buttons, c1810, boxed.
£200–250 *JBB*

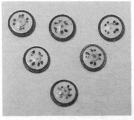

l. A set of 6 Victorian enamel buttons, ⅜in (10mm) diam.
£25–30 *OBS*

A set of 3 French buttons, possibly jet, c1837, 1in (25mm) diam.
£20–40 *MRW*

r. A set of 4 French glass boot/waistcoat buttons, c1860, ¼in (5mm) diam.
£20–30 *MRW*

l. Four Victorian gilt mirror-backed buttons, 1¼in (30mm) diam.
£3–4 each *OBS*

A set of 5 Victorian
opalescent buttons,
¾in (15mm) diam.
£3–4 each *OBS*

A set of 10 dried horn buttons,
inlaid with steel, 1870,
¾in (15mm) diam.
£30–40 *JBB*

A set of 3 Victorian black glass
buttons, c1880, 1½in (35mm) diam.
£25–45 *MRW*

A pair of Victorian Royal
Satsuma buttons,
1in (25mm) diam.
£25–30 *OBS*

A set of 4 Satsuma buttons,
c1890, 1in (25mm).
£70–80 *JBB*

A set of 6 mosaic
waistcoat buttons, c1890,
¾in (15mm) diam.
£80–90 *JBB*

A set of 5 Victorian gilt and
cut-steel buttons,
1½in (35mm) diam.
£3–5 each *OBS*

A set of 8 matt enamel buttons,
c1900, ½in (10mm) diam.
£30–40 *JBB*

l. A set of 6 French sterling silver
buttons, c1900, 1in (25mm) diam.
£55–65 *JBB*

A Victorian silver
bachelor button,
1in (25mm) diam.
£5–6 *OBS*

Two Edwardian
Paris-backs buttons,
1½in (35mm) diam.
£2–3 each *OBS*

A set of 4 Edwardian celluloid and diamanté
buttons, 1½in (35mm) diam.
£3–4 each *OBS*

Cross Reference
Colour Review

A set of 3 silver
buttons, Chester 1901,
¾in (20mm) diam.
£8–10 each *OBS*

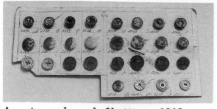

A part sample card of buttons, c1910,
3½ x 7in (9 x 18cm).
£30–40 *MRW*

A mother-of-pearl button,
with a brass Pharaoh's
head, c1920, 1¾in (45mm).
£18–22 *JBB*

A brass wedding ring
advertising button,
inscribed 'You Liar', c1920,
1¾in (45mm) diam.
£17–20 *JBB*

A set of 8 moulded celluloid buttons, c1930,
1in (25mm) diam.
£30–40 *JBB*

A set of 6 Moorcroft buttons, 1930s,
¾in (20mm) square.
£32–42 *JBB*

A pair of Art Deco plastic buttons,
late 1930s, 2¼in (55mm) diam.
£8–10 *MRW*

A pair of celluloid buttons,
1930s, 1¾in (45mm) diam.
£4–5 *OBS*

A metal-coated
moulded plastic
button, c1940,
1in (25mm) diam.
£4–5 *JBB*

A set of 4 London Glass Co buttons,
1930s, ¾in (20mm) diam.
£2–3 each *OBS*

l. A pair of carved
wooden novelty
buttons, c1940,
¾in (20mm) square.
£25–40 *MRW*

A set of 7 Japanese Imari face buttons, depicting
the gods of wisdom, 1950s, ¾in (20mm) diam.
£35–45 *JBB*

Animal & Sporting Subjects

r. A mother-of-pearl button and
brass, with ballooning scene,
c1890, 1½in (35mm) diam.
£20–25 *JBB*

A bronze frog button,
1930s, 1in (25mm) long.
£4–6 *JBB*

A set of 6 plastic-coated buttons, depicting lady golfers, 1940s, 1in (25mm) diam.
£24–28 *JBB*

A set of 11 waistcoat buttons, with photographs of dogs, 1930s, ¾in (20mm) diam.
£30–35 *OBS*

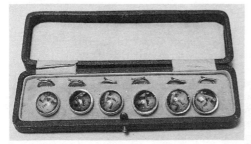

A set of 6 waistcoat buttons, with photographs of bowlers under celluloid, c1910, ½in (10mm) diam.
£65–75 *JBB*

r. A set of 6 reverse-intaglio dog waistcoat buttons, c1920, ¾in (20mm) diam.
£35–45 *JBB*

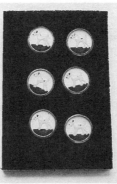

A silver golfing button, by Firmin, London, marked Birmingham 1926, 1in (25mm) diam.
£20–25 *OBS*

Dorset Buttons

A set of Singleton Dorset hand-stitched buttons, c1730, ½in (10mm) diam, on original card.
£3–4 each *OBS*

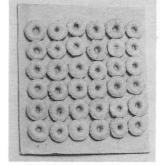

A set of Dorset bird's-eye buttons, c1730, on original card.
£3–4 each *OBS*

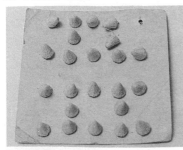

A set of Dorset high top buttons, 1650–1851, recarded.
£10–15 each *OBS*

Dorset Buttons

- Dorset buttons date back to early Georgian times and some of these examples are over 200 years old
- The same manufacturing process was used until the 19thC
- The age can be determined by the type of card on which they are displayed

r. A Dorset button, 1650–1851, ¾in (20mm) diam.
£10–15 *OBS*

Three Dorset knob buttons, 1650–1851, 3in (75mm) diam.
£10–15 each *OBS*

CAMERAS

Many enthusiasts will buy vintage cameras as decorative objects rather than to use, nevertheless the majority of collectors demand that they must work, preferably to their original standard. 'Because they were built like Swiss watches, most vintage cameras can be repaired,' explains specialist dealer John Jenkins. 'Condition is very important and a mint condition camera will fetch three- or four-times more than a poorer example.'

As prices for pre-WWII cameras have escalated out of the reach of many collectors, interest is focusing on Fifties and Sixties items. These are the last of the really well-made cameras when it was a question of individual craftsmanship rather than mass-produced electronics,' claims Jenkins. German, Japanese and British cameras are all collectable and good makers include Leica, Zeiss, Rolleiflex, Canon, Nikon, Ilford and the British firm Reid. 'After WWII, the British forces seized plans from the Leica factory, and brought them back to Britain. Leica copies were made by Reid, but because it was the post-war period, they used better materials and their copies were of a much higher standard than the original,' explains Jenkins.

Though many collectors begin by buying at random, most ultimately specialise, concentrating on cameras of a particular maker, factory or on specific areas such as miniature or spy cameras which can fetch extremely high prices today.

An Agfa Iso-Rapid I cassette loading camera, c1970, 4¼in (11cm) wide.
£5–6 *Gre*

An Agfa Karat 35mm cassette loading camera, c1938, 4¾in (12cm) wide.
£30–50 *Gre*

An Asahi Pentax SV camera and meter, c1962, 5½in (14cm) wide.
£50–70 *VCL*

Locate the Source

The source of each illustration in Miller's can be found by checking the code letters below each caption with the list of contributors.

r. An Ensign Commando rangefinder roll film camera, c1950, 6in (15cm) wide.
£50–70 *Gre*

A Bilora Special Box camera, c1952, 4¾in (12cm) high.
£8–10 *Gre*

l. A Durst Duca 35mm camera, Italian, c1950, 8in (20cm) high.
£50–80 *HEG*

r. An Ensign Selfix 820 f3.8 Ross Xpres camera, c1950, 3½in (9cm) wide.
£50–70 *VCL*

A Kiev II Contax-copy camera, f2 lens, Russian, c1951, 5½in (14cm) wide.
£40–50 *VCL*

An Eastman Kodak Brownie roll film camera, with push-on back and winding key, with Palmer Cox book, *Brownies and other Stories*, c1900.
£525–600 *CSK*

An Ensignette miniature folding strut camera, with 6.8 Tessar lens, c1910, 4in (10cm) high.
£70–90 *Gre*

A Kodak Regent I camera, with f4.5 Tessar lens, c1939, 4in (10cm) wide.
£50–75 *VCL*

A Kodak Jiffy 127 folding rangefinder camera, with Bakelite case, c1950, 5½in (14cm) wide.
£15–20 *Gre*

A Kodak Retinette IB, with coupled meter, c1965, 5in (12.5cm) wide.
£20–30 *VCL*

l. A Korelle 127 strut roll film camera, c1930, 5in (12.5cm) wide.
£50–70 *Gre*

r. A Reflex Korelle single lens reflex camera, c1937, 5½in (14cm) wide.
£80–100 *Gre*

A Leica CL camera,
No. 1331099, with a Leitz
Summicron-C f/2 40mm lens,
No. 2634539, 1973.
£500–600 *CSK*

A Mamiya 6 camera, Japanese,
1950, 2¼in (5.5cm) square.
£60–80 *HEG*

A Luftwaffen Robot 35mm
camera, marked 'Luftwaffen
Eigentum' on lens and body,
1938–40.
£200–250 *HEG*

A Nixette 6 x 6 roll film
camera, c1952,
5½in (14cm) wide.
£50–60 *Gre*

A Minolta-35 Model II camera,
Leica copy, 1954, 5½in (14cm) wide.
£250–275 *HEG*

A Nikon F camera, No. 6822283,
with a Nikon Nikkor-Q Auto
f/3.5 135mm lens No. 975457
and a Nippon Nikkor f/1.2 50mm
lens No. 907309, in maker's
leather ever-ready case, 1959.
£375–450 *CSK*

A Nikon S2 camera,
No. 6157374, with
3 Nikkor lenses, c1956.
£750–900 *P(Ba)*

r. A Rolleiflex 2.8E2
camera, by Franke &
Heidecke, with
Heidosmat viewing
lense, Zeiss Planar
taking lens, and light
meter, in maker's ever-
ready case, c1960.
£350–400 *P(Ba)*

An Ulca STI sub-miniature camera, c1935, 2in (5cm) wide. **£40–60** *Gre*

A Sputnik sub-miniature 16mm camera, c1950, 2in (5cm) wide. **£20–30** *VCL*

A Rolleiflex 3.5 camera, with Heidosmat f/2.8 75mm viewing lens, and Schneider Xenotar taking lens in a Synchro-Compur shutter, in maker's ever-ready case, c1960. **£330–380** *CSK*

r. A Rolleiflex E3 No. 2383415, with Heidosmat f/2.8 75mm viewing lens No. 3676674, and a Carl Zeiss Planar f/3.5 75mm taking lens No. 3673699, in a Synchro-Compur shutter, in maker's shutter, 1962–65. **£260–300** *CSK*

r. A Rolleiflex 2.8F camera, with meter, Heidsomat viewing lens and Zeiss Plana taking lens, in a Synchro-Compur shutter, c1960. **£475–525** *CSK*

A Zeiss Ikon Box Tengor camera, c1950, 4in (10.5cm) high. **£35–45** *Gre*

A Zeiss Ikon 'bull's-eye' Contarex camera, No. Z16818, with a Carl Zeiss Distagon f/4 35mm lens, No. 3703077, c1963. **£330–380** *CSK*

r. A Zeiss Miroflex 9 x 12 plate folding reflex press camera, c1932, 5½in (14cm) high. **£250–350** *Gre*

CERAMICS

As one of Britain's favourite collectables, Ceramics are a major focus in this guide. This year's special features include Cottage ware, Royal Winton and other Chintz ware, as well as Russian ceramics. We look at the pottery of pioneering designer Christopher Dresser, and illustrate popular collecting areas such as Blue and White transfer ware and Cups and Saucers. Demand for twentieth century material is continually expanding. As well as established, and often costly, makers such as Clarice Cliff, Susie Cooper and Royal Doulton, we explore more recent developments in the market. Ceramic cottages, invariably associated with glossy pictures in the Sunday newspaper colour supplements, today have a huge following. For example, the collectors club for Lilliput Lane, founded in 1982, boasts an astonishing 100,000 members, and cottages by this and other firms can be worth three- and even four-figure sums today.

Other new areas featured this year include Pen Delfins, which have been attracting growing interest in the marketplace. For the more traditional in taste, we also devote sections to Victorian and Edwardian pottery and Parian ware.

Animals

l. A Bretby Art Pottery stick stand, in the form of an owl with glass eyes, with green glaze, late 19thC/early 20thC, 36in (91cm) high.
£675–775 *L&E*

l. A pottery dog, inscribed 'Souvenir of London', German, c1910, 2¼in (5.5cm) high.
£20–30 *OD*

A ceramic flower holder, in the shape of a cubist style cat by Louis Wain, c1925, 6in (15cm) high.
£700–800 *WTA*

A set of 3 Winstanley kittens, 1990s, 4¼in (11cm) high.
£14–16 each *CP*

r. A Crown Devon rabbit dish, 1930s, 9in (23cm) wide.
£15–20 *OD*

A pair of Goebel novelty book ends/ashtrays, c1933, 5in (12.5cm) high.
£165–195 *BKK*

A Plichta cockerel, painted with a clover design, 1930s, 6in (15cm) high.
£150–200 *TAR*

A Plichta cat, painted with a thistle design, c1930, 3½in (9cm) high.
£100–120 *TAR*

A ceramic rabbit, 1950s, 11in (28cm) long.
£30–38 *TAC*

A Jemma cat, made in Holland for the gift market, 1950s, 15in (38cm) high.
£20–25 *TAC*

A Midwinter deer, c1950, 5in (12.5cm) high, and Larry the Lamb, modelled by Nancy Great-Rex, c1930, 3½in (9cm) high.
£25–30 each *AND*

A SylvaC rabbit, 1950s, 4in (10cm) high.
£35–45 *BSA*

A SylvaC squirrel jug, 1950s, 20in (50cm) high.
£50–60 *BSA*

r. A Limoges hand-painted box, modelled as 2 frogs on a lily pad, with gilt-metal mounts, signed by artist, 1990s, 2¼in (5.5cm) high.
£100–150 *JPr*

Beswick – Beatrix Potter Figures

l. Duchess, modelled by Graham Orwell, repaired, gilt lettering on base, 1955–67, 3¾in (9.5cm) high.
£530–580 *S*

This rare figure from The Pie and the Patty Pan *is the most sought-after of all the Beswick pieces. Introduced in 1955, it was discontinued in 1967.*

Amiable Guinea Pig, 1974–1985, 4in (10cm) high.
£200–240 *SAS*

Duchess, style 2, holding a pie, 1974–85, 4in (10cm) high.
£140–170 *SAS*

Beswick

- In 1947 John Beswick of Longton obtained copyright from publishers Frederick Warne to produce Beatrix Potter's characters as small scale earthenware figures
- The first piece created by chief modeller Arthur Gredington was Jemima Puddle-Duck, launched in 1948 along with 9 other characters
- By 1954, characters from 21 of the 23 Beatrix Potter stories had been manufactured, by 1977 all the tales had been represented
- The majority are still made today, with new models being introduced annually. Only a few of the figures have been discontinued, and these 'withdrawals' are highly sought after
- Look for early pieces, model and colour variations and the Beswick backstamp, since in 1989 the trade name was changed from John Beswick to Royal Albert for all models in current production

Sir Isaac Newton, 1974–85, 4in (10cm) high. **£190–240** *SAS*

Ginger, 1974–85, 4in (10cm) high. **£325–375** *SAS*

Mr. Jackson, first version, green frog, 1973–74, 2¾in (7cm) high. **£170–220** *SAS*

Johnny Town Mouse with bag, 1988–89, 3½in (9cm) high. **£180–220** *SAS*

Mr Jeremy Fisher Digging, brown frog with grey shoes, 1988–89, 4in (10cm) high. **£130–160** *SAS*

> **Miller's is a price GUIDE not a price LIST**

l. Little Pig Robinson, first version, blue stripes, 1974–85, 3½in (9cm) high. **£130–160** *SAS*

Little Pig Robinson Spying, 1985–88, 3½in (9cm) high. **£120–150** *SAS*

Pickles, 1974–85,
4½in (11.5cm) high.
£120–150 *SAS*

Pig-Wig,
manufacturer's red
enamel mark to
dress on opposite
side to bag, 1974–85,
4in (10cm) high.
£190–240 *SAS*

Simpkin, 1974–85,
4in (10cm) high.
£260–300 *SAS*

Susan, 1985–88,
4½in (11cm) high.
£70–90 *SAS*

Samuel Whiskers and Tailor of
Gloucester, 1955–72, 3½in (9cm) high.
£80–100 *P(B)*

Tabitha Twitchit and
Miss Moppet, 1974–85,
3½in (9cm) high.
£60–80 *SAS*

Tommy Brock, second
version, 1974–85,
3¼in (8.5cm) high.
£80–100 *SAS*

Cross Reference
Colour Review

l. Mrs Rabbit, 1951–current,
and Tom Kitten, 1948–current,
4in (10cm) high.
£60–80 *P(B)*

Mrs Tittlemouse, 1948–current,
3½in (9cm) high, and Peter Rabbit
and his family.
£45–60 *P(B)*

Blue and White

Oriental blue and white ware was imported to Britain from the seventeenth century on. By the end of the eighteenth century reduced imports from China combined with a growing demand for tea and tableware stimulated the development of transfer-printed blue and white pottery.

From the nineteenth century onwards production of blue and white ceramics became a major British industry. Transfer-printed ware was manufactured in huge quantities by many different potteries. Whilst many pieces are unidentified, others can carry the mark of the factory and even the name of the pattern.

Chinese influenced designs were often used, the most famous being the Willow Pattern. Many stories have been invented to explain its significance, but this romantic Oriental design was a British invention attributed to the Spode factory in the late eighteenth century, and endlessly copied, with innumerable variations. Classic elements include a willow tree, a bridge with three figures, a pagoda, a Chinese vessel, a distant island and two birds.

Many European inspired designs were produced including landscapes, classical scenes and floral patterns. In some services, each piece would have a different pattern (unified by the same border), in others, such as Copeland Spode's Italian design, the same view was repeated throughout the service.

A blue and white soup plate, The Piping Shepherd pattern, not marked, c1802, 9¾in (25cm) diam.
£55–65 *HEI*

Three Wedgwood blue and white transfer ware dessert plates, Botanical series, c1805, largest 8½in (21.5cm) diam.
£100–150 each *GN*

l. A blue and white plate, factory unknown, c1880, 10in (25.5cm) diam.
£30–40 *PBi*
This plate is decorated with the Wild Rose pattern, a pattern which was used by a number of different factories.

A Victorian blue and white plate, with garden still life scene imposed over Hampton Court, marked 'De Fete', 10¼in (26cm) diam.
£17–20 *HEI*

A blue and white saucer, with gilt edge, unmarked, c1881, 5½in (14cm) diam.
£7–10 *HEI*

r. A Minton blue and white dish, decorated with Willow pattern, c1900, 5in (12.5cm) diam.
£12–16 *TAC*

l. A Royal Worcester blue and white biscuit barrel, with silver plated lid and handle, c1900, 5½in (14cm) high.
£60–70 *TAC*

A George Jones blue and white trio,
decorated with Casino pattern,
c1907, plate 7½in (19cm) diam.
£20–24 *TAC*

A Swinnertons blue and
white plate, decorated with
Silverdale pattern, 20thC,
10in (25.5cm) diam.
£5–7 *HEI*

A May blue and white platter,
marked on reverse, c1920,
15¾in (40cm) wide.
£22–28 *PSA*

Copeland Spode

A Copeland Spode mini jug and bowl
set, decorated with Italian pattern,
c1911, bowl 3½in (9cm) diam.
£40–50 *TAC*

A Copeland Spode
flask, decorated
with Italian
pattern, dated 1912,
6½in (16.5cm) diam.
£62–72 *TAC*

Two Copeland Spode cream jugs,
decorated with Italian pattern, c1911,
largest 4¾in (12cm) high.
£38–45 each *TAC*

A Copeland Spode jug,
decorated with Italian pattern,
c1919, 7in (18cm) high.
£62–72 *TAC*

A Copeland Spode breakfast
cup and saucer, decorated with
Italian pattern, 1920s, saucer
6½in (16.5cm) diam.
£22–27 *TAC*

A Copeland Spode egg
cup, decorated with
Italian pattern,
1920s, 2in (5cm) high.
£20–25 *TAC*

A Copeland Spode soup bowl and
saucer, decorated with Italian pattern,
1920s, saucer 7in (18cm) diam.
£40–50 *TAC*

r. A Copeland Spode coffee
pot, milk jug and coffee cup
and saucer, decorated with
Italian pattern, 1920s,
coffee pot 8in (20.5cm) high.
Coffee pot **£60–70**
Milk jug **£25–35**
Cup & saucer **£20–25** *TAC*

A Copeland Spode jug, decorated
with Italian pattern, 1920s,
8in (20.5cm) high.
£60–70 *TAC*

l. A Copeland Spode
two-cup teapot, c1928,
7in (18cm) wide.
£70–80 *TAC*

Cross Reference
Colour Review

Two Copeland Spode
miniature jugs, 1930s,
2½in (6.5cm) high.
£30–35 each *PSA*

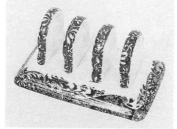

A Copeland Spode toast rack,
decorated with Italian pattern,
1940s, 4½in (11.5cm) wide.
£70–85 *TAC*

l. A Copeland Spode
plate, decorated with
Italian pattern, c1954,
7½in (19cm) diam.
£10–15 *PBi*

Brannam

A Brannam double
bowl, with fish
supports, c1890,
5½in (14cm) high.
£150–200 *NCA*

A Brannam jug and basin set, by
A. Bamflin, c1895, 7in (18cm) high.
£200–250 *NCA*

r. A Brannam tulip vase,
by Braddon, c1909,
5½in (14cm) high.
£125–150 *NCA*

l. A Brannam ovoid vase,
the neck with 3 scroll
handles, incised and
painted with a griffin,
flowers and leaves, on a
blue ground, incised
mark and dated 1899,
12½in (31.5cm) high.
£300–350 *DN*

Burleigh

A Burleigh Ware hand-painted vase, in a geometric double diamond design, c1930, 7¼in (18.5cm) high.
£800–850 *BKK*

A Burleigh jug, The Highwayman, c1933, 7¼in (18.5cm) high.
£200–225 *WTA*

A Burleigh jug, the handle formed as a female tennis player, c1935, 7¼in (18.5cm) high.
£500–550 *WTA*

Burmantofts

l. A Burmantofts lime-green *solifleur* vase, late 19thC, 6in (15cm) high.
£80–100 *NCA*

r. A Burmantofts lime-green single-handled vase, late 19thC, 11in (28cm) high.
£140–160 *NCA*

A Burmantofts two-handled vase, with sunburst motifs, late 19thC, 9in (23cm) high.
£180–200 *NCA*

A Burmantofts Oriental-yellow vase, with a knop neck, c1900, 4½in (11.5cm) high.
£80–100 *NCA*

Candle Extinguishers

A Copeland Parian candlestick and extinguisher of Elizabeth Fry, c1860, 5¼in (13.5cm) high.
£500–550 *TH*

A pair of Copeland white glazed candle extinguishers, entitled Normandy Maid and Man, c1860, 3in (7.5cm) high.
£195–225 *TH*

A Copeland white glazed candle extinguisher, Toby, c1860, 3½in (9cm) high.
£400–450 *TH*

The base becomes a candleholder when the extinguisher is removed.

A Goss white glazed nun candle extinguisher, c1890, 4in (10cm) high.
£150–180 *TH*

A Goss white glazed
Welsh lady candle
extinguisher, c1890,
3¾in (9.5cm) high.
£100–125 *TH*

l. A Grainger white
glazed Tyrolean
hat candle
extinguisher, with
a coloured feather
decoration, c1895,
2¾in (7cm) high.
£110–130 *TH*

r. A Grainger
monkey's head
candle extinguisher,
with blush
decoration and
gilt edges, 1901,
3¾in (9.5cm) high.
£350–400 *TH*

A Kerr and Binns
white glazed kneeling
monk candle
extinguisher, c1855,
4½in (11.5cm) high.
£500–600 *TH*

A Royal Worcester white Parian candle
extinguisher, The Tichbourne Trial, produced
in 3 parts, c1875, lawyer 4in (10cm) high.
£3,200–3,600 *TH*
*This is a tribute to the longest trial in
English history.*

A Royal Worcester
candle extinguisher,
entitled 'Mob Cap',
decorated with gold
edging, c1880,
3½in (9cm) high.
£500–600 *TH*

l. A Royal Worcester
full coloured
Mandarin candle
extinguisher, 1920,
3½in (9cm) high.
£200–225 *TH*

r. A Royal Worcester
candle extinguisher of
an owl, with a coloured
face, white hat and
gold tassel, 1936,
3¼in (8cm) high.
£200–225 *TH*

A Royal Worcester
fully decorated candle
extinguisher, Monsieur
Reynard, 1955,
4¼in (10.5cm) high.
£425–475 *TH*

Carlton Ware

A Carlton Ware vase, c1925, 4¼in (11cm) high.
£40–50 *CSA*

A Carlton Ware coffee can and saucer, marked W & R, 1920s, 2¼in (5.5cm) high.
£10–20 *DgC*

r. A Carlton Ware vase and cover, c1925, 7½in (19cm) high.
£70–80 *CSA*

A Carlton Ware dish, with blackberry design, c1930, 8¾in (22cm) long.
£40–50 *CSA*

A Carlton Ware Anemone preserve pot, c1930, 5in (13cm) high.
£50–60 *CSA*

A Carlton Ware plate, 1930s, 13in (33cm) diam.
£110–130 *BEV*

r. A Carlton Ware coffee service, 1930s, coffee pot 11¾in (30cm) high.
£130–150 *BSA*

l. A Carlton Ware dish, c1935, 11¾in (30cm) long.
£40–50 *CSA*

r. A Carlton Ware ten-piece coffee set, 1970s, coffee pot 13in (33cm) high.
£30–40 *DgC*

Clarice Cliff

A pair of Clarice Cliff Dutch figures, by Wilkinson, c1930, 7in (18cm) high.
£250–350 *WTA*

A Clarice Cliff Conical tea-for-two set, decorated in Crocus pattern, c1932, plate 7in (18cm) diam.
£300–350 *WTA*

A set of 3 Clarice Cliff Bizarre jugs, decorated in Crocus pattern, 1930s, tallest 6¼in (16cm) high.
£425–475 *DN*

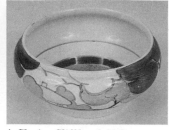

A Clarice Cliff bowl, Yellow Autumn pattern, c1930, 4½in (11.5cm) diam.
£200–250 *PC*

A Clarice Cliff Castellated Circle pattern jug, c1930, 4in (10cm) high.
£350–450 *BKK*

l. A Clarice Cliff Stamford tureen, c1932, 7in (18cm) high.
£400–450 *WTA*

Produced exclusively for Woman's Journal *mail order.*

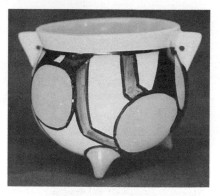

> **Cross Reference**
> Colour Review

r. A Clarice Cliff Bizarre cauldron, decorated in Orange Flower pattern, c1933, 3in (7.5cm) high.
£150–225 *WTA*

l. Two Clarice Cliff plates, Tropic pattern, hand-painted pattern name to reverse of one plate, 1933, 9in (23cm) diam.
£800–1,000 *BKK*

A Clarice Cliff swan flower holder, with printed green factory marks, 1930s, 8in (20.5cm) high.
£250–300 *WTA*

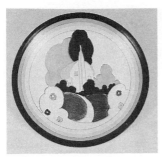

A Clarice Cliff Farmhouse pattern plate, c1931, 10in (25.5cm) diam.
£600–700 *BKK*

A Clarice Cliff Red Autumn pattern plate, c1931, 9in (23cm) diam.
£750–850 *BKK*

A Clarice Cliff plate, Nasturtium pattern, c1933, 6in (15cm) diam.
£100–120 *BKK*

A Clarice Cliff plate, Broth pattern, 1930s, 6½in (16.5cm) diam.
£200–250 *RIC*

r. A set of 6 Clarice Cliff Bizarre tea plates, painted in orange, green and black with a star medallion, on a yellow ground, printed marks in green and black and impressed marks, 1930s, 6¼in (16cm) square.
£900–1,100 *DN*

l. A Clarice Cliff Bizarre plate, colourway Orange Secrets pattern, c1934, 9in (23cm) diam.
£400–450 *WTA*

r. A Clarice Cliff Biarritz plate, Kelverne pattern, c1936, 9in (23cm) wide.
£80–100 *PC*

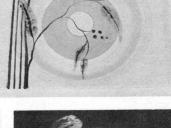

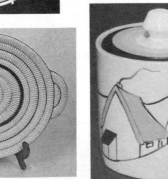

A pair of two-handled cake plates, the ribbed and fluted bands decorated with green and gold stripes, 1930s, 11in (28cm) wide.
£120–140 *PSA*

A Clarice Cliff Bizarre jam pot, House and Bridge pattern, c1931, 3in (7.5cm) high.
£350–400 *WTA*

A Clarice Cliff Fantasque beehive honey pot, 1930s, 3½in (9cm) high.
£150–200 *WTA*

A Clarice Cliff Daffodil shape conserve pot, Poplar pattern, c1932, 5in (13cm) high.
£250–300 *WTA*

A Clarice Cliff sugar shaker, Black Eye Marigold pattern, c1930, 5½in (14cm) high.
£250–300 *TAC*

A Clarice Cliff Conical sugar sifter, Orange Roof Cottage pattern, printed factory marks, c1932, 5in (13cm) high.
£1,000–1,200 *WTA*

A Clarice Cliff Bon Jour shape sugar shaker, Crocus pattern, c1933, 5in (13cm) high.
£170–190 *WTA*

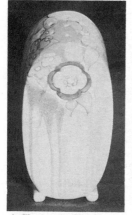

A Clarice Cliff Bon Jour shape sugar sifter, Delicia Lydiat pattern, with Bizarre mark, c1930, 5in (13cm) high.
£250–275 *WTA*

A Clarice Cliff vase, shape No. 369, Latona Knight Errant pattern, painted by John Butler, 1930, 10in (25.5cm) high.
£2,500–3,000 *BKK*

Three miniature Clarice Cliff vases, *l.–r.* Trees and House, Crocus and Secrets patterns, 1930s, 2¾in (7cm) high.
£150–250 each *PC*

l. A Clarice Cliff vase, shape No. 264, Caravan pattern, c1931, 8in (20.5cm) high.
£2,500–3,000 *WTA*

r. A Clarice Cliff Isis vase, Orange Roof Cottage pattern, c1932, 12in (30.5cm) high.
£500–600 *BKK*

A Clarice Cliff Isis vase, Braidwood pattern, c1935, 8in (20.5cm) high.
£400–500 *WTA*

Susie Cooper

A Susie Cooper hand-painted jug, c1928, 7in (18cm) high.
£200–225 WTA

A Susie Cooper geometric cup and saucer, c1930, cup 2½in (6.5cm) high.
£90–120 SCA

A Susie Cooper geometric sauce ladle, 1932, 6in (15cm) long.
£100–125 SCA

A Susie Cooper hand-painted Studio Ware vase, 1930s, 6in (15cm) high.
£90–120 SCA

A Susie Cooper Kestrel shape hand-painted hot water pot, with banded decoration, 1930s, 5in (13cm) high.
£50–60 SCA

A Susie Cooper cruet, Dresden Spray pattern, 1930s, 6in (15cm) long.
£65–75 SCA

A Susie Cooper coffee cup and saucer, Asterisk pattern, 1938, cup 2in (5cm) high.
£25–35 SCA

A Susie Cooper trio, with Sgrafitto pattern, c1945, cup 2in (5cm) high.
£20–30 CSA

A Susie Cooper yellow and white vase, decorated with fish-scale decoration, c1950, 7¾in (20cm) high.
£130–160 DA

l. Two Susie Cooper coffee cups and saucers, c1960, 2in (5cm) high.
£10–15 each CSA

Cottages
Lilliput Lane

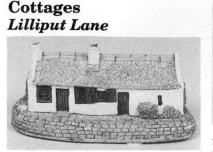

A Lilliput Lane model, Burn's Cottage, Alloway, c1986, 2in (5cm) high.
£60–80 *BGA*

These miniature cottages are often modelled on real buildings and part of the fun for collectors can be tracking down or visiting their original, life-sized inspirations.

A Lilliput Lane model, Burnside, version 2, 1982–85, 3¼in (8cm) high.
£300–350 *ANP*

A Lilliput Lane model, Castle Street, version 2, 1984–86, 7½in (19cm) high.
£250–275 *ANP*

l. A Lilliput Lane model, Dale Farm, version 2, 1982–86, 2½in (6.5cm) high.
£650–675 *ANP*

A Lilliput Lane model, Millers, 1983–86, 2¾in (7cm) high.
£150–175 *ANP*

A Lilliput Lane model, St. Lawrence Church, 1989–current, 5in (13cm) high.
£30–38 *BGA*

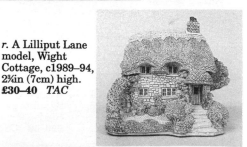

l. A Lilliput Lane model, Sussex Mill, version 2, 1982–86, 2½in (6.5cm) high.
£225–245 *ANP*

r. A Lilliput Lane model, Wight Cottage, c1989–94, 2¾in (7cm) high.
£30–40 *TAC*

l. A Lilliput Lane model, Yew Tree Farm, 1987–88, 3¼in (8cm) high.
£200–225 *ANP*

Legend Lane

l. A Legend Lane model, The Kings Head, 1992–93, 3¾in (9.5cm) high. **£60–70** *LEG*

A Legend Lane model, Keeper's Cottage, 1991–2, 3½in (9cm) high. **£45–50** *LEG*

A Legend Lane cottage, Loveday Antiquities, 1992–3, 2¼in (5.5cm) high. **£40–45** *LEG*

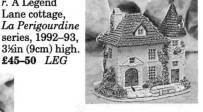

r. A Legend Lane cottage, *La Perigourdine* series, 1992–93, 3½in (9cm) high. **£45–50** *LEG*

A Legend Lane cottage, Oakley Grange, 1992–93, 3½in (9cm) high. **£60–70** *LEG*

r. A Legend Lane model, Briarwood Cottage, 1992–93, 2¾in (7cm) high. **£45–50** *LEG*

A Legend Lane cottage, The Toll House, 1992–93, 2½in (6.5cm) high. **£45–50** *LEG*

David Winter

l. A David Winter cottage, Willow Garden, Regular edition, 1995, 5in (13cm) high, boxed. **£225–275** *BGA*

Two versions of this model were produced. The Premier, limited edition of 2,200 and Regular, limited edition of 4,300.

r. A David Winter model, Candle-maker's Cottage, Guild issue, 1991–92, 4½in (11.5cm) high, boxed. **£45–55** *BGA*

Cottage Ware

In the nineteenth century the Staffordshire potteries produced spill holders, pastille burners and other functional ceramics in the form of houses, but it was not until the 1920s that the vogue for cottage tableware truly took off. Like the ubiquitous crinoline lady that appeared on everything from mirrors to tray cloths during the same period, these cottage designs reflected a romantic fascination with the rural past, as well as meeting contemporary demand for novelty shapes and reasonably priced tea and tableware.

Cottage ware was extremely popular and produced by many different makers –

desirable names today include Price, Greens, SylvaC and Royal Winton. Though British in inspiration, some lines were also manufactured abroad, notably in Japan. Condiment and tea sets are now sought-after and specialist collectors look for the more unusual objects as well as different building designs. Alongside demand for the streamlined shapes and abstract patterns of the Art Deco style, the market for 'pretty' ceramics from the 1920s–30s is currently flourishing. Like period chintz designs, this nostalgic cottage ware has been gaining steadily in price and today attracts collectors across the world.

Biscuit Boxes

A Beswick biscuit box, No. 249, 1920s, 7½in (19cm) high.
£60–70 *PC*

A Carlton Ware biscuit barrel, No. 778973, unmarked, 1920s, 8¾in (22cm) high.
£60–80 *PC*

A Japanese biscuit barrel, in the form of a twin gabled house with a blue roof, 1930s, 6½in (16.5cm) wide.
£40–50 *PC*

A Paramount Pottery biscuit barrel, chipped, 1930s, 7½in (19cm) high.
£20–30 *LA*

A Price Bros biscuit barrel, 1930s, 7in (18cm) high.
£20–28 *WAB*

r. A SylvaC thatched design biscuit barrel, with original label, 1920s, 5in (12.5cm) wide.
£40–50 *LA*

A Price of Kensington biscuit barrel, 1930s, 7½in (19cm) high.
£40–50 *PC*

Cheese & Butter Dishes

l. A Beswick thatched roof cheese dish, 1930s, 7in (18cm) wide.
£40–50 *PC*

An Arthur Wood Morton Old Hall biscuit barrel, 1930s, 6in (15cm) high.
£50–60 *PC*

A Westminster China biscuit barrel, 1930s, 7½in (19cm) high.
£50–60 *PC*

r. A Grimwades Ye Olde Mill butter dish, 1920s, 5½in (14cm) wide.
£40–50 *PC*

A Marutomo ware tiled roof house cheese dish, Japanese, 1920s, 6¾in (17cm) wide.
£40–50 *PC*

A Price of Kensington cheese dish, 1930s, 6½in (16.5cm) wide.
£30–40 *PC*

A Radford thatched cottage cheese dish, 1920s, 9in (23cm) wide.
£50–60 *PC*

> **Cross Reference**
> Colour Review

Cruets

r. A Beswick three-piece cruet set on a stand, in the form of Tudor houses, 1920s, 7in (18cm) wide.
£60–70 *PC*

An unmarked cheese dish, in the form of an inn, 1920s, 7½in (19cm) wide.
£25–30 *PC*

l. A Carlton Ware cruet set, 1920s, 6in (15cm) wide.
£70–85 *PC*

l. A Kensington condiment set, in the form of twin houses, 1920s, 7in (18cm) wide.
£70–80 *LA*

A Price of Kensington three-piece cruet set on a stand, 1920s, 5in (12.5cm) wide.
£50–60 *PC*

A Shorter & Son Ltd three-piece cruet set on a tray, 1920s, 4½in (11.5cm) wide.
£50–60 *LA*

An unmarked three-piece cruet set on a stand, in the form of houses and foliage, 1920s, 5in (12.5cm) wide.
£40–50 *LA*

An imported three-piece cruet set on a tray, in the form of a teapot, milk jug and sugar basin, 1920s, 6in (15cm) wide.
£30–40 *LA*

Jam Pots

A Carlton Ware jam pot, 1920s, 5in (12.5cm) high.
£55–65 *PC*

A Burlington Ware Devon cob jam pot, 1920s, 5in (12.5cm) high.
£25–30 *PC*

A Marutomo ware jam pot, Japanese, discoloured, 1920s, 3½in (9cm) wide.
£15–20 *PC*

A Price of Kensington jam pot, 1930s, 4in (10cm) high.
£15–20 *PC*

A Shorter & Sons Ltd jam pot, 1920s, 6½in (16.5cm) wide.
£25–30 *PC*

l. A Shorter & Sons Ltd jam pot, with pagoda roof, 1920s, 6½in (16.5cm) high.
£25–30 *PC*

A Torquay Pottery jam pot, in the form of a cottage with thatched roof, 1930s, 5½in (14cm) high.
£25–30 *PC*

A Westminster Pottery jam pot, with circular thatched roof lid, 1930s, 6in (15cm) wide.
£25–30 *PC*

l. An unmarked pottery Anne Hathaway's cottage jam pot, 1920s, 4½in (11.5cm) high.
£15–20 *PC*

Jugs

A Carlton Ware cream jug, 1920s, 4½in (11.5cm) wide.
£40–50 *LA*

An Empire Pottery, Tudor design, milk jug, 1920s, 7½in (19cm) wide.
£30–40 *LA*

A Burlington Ware, Devon cob, milk jug, 1920s, 5in (12.5cm) high.
£15–20 *PC*

A Keele Street Pottery Co Ltd miniature cream jug and sugar bowl, 1930s, 3in (7.5cm) wide.
£15–20 *LA*

l. A Royal Winton Tudor house milk jug, 1920s, 6in (15cm) wide.
£25–30 *LA*

Sugar Sifters

l. A Klimax Pottery sugar sifter, in the form of a water tower, 1920s, 5in (12.5cm) high.
£40–50 *LA*

l. A Royal Winton sugar sifter, 1920s, 6in (15cm) high.
£40–50 *PC*

r. An unmarked sugar sifter, in the form of a water tower, 1920s, 7in (18cm) high.
£15–20 *LA*

Toast Racks

A Carlton Ware toast rack, 1920s, 3¾in (9.5cm) wide.
£55–65 *PC*

A pair of Price of Kensington toast racks, 'His' and 'Hers', 1920s, 4in (10cm) wide.
£70–80 *PC*

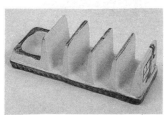

A Westminster Pottery toast rack, 1920s, 5¾in (14.5cm) wide.
£25–30 *LA*

Tea & Coffee Pots

r. A Beswick teapot, in the form of a circular thatched cottage, 1920s, 8in (20.5cm) wide.
£50–60 *LA*

l. A SylvaC Ye Olde Cottage teapot, 1930s, 8½in (21.5cm) wide.
£40–50 *PC*

An Empire Ware Tudor design three-piece tea set, 1930s, teapot 7½in (19cm) wide.
£100–120 *LA*

A Keele Street Pottery Co Ltd teapot, 1930s, 9in (23cm) wide.
£30–40 *LA*

A Kensington Pottery teapot and hot water jug, formed as The Huntsman's Inn, 1920s, 9in (23cm) wide.
£100–120 *PC*

r. An Arthur Wood & Son Morton Old Hall teapot, 1930s, 9in (23cm) wide.
£60–70 *PC*

An unmarked pottery coffee pot, with thatched roof lid, 1930s, 7½in (19cm) high.
£30–40 *PC*

An unmarked pottery beehive-shaped teapot, 1920s, rim chipped, 5in (12.5cm) high.
£8–10 *LA*

An unmarked foreign pottery beehive-shaped teapot, 1920s, 5in (12.5cm) high.
£15–20 *LA*

Cups & Saucers
Victorian & Edwardian

A Grainger & Lee Worcester cup and
saucer, c1820, saucer 6in (15cm) diam.
£18–22 *SnA*

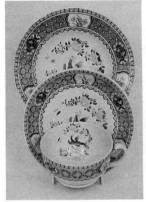

A Minton hand-coloured
trio, c1900, plate 6½in
(16.5cm) diam.
£20–24 *TAC*

An Aynsley gilded trio,
c1910, the plate
7in (18cm) diam.
£14–16 *TAC*

A John and William Ridgway tea cup,
coffee cup and saucer, decorated in
coloured enamels, within gilt borders,
pattern No. 2/974 in red, c1820.
£300-340 *DN*

A Colclough & Co gilded trio,
decorated with blue and
lemon design, c1910, plate
6in (15cm) diam.
£12–14 *TAC*

*The term 'trio', a set of 3, can
refer to either a matching
coffee can, teacup and saucer
or cup, saucer and tea plate.*

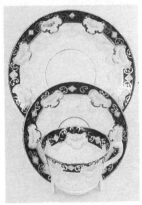

A Royal Albert trio, c1910,
plate 7in (18cm) diam.
£15–18 *TAC*

A Royal Crown Derby blue and
white cup and saucer, c1883,
saucer 5in (12.5cm) diam.
£24–28 *PSA*

An unmarked Victorian cup
and saucer, cup
2½in (6.5cm) high.
£13–16 *PSA*

l. An unmarked Victorian
hand-painted cup and saucer,
in excellent condition, saucer
4¾in (12cm) diam.
£30–37 *TAC*

A Royal Crown Derby cup and
saucer, in cigar pattern No. 1128,
c1887, saucer 5½in (14cm) diam.
£60–70 *VSt*

1920s–'80s

A Carlton Ware coffee cup and saucer, in Chintz pattern, 1920s, saucer 4¼in (11cm) diam.
£80–85 *BEV*

A Clarice Cliff coffee cup and saucer, 1930–36, saucer 4in (10cm) diam.
£100–150 *BEV*

A Carlton Ware trio, decorated in Primrose pattern, 1930s, plate 7in (18cm) diam.
£45–55 *TAC*

A Coalport trio, 1920s, plate 6½in (16.5cm) diam.
£30–35 *PBi*

A Susie Cooper coffee cup and saucer, 1930s, saucer 4¾in (12cm) diam.
£85–90 *BEV*

A Coalport trio, 1920s, plate 7¼in (18.5cm) diam.
£30–35 *PBi*

l. A Royal Crown Derby coffee can and saucer, c1930, saucer 4¾in (12cm) diam.
£30–45 *VSt*

A Susie Cooper coffee cup and saucer, 1930s, 4¾in (12cm) diam.
£65–70 *BEV*

r. A Flosmaron coffee cup and saucer, 1930s, saucer 5in (12.5cm) diam.
£30–35 *BEV*

A Gray's coffee cup and saucer, with silver lustre design, 1930s, saucer 4¾in (12cm) diam.
£30–35 *BEV*

A Royal China coffee cup
and saucer, 1930s, saucer
4¾in (12cm) diam.
£30–35 *BEV*

A Paragon trio, in Rockingham
style, c1957, saucer
5½in (14cm) diam.
£10–15 *VSt*

A Paragon coffee cup and
saucer, 1930s, saucer
4½in (11.5cm) diam.
£75–85 *BEV*

A Plant Tuscan China coffee
cup and saucer, 1930s, saucer
4¼in (11cm) diam.
£25–35 *BEV*

A Plant Tuscan China trio,
1930s, plate 6in (15cm) wide.
£15–25 *DgC*

A Royal Worcester coffee cup
and saucer, 1930s, saucer
4½in (11.5cm) diam.
£40–50 *BEV*

*From the 17thC tea imported
from the East was drunk from
Chinese style bowls. Cups with
handles first appeared in the
1770s and by the mid-19thC
the tea cup had developed its
traditional shape with a
shallow, wide bowl. Since
porcelain was expensive a
single saucer was often
supplied to serve both coffee
can and tea cup.*

A Shelley Queen Anne shape
coffee cup and saucer, c1928,
saucer 4½in (11.5cm) diam.
£45–50 *BEV*

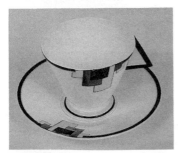

A Shelley Vogue shape cup and
saucer, c1930, saucer
4¾in (12cm) diam.
£85–95 *BEV*

A Standard China trio,
decorated with Pagoda pattern,
1930s, cup 3in (7.5cm) high.
£30–40 *PC*

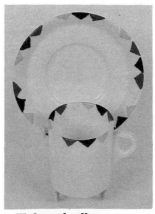

A Wedgwood coffee can
and saucer, signed by
Gail Fox, 1980s, saucer
4¾in (12cm) diam.
£25–30 *BKK*

Denby

A Denby flower trough, 1920s, 11⅕in (29cm) wide.
£80–90 *PC*

A pair of Denby green majolica vases, slight rim chip to one, c1890, 8½in (21.5cm) high.
£120–140 *KES*

A Denby Avocca bulb bowl, with early Orient Ware decorative glaze, crack to base, 1920s, 9in (23cm) diam.
£30–40 *KES*

A Denby Epic *petite marmite* with fish handles, designed by Donald Gilbert, c1930, 5⅕in (13cm) diam.
£12–15 *KES*

A Denby Cottage Blue teapot, with original 'Nevva-drip' patent spout, 1930s, 9¼in (23.5cm) high.
£28–30 *KES*

A Denby Celeste coffee pot, with Art Nouveau style decoration, c1912, 9½in (24cm) high.
£30–35 *KES*

l. A Denby fish novelty ashtray, in pastel blue glaze, 1930s, 4¼in (11cm) wide.
£55–60 *KES*

Cross Reference
Colour Review

r. A Denby majolica pig money box, restored, 1920s, 6in (15cm) long.
£120–130 *KES*

l. A Denby thatched cottage, c1975, 4¼in (11cm) wide.
£60–65 *KES*

Doulton

A Doulton faïence wall plaque, decorated in coloured enamels, within a brown line rim, impressed marks for 1878 and decorators monogram SK, 13¾in (35cm) diam.
£375–425 *DN*

Cross Reference
Bottles

l. A Royal Doulton Dewar's Whisky jug, inscribed 'Falstaff', c1930, 8in (20.5cm) high.
£120–145 *TP*

A Royal Doulton tea-for-two, c1928, plate 5in (12.5cm) diam.
£80–90 *PSA*

A Royal Doulton bone china part-tea set, The Coppice pattern, comprising of 41 pieces, 1960s.
£140–160 *Gam*

A Royal Doulton dish, c1910, 17¾in (45cm) wide.
£30–408 *PSA*

A Royal Doulton Friar teapot, depicting a scene from Dickens with Bill Sykes and his dog, produced 1908–51, 6in (15cm) high.
£200–225 *TP*

A Doulton Lambeth pottery vase, by Hannah Barlow, incised frieze of cattle and horses on moulded blue/green ground, impressed Art Union of London mark, late 19thC, 9½in (24cm) high.
£600–700 *AH*

Animals

A Royal Doulton bulldog
figure, 1940s, 6in (15cm) high.
£300–400 *TP*

*Royal Doulton produced
3 sizes of this model, of which
this is the largest.*

A Royal Doulton flambé cat
figure, Model No. 9, signed
Charles Noke, c1950,
5in (12.5cm) high.
£90–110 *TP*

A Royal Doulton 'Sleepytime'
Bunnykins, designed by Walter
Haywood, 1974–93,
1¾in (4.5cm) high.
£40–45 *PSA*

Four Royal Doulton Bunnykins figures:
Downhill Bunny, 1970s, 3in (7.5cm) wide.
£150–165
Rocket Man, 1970s, 4½in (11.5cm) high.
£50–55
Aerobics Bunny, c1984, 2¾in (7cm) high.
£110–110
School Days, 1970s, 4in (10cm) high.
£10–13 *TP*

Three Royal Doulton drake figures:
l. produced 1923–77, 2in (5cm) high.
£75–85
c. produced 1941–69, 2in (5cm) high.
£75–85
r. c1930, 3in (7.5cm) long.
£100–120 *TP*

Royal Doulton

From the 19thC onwards Doulton
produced ceramics intended for children,
ranging from feeding bottles to doll's
house furnishings, from nursery ware to
the tiled panels illustrating nursery
rhymes that decorated many children's
hospitals built at the turn of the century.
One of their most famous children's lines,
was the Bunnykins series, launched in
1934. The rabbit family was inspired by
the drawings of Barbara Vernon, who
spent her life in a convent, and the
designs were used for both nursery ware
and models. Still in production many
years later, Bunnykins is enormously
popular with adult collectors. Both early
and more recent pieces can command
very grown-up prices.

A Royal Doulton
Bunnykins money bank,
second version, c1980,
9in (23cm) high.
£180–220 *TP*

A Royal Doulton
Bunnykins nurse,
with red cross,
1989–94,
4in (10cm) high.
£60–75 *TP*

*This model was
withdrawn as the
Red Cross objected
to the red cross.
Later produced with
green ones.*

Character Jugs

A Royal Doulton miniature character jug, John Peel, 1940–60, 1¼in (3cm) high.
£50–60 *BGA*

A Royal Doulton character jug, Gulliver, c1963, 4¼in (11cm) high.
£200–225 *TP*

A Royal Doulton character jug, Simple Simon, designed by G. Blower, D6374, printed green mark, 1953–60, 6¼in (16cm) high.
£180–220 *DN*

Figures

l. A Royal Doulton miniature figure, entitled 'Chloe', designed by L. Harradine, Rd No. 764558, 1932–45, 2¾in (7cm) high.
£200–225 *HEI*

A Royal Doulton figure, limited edition, 1945–55, 7in (18cm) high.
£135–165 *HEI*

A Royal Doulton miniature character jug, Pearly Girl, designed by H. Fenton, blue version, printed mark in green, c1946, 2½in (6.5cm) high.
£1,800–2,000 *DN*

A Royal Doulton figure, entitled 'Southern Belle', designed by Peggy Davies, HN2229, 1958–90, 8in (20.5cm) high.
£80–100 *HEI*

A Royal Doulton figure, entitled 'Leading Lady', designed by Peggy Davies, 1965–76, 8½in (21.5cm) high.
£110–130 *TAC*

l. A Royal Doulton figure, entitled 'Child from Williamsburg', designed by Peggy Davies, 1964–83, 5¼in (13cm) high.
£60–80 *VSt*

A Royal Doulton
figure, entitled
'Sandra', designed by
Peggy Davies,
HN2275, 1969–90,
8¼in (21cm) high.
£80–90 *HEI*

A Royal Doulton
figure, entitled
'Wintertime', 1981,
8¼in (21cm) high.
£130–145 *HEI*

*This model was
exclusively
produced for the
Collectors' Club for
one year only.*

A Royal Doulton figure,
entitled 'Miranda',
1987–90, 9in (23cm) high.
£90–110 *TAC*

A Royal Doulton
miniature figure,
entitled 'Town Crier',
designed by Peggy
Davies, HN3261,
1989–1991, 4¼in
(11cm) high.
£65–75 *HEI*

> **Cross Reference**
> Colour Review

A Royal Doulton figure,
entitled 'Amy', Kate
Greenaway Series, designed
by Peter Gee, HN3316,
1991, 8½in (21.5cm) high.
£375–400 *TP*

1991 Figure of the Year.

Three Royal Doulton Snowmen figures:
Snowman with drum, 1988–94,
5¼in (13cm) high.
Snowman playing violin, 1987–94,
5½in (14cm) high.
£40–55 each
Snowman with piano, 1987–94,
piano 3in (7.5cm) wide.
£50–75 *TP*

Tolkien Series Figures

l. A Royal
Doulton Tolkien
figure, entitled
'Gandalf',
Middle-Earth
Series, 1980–84,
7½in (19cm) high.
£120–140 *TP*

*This and the
following figures
are from* Lord of
the Rings
*(1954–55) by
J.R.R. Tolkien.*

l. A Royal
Doulton Tolkien
figure, entitled
'Tom Bombadil',
1981–84,
5½in (14cm) high.
£200–245 *TP*

r. A Royal
Doulton Tolkien
figure, entitled
'Gimli', 1981–84,
5½in (14cm) high.
£75–85 *TP*

Christopher Dresser

Dr Christopher Dresser (1843–1904) is often credited as the first designer 'name'. At a time when William Morris championed the ideals of the Medieval guilds, Dresser was busy designing for industry, producing everything from ceramics to metalware, from linoleum and wallpapers to furniture and textiles. He had a good working knowledge of industrial techniques and his designs could be produced at much less cost than Morris' more labour-intensive products. Like many of his contemporaries Dresser was fascinated by Japanese design, an influence that affected his ceramics. He was art director of the Linthorpe Pottery (near Middlesbrough) 1879–82 and other manufacturers associated with Dresser include Minton, Wedgwood, Ault and Old Hall.

Ault

An Ault vase, with Christopher Dresser signature, c1890, 9in (23cm) high.
£800–1,000 *NCA*

An Ault two-handled vase, with Christopher Dresser signature, c1893, 8½in (21.5cm) high.
£800–1,000 *NCA*

An Ault vase, decorated with Chinese masks, designed by Christopher Dresser, c1893, 8in (20.5cm) high.
£1,000–1,200 *NCA*

An Ault flower holder, with Christopher Dresser facsimile signature, c1893, 4in (10cm) diam.
£180–200 *NCA*

Linthorpe

l. A Linthorpe plate, designed by Christopher Dresser, decorated by W. Davison, c1880, 11½in (30cm) diam.
£400–460 *NCA*

A Linthorpe jardinière, shape No. 533, designed by Christopher Dresser, c1880, 8in (20.5cm) high.
£500–600 *NCA*

A Linthorpe Oriental series moon flask, designed by Christopher Dresser, c1880, 6in (15cm) high.
£700–800 *NCA*

Two Linthorpe salt cellars, shape No. 305, designed by Christopher Dresser, c1880, 3in (7.5cm) diam.
£100–120 each *NCA*

l. A Linthorpe vase, shape No. 105, designed by Christopher Dresser, with a silver collar rim by Dixons, Sheffield, c1880, 12in (30.5cm) high.
£1,000–1,200 *NCA*

A Linthorpe vase or oil lamp base, shape No. 652, designed by Christopher Dresser, c1880, 10in (25.5cm) high.
£500–600 *NCA*

A Linthorpe 'camel' jug, shape No. 347, with C. Dresser and H. Tooth marks, c1880, 7in (18cm) high.
£600–700 *NCA*

A Linthorpe vase, with Christopher Dresser and Henry Tooth signatures, c1880, 3in (7.5cm) high.
£180–220 *NCA*

A Linthorpe Peruvian bottle, shape No. 227, with Christopher Dresser and Henry Tooth signatures, c1880, 7½in (19cm) high.
£800–1,000 *NCA*

A Linthorpe vase, shape No. 227, designed by Christopher Dresser, c1880, 6in (15cm) high.
£340–380 *NCA*

A Linthorpe tankard, shape No. 505, with Christopher Dresser and Henry Tooth signatures, the EPNS rim by Hukin and Heath, c1880, 9½in (24cm) high.
£450–550 *NCA*

A Linthorpe vase, with Christopher Dresser and Henry Tooth marks, c1880, 8½in (21.5cm) high.
£800–850 *NCA*

l. A Linthorpe triangular vase, with centre cut-out, designed by Christopher Dresser, c1880, 7in (18cm) high.
£600–700 *NCA*

A Linthorpe vase, with Christopher Dresser and Henry Tooth facsimiles, c1880, 7in (17.5cm) high.
£550–600 *NCA*

A Linthorpe two-handled vase, shape No. 958, 1883, 5in (12.5cm) high.
£80–100 *NCA*

Linthorpe Copies

A Daison Torquay two-handled vase, after Linthorpe, c1930, 5in (7.5cm) high.
£180–220 *NCA*

A Daison ewer, after Linthorpe, c1930, 9in (23cm) high.
£320–360 *NCA*

Linthorpe Copies

After the Linthorpe factory closed down their moulds were purchased by Daison, who made copies of Dresser's Linthorpe designs, as late as the 1930s.

Old Hall

An Old Hall jug, designed by Christopher Dresser, c1884, 12½in (32cm) high.
£340–380 *NCA*

Six Old Hall Shanghai pattern plates, designed by Christopher Dresser, c1884, 9in (23cm) square.
£550–650 *NCA*

Cross Reference
Colour Review

Elton Ware

An Elton double gourd-shaped vase, decorated with flowers and berries, with a mottled blue/green glaze, painted mark, c1910, 5½in (14cm) high.
£110–130 *DN*

An Elton ewer, with raised floral decoration, c1910, 12in (30.5cm) high.
£400–450 *NCA*

l. An Elton gilt crackle ground vase, c1910, 13½in (34.5cm) high.
£800–900 *NCA*

An Elton gilt crackle ground ewer, c1910, 14½in (37cm) high.
£750–850 *NCA*

r. An Elton gilt crackle ground jug, c1910, 5in (12.5cm) high.
£180–220 *NCA*

l. An Elton gilt crackle ground ewer, with entwined fish handle and spout, painted mark, c1910, 10¾in (27cm) high.
£450–520 *DN*

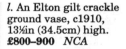

Figures & Groups

A John Bevington hand-painted figure of a gardener, c1850, 8in (20.5cm) high.
£200–250 *VSt*

A pair of Jacob Petit figures, French, c1860, 4in (10cm) high.
£400–500 *VSt*

A Dresden group, crossed swords mark, c1880, 16½in (42cm) high.
£1,500–1,800 *VSt*

A pair of Samson figures, in the style of Meissen, with crossed swords mark, c1860, 5½in (14cm) high.
£400–500 *VSt*

A Vienna mother and children porcelain group, beehive mark, c1880, 8in (20.5cm) high.
£400–465 *VSt*

A Samson porcelain figure, in the style of Chelsea, inscribed 'Caliban', anchor mark, c1880, 4in (10cm) high.
£60–70 *PBi*

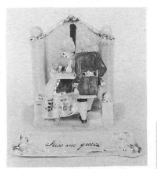

A German fairing, inscribed 'Kiss me quick', c1902, 3¾in (9.5cm) high.
£100–150 *PC*

Two Triart pottery figures of Hansel and Gretel, Italian, 1930s, 5in (12.5cm) high.
£150–180 *VSt*

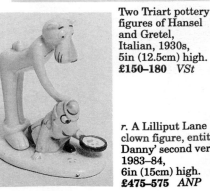

r. Pink Panther, c1981, some damage, 4½in (11.5cm) high.
£8–10 *TAR*

r. A Lilliput Lane clown figure, entitled Danny' second version, 1983–84, 6in (15cm) high.
£475–575 *ANP*

Goss & Crested China
Goss

A Goss Chichester Roman urn, commemorating the Golden Jubilee of Queen Victoria, with Garter star decoration, dated '1887', 3¼in (8.5cm) high.
£75–85 *MGC*

A Goss china replica of Queen Victoria's first shoe, 1890–1930, 4in (10cm) long.
£20–25 *G&CC*

A Goss Hereford kettle with lid, 1910–30, 2¾in (7cm) high.
£20–24 *G&CC*

A Goss vase, with butterfly handles, 1890–1920, 4¾in (12cm) high.
£90–100 *G&CC*

A Goss bowl, with 3 coral feet, commemorating the coronation of King George V and Queen Mary, 1911, 3¾in (9.5cm) diam.
£50–60 *MGC*

l. A Goss bust of Shakespeare, copied from the monument in Stratford-upon-Avon church, 1890s, 4in (10cm) high.
£90–110 *MGC*

r. A Goss Maidstone Roman ewer, 1910–30, 3¼in (8cm) high.
£7–9 *G&CC*

A Goss frilled candleholder, 1910–30, 4¼in (11cm) long.
£15–20 *G&CC*

A Goss character jug of Churchill, 1927, 6¼in (16cm) high.
£200–250 *MGC*

Two Goss preserve pots, decorated with cherries and blackberries, 1920s, 4in (10cm) high.
£85–100 each *MGC*

Though best known for crested ware and cottages, W. H. Goss also produced other ceramic designs.

Crested China

An Arcadian ashtray, with Stratford-upon-Avon crest, 1910–20, 4¼in (11cm) long.
£50–60 *BCO*

A Shelley altar candlestick, with Montrose crest, 1910–24, 4¾in (12cm) high.
£15–18 *BGA*

l. A Carlton treadle sewing machine, c1925, 3¼in (8cm) high.
£25–30 *G&CC*

l. A pair of Victorian shoes, with Portsmouth crest, 6¼in (16cm) long.
£65–70 *TAR*

Crested Animals

A selection of crested animals, 2–4in (5–10cm) wide, from *l.* to *r.*
An Arcadian fish dish. **£15–20**
A German fish. **£7–9**
A German novelty fish. **£15–20**
A Savoy snail. **£35–42**
An Arcadian frog. **£20–24** *CCC*

l. An Arcadian Crowborough hare, 1910–20, 3in (7.5cm) wide.
£19–23 *BCO*

r. A Caledonia Aberlour parrot, 1920, 2½in (6.5cm) high.
£12–15 *BCO*

l. A Grafton duck, with Newbury crest, 1910–20, 2½in (6.5cm) wide. **£10–15** *BCO*

A Grafton mouse, with green bead eyes, c1920, 1¾in (4.5cm) high. **£45–55** *G&CC*

A Foley hare, with Bideford crest, c1920, 3in (7.5cm) wide. **£55–65** *BCO*

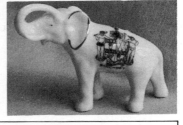

A selection of crested china cats and kittens, 2–4in (5–10cm) wide, 1920s, *l.* to *r.*
A Savoy seated cat. **£75–85**
A Gemma standing kitten. **£20–24**
A Shelley standing cat. **£55–65**
Saxony kittens in a basket and a cat in a bag. **£30–36 each** *CCC*

r. A Willow Art elephant, 1910–20, 3¾in (9.5cm) long. **£30–40** *G&CC*

A Willow Art Bagshot teddy bear, c1910–20, 3¼in (8.5cm) high. **£15–20** *BCO*

An unmarked cat, with Monmouth crest, 1920s, 2½in (6.5cm) high. **£15–18** *BCO*

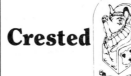

l. A Tourist Art kiwi, c1920, 2½in (6.5cm) high. **£55–65** *G&CC*

 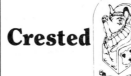

r. An unmarked hare, with Ryde, Isle of Wight crest, 1920s, 3¾in (9.5cm) wide. **£23–28** *BCO*

l. An unmarked elephant, with Bagshot crest, 1900–20, 3in (7.5cm) wide. **£18–22** *BCO*

Crested Buildings & Monuments

l. A Grafton Blackpool Wheel, 3½in (9cm) high. **£30–36**
r. A German North Bar, Beverley, 3in (7.5cm) high. **£55–65** *CCC*

A selection of crested china buildings, 1920s, *l.* to *r.*
A Willow Art Canterbury Cathedral. **£55–65**
An Impero Grimsby hydraulic tower. **£35–45**
A Grafton Houses of Parliament. **£60–75**
A Botolph St. Paul's Cathedral. **£30–36**
An Impero Bootham Bar, York.
£35–65 *CCC*

A Carlton model of Pit Head, with Sunderland crest, 1930s, 4¼in (11cm) high. **£110–130** *MGC*

Crested Figures

r. A Podmore's figure of Edward VIII, copied from a photograph, with City of London crest, 1930s, 5¾in (14.5cm) high. **£80–100** *BCO*

A Savoy bust of John Travers Cornwall, hero of Jutland, c1920, 4¼in (11cm) high. **£250–300** *MGC*

A Grafton Pierrot playing the banjo, with Hereford crest, 1920s, 4in (10cm) high. **£80–100** *MGC*

Hancock

A Hancock's Rubens ware pomegranate vase, c1920, 9in (23cm) high. **£70–80** *CSA*

A Hancock's Ivory ware jug, c1930, 10½in (27cm) high. **£25–30** *CSA*

Hummel

l. A Hummel figure of a boy, 1930s, 4in (10cm) high.
£40–48 *VSt*

A Hummel figure, Umbrella Girl, printed and impressed marks and original label, 1930s, 7¾in (19.5cm) high.
£240–280 *DN*

A Hummel figure, The Photographer, printed and impressed marks and original label, 1930s, 5in (12.5cm) high, together with another figure of a young boy carrying a double base, printed and impressed marks, damaged, 1930s, 6in (15cm) high.
£90–110 *DN*

l. A Hummel group of 2 little girls, one knitting a sock, impressed marks, 1930s.
£150–180 *DN*

l. A Hummel figure, Friends, a girl with a deer, printed and impressed marks and original label, 1930s, 11¼in (28.5cm) high.
£275–325 *DN*

Losol

A Losol ware dressing table set, Blantyre pattern, c1915, tray 15in (38cm) long.
£70–80 *CSA*

A Losol ware preserve jar, Rushton pattern, c1915, 4¾in (12cm) high.
£40–45 *CSA*

A Losol bowl, Gold Brocade pattern, c1925, 8¼in (21cm) diam.
£40–50 *CSA*

A Losol dish, Suntrae pattern, c1925, 8¾in (22cm) wide.
£25–30 *CSA*

A Losol jug, Exotic pattern, c1910, 6¾in (17cm) high.
£35–40 *CSA*

A Losol dish, Waterlily pattern, c1930, 8¼in (21cm) wide.
£15–20 *CSA*

Midwinter

A Midwinter Kingfisher pattern sandwich set, Burslem backstamp, 1930s, platter 13in (33cm) long.
£20–28 *DgC*

A Midwinter Windmill design meat dish, sandwich plates and a jug, 1930s, meat dish 10in (25.5cm) long.
£70–90 *DgC*

A Midwinter celery vase, Salad ware design by Sir Terence Conran, c1958, 7in (18cm) high.
£60–70 *PC*

A Midwinter condiment set, Riviera design by Sir Hugh Casson, c1954, dish 8½in (21.5cm) long.
£20–30 *DgC*

Two Midwinter Stylecraft plates, designed by Jessie Tait, *l*. Fiesta pattern, c1954, 8½in (20.5cm) diam.
£10–12
r. Fantasy pattern, c1953, 9½in (24cm) diam.
£12–14 *AND*

A Midwinter plate, Nature Study design by Sir Terence Conran, c1955, 9½in (24cm) diam.
£10–20 *DgC*

A Midwinter Fashion plate, designed by Sir Hugh Casson, c1960, 9½in (24cm) diam.
£10–12 *AND*

A Midwinter coffee set, with Oranges and Lemons pattern, c1962, designed by John Russell, 7½in (19cm) high.
£45–50 *DgC*

A Midwinter Stonehenge coffee pot, Blue Dahlia pattern designed by Jessie Tait, c1972, 9in (23cm) high.
£15–18 *AND*

Cross Reference
Colour Review

l. A Midwinter Fine 22-piece coffee service, Spanish Garden pattern designed by Jessie Tait, c1966, coffee pot 8in (20.5cm).
£65–75 *AND*

Moorcroft

A MacIntyre Moorcroft salad bowl, with plated rim, tube-lined with a band of growing anemones and leaves picked out in blue, green and brown, on a cream ground, printed mark in brown and registration No. 401753 and green painted signature, c1903, 10¼in (26cm) diam.
£700–800 *DN*

r. A MacIntyre Moorcroft Florian ware vase, tube-lined with anemones and leaves on a shaded blue ground, rim chip, printed mark in brown and registration No. 326471 and signed in green 'W. Moorcroft Dec', 8½in (21.5cm) high.
£200–250 *DN*

A William Moorcroft Florian ware Poppy design vase, in shades of green and pink, c1902, 12in (30.5cm) high.
£1,100–1,300 *RUM*

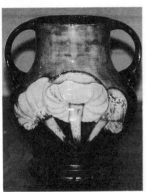

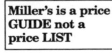

l. A William Moorcroft Landscape design vase, in shades of green, c1913, 6in (15cm) high.
£700–800 *RUM*

l. A William Moorcroft Flambé Toadstool design vase, c1928, 8in (20cm) high.
£1,850–2,100 *RUM*

| Miller's is a price GUIDE not a price LIST |

A Moorcroft vase, tube-lined with lilies and leaves, picked out in colours, on a mottled blue/green ground, impressed and painted signature marks, c1974, 10in (25.5cm) high.
£225–275 *DN*

A Moorcroft Orchid pattern vase, 1950s–60s, 9½in (24cm) high.
£350–450 *HEA*

Bernard Moore

A Bernard Moore red lustre vase, with crab design by Edward R. Wilkes, c1905, 10in (25.5cm) high.
£250–300 *NCA*

A Bernard Moore red lustre vase, with sailing ship sketched in black, 1901–05, 9in (23cm) high.
£250–300 *NCA*

A Bernard Moore red lustre vase, with a dragon in gold, blue and ivory, 1901–05, 7in (17.5cm) high.
£550–650 *NCA*

A Bernard Moore red lustre vase, with a dragon sketched in gold and black, 1901–05, 10in (25.5cm) high.
£500–600 *NCA*

r. A Bernard Moore Arts and Crafts bowl, c1910, 10in (25.5cm) diam.
£400–450 *SHa*

Myott

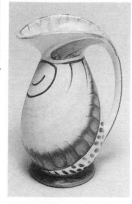

A Myott fruit bowl, decorated with a central flower and leafy branches, 1920–30, 12in (30.5cm) diam.
£85–95 *BEV*

A Myott jug, painted with a cobweb design, c1930, 8in (20cm) high.
£40–50 *CSA*

A Myott jug, painted in yellow, orange brown and green, 1920–30, 9in (23cm) high.
£65–75 *BEV*

Myott

Myott & Son was founded in 1898. During the 1920s and 1930s, the company produced distinctive and colourful Art Deco ceramics, which are highly sought-after today.

l. A Myott water jug, painted in red and green, 1920–30, 8¼in (21cm) high.
£30–40 *BEV*

r. A Myott jug, painted in brown orange and green on a cream background, c1930, 8in (20cm) high.
£30–40 *CSA*

Noritake & Japanese Tableware

A Noritake 22-piece dinner service, c1910, tureen 10¾in (27cm) wide.
£275–325 *BGA(K)*

A Noritake basket ware bowl, decorated in gold, red Komaru backstamp, c1911, 5¼in (13cm) wide.
£15–20 *DgC*

A Noritake trinket dish, green Komaru backstamp, c1920, 3½in (9cm) diam.
£8–12 *DgC*

A Noritake lemon squeezer, with stylised flower design, red M in wreath backstamp, 1920s, 6in (15cm) diam.
£15–20 *DgC*

A Noritake bonbon dish, decorated with a floral pattern, 1920s, 5in (12.5cm) diam.
£15–25 *DgC*

A Noritake bonbon dish, with fluted edge, decorated with a swan, blue Komaru backstamp, c1930, 4in (10cm) diam.
£15–20 *DgC*

l. Two Noritake bonbon dishes, red M in wreath backstamp, c1930, 7¾in (20cm) wide.
£18–25 each *DgC*

r. A Noritake bonbon dish, with floral central pattern and orange edge, green Komaru backstamp, 1930s, 5in (12.5cm) wide.
£15–20 *DgC*

Noritake

- Founded in Japan in 1904, producing hand-painted porcelain on a scale that competed with industrially printed ceramics
- From 1914, specialised in tea and dinner ware, novelty pieces and figurines, primarily for export
- During 1920–30s Noritake's design team based in New York, although still manufactured in Japan. Specific porcelain also designed for European market, often lavishly painted and gilt
- Usually marked 'Noritake' and 'Made in Japan'. Not dated although the backstamp changed over the decades
- Noritake copies were made by smaller Japanese companies for export, and marked 'Nippon' or 'Samurai'

A Noritake condiment set, decorated with sheep in a meadow, green Komaru backstamp, c1930, salt and pepper 3in (7.5cm) high.
£25–35 *DgC*

A Noritake hair tidy, with swan design, green Komaru backstamp, c1930, 4in (10cm) diam.
£25–35 *DgC*

A Noritake three-lobed dish, with pagoda design and gilding, red komaru backstamp, 1930s, 8½in (21.5cm) diam.
£30–50 *DgC*

A Noritake jam pot, with tree by a lake design, blue Komaru backstamp, 1930s, 3in (7.5cm) high.
£15–25 *DgC*

A Noritake cup and saucer, green Komaru backstamp, c1930, 2¾in (7cm) high.
£15–20 *DgC*

l. A Noritake boat-shaped bonbon dish, green M in wreath backstamp, c1930, 7in (17.5cm) wide.
£18–25 *DgC*

A Noritake vase, decorated with peacocks, c1930, 5½in (14cm) high.
£35–48 *DgC*

A pair of Noritake vases, c1910, 5¼in (13cm) high.
£150–180 *BGA(K)*

l. A Noritake hand-painted vase, with embossed decoration on neck, blue Komaru backstamp, c1920, 8½in (21.5cm) high.
£100–150 *PC*

Japanese Tableware

A pair of Nippon hand-painted candlesticks, Kinjo china, 1890s, 5½in (14cm) high.
£40–60 *DgC*

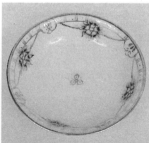

A Nippon bonbon dish, hand-painted in gold with garlands, green backstamp, c1920, 5in (12.5cm) diam.
£15–20 *DgC*

A collection of hand-painted items, decorated with a swan design, marked Nippon, c1920, candlestick 5½in (14cm) high.
Bowls   **£22–25 each**
Plate   **£6–12**
Candlestick   **£25–35**
Powder Bowl **£25–30** *DgC*

Nursery & Children's Ware

A child's brown transfer ware plate, Eureka pattern, by Whittingham Ford & Riley, marked W. F. & R., c1876–82, 7¾in (20cm) diam.
£22–30 *OD*

A child's porcelain part tea set, comprising 17 pieces, late 19thC, plates 5in (12.5cm) diam.
£80–100 *Gam*

A Shelley plate, design by Mabel Lucie Attwell, c1928–34, 6in (15cm) diam.
£75–85 *PC*

l. A Staffordshire child's tea set, comprising 6 pieces, painted with the Noah's Ark pattern, late 1920s, teapot 5in (12.5cm) high.
£100–120 *P(B)*

A Burleigh nursery trio, c1930, plate 6½in (16.5cm) diam.
£100–120 *BKK*

A Shelley mug, design by Mabel Lucie Attwell, c1928, 3in (7.5cm) high.
£85–100 *PC*

A Grimwades Bubbles pattern child's plate, 1930s, 8in (20cm) wide.
£30–38 *WAB*

A Shelley napkin ring, design by Mabel Lucie Attwell, c1928, 2½in (6.5cm) diam.
£75–85 *PC*

A child's transfer printed mug, 1920s, 2¾in (7cm) high.
£5–10 *OD*

A Ridgway pottery child's breakfast set, decorated with Huckleberry Hound and friends, 1950s, plate 7in (18cm) diam.
£35–40 *TAR*

l. A Shelley cup and saucer, c1928, cup 2¾in (7cm) high.
£85–100 *PC*

r Two Hornsea egg cups, decorated with Toffee and Mallow, 1980s, 2in (5cm) high.
£2–3 each *TAR*

Parian Ware

White, semi-matt porcelain, Parian ware was first produced by the Copeland factory c1842–44. It gained its name because its smooth and creamy surface resembled the marble mined by the ancient Greeks on the Aegean island of Paros. Also known as statuary porcelain, Parian was much used for portrait busts and figurines, providing an affordable and high-quality alternative to plaster casts and enabling the middle classes to decorate their homes with sculpture. Portraits of royal, military and political celebrities were extremely popular, as were classical figures. The Art Union of London, a society founded in 1837 to promote the arts by means of a lottery, produced Parian statuettes by leading contemporary sculptors, including J. H. Foley and John Bell, that were distributed to winning members. These finely modelled pieces are much sought-after today. Though statuettes predominate, Parian ware was also used for tableware, vases and other decorative works. Leading manufacturers include Copeland, Wedgwood, Minton, Worcester and Robinson & Leadbeater. The United States Pottery Co at Bennington, Vermont, produced similar biscuit porcelain, and Parian ware was also made in Europe.

Portrait Busts

Lord Randolph Churchill, a Parian bust by Turner & Wood of Stoke, late 19thC, 5in (12.5cm) high.
£60–80 *SAS*

Richard Cobden, a Parian bust by John Adams & Co, sculpted by E. W. Wyon, c1865, 16½in (42cm) high.
£250–300 *JAK*

Geothe, a Parian bust by Robinson & Leadbeater, c1880, 8in (20.5cm) high.
£100–130 *JAK*

Lord William Dargan, a Parian bust by Kerr & Binns, c1855, 9in (23cm) high.
£175–200 *JAK*

Lord Dargan was an Irish entrepreneur and railway builder. He financed the Dublin Exhibition in 1853.

Handel, a Parian bust by Robinson & Leadbeater, c1880, 8in (20.5cm) high.
£100–130 *JAK*

King Edward VII, a Parian bust by W. H. Goss, c1901, 6¼in (16cm) high.
£175–200 *MGC*

Dr Kenealy MP, a Parian bust by George Ash, c1873, 11½in (29cm) high.
£140–160 *JAK*

Dr Kenealy was defender of the Tichborne Claimant which was the longest running trial of its day.

General Gordon, a Parian bust by W. H. Goss, c1885, 7⅞in (19.5cm) high.
£200–250 *MGC*

l. Abraham Lincoln, a Parian bust, possibly American, c1890, 8½in (21.5cm) high.
£65–75 *JAK*

r. Lloyd George, a white Parian bust, late 19thC, 7½in (19cm) high.
£150–180 *SAS*

Kitchener, a Parian bust by Savoy, with the crest of England, 4¾in (12cm) high.
£35–45 *SAS*

Horatio Herbert Kitchener, British Field Marshal, conqueror of the Sudan and Secretary of State for War at the beginning of WWI, died in 1916, when the cruiser taking him to Russia was sunk by a German mine. This bust was produced to commemorate his death.

Mozart, a Parian bust by Robinson & Leadbeater, c1880, 7¾in (20cm) high.
£100–130 *JAK*

Mitchell, a Parian bust by Robinson & Leadbeater, c1895, 8in (20cm) high.
£100–130 *JAK*

Mitchell was Chairman of the Co-operative Wholesale Society from 1874.

Napoleon, a Continental Parian bust, late 19thC, 5½in (14cm) high.
£20–30 *SAS*

Lord Nelson, a Parian bust by Coalport, c1853, 9in (23cm) high.
£450–550 *JAK*

Modelled under the direction of Sir William Parker KCB from a painting by Wichell.

l. Sir Robert Peel, a Parian bust, printed mark 'Published by Samuel Alcock, Hill Pottery, Burslem 1850 from a model by Mr W. Jackson', 11½in (30cm) high.
£275–300 *JAK*

Lord Roberts, a Parian bust by Robinson & Leadbeater, c1900, 8in (20.5cm) high.
£70–100 *SAS*

Lord Salisbury, a white Parian bust by Turner & Wood, 19thC, 5in (12.5cm) high. **£90–110** *SAS*

Lord Salisbury, a tinted terracotta coloured Parian bust by Robinson & Leadbeater, c1880, 8in (20.5cm) high. **£100–130** *JAK*

C. H. Spurgeon, a white Parian bust by Robinson & Leadbeater, late 19thC, 4¾in (12cm) high. **£40–50** *SAS*

John Sumner, a Parian bust by Robinson & Leadbeater, c1800, 12½in (32cm) high. **£275–325** *JAK*

l. William Shakespeare, a Parian bust by Robinson & Leadbeater, c1880, 7½in (19cm) high. **£65–75** *JAK*

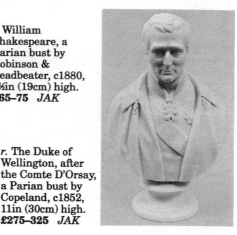

r. The Duke of Wellington, after the Comte D'Orsay, a Parian bust by Copeland, c1852, 11in (30cm) high. **£275–325** *JAK*

Statuettes & Figures

r. A Copeland Parian figure of Storm, sculptor Brodie, minor faults to base, c1858, 18½in (47cm) high. **£450–550** *JAK*

> ### Don't Forget!
> *If in doubt please refer to the 'How to Use' section at the beginning of this book.*

l. A Copeland Parian bust of Miranda, by W. Calder Marshall, c1860, 11in (28cm) high. **£250–300** *JAK*

A Copeland Parian figure of a scantily clade maiden, c1870, 14in (35.5cm) high. **£300–350** *PC*

l. A Minton Parian figure of Miranda, by John Bell, c1865, 15½in (39.5cm) high.
£400–450 *JAK*

Miranda is the daughter of Prospero in Shakespeare's The Tempest.

Miller's is a price GUIDE not a price LIST

l. A Copeland Parian group of Florence Nightingale and the wounded at Scutari, by T. Phyffers, c1858, 13½in (34cm) high.
£500–600
r. An American Parian group of Union Refugees, by John Rogers, c1863, 18in (45.5cm) high.
£1,000–1,200 *JAK*

A Minton Parian group of Babes in the Wood, minor damage, c1855, 12½in (31.5cm) high.
£400–500 *JAK*

A Minton Parian figure of Dorothea, by John Bell, c1860, 13¼in (33.5cm) high.
£400–450 *JAK*

A Parian bust of Clytie, by Robinson & Leadbeater, c1880, 13in (33cm) high.
£400–450 *JAK*

Clytie was a water nymph turned into a sunflower by Apollo the sun god, so that she would always turn towards him in adoration!

Vases & Wine Coolers

r. A Parian vase, decorated with grapes, c1850, 10¾in (27cm) high.
£80–100 *BGA*

l. A Victorian Parian ware vase, encrusted with grapes and flowers on a blue background, 10in (25.5cm) high.
£85–95 *PSA*

A Parian vase, decorated with grapes, c1850, 10¾in (27cm) high.
£80–100 *BGA*

Pendelfins

Pendelfins are a new subject to this guide. These small ceramic figures have been enjoying surprisingly large success in the current market, with some pieces that once sold for shillings fetching hundreds of pounds. The business was started on Coronation Day 1953 in a garden shed, by freelance artist Jean Walmsley Heap and Jeannie Todd, colleagues at Burnley Building Society. Their original intention was little more than to make Christmas gifts for their friends and family. Since their wooden hut was overlooked by Pendle, the legendary Lancashire Witch Hill, they called their clay creations Pendelfins, the second part of the name

inspired by the 'elfin' quality of the figures. Early products included witches, pixies and elves and the mid-1950s saw the introduction of the highly popular Pendelfin rabbit family. The business soon expanded, moving to larger premises and exporting its distinctive animals and figures across the world.

Pendelfin still flourishes in Burnley today, and their collectors' club boasts 15,000 members. Whilst many of the smaller figures are only worth about £20 or less, rare examples dating from the fifties and early sixties have been making large sums, including a recent auction record of £2,650 for an early pair of book ends.

l. Shiner, 1960–67, 5½in (14cm) high.
£325–375 *TP*

r. Rocky, introduced 1959, 4in (10cm) high.
£85–95 *TP*

Bongo, 1964–87, 3¼in (8cm) high.
£30–40 *TP*

Gussie, 1960–68, 3½in (9cm) high.
£325–375 *TP*

FURTHER READING
Heap, Jean Walmsley, *The Pendelfin Story*, Published by Pendelfin, Burnley

Father Mouse, 1961–66, 3½in (9cm) high.
£350–400 *TP*

Mother Mouse, 1961–66, 4in (10cm) high.
£350–400 *TP*

Forty Winks, 1993–95, 4in (10cm) wide.
£25–30 *TP*

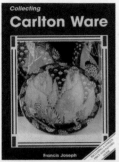

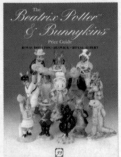
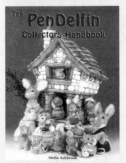

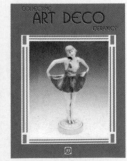
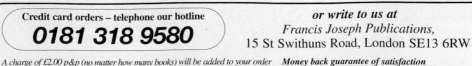

A Carlton Ware cheese dish, 1920s, 6½in (16.5cm) wide.
£25–30 *PC*

A Granville China cheese dish, 1920s, 7in (18cm) wide.
£50–60 *LA*

A biscuit barrel, in the form of a watermill, lid damaged, 1930s, 7in (18cm) high.
£30–40 *PC*

An Empire Ware Tudor Berries design butter dish, in the form of a thatched cottage, 1920s, 6½in (16.5cm) diam.
£30–40 *LA*

A Carlton Ware cheese dish, No. 762479, in the form of a thatched roof house, 1920s, 7in (18cm) wide.
£80–90 *PC*

A Japanese twin-gabled house biscuit barrel, 1920s, 5½in (14cm) wide.
£30–40 *PC*

A Westminster China butter dish, 1930s, 5½in (14cm) wide.
£25–30 *PC*

A biscuit barrel, in the form of a gypsy caravan, designed by Coronet, 1920s, 7½in (19cm) high.
£80–90 *LA*

A biscuit barrel, in the form of a Scandinavian house, 1930s, 7½in (19cm) high.
£40–50 *LA*

A Kensington Pottery condiment set, in the form of 2 thatched roof houses, 1920s, 8in (20.5cm) wide.
£70–80 *PC*

r. A Japanese three-piece cruet set, modelled as pagodas, on a tray, 1920s, 7in (18cm) wide.
£50–60 *LA*

A set of 4 Westminster Pottery egg cups, 1920s, tray 5in (12.5cm) wide. **£30–40** *PC*

A Crown Ducal thatched cottage teapot, 1920s, 7in (18cm) wide. **£80–90** *PC*

A Carlton Ware sifter, 1920s, 5in (12.5cm) high. **£90–110** *PC*

A Beswick three-piece tea set, with matching biscuit box, 1920s, teapot 7½in (19cm) wide. **£100–120** *LA*

An Ebsters & Co Anne Hathaway's cottage three-piece tea set, 1920s, teapot 10½in (26.5cm) wide. **£70–80** *PC*

A Radford tankard, 1920s, 4½in (11.5cm) high. **£40–50** *LA*

A Paramount Pottery teapot, in the form of a thatched roof cottage, 1930s, 9in (23cm) wide. **£30–40** *LA*

A sugar sifter, 1920s, 6in (15cm) high. **£50–60** *LA*

A Crown Ducal vase, with lantern design, c1925, 9in (23cm) high. **£25–35** *DgC*

A pair of Crown Ducal butterfly design lustre vases, c1900, 11in (28cm) high. **£180–200** *TAR*

A Crown Devon coffee service, with Mattajade pattern, c1930, coffee pot 9in (23cm) high. **£300–400** *BKK*

A Davenport cup and saucer, with scenic design, c1820, cup 2½in (6.5cm) high.
£85–95 *PSA*

A Shelley cup and saucer, with Phlox pattern, c1920, saucer 5in (12.5cm) diam.
£20–25 *PBi*

A Royal Doulton cup and saucer, c1900, cup 2¼in (5.5cm) high.
£65–70 *BEV*

A Dartmouth Pottery Motto ware cup and saucer, decorated with a house and tree scene, 1950s, saucer 8¾in (22cm) diam.
£45–50 *TAR*

A Mason's Regency trio, 1930s, plate 7in (18cm) diam.
£10–15 *TAC*

A Burleigh Ware trio, decorated with a fireside scene, 1930s, plate 7in (18cm) diam.
£65–70 *BEV*

r. A Coalport cup and saucer, with Indian Tree pattern, c1930, cup 2¼in (5.5cm) high.
£15–20 *VSt*

A Royal Doulton hand-decorated trio, cup cracked, c1934, plate 7in (18cm) diam.
£18–24 *BKK*

A Crown Devon coffee cup and saucer, 1930s, cup 2in (5cm) high.
£45–55 *BEV*

A Midwinter coffee cup and saucer, with Brama design, 1930s, cup 2in (5cm) high.
£35–40 *BEV*

An Elton gold crackle glaze tyg, c1910, 7in (19cm) high.
£300–400 *NCA*

A Linthorpe jug, by Christopher Dresser, shape No. 597, c1880, 6in (15cm) high.
£700–800 *NCA*

A vase, by Christopher Dresser, with carving and relief floral decoration, marked, c1880, 10½in (27cm) high.
£1,000–1,200 *NCA*

A Sitzendorf bust, cross mark on base, c1880, 6in (15cm) high.
£200–300 *VSt*

An Ault 'Tongues' vase, by Christopher Dresser, shape No. 248, c1893, 13in (33cm) high.
£1,800–2,200 *NCA*

A Linthorpe jardinière, attributed to Christopher Dresser, shape No. 2298, c1880, 7in (18cm) high.
£320–380 *NCA*

An Ernst Bohne bisque group, with blue anchor mark, c1880, 5½in (14cm) high.
£120–150 *VSt*

A Fielding's musical pottery mug, moulded and coloured with a country scene, entitled 'Sarie Marais', 1930s, 4¼in (11cm) high.
£320–350 *SAS*

A Continental porcelain spill vase group of young people, c1910, 5½in (14cm) high.
£55–65 *PSA*

A Goss figure of Lady Betty,
1920–30, 6½in (16.5cm) high.
£275–325 *MGC*

A Losol dish, decorated with Hollyhocks
pattern, c1930, 11in (28cm) long.
£25–30 *CSA*

A Lancaster & Sons cake stand,
1920s, 8in (20.5cm) high.
£15–20 *DgC*

An Arcadian figure of Miss
Holland, 1920s, 5in (12.5cm)
high. **£140–170** *MGC*

A Goss Irish mather,
c1900, 6¼in (16.5cm) high.
£55–65 *MGC*

A Hummel figure of a child
playing a banjo, 1930s,
2½in (6.5cm) high.
£45–55 *VSt*

l. A Longwy charger, c1925,
14½in (37cm) diam.
£300–400 *SUC*

A Hancock's Ivory ware butterfly
dish, c1930, 7in (18cm) wide.
£15–20 *CSA*

A Hancock's Ivory ware jug,
c1930, 6¾in (17cm) high.
£25–30 *CSA*

A Carlton match holder,
1920–30s, 3in (7.5cm) high.
£50–60 *MGC*

A Maling lustreware bowl, pattern No. 5217, 1930s, 8½in (21.5cm) diam.
£100–125 *HEI*

A Myott Son & Co jug, decorated with flowers, 1930s, 8½in (21.5cm) high.
£120–140 *BEV*

A Minton leaf-moulded pottery jug, with flowerhead border to rim, c1900, 8in (20.5cm) high.
£240–280 *HCH*

A Myott geometric-shaped vase, c1933, 8¼in (21cm) high.
£130–150 *BKK*

A Minton jug, decorated in relief, late 19thC, 7¾in (20cm) high.
£130–150 *PC*

A Bernard Moore red lustre vase, c1902, 8in (20.5cm) high.
£240–280 *NCA*

A Noritake lustre sugar bowl, with green Komaru back stamp, 1920s, 5¼in (13cm) diam.
£12–18 *DgC*

A Noritake 5-piece dressing table set, in Bridge Over Lake design, c1930, tray 12in (30.5cm) long.
£110–130 *DgC*

A Japanese hand-painted vase, Nippon back stamp, c1910, 7½in (19cm) high.
£45–55 *DgC*

A pair of Japanese vases, Nippon back stamp, 1890s, 11in (28cm) high.
£350–400 *DgC*

A pair of Quimper plates, decorated with
Annick design, c1930, 9in (23cm) diam.
£55–65 *TAR*

A Quimper ladle, 1950s, 7½in (19cm) long.
£18–22 *TAR*

A Royal Doulton Flambé ware
elephant, signed Noke, c1962,
5½in (14cm) high. **£100–125** *TP*

A Royal Doulton
Bunnykins figure,
1989–93, 4¼in
(11cm) high.
£35–45 *PSA*

A Royal Doulton figure,
entitled 'Past Glory',
1973–79, 8in (20.5cm)
high. **£300–325** *TP*

A Pendelfin,
entitled 'Aunt
Ruby', 1993–95,
8in (20.5cm) high.
£125–145 *TP*

l. A Royal Doulton Series ware
bowl, The Gaffers, 1921–49,
7¾in (20cm) diam.
£100–165 *TP*

A set of 4 limited edition plates,
decorated by Norman Rockwell, 1974,
6in (15cm) diam. **£200–250** *BSA*

A Royal Doulton character jug,
The Fortune Teller, 1959–67,
7in (18cm) high.
£250–300 *TP*

A Royal Doulton figure,
entitled 'Elyse', HN2474,
c1987, 6½in (16.5cm) high.
£100–125 *HEI*

A Royal Doulton figure,
entitled 'Spring Morning',
HN1922, 7½in (19cm) high.
£150–170 *VSt*

Poole Pottery

A Carter Stabler Adams red earthenware fruit plate, shape No. 495, designed by Truda Adams, decorated by Ann Hatchard, impressed 'Carter Stabler Adams, Poole England', 1924–30, 11¼in (28.5cm) diam.
£200–300 *PP*

A Poole Pottery vase, pattern BX designed by Truda Carter, impressed and painted marks and original retailer's paper label for H.V. White Ltd, Minehead, c1930, 11in (28cm) high.
£650–700 *DN*

A Carter Stabler Adams vase, painted by Mary Brown with a version of the Bluebird pattern, c1930, 10in (25cm) high.
£175–225 *Bea*

A Poole Pottery plate, decorated with the portrait of 'The Ship of Harry Paye', the Poole sea captain, drawn by Arthur Bradbury and painted by Ruth Pavely, dated 1948, 15in (38cm) diam.
£450–500 *Bea*

r. A Poole Pottery tea-for-two set, mid-1950s, tray 12¾in (32.5cm) (40.5cm) wide.
£65–75 *GRo*

A Poole Pottery table lamp, c1930, 6¾in (17cm) high.
£40–50 *JO*

A Poole Pottery vase, c1930, 9in (23cm) high.
£70–80 *JO*

A Poole Pottery jam pot and cover, c1930, 4½in (11.5cm) high.
£40–50 *JO*

A Poole Pottery stoneware plate, shape No. 673, Owl from the Bird series in the Wildlife Collection, designed by Barbara Linley Adams, impressed 'Poole England', 1982, 5in (12.5cm) diam.
£5–10 *OD*

Royal Winton Chintz Ware

According to Art Deco ceramics dealer Beverley, whereas a few years ago decorative chintz ware could be purchased for virtually nothing, today the market is literally flowering. 'It is huge in the USA, big in Japan, collected in New Zealand, Canada and South Africa, to say nothing of Britain. It is unbelievably hot!' Collectors' clubs have been formed across the world and rare pieces can sell for hundreds of pounds.

Inspired by decorative textile designs, transfer-printed chintz ware was manufactured by a number of firms in the 1930s, the most famous being Royal Winton. 'They were the Rolls-Royce of chintz,' explains Mr K. C. Glibbery, secretary of the Royal Winton International Collectors' Club. 'Pieces were of extremely high quality, with strong colour and good definition.'

Owned by Grimwades, Royal Winton produced their first lithographed chintz in 1928, named Marguerite, which was eventually to be followed by over 50 other chintz patterns. Designs reflected contemporary fabrics, and according to

legend, the director of Royal Winton would pay his factory girls one shilling a time to be allowed to copy their prettier pinafores. 'Some designs can be compared, or even matched up with period Liberty prints,' explains Beverley. Royal Winton is the most collectable name in the field, other good factories include James Kent, Crown Ducal and Midwinter.

As Beverley explains, collectors, particularly in the United States, like to use their china and to combine various patterns. 'Dinner plate, tea plate, cup and saucer, each one different, will be laid out in a harlequin setting. Tablecloths, napkins and even cutlery are chosen to harmonize with the prevailing colour and the whole effect can look amazing.'

Condition of the ware is important, the design must be sharp, the colours unfaded and beware of seamed or unevenly printed pieces. Certain patterns are rarer than others, designs with a black background, which were produced in a comparatively limited quantity, are particularly sought-after today. Perhaps surprisingly, this feminine and self-consciously pretty china

A Royal Winton plate, decorated with Bedale pattern, 1930s, 7in (18cm) diam.
£40–45 *BEV*

A Royal Winton cup and saucer, decorated with Bedale pattern, 1930s, saucer 5¼in (13cm) diam.
£50–55 *BEV*

A Royal Winton plate, decorated with Cheadle pattern, 1930s, 9¾in (25cm) diam.
£80–90 *BEV*

A Royal Winton table lighter, decorated with Cheadle pattern, 1930s, 4½in (11.5cm) diam.
£200–250 *BEV*

A Royal Winton shell-shaped butter pat, decorated with Eleanor pattern, 1930s, 3¼in (8.5cm) diam.
£15–18 *BET*

A Royal Winton cup and sandwich saucer, decorated with Eleanor pattern, 1930s, saucer 7¾in (20cm) diam.
£55–60 *BEV*

A Royal Winton egg cup, decorated with Estelle pattern, 1930s, 2½in (6.5cm) high.
£30–40 *BEV*

A Royal Winton dish, decorated with Estelle pattern, 1930s, 9¼in (24cm) wide.
£70–80 *BEV*

A Royal Winton egg cup set, decorated with Hazel pattern, 1930s, tray 7in (18cm) wide.
£200–225 *BEV*

A Royal Winton jug, decorated with Hazel pattern, 1930s, 2½in (6.5cm) high.
£60–70 *BEV*

A Royal Winton cup and sandwich saucer, decorated with Marguerite pattern, 1930s, 7¾in (20cm) wide.
£55–65 *MLa*

A Royal Winton butter dish, decorated with Nantwich pattern, 1930s, 6½in (16.5cm) long.
£150–175 *BEV*

A Royal Winton basket, decorated with Marion pattern, 1930s, 5¼in (13cm) wide.
£150–160 *BEV*

A Royal Winton basket, decorated with Marguerite pattern, 1930s, 4in (10cm) diam.
£70–80 *BEV*

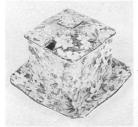

l. A Royal Winton jam pot and cover, decorated with Richmond pattern, 1930s, 2¾in (7cm) high.
£180–200 *BEV*

Two Royal Winton miniature cups and saucers, decorated with Rosina pattern, 1930s, saucer 2in (5cm) diam.
£105–115 each *BET*

A Royal Winton cup and saucer, decorated with Somerset pattern, 1930s, saucer 5½in (14cm) diam.
£60–65 *BEV*

A Royal Winton sifter, decorated with Somerset pattern, 1930s, 3¾in (9.5cm) high.
£80–95 *BET*

A Royal Winton tea service,
comprising 23 pieces, decorated
with Somerset pattern, 1930s.
£850–1,000 *P(O)*

A Royal Winton butter
pat, decorated with
Summertime pattern,
1930s, 3½in (8cm) diam.
£15–18 *BET*

A Royal Winton teapot,
decorated with Summertime
pattern, 1930s, 6¼in (16cm) high.
£200–300 *BEV*

A Royal Winton toast rack, decorated
with Summertime pattern, 1930s,
7in (18cm) long.
£120–140 *BEV*

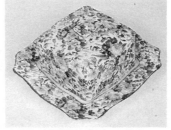

A Royal Winton butter dish,
decorated with Summertime
pattern, 1930s,
5¾in (14.5cm) square.
£130–150 *BEV*

A Royal Winton plate,
decorated with Sweet
Pea pattern, 1930s,
10in (25.5cm) square.
£95–100 *BEV*

A Royal Winton cruet,
decorated with Sweet
Pea pattern, 1930s,
5in (12.5cm) wide.
£120–140 *BEV*

A Royal Winton toast rack,
decorated with Sweet Pea pattern,
1930s, 4½in (11.5cm) long.
£120–140 *BEV*

A Royal Winton dish, decorated with
Sweet Pea pattern, 1930s,
7in (18cm) long.
£70–80 *BEV*

Royal Winton

l. A Royal Winton
basket, decorated
with Tartan pattern,
4in (10cm) wide.
£30–40 *BET*

l. A Royal Winton
cheese dish, 1930s,
6½in (16.5cm) long.
£60–65 *BEV*

r. A Royal Winton comport,
with white rose decoration,
1930s, 10½in (26.5cm) wide.
£15–18 *PSA*

A Royal Winton jam pot
and cover, 1930s,
4¼in (11cm) high.
£20–25 *BEV*

Other Chintz Ware

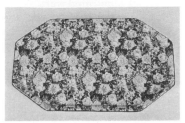

A Crown Ducal dish, decorated with Rose and Peony pattern, 1930s, 14in (35.5cm) long.
£125–150 *BEV*

A Crown Ducal vase, early mark, 1920s, 6in (15cm) high.
£50–60 *BEV*

A Myott teapot, 1930s, 8in (20cm) long.
£50–60 *CSA*

A Nelson Ware jug, decorated with Heather pattern, 1930s, 2¼in (5.5cm) high.
£30–40 *BEV*

A Shelley butter dish, decorated with Melody pattern, 1930s, 7in (18cm) long.
£80–90 *BEV*

A James Kent jam pot and cover, decorated with Du Barry pattern, 1930s, 4⅜in (12cm) high.
£70–80 *BEV*

Russian & Soviet Ceramics

Over the past few years increasing interest has been shown in Russian and Soviet ceramics and more material has appeared on the market. The earliest pieces in this section date from the nineteenth century, manufactured by the Gardner factory at Verbilki, near Moscow. The factory was founded in 1766 by English entrepreneur and timber merchant Francis Gardner, who was encouraged by the Tsar to improve the quality of Russian porcelain. Run by his descendants until the late nineteenth century, the firm was renowned for its statuettes of Russian peasants, produced in limited numbers, and highly sought-after today both in the West and increasingly in Russia. In 1892, Malvei Kuznetsov took over the pottery which was then nationalised after the 1917 October Revolution. Verbilki porcelain is still manufactured today, and over the years the factory has used a wide range of different stamps. 'Under marks and dating can be an absolute minefield for collectors of Russian ceramics,' warns Bob Moore, founder of the British based USSR Collectors' Club.

Many of the ceramics illustrated were produced for export from the 1950s onwards by major Soviet potteries including Gzhel and Lomonosov. 'Ceramics made for the home market tended to be more functional,' explains Moore, 'since the majority of Russians couldn't afford the decorative pieces.' Lomonosov supplied the Russian shop in London (closed 1994) and thanks to the trading relationship established by Prime Minister Callaghan, retailed animal figures through London Zoo. Originally some of these animals might have cost as little as half a crown (12½p), today they can fetch tens or even hundreds of pounds. Marked pieces are worth more than unmarked examples and collectors look both for the factory name (in Russian Cyrillic script) and the words 'Made in the USSR' (written in English), as opposed to the more recent, post-Soviet stamp which reads 'Made in Russia.'

'It is better not to wash Soviet ceramics,' concludes Moore. 'Sometimes the precious factory mark is only an ink stamp and if it is rubbed off, the value of a piece is significantly reduced.'

Dulevo

A Dulevo figure of a dancing girl, from Uzbekistan, old mark, 1940s, 9¾in (24.5cm) high.
£180–220 *SRC*

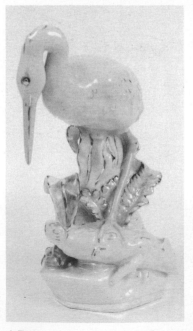

A Dulevo model of a stork and a frog, dove under mark, 1950s, 9½in (24cm) high.
£200–250 *SRC*

A Dulevo figure of a water princess, later dove under mark, 1960s, 13in (33cm) high.
£130–150 *PC*

Gardner

A Gardner figure of a wife with her drunken husband, under mark and impressed in Cyrillic alphabet, 1860–90, 6in (15cm) high.
£500–600 *PC*

A Gardner group of two boys playing by a broken wheel, impressed Gardner in Russian Cyrillic alphabet, 1860–90, 4¼in (11cm) high.
£400–500 *PC*

A Gardner figure of a woman with a child on her shoulders, under mark and impressed, 1860–80, 12¼in (31cm) high.
£550–650 *PC*

l. A Gardner six-person tea service, George and dragon topped by double headed Imperial eagle under mark in red, 1860–90, teapot 6¼in (16cm) high.
£350–400 *PC*

A Gardner biscuit figure of a fisherman breaking a hole in the ice to fish, under mark and impressed, 1860–90, 11½in (29cm) high.
£550–650 *PC*

A Gardner six-person tea service, all under marked, 1860–90, teapot 6¼in (16cm) high.
£360–400 *PC*

Gzhel

Three Gzhel figures from Russian fairy tales, special under mark, 1942–55, tallest 7in (18cm) high.
£120–200 each *PC*

A Gzhel trial figure of Ivan Tsarevich and his princess on the magic grey wolf, 1940–55, 10¼in (26cm) high.
£400–500 *PC*

Three Gzhel ornaments, under marked 'made in USSR', 1960–70s, clock 6in (15cm) high.
Clock and jar **£80–100 each**
Lidded Dish **£40–50** *PC*

Three Gzhel models, 1960-70s, back stamped, lady 8¼in (21cm) high.
Birds **£30–40 each**
Lady **£45–65** *SRC*

l. A selection of Gzhel figures, under marked, 1960–70s, Magic Pike 3¼in (8.5cm) high.
£20–65 each *SRC*

A selection of Gzhel figures, 1960-70s, 3in (8cm) high.
£15–20 each *SRC*

Lomonosov

Two Lomonosov figure groups, 1940–50s, smallest 7¾in (19.5cm) high.
l. **£150–180**
r. **£120–150** *PC*

A Lomonosov figure of Vakoula on the Diable, sculptor B. Ya Vorobjen, artist L. K. Blak, marked, 1940s, 6in (15cm) high.
£150–200 *SRC*

A Lomonosov figure of a seamstress, embroidering one of the first Revolutionary flags, 1950s, 6in (15cm) high.
£130–180 *PC*

This is a Lomonosov copy.

Two Lomonosov bear groups, blue under marks, 1948–50, tallest 4¾in (12cm) high.
£150–200 *PC*

l. A Lomonosov group of a lion and a hare, 1948–50, 5¼in (13.5cm) high.
£150–200 *SRC*

A Lomonosov figure of a leopard cub 4in (10cm) high and mother leopard, 1950–85, USSR mark.
Cub   **£18–28**
Mother **£100–140**
Russian mark, 1990.
Cub   **£10–15**
Mother **£40–50** *SRC*

The earlier versions with the Soviet mark and stamped 'made in the USSR' are worth more than the later examples marked 'made in Russia'.

Three Lomonosov figures, 1950s, 7¼in (18.5cm) high.
£90–140 each *PC*

A set of Lomonosov figures of hares, 1950s, tallest 6½in (16.5cm) high.
£450–500 *SRC*

Three Lomonosov figures of cats, back stamped 'made in USSR', 1950–85, tallest 6¾in (17cm) high.
£50–80 each *SRC*

The price for pieces made in 1990 is £20–30 each.

A Lomonosov white figure of a male elk, sculptor Y.A. Vorobjen, 1950–70s, 12in (31cm) high.
£100–130 *SRC*

A Lomonosov figure of an elk calf, marked 'made in USSR', 1960, 6in (15cm) high.
£180–220 *SRC*

A Lomonosov tiger cub, c1960, 5in (12.5cm) high.
£15–25 *DgC*

Taiwanese copies of this piece exist, but are of a lighter weight and with poorer quality painting.

Three Lomonosov Himalayan bears, under marked 'made in USSR', 1960s, tallest 6¾in (17cm) high.
l. **£150–200**
c. **£70–80**
r. **£70–80** *SRC*

A Lomonosov mammoth, 1960s, 4¼in (11cm) high.
£180–250 *SRC*

This is a rare model.

Revolutionary Factories

A Revolutionary factory figure of a Yakut girl in a long coat, sitting on a tree stump, hammer and sickle impressed mark, 1920, 6in (15cm) high.
£150–180 *PC*

A Revolutionary factory figure of a Yakut girl in a long coat, hammer and sickle impressed mark, 1920, 6in (15cm) high.
£200–250 *PC*

A Revolutionary factory plate, with Russian slogan, hammer and sickle under mark, 1950s, 9½in (24cm) diam.
£300–400 *PC*

Made in the 1950s, these plates are not made to deceive but are genuine copies of 1920s Revolutionary plates. Their marks explain that they are 'made in the style of . . .'.

r. A Revolutionary factory plate, under marked in light blue, 1950s, 10in (25cm) diam.
£360–460 *PC*

A Revolutionary factory plate, under marked, 1950s, 10in (25cm) diam.
£360–460 *PC*

Verbilki

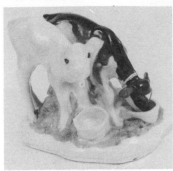

A Verbilki group of 2 calves, marked 'made in USSR', 1940–50s, 6in (15cm) high.
£180–220 *PC*

l. A Verbilki biscuit figure of a rural housewife in traditional costume, under marked, 1920–25, 10in (25cm) high.
£400–500 *PC*

A Verbilki group of fighting snow leopards, 1950–60, 5¾in (14.5cm) high.
£160–220 *SRC*

Various Factories & Unmarked Pieces

l. A figure of a girl with a kid, early 1935, 6¾in (17cm) high.
£150–200
r. A figure of a bongo drummer, 1950s, 7¾in (19.5cm) high.
£120–160 *SRC*

The factory which produced these figures burned down and was not re-opened.

A figure of a girl holding a mirror, wearing a gold necklace, mid-1930s, 6in (15cm) high.
£175–225 *SRC*

A clown ashtray and a trinket box, c1940, ashtray 4¼in (11cm) wide.
£75–95 each *SRC*

Two figures of the drunken general, 1948–55, tallest 8¾in (22cm) high.
£130–200 each *PC*

Four figures of Mishka the bear, 1980s, tallest 8in (20cm) high.
£50–90 each *SRC*

Mishka the bear was the symbol for the 1980 Summer Olympics held in Moscow. The Olympics were boycotted and only a few of these figures were brought to the West. They are very sought-after today.

A selection of bears, all USSR marked, 1950–1970, tallest 5½in (14cm) high.
Small **£25–35 each**
Large **£50–70 each** *PC*

Rye Pottery

A ceramic industry has existed in Rye, Sussex, since the thirteenth century. Rye Pottery, however, came to national attention in the late nineteenth century under the Mitchell family, when firstly Sussex Rustic Ware (1869–1920) and then Sussex Art Ware (1920–39) were marketed. The pottery closed in 1939 and reopened in 1947 under the Cole Brothers, Walter and John. Post-WWII Rye concentrated on decorative items for the home at affordable prices, and in a distinctive style. Potters included David Sharp, Dennis Townsend, Ray Everett and Jimmy Elliott. In the late 1950s, many of these artists left to establish their own individual potteries.

A Rye Pottery model of a carpenter's bag, no mark, c1890, 5in (12.5cm) high.
£130–150 *NCA*

A Rye Pottery cut-out bowl, decorated with coiled grass snakes, c1900, 6in (15cm) diam.
£500–575 *NCA*

A Rye Pottery dish, decorated with hops, c1910, 4½in (11.5cm) diam.
£70–85 *NCA*

A Rye Pottery miniature green and white posy bowl, c1920, 1½in (3.5cm) high.
£35–45 *NCA*

A Rye Pottery studio plate, by John Cole, decorated with a white, black and blue pattern, c1951, 10in (25.5cm) diam.
£150–180 *NCA*

A Rye Pottery studio plate, decorated with a white, black, brown and green pattern, c1955, 9in (23cm) diam.
£150–180 *NCA*

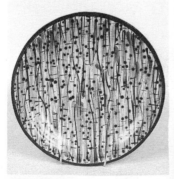

A Rye Pottery studio plate, decorated with a red, black and white pattern, c1955, 11in (28cm) diam.
£110–130 *NCA*

A Rye Pottery 'Cock' vase, early 1950s, 6in (15cm) high.
£90–100 *NCA*

A Rye Pottery bowl, decorated with a grey and white pattern, 1950s, 10in (25.5cm) high.
£110–130 *NCA*

A Rye Pottery bowl, decorated with a white, black, yellow and red pattern, 1950s, 4in (10cm) high.
£35–45 *NCA*

A Rye Pottery bottle, decorated with a white, black, blue and yellow pattern, 1950s, 3in (7.5cm) high.
£40–50 *NCA*

A Rye Pottery vase, decorated with multi-coloured stripes, 1950s, 4in (10cm) high.
£30–40 *NCA*

A Rye Pottery green lamp base, decorated in a filament pattern, 1950s, 12in (30.5cm) diam.
£100–120 *NCA*

A Rye Pottery floral 'A' pattern plate, 1960s, 10in (25.5cm) diam.
£8–10 *JR*

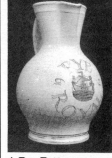

A Rye Pottery jug, by Dennis Townsend, 1951, 10in (25.5cm) high.
£500–600 *PC*

A Rye Pottery vase, by Tarquin Cole, c1951, 10in (25.5cm) high.
£500–600 *PC*

These two vases were exhibited at the Festival of Britain in 1951, and their value reflects their historical interest

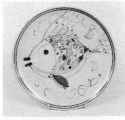

A Rye Pottery studio plate, with a blue and red fish design, c1960, 9in (23cm) diam.
£80–100 *NCA*

A Rye Pottery floral 'A' pattern cup and saucer, 1960s, 3¾in (9.5cm) high.
£4–6 *JR*

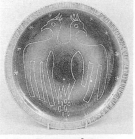

A Rye Pottery plate, designed by Walter Cole, c1980, 11in (28cm) diam.
£200–220 *NCA*

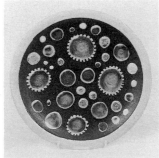

An Iden Pottery plate, by Dennis Townsend, c1965, 10in (25.5cm) diam.
£100–120 *NCA*

An Iden Pottery dish, by Ray Everett, c1960, 11½in (29cm) wide.
£30–35 *NCA*

FURTHER READING

Rye Pottery Catalogue 1950s–60s, New Century Gallery, Kensington Church Street, London, NW8

r. A Rye Pottery dish, by Walter Cole, c1980, 11½in (29cm) diam.
£80–100 *NCA*

Staffordshire
Animals

A pair of Staffordshire figures of greyhounds, with hares in their mouths, 19thC, 7¾in (19.5cm) high.
£200–220 *ACA*

A Staffordshire miniature model of a dog and kennel, c1860, 1½in (3.5cm) high.
£100–125 *JO*

A Staffordshire figure of a spaniel, with fan tail, 19thC, 12½in (32cm) high.
£145–165 *ACA*

A Samson copy of a Staffordshire figure of a French poodle, gold anchor mark, c1900, 2¾in (7cm) high.
£60–70 *JO*

A Staffordshire figure of a poodle, on a cobalt blue base, 19thC, 3¼in (8cm) high.
£90–100 *ACA*

A Staffordshire group, with kennel, c1860, 4in (10cm) high.
£130–150 *JO*

A Staffordshire group of a cherub and spaniel, 19thC, 6¼in (16cm) high.
£200–225 *ACA*

A Staffordshire figure of a dalmation, 19thC, 3½in (9cm) high.
£90–110 *ACA*

A pair of Staffordshire figures of cats, c1900, 4in (10cm) high.
£250–300 *ACA*

A Staffordshire miniature group of sheep, 19thC, 2¼in (5.5cm) high.
£100–120 *ACA*

A Staffordshire figure of a stag, bocage restored, 19thC, 5½in (14cm) high.
£150–200 *ACA*

r. A Staffordshire group of a sheep and lamb, c1850, 5¼in (13cm) high.
£150–180 *JO*

l. A Staffordshire figure of a sheep, on a cobalt blue base, slight restoration, 19thC, 3¼in (8cm) high.
£90–100 *ACA*

Figures

A Staffordshire bust, probably portraying Daniel O'Connell, c1850, 7½in (19cm) high.
£320–360 *RWB*

SPRING

A Staffordshire figure, inscribed 'Spring', 19thC, 7¾in (20cm) high.
£125–145 *ACA*

A Staffordshire figure, Nightwatchman, 19thC, 9in (23cm) high.
£200–250 *ACA*

A Staffordshire figure of John Philip Kemble as Hamlet, c1852, 11¼in (28.5cm) high.
£500–550 *RWB*

l. A Staffordshire figure of a Classical lady making a sacrifice, 19thC, 7½in (19cm) high.
£165–185 *ACA*

A Staffordshire figure, Sloth, possibly by Ralph Wood, 19thC, 7¾in (20cm) high.
£125–155 *ACA*

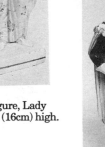

l. A Staffordshire figure, Lady Archer, 19thC, 6¼in (16cm) high.
£130–150 *ACA*

A Staffordshire figure, Prince Albert, restored, 19thC, 11½in (29cm) high.
£125–150 *ACA*

Cross Reference
Colour Review

A pair of Staffordshire figures of Shakespeare and Milton, c1850, 13in (33cm) high.
£700–800 *JO*

l. A Staffordshire group, inscribed 'John Brown', 19thC, 11in (28cm) high.
£500–535 *ACA*

l. A Staffordshire figure, Winter, 19thC, 7¼in (18.5cm) high.
£145–165 *ACA*

A pair of Staffordshire figures, Sand and Beesoms, c1880, 9in (23cm) high.
£400–500 *JO*

A Staffordshire figure, Mazeppa, 19thC, 5¼in (13cm) high.
£120–135 *ACA*

A Staffordshire group of a child and goat, c1840, 4½in (11.5cm) high.
£120–140 *JO*

A Staffordshire group, by Lloyd of Shelton, depicting a shepherd and shepherdess with their sheep, c1835, 5½in (14cm) high.
£240–280 *JO*

A pair of Staffordshire figures of children riding on goats, c1845, 6in (15cm) high.
£350–400 *MSA*

r. A Staffordshire group, inscribed 'Rural', 19thC, 7in (18cm) high.
£200–250 *ACA*

Houses, Castles & Cottages

A Staffordshire pastille burner, modelled as a cottage scene, 19thC, 6in (15cm) high.
£145–165 *ACA*

A Staffordshire pastille burner, modelled as a cottage, c1820, 5in (12.5cm) high.
£150–200 *JO*

r. A Staffordshire lilac pastille burner, modelled as a castle, c1840, 5¾in (14.5cm) high.
£200–225 *JO*

l. A Staffordshire miniature model of a castle, c1840, 2¼in (5.5cm) high.
£80–100 *JO*

A Staffordshire pastille burner, modelled as a cottage, c1820, 4in (10cm) high.
£150–180 *JO*

A Staffordshire pastille burner, c1835, 3¾in (9.5cm) high.
£120–140 *JO*

A Staffordshire pastille burner, c1840, 6in (15cm) high.
£200–225 *JO*

A Staffordshire pastille burner, modelled as a folly, c1840, 6½in (16.5cm) high.
£130–150 *JO*

A Staffordshire pastille burner, modelled as a cottage, c1845, 4½in (11.5cm) high.
£100–125 *JO*

A Staffordshire pastille burner, modelled as a castle, c1855, 10¼in (26cm) high.
£200–220 *JO*

A Staffordshire spill holder, modelled as a castle, 19thC, 5¼in (13cm) high.
£80–95 *JO*

A Staffordshire pastille burner, Swan Cottage, c1860, 6¾in (17cm) high.
£80–95 *JO*

A Staffordshire model of a mansion, c1860, 7¼in (18.5cm) high.
£100–125 *JO*

A Staffordshire spill vase, modelled as a castle, c1860, 12in (30.5cm) high.
£80–90 *RWB*

A Staffordshire pastille burner, modelled as a folly, c1860, 5in (12.5cm) high.
£100–125 *JO*

A Staffordshire miniature model of a castle, c1870, 3¾in (9.5cm) high.
£80–95 *JO*

Pen Holders

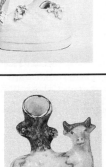

l. A Staffordshire quill holder, modelled as a parrot on a perch, 19thC, 5in (12.5cm) high.
£165–185 *ACA*

r. A Staffordshire pen holder, modelled as a stag, c1840, 4in (10cm) high.
£100–125 *JO*

A Staffordshire group pen holder and inkwell, c1860, 4½in (11.5cm) high.
£60–75 *JO*

Spill Vases

l. A Staffordshire spill vase, modelled as a cow and dairy maid, c1840, 5½in (14cm) high.
£200–220 *JO*

r. A Staffordshire spill vase, modelled as a shepherdess with a Jacob sheep, c1850, 6in (15cm) high.
£120–140 *JO*

l. A Staffordshire porcellaneous spill vase, modelled on an *Aesop's Fable*, c1830, 6½in (16.5cm) high.
£360–400 *RWB*

Tableware

r. A Staffordshire tureen, modelled as a dove, 19thC, 6in (15cm) high.
£400–475 *ACA*

Two Staffordshire cow creamers, 19thC, 4¾in (12cm) high:
l. Willow pattern. **£200–230**
r. Brown and white. **£175–200** *ACA*

Studio Ceramics

A charger, designed by Alan Caiger-Smith, 1960s, 14in (35.5cm) diam.
£250–300 NCA

A blue glazed stoneware vase, by Joan Calver, 1996, 9¾in (25cm) high.
£100–120 ELG

l. A Crowan Pottery 12-piece coffee service, by Harry and May Davis, some damage, c1950, coffee pot 6½in (16.5cm) high.
£150–180 IW

A porcelain ginger jar, by Russell Coates, glazed and enamelled in kutani colours, 1996, 10¼in (26cm) high.
£150–200 ELG

A porcelain dish, by Bridget Drakeford, green glaze with bronze crystals, 1996, 7½in (19cm) diam.
£100–120 ELG

A salt glazed jug, by Jane Hamlyn, c1980, 7in (18cm) high.
£80–90 IW

A Carne vase, 1960, 8in (20.5cm) high.
£30–40 PC

A stoneware jug, by Sheila
Fournier, with white glaze
and Japanese style
brushwork, 1960–70s,
5½in (14cm) high.
£30–40 SnA

Cross Reference
Colour Review

l. A stoneware vase,
by Janet Leach, c1980,
13in (33cm) high.
£250–300 IW

A stoneware pot with lid,
by Emily Myers, vivid
blue glaze, c1995,
7in (18cm) diam.
£110–130 ELG

Two ceramic vases, by Tessa
Wolfe Murray, flat shape,
with elliptical
curves, decorated with
slips, stain
and glazes, 1990s.
l. 8in (20.5cm) high.
£60–70
r. 10½in (26.5cm) high.
£120–140 ELG

A St Ives Pottery,
Cornwall, stoneware
mug, 1940–70,
4¾in (12cm) high.
£55–65 SnA

A stoneware torso, by
Juliet Thorne, 1996,
8¾in (22cm) high.
£80–100 ELG

l. A bowl, by Dame
Lucie Rie, in
'American' yellow,
impressed LR seal,
c1960, 6½in
(16.5cm) diam.
£4,500–5,000 Bon

A carved and
burnished stoneware
dish, by Antonia
Salmon, c1995,
11in (28cm) diam.
£140–165 ELG

r. A Troika vase, 1960s,
4¾in (12cm) high.
£30–40 PC

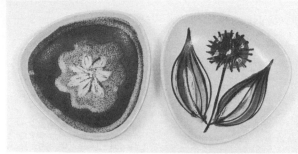

Two white glazed and painted flat dishes, by Marianne de Trey for Dartington Pottery, c1950–60, 5½in (14cm) diam.
£24–28 *SnA*

A celadon glazed bowl, by James Walford, c1950, 5¾in (14.5cm) diam.
£90–100 *IW*

A Raku vase, by John Wheeldon, 1990s, 8in (20cm) high.
£55–65 *ELG*

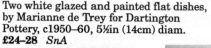

A pair of stoneware 'Duelling Birds' vases, by Maggie Williams, 1990s, 17¾in (45cm) high.
£400–500 *ELG*

r. A stoneware bowl, by George Wilson, jade green with black dragonfly decoration, c1995, 11in (28cm) diam.
£80–90 *ELG*

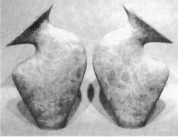

A stoneware 'Angel Bird' vase, by Maggie Williams, with blue textured surface, c1995, 12¼in (31cm) high.
£40–50 *ELG*

A vase, by Michael Cardew, Winchcombe Pottery, some damage, c1930, 5½in (14cm) high.
£120–140 *IW*

A Winchcombe Pottery coffee jug, c1940, 8in (20.5cm) high.
£90–110 *IW*

A Winchcombe Pottery jug, 1930s, 11¾in (30cm) high.
£150–200 *IW*

Victorian & Edwardian

Two German porcelain menu holders, c1900, 4½in (11.5cm) long.
£35–45 each *VSt*

A Paris porcelain shoe, decorated with cherubs, c1880, 5¼in (13cm) high.
£110–130 *VSt*

A Victorian toothbrush holder, with registration No. c1891, 8in (20.5cm) wide.
£24–28 *TAC*

Two slippers, c1890, 5in (13cm) long:
l. green porcelain, with gilt decoration.
£40–50
r. Dresden, hand-painted.
£80–100 *VSt*

A porcelain basket, c1845, 10½in (27cm) wide.
£250–300 *VSt*

l. A Dresden letter holder, with hand-painted scenes, c1900, 6½in (16.5cm) wide.
£350–400 *VSt*

r. A Hulme & Christie sauce tureen on stand, c1900, 8½in (21.5cm) wide.
£35–45 *TAC*

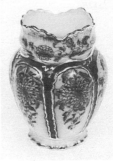

A Victorian toothbrush holder, by Salt Bros, Tunstall, with blue transfer and gilt decoration, 5¼in (13cm) high.
£28–32 *TAC*

A Sitzendorf encrusted basket, c1880, 6¾in (17cm) high.
£70–80 *VSt*

Bowls

A late Victorian celadon jardinière, painted with bluebirds and blossom, 13in (33cm) diam.
£325–365 *PSA*

A Samson Chinese export punchbowl, decorated with flower-sprays, c1890, 10¾in (27.5cm) diam.
£150–180 *PC*

A spongeware bowl, c1900, 6in (15cm) diam.
£40–50 *IW*

Cups

An unmarked coffee can, decorated in blue, red, green and gilt, 19thC, 2¼in (5.5cm) high.
£52–62 *PSA*

A Pratt ware coffee can, decorated with a rural scene, c1885, 2¾in (7cm) high.
£90–110 *PSA*

A Coalport mug, inscribed 'James Thornton, Spalding, 1855', 4in (10cm) high.
£150–200 *VSt*

Jugs

A Bretby ewer, decorated with flowers, c1895, 9½in (24cm) high.
£150–200 *PC*

A Ford & Sons water jug, c1910, 8in (20.5cm) high.
£30–35 *TAC*

A Minton jug, decorated with blue, white and gilt, c1898, 5½in (14cm) high.
£30–35 *TAC*

A Sarreguemines jug, 'Judge', No. 4502, c1902, 6½in (16.5cm) high.
£100–120 *PC*

Plates

r. A set of 6 Brown-Westhead, Moore & Co dessert plates, c1885, 8in (20.5cm) diam.
£130–150 *PC*

A Dresden ribbon plate, marked Germany, c1910, 7in (18cm) diam.
£15–18 *HEI*

A pair of Bodley, Staffordshire, porcelain dessert plates, depicting marine life, c1890, 9in (23cm) diam.
£90–110 *BSA*

l. A Minton hand-painted plate, c1870, 9in (23cm) diam.
£80–90 *VSt*

Cross Reference
Colour review

A Minton hand-painted comport, c1870, 9in (23cm) diam.
£80–90 *VSt*

A Paragon cabinet plate, hand-painted with game birds, c1906, 8½in (21.5cm) diam.
£100–120 *VSt*

A Pratt ware plate, No. 319, depicting 2 boys drinking and eating, c1860, 7in (18cm) diam.
£25–35 *SER*

l. A Spode Feldspar plate, c1815, 8¾in (22cm) diam.
£100–120 *VSt*

r. A Royal Crown Derby plate, Scissor pattern, c1885, 8½in (21.5cm) diam.
£50–60 *VSt*

This pattern is not so desirable because the centre of the plate has been left undecorated.

l. A W. F. & Co transfer printed plate, with portrait of Sir J. York Scarlet in the centre, c1870, 9½in (24cm) diam.
£130–150 *PC*

r. A plate with coloured transfer hunting scene, maker unknown, late 19thC, 6in (15cm) diam.
£20–30 *OD*

l. A plate, decorated in blue, red, green and gilt, unmarked, early 19thC, 9in (23cm) diam.
£38–48 *PSA*

Teapots

A Bell Pottery teapot and cover, c1880, 6½in (16.5cm) high.
£50–60 *PC*

A Staffordshire porcelain teapot on stand, c1880, 8½in (21.5cm) high.
£120–140 *RA*

A Measham ware teapot, the lid with acorn finial, cartouche to the side bearing the name of the original owners and date, c1882, 15in (38cm) high.
£250–300 *JBL*

Vases

A Derby vase, with gilded decoration, c1887, 6½in (16.5cm) high.
£180–220 *VSt*

A pair of Sarreguemines stoneware vases, c1890, 9¼in (23.5cm) high.
£250–300 *PC*

r. A Dresden vase, with painting of a stork, marked, c1880, 9in (23cm) high.
£150–180 *VSt*

A Baron vase, marked Barnstaple ware, c1894, 11in (28cm) high.
£130–150 *NCA*

Wall Pockets

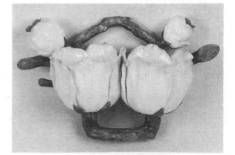

A Victorian magnolia-shaped wall pocket, marked W. & R., Reg. 101007, 10½in (26.5cm) wide.
£100–125 *PSA*

l. A French wall pocket, made in Desvres, c1880, 8in (20.5cm) high.
£100–125 *PSA*

A pair of Volkstedt porcelain wall pockets, marked JR in blue, c1900, 8in (20.5cm) high.
£200–250 *VSt*

l. An Arthur Wood hand-painted wall pocket, c1930, 9in (23cm) high.
£30–35 *BKK*

r. A Burleigh Ware wall vase, c1935, 7¾in (20cm) high.
£20–30 *CSA*

Cross Reference
Royal Winton
Chintz Ware

A Crown Devon wall vase, c1935, 7½in (19cm) high.
£20–30 *CSA*

A Kensington Pottery wall vase, c1935, 7½in (19cm) high.
£20–30 *CSA*

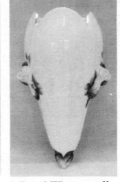

A Royal Winton wall vase, c1940, 8¾in (22cm) high.
£35–40 *CSA*

A Shorter wall pocket, c1940, 7in (18cm) high.
£15–20 *CSA*

Wedgwood

A Wedgwood encaustic decorated black basalt bough pot, with flower holder, c1770, 7in (18cm) diam.
£500–600 *PC*

A Wedgwood blue jasper ware pot with lid, applied with lions' masks and classical figure design, c1900, 6¼in (16cm) high.
£75–85 *PSA*

A Wedgwood Feldspathic stoneware jug, moulded in relief with figures within blue bordered panels, with angled scroll handle, c1800, 5in (12.5cm) high.
£90–110 *TMA*

Worcester

A Worcester tea cup and saucer, decorated in kakiemon style, within blue ground fan-shaped bands, decorated with flower roundels and gilt leaf scrolls, blue seal mark, c1770, 5in (12.5cm) diam.
£330–380 *DN*

A Worcester ewer, decorated with a floral design, c1885, 10¼in (26cm) high.
£900–1,000 *OBS*

A Locke Worcester miniature vase, decorated with a mirror image pattern, c1900, 3¼in (8cm) high.
£40–50 *TVA*

l. A Royal Worcester figure of a King Charles spaniel, seated on a light green cushion with gold tassels, c1911, 1½in (3.5cm) wide.
£300–400 *TH*

r. A set of 4 Royal Worcester tropical fish series models, by Ronald Van Ruyckevelt, shape Nos. 3602–6, 1956, 10in (25.5cm) high.
£2,000–2,500 *TVA*

r. A Royal Worcester white jug, 1950s, 5in (12.5cm) high.
£25–35 *TAC*

A Royal Worcester blush-ivory flatback jug, painted with English flowers, with gilded handle and highlights, c1912, 4¾in (12cm) high.
£160–190 *QSA*

r. A Royal Worcester vase, signed Kitty Blake, c1936, 6in (15cm) high.
£200–300 *VSt*

A Royal Worcester figure of a boy, by Freda Doughty, entitled 'Wednesday's Child', teddy's leg broken, c1940, 7in (18cm) high.
£85–95 *QSA*

A Royal Worcester figure of a girl with a cat, by Freda Doughty, entitled 'Saturday's Child', c1940, 5¾in (14.5cm) high.
£150–170 *VSt*

COMICS

American comics have long been popular. Collectors are prepared to pay thousands of dollars for comics that heralded the launch of such figures as Superman, Batman and Spider-Man. These super heroes are famed across the world and kept perpetually young and desirable through their continued appearance on film, TV and in contemporary comics.

Until recently demand for British comics has lagged far behind their US equivalents. Over the past two years, however, the market has boomed. Recent auction records include £4,200 for *The Beano* comic No. 1, and £4,000 for *The Dandy Monster Comic*, the first *Dandy* annual.

'D. C. Thomson's *Beano* and *Dandy* are the great classics of the field,' explains comic book auctioneer Malcolm Phillips. 'Their characters have become part of British culture. Most people know that Dennis the Menace's dog is called Gnasher and that Desperate Dan's favourite meal is cow pie.'

Launched respectively in 1937 and 1938, *The Dandy* and *The Beano* are still published today. As these comics have been read for over half a century vintage issues appeal to a wide range and age group of collectors. With comics that have not remained in print over the years demand is fuelled by those who read them as children and the market changes as a new generation of collectors comes to maturity.

'Material relating to some pre-WWII favourites was more valuable twenty years ago than it is today,' explains Malcolm Phillips. 'Many of today's collectors grew up reading fifties and sixties comics and that is what they want to buy as adults.' The first *Eagle* comic (14th April, 1950) can be worth £200 or more whilst fine first issues of such sixties favourites as *Valiant* and *Hurricane* can fetch around £60–70.

From the launch in 1874 of *Funny Folks*, generally acknowledged as the first British comic, each decade has produced its collectable comics. Number one issues, special or celebration numbers and comics introducing famous characters tend to be the most desirable. Value depends on rarity, condition and that most elusive and precious of attributes the presence of an original free gift. *Dandy* was launched with a free Express Whistler, *Beano* with a Whoopee Mask, whilst the first *Beezer* (21st January, 1956) came complete with a Whizz Bang. 'It is incredibly rare to find comic and gift complete,' concludes Malcolm Phillips. 'These toys may have been freebies but if today they are in their original condition they can raise the value of a comic by as much as seventy per cent.'

l. Various overseas editions of *All In Pictures*, Amalgamated Press, 1951–52, 7 x 5¼in (18 x 13.5cm).
£10–15 each *NOS*

r. Amazing Fantasy, Marvel Comics Group, featuring the first appearance of Spider-Man, August 1962, 10 x 7in (25.5 x 18cm).
£2,500–2,750 *NOS*

Cross Reference
Colour Review

The Avengers, Marvel Comics Group, featuring the first appearance of The Vision, October 1968, 10 x 7in (25.5 x 18cm).
£12–15 *NOS*

Angela, Image Comics, a limited edition premium comic, June 1995, 10 x 7in (25.5 x 18cm).
£20–25 *NOS*

l. The Beano No. 21, D. C. Thomson, the first Christmas issue, with snow-capped titles throughout, 1938, 11¾ x 8⅝in (30 x 22cm).
£360–420 *CBP*

Three *Beano* books, D. C. Thomson,
11 x 8in (28 x 20.5cm):
l. Everyone's Gone to the Moon, 1951.
*c. Biffo, Magic Lollipops in danger from
Pansy Potter,* 1952.
r. Biffo Rodeo, 1953.
£70–100 each *CBP*

Beezer No. 1, D. C. Thomson,
with unused free gift Whizz
Bang, 1956, 16½ x 12in
(42 x 30.5cm).
£350–400 *CBP*

*Cinefantastique, Star
Trek,* 20th anniversary
edition, March 1987,
11 x 8¼in (28 x 21cm).
£12–15 *NOS*

Eight copies *Buck Jones,*
Cowboy Comics, Amalgamated
Press, one heavily worn, 1950,
7 x 5¼in (18 x 13.5cm).
£175–200 *CBP*

Dan Dare's Anastasia Jet Plane,
a Presso book by Wallis Rigby,
1950s, 9¾ x 15in (25 x 38cm).
£120–140 *CBP*

*Make your own model of Anastasia
and read the illustrated story by
Frank Hampson.*

Two *Dandy* books, D. C. Thomson,
11 x 8in (28 x 20.5cm):
l. Korky's Toyshop, the last
Monster title, 1952.
£110–130
r. Hats Off to Korky, 1954.
£80–100 *CBP*

The Fantastic Four
No. 1, Marvel Comics,
with The Thing, Mr
Fantastic, Human
Torch and Invisible
Girl, 1961, 10¼ x 7in
(26 x 18cm).
£1,400–1,600 *CBP*

*l. Fantastic
Four* No. 48,
Marvel Comics
Group, the
debut of Silver
Surfer, 1966,
10¼ x 7in
(26 x 18cm).
£250–300 *CBP*

Two copies of *Flynn of the FBI*, Atlas
Publications, with original strips by
Arthur Mather, 1952, 9¾ x 6¾in
(25 x 17.5cm).
£10–12 each *NOS*

r. Gen Thirteen, Image
Comics, a pulp fiction
pastiche variant,
March 1995, 10 x 7in
(25.5 x 18cm).
£16–20 *NOS*

*r. Two copies of
Headline Comics,*
Atlas
Publications,
reprints, 1952,
10½ x 7½in
(27 x 19cm).
£5–6 each *NOS*

Two copies of *The Hotspur*, 1933, 11¾ x 8¾in (30 x 22cm): *l.* No. 1, introducing the Swooping Vengeance and Buffalo Bill's Schooldays. **£250–300** *r.* No. 2, The Big Stiff and The Colorado Kid. **£50–60** *CBP*

Journey Into Mystery No. 16, Atlas Publications, 1954, 10¼ x 7in (26 x 18cm). **£140–160** *CBP*

Two copies of *Journey Into Mystery*, Atlas Publications, 10¼ x 7in (26 x 18cm): *l.* No. 21, 1955. **£75–85** *r.* No. 40, 1956. **£55–65** *CBP*

Two copies of *Journey into Mystery*, Atlas Publications, 10¼ x 7in (26 x 18cm): *l.* No. 57, 1960. **£140–160** *r.* No. 70, 1961. **£70–80** *CBP*

r. Justice No. 3, Youngs Merchandising, reprints of US Marvel strips, 1952, 10½ x 7in (27 x 18cm). **£6–8** *NOS*

l. Ken Shannon Private Eye No. 7, Ayers & James Pty, reprints, 1952, 10¾in x 7in (27.5 x 17.5cm). **£5–6** *NOS*

Lady Death, Chaos Comics Premium edition, limited to 10,000 copies, leather cover variant, August 1995, 10 x 7in (25.5 x 18cm). **£40–50** *NOS*

Five copies of *Lilliput*, Pocket Publications Ltd, 1945/46, 7¾ x 5½in (20 x 14cm). **£35–45** *CBP*

Lilliput was a pocket magazine including short stories, cartoons, photographs, news, colour reproductions with front cover illustrations by Walter Trier.

Larry Kent's Comic,
Youngs Merchandising,
all original Australian
artwork, 1952,
10½in x 7in (26.5 x 18cm).
£8–10 *NOS*

Marc Brody Illustrated
No. 2, Horowitz
Publications, original
strips, 1956, 9½ x 7in
(24 x 18cm).
£8–10 *NOS*

*Picture Stories from the
Bible*, DC Publications,
New Testament edition
No. 1, 1944, 10¼ x 7¼in
(26 x 18cm).
£100–120 *CBP*

*Picture Stories from
the Bible*, Bible
Pictures Ltd, a
hardback book reprint
of US Bible comics,
1943, 10 x 7in
(25.5 x 18cm).
£38–48 *NOS*

Doc Savage No. 9, *Rangers Comics* No. 11
and *Shadow Comics* No. 7, propaganda
issues, 1942/43, 10¼ x 7in (26 x 18cm).
£135–155 *CBP*

Police Against Crime
No. 18, Rosnock Pty Ltd,
reprint, 1956, 10¼ x 7½in
(26 x 19cm).
£3–4 *NOS*

Famous Yank Police Comics
No. 21, Ayers & James Pty,
reprint, 1952, 10½ x 7¾in
(27 x 20cm).
£6–8 *NOS*

Shock SuspenStories No. 1, and *The Haunt
of Fear* No. 27, EC Comics, 1952/54,
10¼ x 7in (26 x 18cm).
£135–155 *CBP*

Radio Fun No. 17, with Big
Hearted Arthur, Flanagan &
Allen, Clark Gable, 1939,
10 x 7in (25.5 x 18cm).
£70–80 *CBP*

*Sergeant Pat of the Radio
Patrol*, Atlas Publications,
original and reprint, 1953.
9¾ x 6¾in (25 x 17.5cm).
£6–8 *NOS*

*r. Showcase
presents Doctor
No*, No. 43,
National
Comics, 1963,
10¼ x 7in
(26 x 18cm).
£55–65 *CBP*

The Silver Surfer, premier issue, Marvel Comics Group, 1968, 10 x 7in (25.5 x 18cm).
£200–225 *NOS*

Two copies of *The Skipper*, 1930, 11¾ x 8¾in (30 x 22cm):
l. No. 3, The Texas Terror and the First Men to Fly the Atlantic.
r. No. 2, Red Rock Baxter, The Hooded Spy and Quaint Barbers of the World.
£20–30 each *CBP*

Star Wars, Official Collectors edition, Marvel Comics Group, 1977, 11 x 8¼in (28 x 21cm).
£8–10 *NOS*

Supercar, No. 1, Gold Key, 1962, 10¼ x 7in (26 x 18cm).
£120–140 *CBP*

Giant Secret Origins, No. 8 and *Giant Superman*, No. 11, National Comics, 1965, 10¼ x 7in (26 x 18cm).
£100–125 *CBP*

Giant Superman Annual, No. 1, National Comics, 1964, 10¾ x 7in (27 x 18cm).
£55–65 *CBP*

Thriller Comics, No. 1, *The Three Musketeers*, 1951, 7 x 5¼in (18 x 13.5cm).
£90–100 *CBP*

Four copies of *Thriller Comics*, Nos. 2–5, 1951, 7 x 5¼in (18 x 13.5cm).
£100–120 *CBP*

r. The Topper Book, No. 1, D. C. Thomson, with Beryl the Peril, Mickey the Monkey, Flip McCoy and Uncle Dan the Menagerie Man, 1954, 8½ x 12in (21.5 x 30.5cm).
£90–100 *CBP*

New Triumph, No. 772, cover and first issue of Superman reprints from US daily strips, 1939, 13 x 11¾in (33 x 29.5cm).
£160–180 *CBP*

TV Century 21, No. 1 Universe edition, with free *Special Agent Identicode* book, 1965, 14¼ x 9¾in (36 x 25cm).
£220–240 *CBP*

2000AD, Prog. 539, full colour front cover original artwork, by Steve Dillon, with acetate text overlay, 1987, 21 x 11¾in (53 x 30cm).
£60–80 *CBP*

Vampirella, No. 1, IPC Magazines, reprints of US Vampirella Stories, 1975, 11¾ x 9in (30 x 23cm).
£8–10 *NOS*

White Indian, No. 11, Magazine Enterprise, 1953, 10¼ x 7¼in (26 x 18.5cm).
£45–55 *CBP*

Although this is No. 11, it is, in fact, the first White Indian issue.

The X Files, No. 1 Special 'Ashcan' edition, black and white, Topps Comics, 1995, 10 x 7in (25.5 x 18cm).
£15–20 *NOS*

X Force, Special Anniversary issue, Marvel Comics Group, with variant cover, illustrated by creator Rob Liefeld, 1996, 10 x 7in (25.5 x 18cm).
£20–24 *NOS*

Giant-Size X-Men, No. 1, Marvel Comics Group, 1975, 10 x 7in (25.5 x 18cm).
£125–150 *NOS*

'Senses-shattering 1st issue' in which the new X-Men appear for the first time and Wolverine for the second time.

Comic Artwork & Collectables

l. Desperate Dan, original artwork, signed by Dudley Watkins, together with *The Dandy*, No. 1026, 1961, 21¼ x 14¼in (54 x 36cm).
£850–1,000 *CBP*

l. Amazing Spider-Man Annual, No. 14, pages 32 and 33 centre spread original artwork, by Frank Miller, 1980, 16¼ x 21¾in (41 x 55cm).
£300–340 *CBP*

r. Four commemorative tokens, 1905, 2½in (6.5cm) high.
£20–22 *WAB*

Given free with comics to commemorate Nelson and the Battle of Trafalgar in 1805.

COMMEMORATIVE WARE

Ceramics dominate the commemoratives market and the following section. During the late eighteenth and early nineteenth centuries new industrial techniques and the improvement of transport allowed commemorative wares to be mass-produced and distributed around the country. From the Victorian period onwards vast numbers of ceramics were manufactured to celebrate significant events and prominent personalities. 'Commemoratives are a populist art form,' says Andrew Hilton from Special Auction Services. 'Though objects can be attractive they were often cheaply made. Unlike other areas of the ceramics market, their value today lies not primarily in their surface beauty or great aesthetic quality, but in who and what they represent.' As Hilton explains, the attraction of commemorative ware is above all historical. 'Most of us have sat through history lessons, learning the dates of the kings and queens and fallen asleep because it seemed so boring. When you hold a Coronation mug or a bust of Wellington in your hand, it makes history come alive.'

During the 1980s, the antiques market was largely driven by interior decorators and prices boomed for the most visually attractive commemoratives. In the leaner, and perhaps more rational 1990s, though demand is still strong, it is primarily fuelled by academic collectors, with a scholarly interest in a specific subject. Popular fields at the moment include political commemoratives. Great politicians always have their admirers and there is currently growing enthusiasm for objects connected with Margaret Thatcher. Military subjects have a strong following, WWI resulted in a vast number of commemoratives and Crimean material has been making very good prices. 'People are also looking for the more unusual pieces, for example, objects recording mining disasters,' adds Hilton. 'Rare and esoteric subject matter is attracting a lot of interest today.'

The field, however, is dominated by royal commemoratives. Though contemporary royal crises do not affect demand for historical ware they can influence the values of more recent creations. 'There is very little interest now in pieces celebrating the Duke and Duchess of York,' admits Hilton, 'the second-hand market for material relating to the Queen Mother, however, remains good because she is such a popular figure.'

r. A pottery plate, printed in sepia with entitled portrait of Revd C.H. Spurgeon, gilt rim, 19thC, 11in (28cm) diam.
£70–80 *SAS*

A Challinor & Co plate, printed with central portrait of John Wesley within a border of Wesleyan trophies, inscribed and dated 'John Wesley born June 17, 1703, died March 2, 1791', 10¼in (26cm) diam.
£170–200 *SAS*

A Clementson plate, printed in brown with a view of Powys Castle, Welshpool, inscribed 'Viscount Clive Attaining his majority, November 5th, 1839', 10¾in (27cm) diam.
£30–35 *SAS*

r. A pottery plate, printed in black with portrait of HM Stanley, views and map of Africa, inscribed with details of Stanley's expedition in 1887, gilt rim, 9½in (24cm) diam.
£120–150 *SAS*

r. A pewter tankard, with monogram 'CD' for Charles Dickens, and 'Gad's Hill 1870', base rim engraved 'HNP from GH 1889', with an autographed letter by Georgina Hogarth presenting the tankard to Horace Pym.
£5,000–5,500 *S*

Three china coffee cups,
inscribed 'The First Aviation
Week Held in Gt Britain',
1909, 2½in (6.5cm) high.
£250–300 *CSK*

A Cauldon plate, the centre
decorated with a cartouche of
Britannia, inscription for
Wembley Exhibition 1924, with
gilt rim, 10⅝in (27cm) diam.
£90–110 *SAS*

A Royal Doulton beaker,
printed in sepia with a
portrait of the 16th Duke of
Norfolk, inscribed 'May
30th, 1929', the reverse with
a named view of Arundel
Castle, 3½in (9cm) high.
£25–35 *SAS*

A Delft dish, with a portrait of
Baden-Powell in scouts
uniform, inscribed 'Vogelenzong
Bloemendaal, 1937 Holland',
5¼in (13cm) diam.
£80–100 *SAS*

Military

A Staffordshire pottery
tobacco jar and cover, in
the form of the Duke of
Wellington, decorated in
coloured enamels and gilt,
19thC, 7½in (19cm) high.
£350–400 *DN*

A mug, commemorating the
end of the Crimean War,
1854–56, 3½in (9cm) high.
£100–120 *MGC*

Miller's is a price
GUIDE not a price LIST

A porcelain mug, printed
with a scene depicting
soldiers in battle, entitled
'Sergeant Thomas
Defending the Colours at
Inkermann', gilt lining
and decoration to handle,
mid-19thC, 4in (10cm) high.
£800–900 *SAS*

r. A Coalport plate, printed in
blue with portrait of Roberts
within a Maltese cross design,
inscribed with place names
against a background of
anchors, chains, foliage and
trailing ribbon, the reverse
printed in blue and
No. 802, Boer War, 1900,
10½in (26.5cm) diam.
£150–180 *SAS*

Three pieces of Foley China, c1902, tallest jug 3½in (9cm) high.
£40–50 each *MGC*

l. A Copeland Spode beaker, printed in colours with RAF wings, inscribed 'British War Relief Society', c1945, 4½in (11.5cm) high.
£25–30 *SAS*

A Wedgwood Carrara ware bust of Viscount Montgomery of Alamein, limited edition of 250, 1976, 7½in (19cm) high.
£70–80 *MGC*

Cross Reference
Colour Review

A figural group, by Michael Sutty, depicting hoisting of the flag at Goose Green, 1980s, 18in (45.5cm) high.
£200–300 *PC*

World War I

l. A Limoges porcelain plate, transfer printed in colours with 4 portrait medallions, against a background of Allied flags with berried laurel leaves and ribbon and lined borders, dated '1914', 10½in (26.5cm) diam.
£50–60 *SAS*

A Lloyd George jug, commemorating the outbreak of WWI, inscribed 'My object is to win the War', 1914, 6½in (16.5cm) high.
£30–40 *TAC*

A Rosenthal plate, decorated in blue with a scene of German soldiers, entitled 'Unsere Artillerie 1914', 9½in (24cm) diam.
£100–120 *SAS*

A Hindenburg porcelain decagonal ribbon plate, printed with central portrait, surmounted by the Maltese cross, within red, white and black lining and gilt border, inscribed and initialled 'W' and dated '1914', 10¼in (26cm) diam.
£90–110 *SAS*

A Booths mug, printed in blue with soldiers of the Allies marching, interior rim inscribed, 1914, 3⅜in (9.5cm) high.
£90–110 *SAS*

A pottery ewer, printed in blue with portraits of the Duke of Wellington dated '1815' and Kitchener of Khartoum dated '1915', inscribed in a gilt cartouche 'Jas. Watson & Co', 8¼in (21cm) high.
£110–130 *SAS*

Two Bairnsfather Ware jugs, inscribed, c1919, 6¼in (16cm) high.
£80–90 *PC*

A Bairnsfather Ware pottery vase, with scenes entitled 'Keeping his hand in' and 'At present we are staying at the Farm', the neck with border of WWI trophies and gilt rim, souvenir mark, c1919, 7½in (19cm) high.
£100–120 *SAS*

A pottery plate, printed in black and decorated in coloured enamels with the British lion standing on the chest of the defeated German eagle against a background of the Allied flags, inscribed 'Victory', 1918, 10in (25.5cm) diam.
£80–100 *SAS*

A wooden memorial board, commemorating those who served in the Great War, dedicated in 1919, 31 x 47in (78.5 x 119.5cm).
£90–110 *COB*

A pair of Bairnsfather Ware bowls, with scenes on one side, the reverse with coloured Royal Standard, gilt rims, printed Grimwades mark, c1919, 6¾in (17cm) diam.
£70–80 each *SAS*

Character Jugs

The following WWI character jugs were produced by Wilkinson Ltd and designed by Sir Francis Carruthers Gould. Each caricature represents a famous commander. The pottery bodies are painted in underglaze colours, coloured enamels and gilded. The base of each jug is printed in black with the maker's mark, facsmile signature of the designer and the retailers name and address. These jugs all came from a single owner collection, purchased when new, and were in perfect condition, with the exception of Lloyd George.

An Admiral Jellicoe character jug, 10in (25.5cm) high. £325–375 *SAS*

A Marshal Joffre character jug, 10in (25.5cm) high. £350–400 *SAS*

> **Cross Reference**
> Militaria

A Lloyd George character jug, handle restored, 10¼in (26cm) high. £225–275 *SAS*

An Earl Haig character jug, 10¾in (27cm) high. £375–425 *SAS*

FURTHER READING

Knowles, Eric, *Royal Memorabilia* Millers Publications, 1994

Miller & Pinchin *Character Jug Collectors Handbook,* Francis Joseph Publications, 1995

l. An Admiral Beatty character jug, 10¾in (27cm) high. £325–375 *SAS*

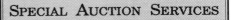

Politics

A plate, printed in black, entitled 'F.B. Mildmay Esq MP' inscribed 'Elected for South Devon Dec 5th 1885', gilt lining, 6in (15cm) diam.
£30–40 *SAS*

An octagonal plate, printed in black with a titled portrait of Sir John A. MacDonald, gilt rim slightly rubbed, c1890, 9½in (24cm) diam.
£500–550 *SAS*

A white parian jug, printed with 2 portraits of Ernest Jones the patriot, poet and politician, 6½in (16.5cm) high.
£200–250 *SAS*

Ernest Jones was born in 1819 at Holstein, he returned to England in 1841, was called to the Bar in 1844 but chose to join the Chartists in 1846. In 1847 he became editor of The Northern Star. *He was a revolutionary and in 1848 was imprisoned. Upon his release he became leader of the then declining Chartist movement, making a number of unsuccessful attempts to enter the House of Commons. Latterly he joined* The Northern Circuit *also writing novels and poetry. He died in 1869 when an imposing public funeral was held at Ardwick Cemetery, Manchester.*

A Booths pottery plate, printed with portrait of Chamberlain in black, within a floral and scroll moulded border, c1938, 10½in (26.5cm) high.
£50–60 *SAS*

A Royal Doulton two-handled loving cup, with portrait of Margaret Thatcher, 1977, 4in (10cm) high.
£18–22 *MGC*

This cup was made to commemorate Margaret Thatcher becoming the first woman prime minister of the UK.

A Copeland Spode pottery plate, printed in blue with 3 portraits of Joseph, Austen and Neville Chamberlain, within a border of flowers and foliage, the reverse inscribed 'To commemorate the security of peace', Munich Crisis 1938, 10½in (26.5cm) diam.
£100–120 *MGC*

A white pottery mask head teapot and cover, formed as the caricature of Margaret Thatcher by Luck & Flaw, creators of *Spitting Image*, 1970/80s, 7¼in (18.5cm) high.
£120–140 *SAS*

Two *Spitting Image* squeaker rubber puppets, depicting Margaret Thatcher and Neil Kinnock, 1986, 6in (15cm) high.
£8–10 each *MGC*

Winston Churchill (1874–1965)

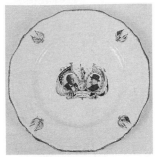

A quatrefoil plate, printed with sepia portraits of Roosevelt and Churchill, against a background of coloured flowers and the Statue of Liberty within a border of crossed flags, 10in (25.5cm) diam.
£15–25 *SAS*

A Burleigh Ware white pottery two-handled loving cup, with portrait of Churchill, the rim inscribed 'Champion of Democracy', the base printed in blue, 6¾in (17cm) high.
£100–125 *SAS*

A Copeland Spode jug, printed in black with portrait medallion of Churchill, quotations from speeches, tanks, ships and aircraft, the reverse with a map of the world and British bulldog, 6½in (16.5cm) high.
£80–100 *SAS*

A porcelain plate, printed with sepia photographic portraits of Churchill and Roosevelt, inscribed 'Atlantic Meeting, 1941', 8in (20.5cm) diam.
£150–180 *SAS*

A compilation of 12 Decca records, entitled 'His Memoirs and His Speeches 1918 to 1945', 1966, 13 x 12¼in (33 x 31cm).
£50–60 *NW*

r. A black moulded plastic bust of Winston Churchill, on a plinth base impressed 'Winston S. Churchill', 1965, 5¼in (13cm) high.
£10–20 *SAS*

Royalty

A jug, commemorating the death of King George IV, c1830, 7in (17.5cm) high.
£225–275 *MGC*

A pottery bowl, commemorating the death of Queen Charlotte, printed in black with portraits and memorial urn initialled 'C', inscribed, with pink lustre banding, c1817, 6½in (16.5cm) diam.
£30–35 *SAS*

A pearlware mug, commemorating the coronation of King William IV and Queen Adelaide, with portraits flanking a crown and national emblems, inscribed, c1831, 4¼in (11cm) high.
£200–250 *DN*

Victoria (1837–1901)

A salt glazed tyg, the handles modelled as greyhounds, moulded in relief with portraits between cornucopiae, impressed mark, chipped, 1840, 6¼in (16cm) high.
£450–500 *WL*

An Old Hall jug, commemorating the death of Prince Albert, c1861, 7½in (19cm) high.
£200–250 *MGC*

A porcelain mug, by William Lowe, commemorating the Diamond Jubilee of Queen Victoria, inscribed in gilt 'God Save the Queen', c1897, 3¼in (8cm) high.
£110–130 *SAS*

r. A two-handled loving cup, commemorating Queen Victoria's Diamond Jubilee, c1897, 4in (10cm) high.
£75–85 *TAC*

A Foley China trio, commemorating Queen Victoria's Diamond Jubilee, c1897, plate 6in (15cm) diam.
£55–65 *MGC*

Edward VII (1901–10)

r. A Foley China teapot, commemorating the coronation of Edward VII, c1902, 6½in (16.5cm) high.
£80–100 *TAC*

r. A Foley China moustache cup and saucer, commemorating the coronation of Edward VII, c1902, saucer 6in (15cm) diam.
£90–110 *MGC*

George V
(1910–36)

A Shelley jug and bowl, commemorating the coronation of King George V and Queen Mary, c1911, jug 2½in (6.5cm) high.
£40–50 MGC

A CWS teapot and cover, commemorating the coronation of King George V and Queen Mary, c1911, 5½in (14cm) high.
£50–60 SAS

A porcelain mug, commemorating the visit to Pretoria, South Africa by HRH Edward Prince of Wales, c1925, 3¼in (8cm) high.
£90–110 SAS

A Shelley two-handled cup, commemorating the coronation of King George V and Queen Mary, c1911, 4½in (11.5cm) high.
£40–50 SAS

A Continental porcelain mug, commemorating the coronation of King George V and Queen Mary, with lithophane base, c1911, 2¾in (7cm) high.
£300–400 SAS

l. A porcelain mug, commemorating the visit to Pretoria, South Africa by HRH Edward Prince of Wales, c1925, 3¼in (8cm) high.
£90–110 SAS

A plate, commemorating the coronation of King George V and Queen Mary, inscribed, c1911, 8¼in (21cm) diam.
£20–30 SAS

A Royal Winton mug, commemorating the investiture of HRH Edward Prince of Wales, c1911, 3½in (9cm) high.
£80–100 SAS

Edward VIII
(1936–abdication)

A teapot, commemorating the coronation of King Edward VIII, c1937, 5in (12.5cm) high.
£25–30 TAC

A Minton bowl with cover, commemorating the coronation of King Edward VIII, inscribed, printed mark in gilt and No. 31 of 300, c1937, 2½in (6.5cm) diam.
£275–325 DN

A Minton porcelain beaker, decorated in coloured enamels and gilt, inscribed, base marked and No. 347 of 2000, c1937, 4¼in (10.5cm) high.
£180–200 SAS

George VI (1936–52)

A Collingwoods porcelain mug, commemorating the coronation of 1937, printed in sepia with portraits of Princesses Elizabeth and Margaret Rose, with gilt rim, 2½in (6.5cm) high.
£100–125 *SAS*

A Royal Doulton mug, commemorating the coronation of King George VI and Queen Elizabeth, c1937, 3¼in (8cm) high.
£30–35 *MGC*

An Art Deco style pottery jug, commemorating the coronation of King George VI and Queen Elizabeth, inscribed, 1937, 7½in (19cm) high.
£130–150 *SAS*

l. A Wadeheath pottery loving cup, in Art Nouveau style, commemorating the coronation of King George VI and Queen Elizabeth, inscribed, plays the National Anthem, marked, c1937, 5in (13cm) high.
£60–80 *SAS*

r. A Gray's pottery plate, commemorating the South African visit by King George VI and Queen Elizabeth, inscribed, with gilt rim, c1947, 10½in (26.5cm) diam.
£25–35 *SAS*

Elizabeth II (1952–to present)

An Aynsley cup and saucer, commemorating the coronation of Queen Elizabeth II, c1953, saucer 6in (15cm) diam.
£30–40 *MGC*

A Paragon loving cup, with 2 silver lion's handles, commemorating the Silver Wedding of Queen Elizabeth II and HRH the Duke of Edinburgh, decorated in colours and silver, coat-of-arms, monograms and inscriptions, No. 472 of 750, c1972, 5¼in (13cm) high.
£120–140 *SAS*

A Royal Albert plate, commemorating the 80th birthday of the Queen Mother, c1980, 4¾in (12cm) diam.
£10–12 *TAR*

l. A mug, commemorating the marriage of Prince Charles and Lady Diana Spencer, c1981, 3½in (9cm) high.
£5–10 *FAL*

r. A pair of Carlton Ware figures, by Malcolm Gooding, modelled as the Queen and Prince Charles, c1984, 4¼in (11cm) high.
£10–12 each *TAR*

COMPACTS

This selection of compacts comes from a variety of private collectors. Though the earliest examples shown date from the early twentieth century, it was not until the 1920s, with the growing acceptability of cosmetics, that the compact became an essential element of every lady's handbag. As compact historian Juliette Edwards notes, two origins have been suggested for the compact's name: that the box held solid compacted powder or, more likely, that it provided a small compact container, that was easily portable. Reflecting their function, these decorative boxes were also referred to as vanities or vanity cases, though from c1950 these terms were only used if the box was designed to include lipstick, rouge, cigarettes or other materials in addition to face powder.

The 1920s and 30s was a golden age for compacts. Many fine Art Deco designs were created whilst the fashion for novelty gadgets led to the development of compacts and vanity cases with various internal mechanisms designed to release powder with the push of a lever or cigarettes at the press of a button. During WWII cosmetics were unobtainable and the manufacture of compacts was halted in Britain. The 1950s saw renewed desire for luxury and elegance, reflected both in fashion and make up. Many beautiful and imaginative compacts were produced, their design reflecting current crazes including the contemporary fascination with space and flying saucers, and exploiting new materials such as plastic.

Compact collecting is growing in popularity. Though fine examples can be expensive, there is still a wide selection of examples available for under £50. Condition is important and compacts that preserve their original pouch, puff and sifter will command a premium. Compacts should be cleaned with care, 'Never wash compacts which have glass mirrors; water will get behind the mirror and damage its reflective coating,' warns Juliette Edwards. She recommends using a dry toothbrush to dislodge old powder and cleaning mirrors and metal parts with a good quality silicone furniture polish and a soft cloth.

A silver-plated heart-shaped compact, with finger ring and chain, c1900, 1¼in (3cm) wide.
£65–75 *PC*

Two vanity compacts, both on chains, one brass and one silvertone with Art Nouveau decoration, c1905, 2½in (6.5cm) wide.
£60–70 each *PC*

FURTHER READING

Edwards, Juliette, *A Collectors' Manual*, printed privately 1994

An Italian engraved silver compact, with romantic scene enamelled on the lid, c1900, 3in (7.5cm) diam.
£120–140 *PC*

A silver compact and perfume bottle on a chain, with heavy repoussé decoration, c1905, 2¼in (5.5cm) wide.
£100–120 *PC*

l. A sterling silver compact, with enamelled seascape on the lid and gilded interior, c1927, 2in (5cm) diam.
£65–75 *PC*

Two fob watch-shaped compacts, both 1¾in (4.5cm) diam:
l. Estée Lauder, date unknown.
£35–45
r. Sterling silver, with lilac guilloché enamel lid and gilded interior, 1912.
£90–105 *PC*

A sterling silver compact, the red and blue enamel lid with silver Royal Artillery insignia, Birmingham hallmark for 1929, 2in (5cm) diam.
£50–60 *PC*

Three American silvertone compacts:
l. A vanity compact, on a chain with floral enamel motif, with integral perfume bottle, 1920s, 2¼in (5.5cm) wide. **£65–75**
c. A Norida compact, with floral enamel motif, 1930s, 2½in (6.5cm) diam. **£75–85**
r. An Elgin vanity compact, with Art Deco bird design, 1930, 1¾in (4.5cm) wide.
£85–95 *PC*

A collection of compacts for pressed powder, c1930, 2in (5cm) diam.
£15–45 each *PC*

A French carved beige plastic compact, with brown cord and tassel, 1920s, 3in (7.5cm) diam.
£100–120 *PC*

Two Houbigant goldtone hexagonal compacts, c1930, 2in (5cm) wide.
£40–48 each *PC*

A sterling silver compact, the red guilloché enamel lid with marcasite Art Deco motif, gilded interior, c1930, 2½in (6.5cm) diam.
£80–90 *PC*

Two American compacts with enamel lids and pouch bases, 1930s:
l. Green lid and goldtone mesh base, 2½in (6.5cm) diam.
r. Evans, cream lid and diamanté encrusted fabric base, 2¾in (7cm) diam.
£65–80 each *PC*

An Art Deco compact, in pink guilloché enamel on chrome, in original black grosgrain pouch and jeweller's box, 1930s, 2½in (6.5cm) square.
£40–48 *PC*

Three silvertone and black enamel compacts, early 1930s, 2in (5cm) wide:
l. Dubarry. **£30–35**
c. Innoxa. **£35–40**
r. Morny. **£24–28** *PC*

Two compacts with petit-point inserts and enamel bases, 1930s:
l. 3in (7.5cm) square. **£20–25**
r. Rowenta, 4in (10cm) wide. **£30–40** *PC*

A Park Lane goldtone and cream enamel vanity compact, the interior with clips for stamps and matches, space for cigarettes and holder, comb, powder, rouge and lipstick, 1930s, 4¼in (11cm) long. **£70–80** *PC*

A Gwenda compact, with butterfly-wing backed design under transparent plastic lid and black enamel base, 1930s, 3¼in (8.5cm) diam. **£35–45** *PC*

An octagonal silvertone compact, with portrait on the lid and black enamel base, 1930s, 3in (7.5cm) wide. **£40–50** *PC*

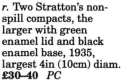

Two red plastic compacts, 1930s:
l. French, with inset print of Notre Dame on the lid, 3in (7.5cm) wide.
r. With raised St George's cross and 2 swords, 2½in (6.5cm) wide. **£35–40 each** *PC*

r. Two Stratton's non-spill compacts, the larger with green enamel lid and black enamel base, 1935, largest 4in (10cm) diam. **£30–40** *PC*

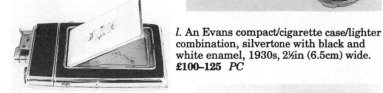

l. An Evans compact/cigarette case/lighter combination, silvertone with black and white enamel, 1930s, 2½in (6.5cm) wide. **£100–125** *PC*

l. A Gwenda silvertone compact, with butterfly-wing picture to the lid, 1930s, 1¾in (4.5cm) wide. **£40–50** *PC*

r. A brown plastic compact, with gold badge, in the form of an American Army officer's cap, 1940s, 3in (7.5cm) diam. **£80–100** *PC*

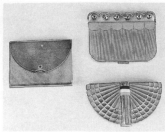

l. An American Trio-ette plastic vanity compact for powder, with lipstick in the handle, 1940s, 4½in (11.5cm) long. **£65–75**

c. A sterling silver and blue guilloché enamel compact, Birmingham 1923, 3½in (9cm) long. **£80–90**

r. A French cream plastic compact, with transfer design, c1937, 4¼in (11cm) long. **£50–60** *PC*

Three American goldtone compacts, largest 4in (10cm) wide:
l. 1950s. **£45–55**
r. 1940s.
£80–100 each *PC*

> **Cross Reference**
> Colour Review

A compact and lipstick set, 1940s, 4¼in (11cm) wide. **£55–65** *TCF*

A Vogue Vanities goldtone compact, with enamelled lid depicting a Regency couple on a grey horse, c1950, 3¾in (9.5cm) diam. **£30–38** *PC*

Two Kigu Chérie heart-shaped compacts, one black enamel with marcasite motif, one sterling silver, together with grosgrain drawstring pouch, 1950s, 3in (7.5cm) wide.
l. **£45–55**
r. **£65–75** *PC*

An American Ciner matching goldtone compact and lipstick case, decorated with diamanté and pearls, in original fitted gold brocade case, c1950, 2½in (6.5cm) long. **£70–80** *PC*

l. A Kigu Flying Saucer compact, blue enamel and goldtone, with inner lid, 1950s, 2½in (6.5cm) diam. **£140–160**

c. A Kigu bolster-shaped compact, pink enamel on goldtone, with inner lid, 1950s, 2in (5cm) wide. **£50–60**

r. A Pygmalion goldtone globe compact, engraved with a world map, 1950s, 1½in (4cm) diam. **£80–100** *PC*

l. A Kigu Concerto musical compact, in goldtone and black enamel, with inner lid, musical movement plays La Ronde, in original presentation box, 1950s, 2¾in (7cm) diam. **£75–85** *PC*

r. Two Mascot goldtone handbag-shaped compacts and one Kigu suitcase-shaped compact, 1950s, 2½in (6.5cm) wide. **£40–50 each** *PC*

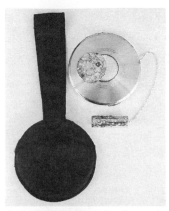

A Le Rage goldtone vanity compact, with inner lid, clothes brush, powder compartment and perfume bottle, the lid with central recess for rouge or photograph, with original black grosgrain carrying case, c1951, 4in (10cm) diam.
£80–90 *PC*

A Stratton party case goldtone metal handbag, with fitted matching compact, cigarette case, lipstick and comb, black and gold enamel exterior, 1952, 6in (15cm) wide.
£80–90 *PC*

An Elizabeth Arden black enamel on goldtone compact, for cream powder, the lid design based on a Napoleonic snuff box, 1953, 2¾in (7cm) diam.
£30–35 *PC*

A Kigu party case, one side contains powder compartment with inner lid, cigarette case on reverse, lipstick clipped to the top, 1955, 3in (7.5cm) wide.
£45–55 *PC*

A Stratton Petite compact, goldtone with black enamel lid and marcasite motif, inner lid, with original black pouch and box, 1960, 2½in (6.5cm) diam.
£30–35 *PC*

A sterling silver compact, the lid with fuchsias on white guilloché enamel, inner lid with Birmingham hallmark for 1961, 3in (7.5cm) diam.
£60–70 *PC*

A Thai silver compact, with niello figure design on the lid, 1960s, 2in (5cm) diam.
£40–50 *PC*

l. A Stratton Empress goldtone compact, with jewel design and inset lipstick, automatic opening inner lid, in original black taffeta pouch, 1961, 2¾in (7cm) wide.
£30–40 *PC*

A Stratton Queen goldtone compact, for loose or cream powder, with Wedgwood china insert on the lid, 1966, 3¼in (8.5cm) diam.
£25–30 *PC*

CORKSCREWS & BOTTLE OPENERS

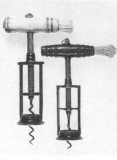

A double-action corkscrew of the type patented by Sir Edward Thomason in 1802, with four-pillar brass barrel and bone handle, c1820, 7½in (19cm) long.
£200–250 *CS*

A King's Screw bone handled corkscrew, the brass barrel with plaque bearing royal coat-of-arms and maker's name, 'Dowler', c1820, 7in (18cm) long.
£150–180 *CS*

Two corkscrews with steel frames:
l. With turned bone handle and brush, c1830, 8in (20.5cm) long.
r. With turned rosewood handle, c1820, 6¾in (17cm) long.
£80–95 each *CS*

A King's Screw corkscrew, with turned bone handle and steel side-wind handle, early 19thC, 8in (20.5cm) long.
£200–250 *CS*

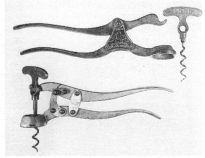

A Lund two-part corkscrew, cast steel with bronzed copper finish, and a Wolverson's design corkscrew, The Tangent Lever, c1870, 8in (20.5cm) long.
£30–50 each *CS*

A London Rack corkscrew, with wooden handle and metal side-wind handle, c1855, 7½in (19cm) long.
£55–65 *Bar*

An all-steel corkscrew, patented by Twigg in 1867, 6¾in (17cm) long.
£210–250 *CS*

> **Cross Reference**
> Bottles

r. Two metal multi-tools:
Regd 689051, c1905, 6¼in (16cm) long.
An Andress tool, c1875, 5½in (14cm) long.
£20–25 each *Bar*

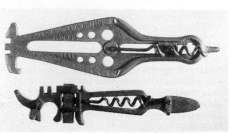

A French nickel-plated all-steel single lever corkscrew, Le Presto, by Perille, c1880, 7in (18cm) long.
£120–140 *CS*

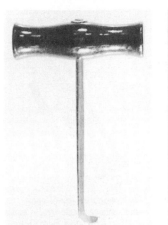

A Greeley patent cork puller, 1888, 3¾in (9.5cm) long.
£60–70 *Bar*

A bar corkscrew, the screw missing, c1890, 9½in (24cm) high.
£55–65 *WAB*

A complete bar corkscrew would be worth £75–85.

A German all-steel folding pocket corkscrew, by Hollweg, c1895, 2¾in (7cm) long.
£25–30 *CS*

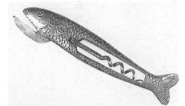

A cast iron fish combination corkscrew and can opener, c1883, 5½in (14cm) long.
£80–95 *CS*

An all-steel corkscrew, Bodega, patented in Frankfurt in 1899 by Ernst Scharff, 6¼in (16cm) long.
£230–280 *CS*

A German legs corkscrew, with flesh-coloured thighs and striped stockings, c1890, 2½in (6.5cm) long.
£280–325 *BSA*

Cross Reference
Advertising and
Packaging

l. A Thomason type bone-handled corkscrew, the barrel embossed with Gothic window design, 19thC, 7in (18cm) long.
£320–340 *CS*

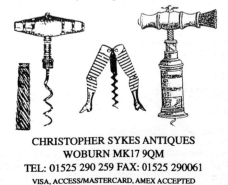

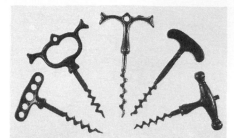

Five French simple type steel corkscrews,
late 19thC, 4in (10cm) long.
£20–25 each *Bar*

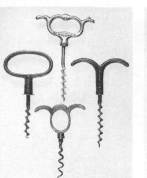

Four all-steel corkscrews,
c1900, longest
5in (12.5cm) long.
£5–12 each *CS*

A French all-steel rack
corkscrew, made by J. Perille,
c1920, 5¾in (14.5cm) long.
£45–55 *CS*

A French Zig Zag
concertina corkscrew,
c1920, 6in (15cm) long.
£25–35 *CS*

Five French and German cork extractors,
20thC, 3½in (9cm) long.
£12–15 each *Bar*

A Norwegian metal
corkscrew, 20thC,
4¼in (11cm) long.
£12–15 *Bar*

A selection of brass figural corkscrews, 20thC, 3½in (9cm) long.
£5–25 each *CS*

A brass key-shaped
corkscrew, 20thC,
5½in (14cm) long.
£15–20 *TAC*

An Austrian carved
and painted wood
Friar, with corkscrew
head, 20thC,
6½in (16.5cm) high.
£20–24 *TAC*

A metal bottle
opener, with
standing figure
of a man, c1925,
4¾in (12cm) long.
£10–12 *WAB*

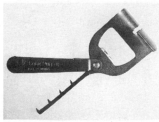

An American combination cork
drawer and crown cap lifter,
20thC, 5½in (14cm) long.
£35–45 *CS*

Cross Reference
Breweriana

DOLLS

A German paper fashion doll, The Girl's Doll, with wooden stand and 8 outfits, in original box marked 'GWF & W', c1860, 6¾in (17cm) high.
£1,700–2,000 *CSK*

A set of carved wood painted circus dolls, comprising 4 acrobatic clowns, in original clothing, c1920, 8in (20.5cm) high, with 3 animals and apparatus.
£550–650 *AH*

l. An English poured wax doll, probably by Lucy Peck, with wax shoulder-head, wax arms and legs, glass eyes, inset mohair, original silk bride's outfit, c1880, 18in (46cm) high.
£600–700 *YC*

r. A German china-headed doll, with cloth body and original outfit, maker unknown, c1860, 27in (68.5cm) high.
£400–450 *YC*

FURTHER READING

Alison Beckett, *Collecting Teddy Bears & Dolls* Miller's Publications, 1996

r. A Frozen Charlotte, c1890, 3¼in (8cm) high.
£50–60 *AmD*

Three pincushion dolls, 1920s, 3½in (9cm) high.
£30–35 each *VSt*

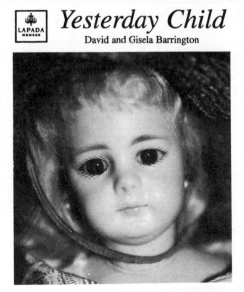

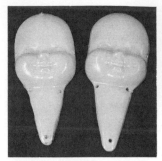

Two china faces for rag dolls,
1930s, 5½in (14cm) high.
£5–6 each *PSA*

Bisque Dolls

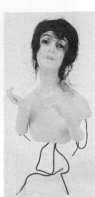

A half doll, 1920s,
4½in (11.5cm) high.
£35–45 *AmD*

A Bruno Schmidt baby
doll, with celluloid head
and composition body,
all original, c1910,
17¼in (44cm) high.
£225–275 *YC*

A fully-jointed plastic
doll, by Sasha
Morgenthaler, c1970,
12in (30.5cm) high.
£90–120 *YC*

l. An SFBJ character
doll, Paris, c1900,
20in (51cm) high.
£700–850 *AnS*

A Bébé Jumeau
swivel-headed doll,
with jointed
composition body,
head marked 'Déposé
Tête Jumeau Bt
SGDG', c1890,
19¾in (50cm) high.
£3,000–3,500 *YC*

A Jumeau open-mouth
girl doll, with fixed
paperweight eyes,
original hair, jointed
composition body,
period dress, c1890,
25in (63.5cm) high.
£1,500–1,700 *YC*

> **Cross Reference**
> Colour Review

l. A laughing
Jumeau doll, marked
SFBJ Paris, c1900,
21in (53.5cm) high.
£700–850 *AnS*

An all-bisque baby doll in a basket, with celluloid mirror and brush and rubber bottle, c1900, basket 6½in (16.5cm) long.
£150–175 *AnS*

A bisque baby doll, c1910, re-dressed, 3¼in (8.5cm) high.
£60–70 *AmD*

A Bébé Tête Jumeau doll, with closed mouth and original dress, c1890, 15in (38cm) high.
£2,000–3,000 *AmD*

A French jointed doll, with cork pate and original wig, marked '476', c1910, 21in (53cm) high.
£475–525 *AmD*

r. A bisque doll, with painted eyes and mohair wig, c1920, 2¾in (7cm) high.
£25–30 *AmD*

An SFBJ character doll, with sleeping eyes, open-closed mouth with moulded teeth, jointed composition toddler body, all original, c1912, 20in (51cm) high.
£800–900 *YC*

A jointed doll, possibly French, marked 'B', c1910, 11½in (29cm) high.
£200–250 *AmD*

FURTHER READING

Pearson, Sue, *Dolls & Teddy Bears Antiques Checklist*
Miller's Publications 1992

r. A Googly type all-bisque doll, Japanese, c1920, 4in (10cm) high.
£25–30 *YC*

Select Glossary of Terms and Makers

Bisque: Unglazed, usually tinted porcelain, fired twice (before and after painting) and used from the mid-19thC and into 20thC for making dolls' heads, limbs and complete dolls, known as all-bisque.

Composition: A substance comprised of papier mâché, sawdust and other ingredients used for the heads and bodies of dolls.

Frozen Charlotte: Glazed china doll that came in a variety of sizes from under one inch (2.5cm) to 18in (45.5cm) high. Like silver charms and sixpences, miniature Frozen Charlottes were hidden in Christmas puddings as good luck tokens and they were also known as pudding dolls.

Googlies: Dolls, often bisque, with round 'googly' eyes, snub noses and an impish expression, first produced c1911 and inspired by the drawings of American illustrator Grace Gebbie Drayton.

Heubach, Gebrüder (1820–1920s): A prolific German manufacturer of porcelain and bisque dolls' heads and dolls, including piano babies.

Jumeau: The Parisian firm of Jumeau (1842–99) was at the forefront of the French doll industry, and its wares are highly collectable today. In 1899 Jumeau merged with other French companies to form the Société Française de Fabrication de Bébés et Jouets (SFBJ).

Kämmer & Reinhardt (1886–1940): German doll manufacturers based in the Walterhaüsen region. The firm specialised in character dolls using both bisque or celluloid heads.

Kewpies: First produced c1913, the Kewpie doll was based on the cupid-like figures of American illustrator Rose O'Neill, published in the *Ladies Home Journal*. All-bisque Kewpies (the most sought-after examples today) were made by the Kestner factory, but this popular doll was also produced by other manufacturers in Germany, the USA and across the world, and in other materials including celluloid, fabric and rubber.

Marotte: A doll's head mounted on a stick, which often plays music when twirled.

Marseille, Armand (1890s–1930s): Born in Russia, moved to Thuringia in Germany. He bought a porcelain factory and from the 1890s began producing bisque dolls' heads. Armand Marseille became the most prolific of all the German doll manufacturers supplying heads to many other companies.

Piano Babies: As their name suggests, these all-bisque figurines were designed as decorative objects to stand on the piano. Prominent makers include Gebrüder Heubach.

Pin Dollies: Porcelain half dolls, made to be mounted on a pincushion, hence the holes in the base, popular in the 1920s and produced mainly in Germany.

Sasha Dolls: Vinyl dolls created by Swiss designer Sasha Morgenthaler and first produced by Trendon Ltd of Stockport, Cheshire in 1965. Dolls had different skin tones, depending on hair colouring.

German Bisque

A Catterfelder Puppen jointed doll, with original wig, c1900, re-dressed, 8in (20.5cm) high. **£180–220** *AmD*

A musical marotte, with bisque shoulder-head, all original, c1890, 15in (38cm) high. **£400–500** *YC*

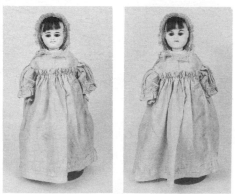

A Bartenstein two-faced doll, head turns under bonnet, with glass eyes, cloth body, papier mâché shoulder plate, original outfit, c1885, 15in (38cm) high. **£750–850** *YC*

r. A Kaiser Baby, possibly Einco, c1920, 9in (23cm) high. **£245–285** *AmD*

An Ernst Heubach black bisque doll, with closed mouth, weighted brown glass eyes, black mohair wig, jointed 5-piece composition body, in green 'grass' skirt, impressed '399.1', 18in (45.5cm) high, and an Armand Marseille black bisque doll, impressed '351', both c1930.
£450–550 *S*

l. A Simon & Halbig bisque-headed girl doll, with sleeping blue glass eyes, open mouth, brown mohair wig, pierced ears, jointed composition body, marked, c1910, 6½in (16.5cm) high.
£450–550
r. A Heinrich Handwerck bisque-beaded girl doll, with blue glass sleeping eyes, open mouth, dimpled chin, pierced ears, brown mohair wig and jointed composition limbs, marked, c1910, 22in (56cm) high.
£500–600 *AH*

A Max Handwerck jointed Bébé Elite, with original dress and bonnet, c1910, 26½in (67.5cm) high.
£550–650 *AmD*

A Gebrüder Heubach character boy doll, with intaglio eyes, open-closed mouth, jointed composition body, No. 7604, c1915, 19in (48cm) high.
£800–900 *YC*

A Kämmer & Reinhardt character baby, with sleeping eyes, open mouth, mohair wig, composition baby body, all original, No. 122, c1915, 14½in (36.5cm) high.
£800–900 *YC*

A Kämmer & Reinhardt girl doll, with sleeping eyes, jointed composition body, all original, c1900, 21in (53cm) high.
£600–700 *YC*

r. A Kämmer & Reinhardt character doll, all original, No.117A, marked 'Mein Liebling', c1915, 21in (53cm) high.
£3,800–4,200 *YC*

A Kestner closed
mouth girl doll,
with bisque head,
sleeping eyes,
jointed
composition body,
all original,
No. 168, c1895,
15in (38cm) high.
£1,300–1,500 *YC*

Three Kestner all-bisque Kewpies,
each marked on foot 'Rose O'Neill',
c1920, largest 9in (23cm) high.
l. **£300–350**
c. **£400–450**
r. **£200–220** *YC*
*The prices of Kewpies vary according
to size, quality and material.*

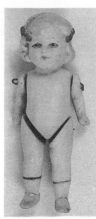

An all-bisque doll,
'Limbach', with
moulded shoes
and socks,
moulded hair with
blue bows,
c1930, 4½in
(11.5cm) high.
£40–50 *AmD*

An Armand Marseille
Red Riding Hood doll,
all original, c1900,
11in (28cm) high.
£200–245 *AnS*

An Armand Marseille
bisque headed doll,
with sleeping blue
eyes, open mouth and
teeth, composition and
kid jointed body,
replacement wig,
impressed mark
'Germany 370 A1M',
early 20thC,
18in (45.5cm) high.
£225–250 *HCH*

An Armand Marseille bisque-
headed doll, with sleeping
blue eyes, open mouth, on a
composition ball-jointed body,
brown mohair wig, wearing
blue crocheted wool outfit and
lace-up boots, one finger
chipped, incised '390n A13 M',
c1920, 27½in (70cm) high.
£400–450 *DN*

An Armand
Marseille girl doll,
No. 390, all original,
boxed, mint
condition, c1912,
15in (38cm) high.
£300–350 *YC*

r. An Armand Marseille
bisque-headed doll,
with sleeping blue eyes,
open mouth with 4 teeth,
blonde mohair wig,
composition ball-jointed
body, contemporary
outfit, marked
'A O½ M 390', c1920,
16½in (42cm) high.
£250–350 *DN*

An Armand Marseille
character boy doll,
mould 996, 1920s,
24in (61cm) high.
£350–425 *AnS*

r. An Armand
Marseille
Mulatto baby
doll, with
bisque head,
sleeping eyes,
jointed
composition
baby body,
No. 341, c1920,
9in (23cm) high.
£250–300 *YC*

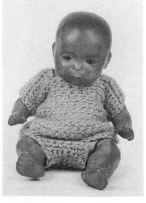

Three Armand Marseille bisque dolls, with closed mouths, weighted blue glass eyes, moulded blonde hair, jointed 5-piece composition bodies, in matching outfits, impressed '341', c1926, largest 18in (45.5cm) high.
£550–650 *S*

A Franz Schmidt bisque-headed doll, with sleeping blue eyes, lashes and open mouth with 2 teeth, on a jointed bent-limbed composition body, wig worn, marked 'F S & C 1295', c1920, 22in (56cm) high.
£240–280 *DN*

l. A Schoenau & Hoffmeister bisque Princess Elizabeth doll, with open smiling mouth and upper teeth, weighted blue glass eyes, blonde mohair wig, chunky 5-piece composition body, in original pink dress with embroidered flowers, c1932, impressed 'Porzellanfabrik Burggrub, Princess Elizabeth 3½', 16½in (42cm) high.
£650–750 *S*

An Armand Marseille bisque-headed character Googly doll, with weighted brown glass eyes, closed mouth, brown mohair wig, on a 5-piece composition character body, wearing knitted dress and leather shoes, incised 'Germany, 323, AOM', c1920, 14in (35.5cm) high.
£1,200–1,400 *Bon*

A Bruno Schmidt character boy doll, Tommy Tucker, with brown sleeping eyes, closed mouth, painted hair and jointed toddler body, c1910, 21in (53.5cm) high.
£1,800–2,000 *YC*

A Simon & Halbig girl doll, with swivel head, jointed composition body, original mohair wig, No. 1079, c1900, 17¾in (45cm) high.
£500–600 *YC*

A Walther & Söhn Googly bisque doll, with smiling closed mouth, weighted blue googly eyes and 5-piece composition body, wig worn, stringing loose, impressed '208-2/o', c1920, 6¾in (17cm) high.
£600–700 *S(S)*

Piano Babies

An all-bisque piano baby, with gold painted trumpet, c1910, 5in (12.5cm) high.
£100–120 YC

A Heubach all-bisque piano baby, with sunburst mark, c1910, 6½in (16.5cm) long.
£150–200 YC

A Gebrüder Heubach all-bisque piano baby, with sunburst mark, c1910, 7½in (19cm) long.
£200–250 YC

A Gebrüder Heubach all-bisque piano baby, with sunburst mark, c1910, 5½in (14cm) long.
£150–200 YC

l. A Gebrüder Heubach all-bisque piano baby, c1910, 4½in (11.5cm) long.
£100–120 YC

A French piano baby, 1920s, 7¼in (18.5cm) high.
£35–45 VSt

A German bisque piano group, c1900, 17½in (44.5cm) high.
£100–150 PC
This piano toddler is a variation on the usual baby theme.

r. A pair of French bisque piano babies, 1920s, 4in (10cm) high.
£40–50 VSt

Dolls' Accessories

A Victorian mahogany doll's cradle, c1880, 20in (51cm) long.
£185–200 AnS

A doll's pram, with stained inlaid wood coach body and single green lining, on sprung four-wheel chassis, double-end black leather cloth interior and hinged folding hood, early 20thC, 30in (76cm) long.
£140–160 Bea(E)

A Victorian doll's cradle, covered in scraps, 17in (43cm) long.
£50–65 AnS

A German doll's tin bath tub, c1900, 8½in (21.5cm) long.
£70–85 *MSB*

A set of German tin store scales, c1900, 1½in (4cm) high.
£25–30 *MSB*

A German painted tin stove, with 2 covered pots, 1900s, 4¾in (12cm) high.
£70–85 *MSB*

A German tin food carrier, c1900, 4½in (11.5cm) high.
£70–90 *MSB*

Four German miniature tin food moulds, c1900, longest 2½in (6.5cm) long.
£10–14 each *MSB*

A selection of German doll's tin kitchen utensils, c1900, largest 4in (10cm) long.
£15–20 each *MSB*

A German miniature tin skillet and 2 ladles, c1900, skillet 4in (10cm) long.
£15–20 each *MSB*

l. A German tin and brass fish steamer, c1900, 4½in (11.5cm) long.
£35–45 *MSB*

l. A doll's Bisto pattern dinner service, comprising 17 pieces, early 1880s, tureen 5in (12.5cm) wide.
£165–185 *PSA*

A doll's dessert service, comprising 8 pieces, 1920–30s, plate 3½in (9cm) diam.
£24–28 *PSA*

Dolls' House Furniture & Fittings

A doll's house cast iron washstand, by Stevens & Brown, with white china pitcher and basin, American, 1860s, stand 6½in (16.5cm) high.
£80–100 *MSB*

Two German doll's house painted wood chairs, with velvet seats and paper borders, c1840,
l. 5in (12.5cm) high. **£35–45**
r. 2in (5cm) high. **£10–15** *YC*

An Art Nouveau doll's house dressing table and wardrobe, c1900, tallest 7in (18cm) high.
£18–24 each *PSA*

A doll's house cast iron radiator, possibly German, 1900s, 2½in (6.5cm) high.
£35–45 *MSB*

An American doll's house cast iron sorting table desk, 1930s, 2in (5cm) high.
£14–16 *MSB*

An American doll's house cast iron rocking chair, 1930s, 2¾in (7cm) high.
£15–20 *MSB*

A selection of doll's house tôle washing accessories, c1900, largest 4in (10cm) high.
£100–135 *MSB*

An oak doll's house secretaire bookcase, with fall flap and simulated books, c1910, 8¾in (22cm) high.
£120–150 *YC*

A doll's house metal tea set, c1890, teapot 1¼in (3cm) high.
£24–28 *PSA*

A doll's house carpet sweeper, 1900s, 6½in (16.5cm) high.
£35–45 *MSB*

A doll's house silver coin table, c1930, 1½in (4cm) diam.
£25–30 *PSA*

A doll's house wooden tea set, c1860, tray 2½in (6.5cm) wide.
£30–38 *PSA*

r. Three doll's house glass tumblers, c1870, 1in (2.5cm) high.
£20–25 *PSA*

EPHEMERA

The term ephemera means lasting only for a short while. In collecting terms it applies to printed or handwritten items on paper (other than books). Many of the following collectables were intended to be discarded after use, some were distributed freely for advertising purposes, and others, such as autographs, were originally obtained for nothing. The following selection includes general printed matter, autographs, cigarette and trade cards, postcards and posters.

A cinema programme for the Rialto Theatre, Woodbury, N. J., featuring Lon Chaney in *The Road to Mandalay*, 1920s, 8 x 5¼in (20.5 x 13.5cm).
£6–8 BBR

A printed card box ticket for the Theatre Royal, Drury Lane, to admit Mrs H. Clive to the King's Private Box this Evening, 1822, 3 x 5in (8 x 12.5cm).
£95–115 BAL

A Souvenir Edition of *The Daily Sketch*, V E Day, May 9th, 1945.
£5–10 COB

A Souvenir brochure of the British Empire Exhibition, c1924, 11½ x 8½in (29 x 21.5cm).
£8–12 COB

Cross Reference
Colour Review

Modern Woman, published by George Newnes Ltd, London, January 1946, 8 x 5½in (20.5 x 14cm).
£2–4 PC

Two matchbooks, Universal Match Corp, St Louis, 1940s.
£4–5 each HUX

These matchbooks were distributed to American GIs during WWII and carry warnings about sexually transmitted diseases. Also inscribed on reverse 'Don't get burnt – use cover.'

A reproduction of a 1920s designed greetings card with letter on reverse, 1990s, 8 x 6in (20.5 x 15cm).
£2–3 MAP

A cut paper panel, with 2 fish within a border of basketwork, the outer border with 2 squirrels on scrolling vines issuing from an urn, 19thC, 5in (12.5cm) square.
£100–120 DN

Autographs

Abba, a photograph
signed by all four
members, 1980s,
10 x 8 (25.5 x 20.5cm).
£230–260 *VS*

Enrico Caruso, a
signed postcard, also
with facsimile
signature, c1910.
£250–300 *VS*

James Cagney, a
photograph, dedicated and
signed in full, 1930s.
£80–90 *AAV*

Robert De Niro,
a signed colour
photograph, 1990s,
10 x 8in (25.5 x 20.5cm).
£70–80 *VS*

| **Cross Reference** |
| Books |
| Rock & Pop |

l. Walt Disney,
a signed sheet
of Dorchester
Hotel note-
paper, laid
down, 1950s.
£550–650 *VS*

Charles Chaplin, a signed
sepia photograph,
contemporarily over-
mounted in ivory, framed
and glazed, 1935,
15 x 10in (38 x 25.5cm).
£450–550 *VS*

r. Arthur Conan Doyle, a menu
from the New Vagabond Club,
27th November, 1902, signed in
pencil, and also by Gen Ian
Hamilton, Anthony Hope
Hawkins and others,
7 signatures in total, adhesion
marks to reverse.
£150–175 *VS*

Arthur Conan Doyle, an
autographed letter, with
pencil sketch by Ollier at
head, sticker marks to
reverse, 1900.
£275–350 *VS*

l. Clark Gable, a
signed and inscribed
photograph, 1940s,
7 x 8in (18 x 20cm).
£400–450 *VS*

Cary Grant, an early sepia photograph signed later, 1960s, 7 x 5in (18 x 12.5cm).
£230–270 *VS*

Jimi Hendrix, a piece of paper signed and inscribed in black biro, 1960s, 14¾ x 13¾in (37.5 x 35cm).
£900–950 *CSK*

Rock Hudson, a signed photograph, 1960s, 10 x 8in (25.5x 20cm).
£80–90 *VS*

Al Jolson, a signed and inscribed photograph, slight foxing, c1960s, 6 x 4½in (16 x 11.5cm).
£75–90 *VS*

Paul McCartney, a signed colour postcard over-mounted in black, c1988, 8 x 10in (20 x 25.5cm).
£100–120 *VS*

r. Elvis Presley, a signed and inscribed record album sleeve '*How Great Thou Art*', record still present, some scuffing and staining affecting signature, 1970s.
£200–250 *VS*

Vivien Leigh, a signed programme to inside photo page, '*Look After Lulu*', 1957, also signed by Max Adrian.
£90–110 *VS*

Shirley Temple, a postcard signed in full, 1930s.
£100–120 *AAV*

Spencer Tracy, a signed and inscribed photograph, very slight wrinkling, 1940s, 10 x 8in (25.5 x 20cm).
£200–250 *VS*

r. Orson Welles, a signed photograph, c1950, 7 x 5in (18 x 12.5cm).
£230–280 *VS*

Cigarette & Trade Cards

Cigarette card collecting is over 100 years old, dating from the second half of the nineteenth century when tobacco companies first began to produce lithographed cards to advertise their wares. What makes a desirable set of cards? 'Good artwork, good condition and the right subject matter,' explains specialist dealer John Wooster. Certain themes such as sport and transport are always popular, attracting not only cigarette card collectors but also sporting and transport enthusiasts. More obscure subjects, such as 'household hints', have a correspondingly limited appeal. Condition is crucial and prices vary accordingly. Completeness is also an important factor, especially in the UK. In America they often break up sets and sell cards individually, perhaps focusing on a specific celebrity. In Britain collectors prefer the whole run, with the exception of very specific rarities.

Generally speaking trade cards tend to fetch lower prices than their tobacco equivalent. 'Cigarette cards were issued for adults, quality was high and subjects were chosen for the adult market,' says Wooster. 'Cards issued with sweets or gum were designed for children, images can be comparatively poor and do not necessarily attract the grown-up collector.' Nevertheless, some trade cards are desirable, ranging from traditional favourites such as sporting themes to more recent areas such as science fiction, (which is attracting a growing band of collectors across the world).

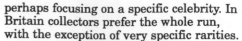

W. D. & H. O. Wills Ltd,
Nelson Series, set of 50, 1905.
£68–130 *MUR*

W. D. & H. O. Wills Ltd,
Borough Arms, 2nd
edition, set of 50, 1906.
£30–65 *ACC*

Carreras Ltd, Black Cat
cigarettes, School
Emblems, set of 50, 1929.
£35–60 *ACC*

l. J. A. Pattreiouex
Ltd, Senior Service
cigarettes, Coastwise,
set of 48, 1939.
£11–20 *ACC*

r. Godfrey Phillips
Ltd, Old Masters,
set of 36, 1939.
£11–18 *ACC*

W. D. & H. O. Wills
Ltd, Lucky Charms,
set of 50, 1923.
£14–28 *ACC*

Cigarette Cards

The price range given for cigarette cards covers the value of sets in good/average condition to the best possible condition. If a set is in excellent/mint condition it can be worth twice or even three-times as much as an example that it only fair, especially when cards are rare. If a set is in poor or damaged condition it will be worth less than the good/average price.

Animals

W. D. & H. O. Wills Ltd,
Animals and Their
Furs, set of 25, 1929.
£45–85 *ACC*

John Player & Sons,
British Live Stock,
set of 25, 1915.
£20–40 *MUR*

A Royal Winton breakfast set, decorated with Spring pattern, 1930s, tray 10in (25.5cm) wide. **£800–900** *BEV*

A Royal Winton teapot, decorated with Hazel pattern, 1930s, 5in (12.5cm) high. **£300–350** *BEV*

A Royal Winton stacking set, 1930s, 6¼in (16cm) high. **£150–200** *BEV*

A Royal Winton plate, decorated with Somerset pattern, 1930s, 8in (20.5cm) square. **£70–80** *BEV*

A Royal Winton butter dish, decorated with Marguerite pattern, 1930s, 6in (15cm) long. **£65–75** *SCA*

A Royal Winton heart-shaped trinket box, 1930s, 4in (10cm) wide. **£85–95** *PC*

A James Kent toast rack, decorated with Primula pattern, 1930s, 7in (18cm) wide. **£85–95** *BEV*

A Royal Winton coffee jug, 1930s, 5½in (14cm) high. **£130–150** *BET*

A Royal Winton cruet, decorated in Hazel pattern, c1930s, 8in (20.5cm) wide. **£200–225** *BEV*

A Royal Winton fruit bowl, decorated in Hazel pattern, 1930s, 9in (23cm) wide. **£150–175** *BET*

A set of 3 Shelley jugs, decorated with Melody pattern, c1930, largest 5½in (14cm) high. **£200–225** *BEV*

A Barker Bros sugar shifter, 1930s, 6½in (16.5cm) high. **£90–100** *BEV*

A Virbilki ceramic figure of Popov,
1950–60, 14½in (37cm) high.
£850–1,000 *PC*

A Revolutionary factory plate,
under marked in blue, 1950s,
10in (25cm) diam.
£300–400 *PC*

A Lomonosov pitcher or face
mug, with the face of a dancing
girl, c1950, 5½in (14cm) high.
£150–200 *SRC*

A Virbilki figure of a Japanese
girl dancer, under marked,
1950s, 10½in (27cm) high.
£150–200 *PC*

A Russian ceramic model of children
at a well, by Francis Gardner, under
marked, c1880, 4¼in (110cm) wide.
£450–550 *PC*

A Rye Pottery bowl, designed
by David Sharp, c1970,
10in (25.5cm) diam.
£125–150 *NCA*

r. A Rye Pottery jug,
c1900, 7in (18cm) high.
£200–250 *NCA*

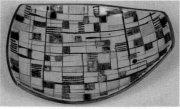

A Rye pottery mosaic pattern
dish, with 4 small feet, 1950s,
10in (25.5cm) wide.
£70–80 *NCA*

A Lomonosov 24-piece tea set, decorated with
fishnet pattern, 1960s, teapot 5in (13cm) high.
£400–500 *SRC*

Five figures of Mishka, produced for the
Moscow Olympics, 1980, largest 5in (13cm) high.
£50–60 each *SRC*

A Staffordshire figure, marked Gardners, 19thC, 5½in (14cm) high. **£175–215** *ACA*

A pair of Staffordshire Crimean war patriotic figures, c1854, 8¾in (22cm) high. **£250–280** *RWB*

A Staffordshire figure of the Hairdresser, 19thC, 6¾in (17cm) high. **£240–260** *ACA*

A Staffordshire figure of Athene, holding Gorgon's head, c1790, 6in (15cm) high. **£200–245** *ACA*

A Staffordshire Crimean war group, 19thC, 9in (23cm) high. **£160–190** *ACA*

A Staffordshire sheep and lamb spill holder, 19thC, 5½in (14cm) high. **£200–245** *ACA*

A Staffordshire figure of a dog, 19thC, 3¾in (9.5cm) high. **£100–120** *ACA*

A Staffordshire model of a house, c1875, 7¾in (20cm) high. **£125–150** *JO*

A Staffordshire model of a castle, c1840, 7¼in (18.5cm) high. **£125–150** *JO*

A Torquay Pottery vase,
c1920, 6in (15cm) high.
£50–60 *JO*

A French porcelain box,
c1870, 1¾in (4.5cm) high.
£200–300 *VSt*

A Naples porcelain casket, crown
mark, c1880, 5½in (14cm) wide.
£250–300 *VSt*

A Paragon dish, gilded and painted,
c1900, 10in (25.5cm) wide.
£150–200 *VSt*

A Torquay Pottery bowl, c1880,
some damage, 6in (15cm) high.
£8–12 *OD*

A Royal Worcester figure,
c1950, 5in (12.5cm) high.
£150–170 *VSt*

Three Arthur Wood Pottery jugs, with floral
decoration, c1950s, largest 7½in (19cm) high.
£25–35 *LA*

A SylvaC matt-glazed planter, No. 2061,
1950s, 11in (28cm) wide.
£35–42 *BSA*

A Victorian majolica dog's bowl, attributed to
George Jones, 9¾in (25cm) diam.
£150–250 *PC*

A Wilkinson, Burslem, dressing table set,
1930s, tray 12½in (32cm) wide.
£60–70 *PSA*

A Copeland commemorative coffee pot, retailed by Thos Goode, dated '1887', 10½in (26.5cm) high.
£120–180 *PC*

A Whittingham, Ford & Riley pottery teapot, depicting President Garfield, with hinged pewter lid, 1880s, 7½in (19cm) high.
£35–45 *SAS*

A Wilkinson Ltd Toby jug, depicting Sir John French, c1914–18, 10in (25.5cm) high.
£325–375 *SAS*

A Wilkinson Ltd Toby jug, depicting King George V, c1918, 12in (30.5cm) high.
£800–1,000 *SAS*

A Copeland for Thos Goode subscribers' tyg, commemorating 1900 Transvaal war, handle restored, 5½in (14cm) high.
£550–650 *SAS*

A Wilkinson Ltd Toby jug, depicting President Wilson, c1918, 10¾in (27.5cm) high.
£450–500 *SAS*

A Delft plate, commemorating Maastricht 1944 Liberation, with inscription, 9in (23cm) diam.
£50–60 *SAS*

A Coronation 'Cheerio' advertising card, 1937, 14in (35cm) high.
£8–10 *GL*

r. A Prices gurgling jug, depicting Harold Wilson, mid-1970s, 7½in (19cm) high. **£75–85** *MGC*

Action Comics, DC Comics,
Feb 1962, 10 x 7in (25.5 x 18cm).
£20–25 *NOS*

Batman, DC Comics, June
1971, 10 x 7in (25.5 x 18cm).
£12–15 *NOS*

The Beano Comic, No. 5,
August 1938, 11¾ x 8¾in
(30 x 22cm).
£475–525 *CBP*

The Dandy, No. 1, 1937,
11¾ x 8¾in (30 x 22cm).
£2,500–3,000 *CBP*

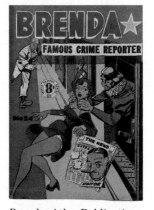

Brenda, Atlas Publications,
10 x 7in (25 x 17.5cm), 1953.
£8–10 *NOS*

Green Lantern, DC Comics,
1955, 10¼ x 6⅝in (26 x 17cm).
£110–140 *CBP*

Headline Comics, No. 6, Atlas
Publications, 1952, 10¾ x 7½in
(27 x 19cm).
£4–6 *NOS*

I Hate Crime, No. 13, Youngs
Merchandising, 1951,
11 x 7½in (28 x 19cm).
£3–4 *NOS*

Incredible Hulk, No. 181,
1974, 10¼ x 6⅝in
(26 x 17cm).
£175–200 *CBP*

Journey Into Mystery,
No. 1, Atlas, Russ Heath
front cover, June 1952,
10¼ x 7in (26 x 18cm).
£1,400–1,600 *CBP*

Lady Penelope, No. 1, with
free Lady Penenlope
signet ring, 1966,
14¼ x 10½in (36 x 27cm).
£100–120 *CBP*

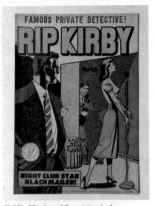

RIP Kirby, No. 15, Atlas
Publications, 1954, 10 x 7in
(25 x 17.5cm).
£8–10 *NOS*

The Amazing Spider-Man,
annual No. 1, Marvel, 1964,
10 x 7in (25 x 18cm).
£55–65 *NOS*

The Three Musketeers, No. 1,
Classic Comics, 1941, 10¼ x 7in
(26 x 18cm). **£40–50** *CBP*

Treasure Comics, No. 8, Frank
Frazetta four-page story, 1946,
10¼ x 7in (26 x 18cm).
£35–45 *CBP*

TV Fun, No. 1, 1953,
12 x 9in (30 x 23cm).
£55–65 *CBP*

Wham, No. 1, Odhams, 1964,
12 x 9in (30 x 23cm).
£150–170 *CBP*

The X-Men, No. 1, Marvel Comics,
Sept 1963, 10 x 7in (25.5 x 18cm).
£350–375 *NOS*

l. A gilded silver filigree compact, with enamel decoration, c1920, 2in (5cm) wide.
r. A brass cosmetic pot, with inset hand-painted portrait, late 19thC, 1¾in (4.5cm) wide.
£45–55 each *PC*

Two enamel on brass compacts, with rotating inner lids/sifters, 1920s, 2½in (6.5cm) wide.
£50–60 each *PC*

An engraved silver compact, with enamelled pastoral scene of dancing cherubs, c1900, 4¼in (11cm) wide.
£250–300 *PC*

A goldtone and multi-coloured brocade vanity compact, to hold powder, lipstick and cigarettes, c1934, 4in (10cm) wide.
£45–55 *PC*

A Stratton goldtone compact, with signed enamelled picture, c1950, 2in (5cm) wide.
£30–40 *PC*

A Volupté goldtone hand-shaped compact, with red enamelled nails, American, 1940s, 4½in (11.5cm) long.
£170–190 *PC*

An Elgin coloured stone powder compact, American, 1950s, 3in (7.5cm) wide.
£70–80 *TCF*

A Stratton red enamel on goldtone compact, c1960, 3in (7.5cm) wide.
£40–50 *PC*

A Kanebo goldtone compact, Japanese, c1993, 3in (7.5cm) wide.
£45–55 *PC*

A Dandymate red and white plastic combined compact and cigarette case, with musical movement, Japanese, 1970s, 4in (10cm) long.
£40–50 *PC*

A Stratton goldtone compact, with floral petit point insert, with original grosgrain pouch, 1960s, 3½in (9cm) wide.
£35–45 *PC*

A bisque baby doll in a bath tub, c1910, 3½in (9cm) high.
£50–60 *VSt*

A Heubach Mulatto baby, with bisque head, sleeping eyes and composition baby body, No. 399, c1912, 12in (30.5cm) high.
£350–400 *YC*

A French bisque piano baby, 1920s, 7¼in (18.5cm) high.
£35–45 *VSt*

A Gebrüder Heubach character doll, c1920, 10in (25.5cm) high.
£350–400 *AmD*

A ceramic pin doll, 1920s, 3½in (9cm) high.
£50–60 *VSt*

A Simon & Halbig bisque-headed character doll, with ball-jointed composition body, marked, c1920, 23in (58.5cm) high.
£450–500 *Bea*

A Revalo bisque-headed doll, Coquette, with 5-piece straight limbed body, c1920, 11in (28cm) high.
£350–400 *YC*

A Lenci felt doll, with painted face, jointed body, mohair hair and gauze dress, c1930, 19in (48.5cm) high.
£700–800 *YC*

A Käthe Kruse cloth doll, with painted face, stuffed jointed cloth body, original box, c1937, 20in (50.5cm) high.
£800–1,000 *YC*

A Triangtois half-Tudor dolls' house, with painted decoration and contents, 1930s, 26¾in (68cm) wide.
£120–150 *Gam*

A Lines Bros dolls' house, with contents, c1890, 34in (86.5cm) wide.
£2,500–3,000 *Bon*

A wooden dolls' house, c1920, 18in (45.5cm) wide.
£90–150 *FOX*

A wooden dolls' house, 1950s, 23½in (60cm) wide.
£18–25 *OD*

A late 19thC style dolls' summer dress and hat, 1990s, dress 15½in (39.5cm) long.
£140–160 *JPr*

A German painted wood sofa, with velvet upholstery and paper border, c1840, 5in (12.5cm) wide.
£35–45 *YC*

A dolls' house screen and a three-piece suite, c1900, screen 4½in (11.5cm) high. Screen **£10–12** Suite **£24–28** *PSA*

r. A dolls' house telephone, 1930s, 1¼in (3cm) high.
£18–23 *MSB*

Eleven pieces of salon furniture, c1890, settee 6½in (16.5cm) long.
£320–350 *YC*

A set of dolls' house furniture, with glass ware and tea set, c1920, sideboard 6½in (16.5 cm) high.
£10–22 each *PSA*

Four pieces of painted wood dolls' house furniture, 1940s, tallest 3½in (9cm) high.
£30–40 *OD*

A. B. & C. gum cards, Flags of the World, set of 80, 1960.
£54–64 *MUR*

W. D. & H.O. Wills Ltd, India, Scissors Cigarettes, Beauties, set of 52, 1911.
£125–250 *ACC*

W. Duke, Sons & Co, USA, Coins of all Nations, set of 50, 1889.
£600–1,200 *ACC*

Amalgamated Press Ltd trade cards, Football Fame series, set of 32, 1936.
£70–80 *MUR*

Gallaher Ltd, Dogs, first series, set of 48, 1936.
£19–38 *MUR*

Lyons Tea trade cards, Wings Across the World, set of 24, 1961.
£1–2 *ACC*

John Player & Sons, Racing Yachts, series of 25, 1938.
£40–80 *MUR*

Cohen, Weenen & Co, Celebrities, set of 45, c1901.
£3.50–7.00 each *ACC*

John Player & Sons, Aviary and Caged Birds, set of 25, 1935.
£60–75 *MUR*

Snap Cards Products Ltd, ATV Stars, series 2, set of 48, 1960.
£18–36 *MUR*

Whitbread & Co Ltd, Inn Signs, c1973.
£1.50–2.50 each *ACC*

Mickey Mouse chocolate cards, set of 60, 1930s.
£250–300 *CBP*

A harlequin set of 8 green glasses, c1830,
5in (13cm) high.
£300–350 *FD*

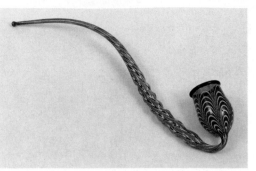

A Nailsea red and white combed glass pipe, 19thC,
20½in (52cm) long.
£180–210 *FD*

A glass vase, depicting Queen
Victoria, c1850, 7½in (19cm) high.
£85–100 *TAR*

Three Victorian pressed glass piano
rests, 4¼in (11cm) diam.
£5–7 each *FD*

l. A clear glass rolling pin, with
marvered red and blue splashes,
c1860, 13½in (34.5cm) long.
£80–110 *Som*

A 'Nailsea' blue and white
glass flask, slight damage,
c1860, 8½in (21.5cm) long.
£90–110 *Som*

r. An amethyst glass pen
tray, with pen, c1880,
9½in (24cm) long.
£125–145 *MJW*

A ruby flash decanter,
19thC, 7¾in (19.5cm) high.
£80–110 *PSA*

A Victorian multi-coloured millefiori
glass jug, 3¼in (8.5cm) high.
£75–85 *PSA*

A Victorian vaseline glass vase,
3¼in (8cm) high.
£35–40 *TAR*

A glass bottle by Ludwig Moser & Söhne, c1880, 3½in (9cm) high.
£170–200 *MJW*

A pair of wine glasses, with gilt rims, c1890, 5½in (14cm) high.
£60–70 *MJW*

A pair of glass candlesticks, 19thC, 6¼in (16cm) high.
£170–210 *PSA*

A Victorian cranberry glass decanter and stopper, 16in (41cm) high.
£140–160 *OBS*

A Sowerby glass jug and 2 matching beakers, c1860, jug 5¾in (14.5cm) high.
£35–45 *PSA*

A pair of John Derbyshire & Co pressed glass figures of Mr & Mrs Punch, c1880, 6¾in (17cm) high. **£150–200** *PC*

A St Louis cranberry and green overlay glass perfume bottle, 19thC, 7½in (19cm) high.
£375–425 *MAT*

A Venetian wine glass, c1890, 4½in (11.5cm) high.
£150–170 *MJW*

A Venetian glass plate, c1900, 7in (18cm) diam.
£135–165 *MJW*

A crystal posy vase, c1890, 8¼in (21cm) high.
£185–225 *MJW*

Two Gallé glass vases, with floral decoration, c1900, tallest 5¾in (14.5cm) high.
£350–450 each   *PC*

A pair of Murano blown glass fish, 1930s, largest 11in (28cm) high.
£120–150   *FD*

An Art Deco glass ashtray, French, c1932, 5¼in (13.5cm) wide.
£32–42   *BKK*

A Bagley frosted glass boat-shaped bowl, Salisbury 2832, c1932, 8¾in (22cm) wide.
£15–25   *PC*

A Bagley frosted glass garniture, clock Wyndham 1333, posy vases Grantham 334, c1934, clock 5½in (14cm) high.   **£65–80**   *PC*

A Bagley frosted glass 7-piece trinket set, Wyndham 1333, c1933, tray 11in (28cm) wide.
£80–100   *PC*

A Bagley clear glass 3-piece flower set, Wyndham 1333/D, c1934, 11in (28cm) wide.
£50–70   *PC*

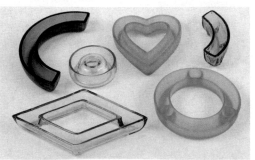

A collection of Bagley glass bloom troughs, c1936, largest 11in (28cm) wide.
Small **£4–8 each** Large **£10–20 each**   *PC*

A Sowerby pressed glass bowl,
c1935, 8¼in (21cm) diam.
£65–75 *BKK*

A Bagley glass lamp, 1930s,
8in (20.5cm) high.
£95–100 *BEV*

A Sowerby pressed glass bowl,
c1936, 7in (18cm).
£50–60 *BKK*

A Bagley clear glass 4-piece
flower set, Queen's Choice 1122,
c1936, 9¼in (23.5cm) diam.
£70–80 *PC*

A Bagley clear glass ashtray,
made to commemorate Edward
VIII's coronation, 1936,
4in (10cm) diam.
£40–50 *PC*

A Bagley frosted glass cake
stand, Fish Scale 3067, c1938,
9½in (24cm) diam.
£25–35 *PC*

A cloud glass footed bowl,
1930s, 6in (15cm) diam.
£20–25 *BEV*

A Gray-Stan glass vase, decorated
with red swirls over white, cased
in clear glass, engraved signature,
1930s, 9in (23cm) high.
£350–450 *CMO*

l. A cloud glass vase, 1930s,
6in (15cm) high.
£90–95 *BEV*

A Gray-Stan glass vase,
decorated with green swirls
over white, cased in clear
glass, engraved signature,
1930s, 9¾in (25cm) high.
£250–350 *CMO*

A limited edition souvenir goblet of RMS Elizabeth, 1940–68, 8¼in (21cm) high.
£140–160 *OBS*

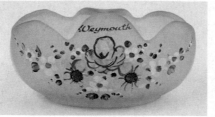

A Bagley frosted glass bowl, Tulip Posy 3169, Rd No. 870054, c1953, 5½in (14cm) diam.
£20–25 *PC*

Bagley glass was produced in a variety of colours, both decorated and undecorated.

A selection of Italian glass vases and an egg timer, 1950s, tallest 8in (20.5cm) high.
Vases   **£120–500 each**
Egg timer **£580–650** *Bon*

A pair of glass vases, 1950s, 9¾in (25cm) high.
£25–35 *CaL*

A pair of Murano style glass clowns, 1990s, 9in (23cm) high.
£25–30 each *HEI*

A pair of Murano glass decanters in the form of clowns, 1950s, 13in (33cm) high.
£120–150 each *FD*

A Chance Bros glass vase, 1970s, 4in (10cm) high.
£7–10 *FD*

A glass vase, 1960s, 13in (33cm) wide.
£25–35 *CaL*

A Glassform bowl, signed and numbered 4303, 1994, 6in (15cm) diam.
£60–80 *GLA*

Two Glassform vases, Nos. 4486 and 4485, signed, 1995, 4in (10cm) high.
£20–30 each *GLA*

A Glassform vase, 1994, 7in (18cm) high.
£40–50 *GLA*

A Glassform ashtray, No. 4422, signed, 1995, 7in (18cm) diam.
£45–55 *GLA*

John Player & Sons, Boy Scout & Girl Guide Patrol Signs & Emblems, set of 50, 1933.
£16.50–33 *ACC*

W. D. & H. O. Wills Ltd, Animals and Their Furs, set of 25, 1929.
£45–85 *ACC*

John Player & Sons, Birds & Their Young, set of 50, 1937.
£12–22 *ACC*

Beauties

Taddy & Co, Actresses, one from a set of 20, c1898.
£180–360 each *ACC*

l. Ogden's Ltd, Beauty Series, with domino set on reverse, one card from a set of 52, c1900.
£21–42 *ACC*

Many series of cigarette cards were duplicated as games, either as an inset or on the reverse.

John Player & Sons, Poultry, set of 50, 1931.
£35–70 *MUR*

r. Universal Tobacco Co, Madras, Actresses, c1900.
£20–40 *ACC*

These cards were never issued as a set but were produced at random.

l. W. Duke, Sons & Co, USA, Holidays, set of 50, 1890.
£580–1,200 *ACC*

Caricatures

John Player & Sons, Straight Line
Caricatures, set of 50, 1926.
£22–44 *ACC*

r. Stephen Mitchell & Son,
Humerous Drawings, set of 50, 1924.
£96–166 *ACC*

W. A. & A. C. Churchman,
Howlers, set of 16, 1936.
£8–16 *ACC*

Military

W. D. & H. O. Wills Ltd, India,
Scissors Cigarettes, Types of the
British Army, set of 50, 1908.
£210–420 *ACC*

W. D. & H. O. Wills Ltd, Overseas,
Pirate Cigarettes, China's Ancient
Warriors, 4 sets of 25, 1911.
£35–76 per set *ACC*

V.C. HEROES – BOER WAR
Nº 87

Serg Major A Young V.C. Cape Police
Awarded the Victoria Cross for conspicuous
bravery at Koffers Kraal. With a few men he
rushed some Kaposis and afterwards captured
Commandant Erasmus single handed.

Taddy & Co, VC
Heroes – Boer War,
set of 20, 1902.
£350–700 *ACC*

Gallaher Ltd,
Regimental Colours
& Standards,
set of 50, 1912.
£265–530 *ACC*

THE LATE EARL ROBERTS.

J. S. Billingham,
Army Pictures,
Cartoons, etc, 1916.
£70–140 each *ACC*

r. W. D. & H. O.
Wills Ltd,
India, Scissors
Cigarettes, Indian
Regiment Series,
set of 50, 1912.
£270–540 *ACC*

Sporting

John Player & Sons, Player's
Navy Cut Cigarettes, Riders
of the World, set of 50, 1905.
£35–70 *MUR*

Ogden's Ltd, Trainers and Owner's
Colours, 1st series, set of 25, 1925.
£25–50 *MUR*

W. D. & H. O. Wills
Ltd, proof cards, 1908.
£16–32 each *ACC*

Transport

r. Carreras Ltd,
Post 1945 Issues,
Vintage Cars,
set of 50, 1976.
£6–7 *ACC*

l. W. D. &
H. O. Wills
Ltd, Railway
Locomotives,
set of 50, 1930.
£35–65 *MUR*

*These are often cut
from large sheets but
command similar
prices to standard
issues. There are many
variations with the
reverse plain and some
with or without
typesetting. Beware
of reproductions.*

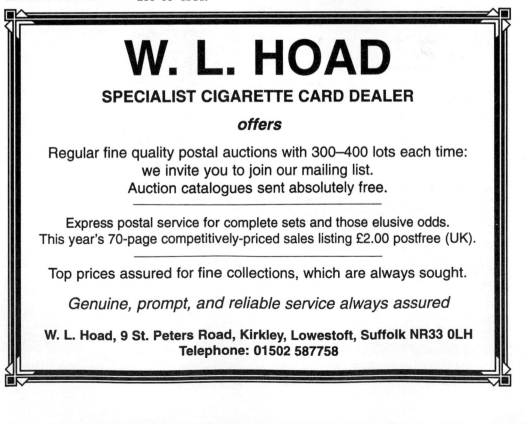

Trade Cards

Liebig Extract of Meat Co
Ltd, Useful Insects, set of
6 cards, 1903.
£5.00–11.50 *MUR*

*The Liebig Extract of Meat Co
Ltd was formed in 1856 and
was acquired by Brooke Bond
in 1971. In Britain their
product was renamed Oxo,
which it is known as today.
In a period of 100 years from
1872 the company issued a
large number of sets of cards,
including postcards, menus,
calendars, place cards and
other novelty issues.*

Liebig Extract of Meat Co Ltd,
The Tale of Mother Holle
(a fable), set of 6 cards, 1906.
£17.50–45 *MUR*

Geo. Bassett & Co Ltd, Football
1987–88, set of 48, 1988.
£3–5 *ACC*

Liebig Extract of Meat Co
Ltd, National Dances,
set of 6, 1889.
£27.50–55 *MUR*

Victoria Gallery, London, Olympic
Greats, set of 25, 1992.
£5.50–7.50 *MUR*

*Victoria Gallery were officially
authorised to do reprints of the
Imperial Tobacco Company series.*

l. Whitbread & Co
Ltd, Inn Signs, 1st,
2nd and 3rd Series,
sets of 50, c1951.
£2–3 each *JMC*

r. Skybox International
Inc, USA, Star Trek, The
Next Generation, Season
Two, set of 96, 1995.
£7–14 *MUR*

Victoria Gallery, London, American Civil War
Leaders, set of 20, 1992.
£5–6 *MUR*

Topps Chewing Gum Inc, USA, The X Files,
set of 72, 1995.
£7–14 *MUR*

Postcards

A set of 10 postcards, issued by the
Post Office, 1993.
£3–4 *JMC*

*Titled The Bash Street Kids, The Wind
in the Willows, The Big Friendly Giant,
The Snowman, Long John Silver,
Tweedledum & Tweedledee, Peter
Rabbit, Aladdin and the Genie, Just
William, Rupert Bear and Bill Badger.*

A set of 13 postcards, Famous Passenger Lines,
reproduced from posters, 1990s.
£5–8 *MAP*

Posters

A Japanese paper poster,
No. 133, by Lucy Kemp-Welch,
c1914, 30 x 20in (76 x 51cm).
£700–800 *ONS*

A Russian linen poster, artist
unknown, 'Comrades – Workers!
Hurry up on Revolutionary Front!'
c1917, 27¼ x 18½in (70 x 47cm).
£250–350 *ONS*

An LMS linen poster, by Christopher
Clark, printed by Horrocks, c1924,
40¼ x 50in (102 x 127cm).
£650–750 *ONS*

An LMS linen poster, RA Series
No. 6, by Sir David Murray,
printed by McCorquodale, c1925,
40¼ x 50in (102 x 127cm).
£300–400 *ONS*

An LMS poster, Best Way Series
No. 58, printed by McCorquodale,
c1925, 40¼ x 50in (102 x 127cm).
£1,000–1,200 *ONS*

A Russian linen poster, artist
unknown, published by Odessa
Propaganda Department,
c1918, 28¼ x 21in (72 x 53cm).
£325–425 *ONS*

An LNER linen poster, by Frank H. Mason, printed by Jarrold, c1938, 40¼ x 50in (102 x 127cm). **£450–550** *ONS*

A concert poster, designed by Caron, 1930s second printing, some creasing, 31½ x 25¼in (80 x 64cm). **£1,800–2,000** *S*

An LMS poster, by Norman Wilkinson, printed by David Allen, slight damage, c1925, 40¼ x 50in (102 x 127cm). **£800–1,000** *ONS*

Two concert posters, advertising Henry Cotton at an evening of Varieties at the Coliseum, Charing Cross, 1938, 29½ x 19¾in (75 x 50cm). **£225–275** *S*

An LNER poster, by Frank H. Mason, printed by Jarrold, some damage, c1940, 40¼ x 50in (102 x 127cm). **£350–450** *ONS*

A GWR poster, by Ronald Lampitt, printed by J. Weiner, some damage, c1946, 40¼ x 50in (102 x 127cm). **£450–550** *ONS*

Film

A film poster, *Alien*, Felden Productions, 1979, 11 x 8½in (28 x 21.5cm). **£20–25** *NOS*

A film poster, *Barbarella*, Paramount, linen-backed, 61½ x 45in (156 x 114cm). **£900–1,100** *CSK*

A film poster, *Deadline*, 20th Century Fox, double-crown tie-in, good condition, 1952. **£100–120** *VS*

A one-sheet film poster,
Forbidden Planet, MGM,
linen-backed, 1956, 41 x 27in
(104 x 68.5cm).
£1,800–2,000 *S*

A French film poster, *From
Russia with Love*, some damage,
1964, 24¾ x 18in (63 x 46cm).
£50–60 *VS*

A French film poster, *Gilda*,
very good condition, 1946,
24½ x 18in (62 x 46cm).
£90–110 *VS*

A film poster, *I married a
Woman*, Universal International
Release, very good condition,
1958, 8¾ x 5½in (22 x 14cm).
£35–45 *VS*

A film poster, *Goldfinger*,
British Quad, linen-backed,
1964, 30 x 39½in (76 x 100cm).
£1,200–1,500 *CSK*

A one-sheet poster featuring
Joan Crawford, *Johnny Guitar*,
1953, 41 x 27in (104 x 69cm).
£250–280 *CNY*

A film poster, *Thunderbird 6*,
designed by Frank Bellamy,
paper-backed, c1970,
30 x 40in (76 x 102cm).
£150–200 *CSK*

A one-sheet poster featuring
Marilyn Monroe, *Niagara*,
linen-backed, 1952,
41 x 27in (104 x 69cm).
£460–500 *CNY*

A six-sheet film poster, *Love
in the Afternoon*, designed by
Saul Bass, linen-backed, 1957,
81in (206cm) square.
£750–850 *CSK*

Rock & Pop

A concert poster, for the Beatles rock gala at 'Knotty Ash Hall', printed in green and black, damaged, 1962, 28 x 19¾in (71 x 50cm).
£1,700–2,200 *S*

A concert poster, for the Beach Boys and The Maharishi Mahesh Yogi at Boston Garden, printed in red, black and white, excellent condition, 1968, 22 x 14in (56 x 35.5cm).
£400–500 *S*

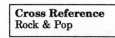

Cross Reference
Rock & Pop

A coloured concert poster, for the Beatles tour in Stockholm, signed by the band, some damage, 1964, 39¼ x 27½in (100 x 70cm).
£17,000–20,000 *S*

At auction this poster trebled its estimate, selling to a Radio 1 disc jockey and TV personality.

A concert poster, for Jimi Hendrix at the Washingtion Hilton, printed in blue and fluorescent orange on yellow, some damage, 1968, 23 x 17½in (58.5 x 44.5cm).
£1,800–2,200 *S*

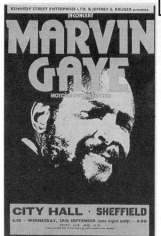

A concert poster, for Marvin Gaye at Sheffield, 1978, 30 x 20in (76 x 51cm).
£500–600 *CSK*

A concert poster, for Eric Clapton and his new group at Torquay, 1970, 30 x 20in (76 x 51cm).
£350–450 *CSK*

FURTHER READING
Stephen Maycock, *Rock & Pop Memorabilia* Miller's Publications 1995

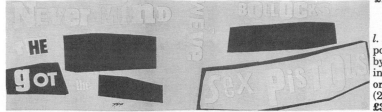

l. A promotional banner poster, for The Sex Pistols, by Warner Bros, printed in fluorescent green and orange, 1977, 11 x 34in (28 x 86.5cm).
£350–450 *CSK*

FAIRIES

The feature in our last edition of *Miller's Collectables* on gnomes excited a massive amount of interest. We follow it up this year with a small section on fairies and other elfin folk. Since the Victorian period, fairy painting has been a British speciality, images often inspired by or linked to a literary theme. William Shakespeare's *A Midsummer Night's Dream*, has been portrayed by many artists, including Arthur Rackham (1867–1939). Master of the fantasy field, his illustrated children's books are highly collectable.

Cicely Mary Baker (1895–1973) was one of a number of artists who concentrated on painting fairies. Flower Fairies, her most famous creation, produced in book form as well as prints and cards, has helped establish the popular image of the fairy; believe in them or not, everyone knows what a fairy looks like. As the following selection of tins shows, fairies have long been used in advertising, and the tradition continues into the present, with the name of a famous brand of washing-up liquid.

A pair of watercolours, by William Stephen Coleman (1829–1904), signed, 15in (38cm) diam.
£4,000–4,500 *HO*

These watercolours were probably produced for use on Minton plaques.

A nursery print, by Margaret Tarrant (1888–1969), depicting a pixie market, 1930s, framed 22½ x 20in (57 x 51cm).
£55–65 *HEI*

Seven Wedgwood tiles, depicting characters from *A Midsummer Night's Dream*, 19thC, 8in (20.5cm) square.
£100–125 *PSA*

William Shakespeare's, A *Midsummer Night's Dream*, with illustrations by Arthur Rackham, published by Heinemann, 1908, 10 x 7½in (25.5 x 19cm).
£180–230 *HB*

A collection of Flower Fairy prints, by Cicely Mary Baker, with appropriate verse written by the artist on reverse, c1925, framed 11 x 9¼in (28 x 23.5cm).
£40–50 each *PC*

A tin, illustrated with a fairy, c1920, 3½in (9cm) wide.
£9–11 *HUX*

A Fairy Nougat tin, by George W. Horner & Co Ltd, 1930s, 7in (18cm) diam.
£24–28 *WAB*

A glass powder bowl, illustrated with a fairy, 1920s, 6½in (16.5cm) high.
£85–95 *PSA*

A tea caddy, by Huntley & Palmers, illustrated with gnomes, c1930, 5in (12.5cm) high.
£15–18 *HUX*

A Sovereign – King of all Toffees tin, c1930, 17in (43cm) wide.
£22–26 *HUX*

r. A Clarecraft Faerie Realm ceramic fairy figure, No. FY03, 1990s, 6¼in (16cm) high.
£40–50 *FMN*

Two ceramic figures from The Fairy Collection, Chinese:
l. Enchanted, No. 5579.
r. Bountiful Spirit, No. 5593.
1990s, 3½in (9cm) high.
£9–12 each *FMN*

Two silver fairy brooches, 1990s, largest 2in (5cm) high.
£9–13 each *FMN*

Gnomes

l. A Victorian ceramic gnome hat pin holder, 6in (15cm) high.
£24–28 *TAC*

For a further selection of gnomes please refer to *Miller's Collectables Price Guide 1996–97*, page 244.

r. A grey painted stone gnome, marked, c1900, 11in (28cm) high.
£75–85 *BGA*

A grey painted stone gnome, 1950s, 13in (33cm) high.
£25–35 *BGA*

FANS

A Japanese embroidered fan, with a copy of a Canton dress design, 1865, 8in (20.5cm) wide.
£95–100 *BSA*

A painted leaf fan with 2 ladies watching putti setting up a trap with a net across a bridge, signed J. Donzel, the verso with monogram A.M., with carved and pierced mother-of-pearl sticks, damaged and repaired, c1885, 11in (28cm) wide.
£1,750–2,000 *CSK*

r. A lace and cut-steel decorated fan, with bone sticks, c1880, 14in (35.5cm) long.
£60–70 *BSA*

A Japanese hand-painted black and gold lacquered fan, on wooden sticks, 19thC, 12in (30.5cm) long.
£550–625 *BSA*

A marriage fan, by Alexandre and signed Donzel, painted with the marriage contract, the verso with monogram F.R., and Continental Baroness's coronet, pierced and gilt mother-of-pearl sticks, c1880, 12in (30.5cm) wide, with leather fan box lined with blue silk.
£8,500–9,500 *CSK*

A Japanese ivory brisé fan, lacquered in two tones of gold with sailing boats between islands, the verso with a similar scene, c1880, 11in (28cm) wide.
£1,500–1,800 *CSK*

A Japanese tortoiseshell brisé fan, lacquered in gold, with an owl perched in a tree and other birds, the guardsticks decorated with *shibayama*-work birds and flowers, late 19thC, 10in (25.5cm) wide, with Canton lacquered box.
£3,500–4,000 *CSK*

A painted leaf fan, with a nymph and putti, the reserves of Brussels lace, with carved and pierced mother-of-pearl sticks, c1890, 14in (35.5cm) wide, with box.
£650–750 *CSK*

A leaf painted fan, with mother-of-pearl sticks, signed, c1890, 12in (30.5cm) wide.
£1,400–1,450 *CSK*

A Chinese fan, decorated by 4 different artists and 4 types of calligraphy, with gold lacquered sticks, c1910, 12in (30.5cm) wide.
£200–225 *BSA*

A pink ostrich feather fan, with mother-of-pearl sticks, c1920, 27½in (70cm) long.
£80–85 *TAR*

A painted silk and satin fan, with wooden painted sticks, c1890, 12in (30.5cm) wide.
£30–40 *GWA*

A handmade lace leaf fan, with mother-of-pearl guardsticks, c1910, 8in (20.5cm) with Dickins & Jones Ltd box.
£80–90 *GWA*

A black ostrich feather fan, with celluloid sticks, c1910, 12in (30.5cm) long.
£20–30 *BSA*

A dyed ostrich feather fan, with cellulose tortoiseshell sticks, c1920, 12in (30.5cm) long.
£30–35 *CCO*

r. A shaped silk leaf fan, painted with a white peacock, with horn sticks carved and pierced to resemble peacock feathers, signed 'A. Thomasse', slight wear, c1908, 10¼in (26cm) wide.
£450–550 *CSK*

A gauze, ribbon and sequinned fan, with carved and painted sticks, c1900, 14in (35.5cm) wide.
£50–60 *GWA*

A chromolithographic fan, advertising the Brasserie Universelle, decorated with 2 cat portraits, wooden sticks, c1910, 10in (25.5cm) wide.
£210–250 *CSK*

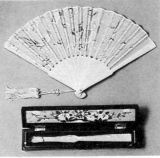

An Oriental embroidered gauze fan, with bone sticks and original tassel, c1920, 10in (25.5cm) wide, with original lacquered box.
£90–100 *GWA*

FIFTIES STYLE

A cotton print summer dress, 1950s.
£10–20 *PC*

A puff ball dress, 1950s.
£25–45 *TCF*

A ball gown, labelled 'Marshal and Snellgrove', 1950s.
£55–65 *TCF*

An American western style embroidered cream coloured shirt, together with a pair of gabardine trousers.
Shirt **£65–75**
Trousers **£45–55** *SPS*

An American beaded needlepoint handbag, with applied fruit and a chain handle, 1950s.
£40–45 *SBT*

A transparent Lucite handbag, 1950s, 11½in (29cm) high.
£100–120 *TCF*

FURTHER READING

Madeleine Marsh,
Collecting the 1950s
Miller's Publications, May 1997

A chrome metal and black plastic handbag, 1950s, 5½in (14cm) wide.
£75–85 *TCF*

A French green and white painted metal patio chair, 1950s.
£70–100 *CSK*

A Lucite bangle, incorporating brightly coloured patches, 1950s, 10in (25.5cm) diam.
£42–52 *SnA*

A coffee table, with a glass top decorated with a black and white abstract pattern, 1950s.
£25–30 FLD

An acorn sugar shaker, 1950s.
£24–28 TAC

A Murano glass fish, on a stand, 1950s, 10¾in (27cm) high.
£65–75 FD

A Midwinter plate, Riviera pattern, by Sir Hugh Casson, c1954, 7½in (19cm) diam.
£12–14 AND

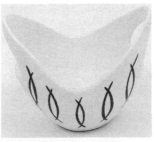

A Jersey Pottery freeform vase, 1950s, 7½in (19cm) high.
£8–10 REN

A ceramic wall plaque, depicting a girl, by Jena, 1950s.
£35–45 FLD

l. A Burleigh Ware vase, decorated with harbour scene, 1950s, 13in (33cm) high.
£24–28 DGP

A Poole Pottery plate, inscribed 'Festival of Britain', dated '1951', 10in (25.5cm) diam.
£60–70 SAS

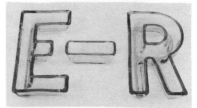

A Bagley glass bloom trough set, incomplete, c1953, 4in (10cm) wide.
£50–70 PC

This trough should read EIIR and was made for the Queen's Coronation.

A Lesney Coronation coach, drawn by 8 horses, 4 mounted, good condition,
£110–130 TMA

GLASS
Bagley Glass

Bagley, the glass company based in Knottingly, West Yorkshire, started making bottles in 1871 and in 1913 diversified into domestic and pub glassware under the name of The Crystal Glass Co Ltd.

Queen's Choice, a design influenced by Chippendale, was introduced in 1922, soon to be followed by several other very successful patterns. The heyday of the company was the mid-1930s when under the management of Dr Stanley Bagley and Mr Percy Bagley. A number of excellent Art Deco patterns were created, initially by designer Alexander Hardie Williamson, but also by in-house artists. Crystaltynt, a range of delicately coloured glass, both clear and frosted, was introduced at the same time. This period of innovation ended with the war.

In 1947, an opaline glass, Crystopal, was produced and many post-war designs were made from this material. Ten years later the company began to manufacture Jetique, a rich black glass, which proved highly popular. Many articles were decorated either by hand or by transfer and often metal-mounted but in general such decoration did little to enhance the beauty of the glass.

Stanley and Percy Bagley both died in the late 1950s. The factory subsequently changed hands several times and recently has been completely modernised. It is now producing high quality glassware for the cosmetics industry. The period of interest for Bagley glass collectors runs from the early 1920s to the early 1960s.

1920s & 30s

A Bagley green pressed glass bowl and cover, 1929, 4in (10cm) high.
£8–10 *BKK*

A Bagley amber glass vase, with plinth and insert, 1932, 5in (12.5cm) high.
£15–20 *BKK*

A Bagley clear flint glass salver, pattern No. 2, 1922, 6in (15cm) high.
£15–25 *PC*

A Bagley blue glass bowl, with painted decoration, 1930, 6¼in (16cm) diam.
£15–20 *BKK*

r. A Bagley 13-piece clear flint glass fruit set, Pendant 742, with intaglio base, RD 742290, 1932, largest bowl 9in (23cm) diam.
£50–75 *PC*

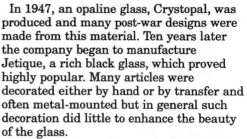

A pair of Bagley green pressed glass candlesticks, 1929, 5¼in (13cm) high.
£12–15 *BKK*

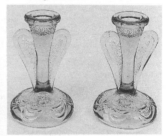

A Bagley Queen's Choice blue pressed glass bowl, 1933, 4¼in (11cm) diam.
£8–10 *BKK*

A set of 3 Bagley clear flint glass jelly moulds, in the shape of rabbits, 1934, largest 6in (15cm) wide.
£30–40 *PC*

A Bagley clear flint glass two-piece comport, Empress 5234, comprising celery vase and salad bowl, 1934, 9¼in (23.5cm) high.
£50–60 *PC*

l. A Bagley frosted pink glass three-piece flower set, Wyndham 1333/0, 1934, 7in (18cm) high.
£80–95 *PC*

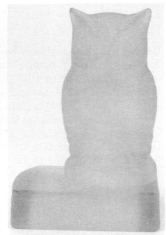

A pair of Bagley frosted peach glass owl book ends, RD 798842, 1934, 6in (15cm) high.
£90–110 *PC*

A Bagley frosted green glass clock and 2 clear glass vases, Bamboo 3007, 1934, 5in (12.5cm) high.
£65–80 *PC*

A Bagley frosted green glass seven-piece trinket set, pattern 3002, 1934, tray 15in (38cm) wide.
£70–80 *PC*

l. A Bagley amber clear glass marine bowl, pattern 3000, RD 798843, designed by Alexander H. Williamson, 1934, 12in (30.5cm) diam.
£50–60 *PC*

A Bagley green glass leaf vase with centre, pattern 3001, RD 798844, designed by Alexander H. Williamson, 1934, 7½in (19cm) high.
£90–110 *PC*

A Bagley green glass four-piece trinket set, pattern 3008, 1934, tray 13in (33cm) wide.
£80–100 *PC*

A Bagley green pressed glass marine plate, 1934, 9in (23cm) square.
£15–20 *BKK*

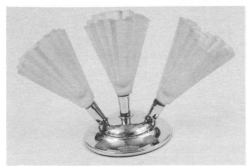

A Bagley frosted blue glass *épergne*,
Grantham 334, posy 'Peg' version, 1934,
5½in (14cm) high.
£30–40 *PC*

A selection of Bagley glass ashtrays/butter pats,
pattern 3016, 1936–56, 4in (10cm) diam:
EIIR. **£8–12**
Festival of Britain and ER. **£18–20 each**
Royal visit and ER. **£60–80** *PC*

A Bagley green glass lamp,
1930s, 8in (20.5cm) high.
£85–95 *BEV*

Two Bagley clear flint glass
commemorative plates,
c1937, 9¾in (25cm) diam:
Coronation. **£8–15**
Royal Visit. **£40–50** *PC*

A Bagley frosted blue glass
two-piece flower set, decorated
with painted leather flowers,
Queen's Choice 1122, 1937,
4½in (11.5cm) diam.
£40–50 *PC*

A Bagley amber glass vase
with flower holder, decorated
with koala bears, 1937,
8in (20.5cm) high.
£180–220 *PC*

A Bagley amber pressed glass
heart-shaped posy ring bowl,
1939, 7in (18cm) long.
£8–10 *BKK*

A Bagley frosted amber glass
flower jug, Sunburst 3072,
1939, 9½in (24cm) high.
£30–40 *PC*

1940s & 50s

A Bagley clear glass seven-piece fruit set, hand-decorated, Adelphi 3162, 1946, large bowl 8in (20.5cm) diam.
£30–40 *PC*

A Bagley clear amber glass seven-piece fruit set, Carnival 3141, RD 849118, 1946, large bowl 8½in (21.5cm) diam.
£20–30 *PC*

A Bagley clear blue glass sweet dish, Alexandra 3121/3, 1940, 11in (28cm) wide.
£10–20 *PC*

A Bagley frosted pink glass three-piece flower set, Bristol 3145, 1947, 8in (20.5cm) wide.
£30–40 *PC*

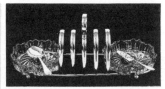

A Bagley toast rack set, with chrome stand and clear green glass dishes, pattern 3184, 1950, 10in (25.5cm) long.
£15–25 *PC*

A Bagley clear flint glass sugar bowl, Katherine 3187, 1955, 5½in (14cm) high.
£15–20 *PC*

A Bagley Jetique polka dot wall vase, pattern 3193, 1957, 5in (13cm) wide.
£12–18 *PC*

A Bagley Jetique mushroom posy with centre flower holder, pattern 3195, 1957, 7½in (19cm) diam.
£15–20 *PC*

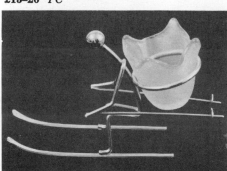

r. A Bagley glass bowl with Jetique figure of Andromeda, Equinox 3161/T, 1957, 8in (20.5cm) high.
£60–70 *PC*

l. A Bagley skier, with green frosted glass handkerchief, posy/match holder, on chromium mount, 1957, 6in (15cm) long.
£2–5 *PC*

Bowls & Dishes

An amethyst glass sugar bowl, the hollow conical foot with folded rim, c1810, 4in (10cm) high.
£140–160 *Som*

A Victorian bonbon dish, 8½in (21.5cm) wide.
£50–60 *AnS*

A Schneider etched glass bowl, c1939, 14in (35.5cm) diam.
£100–150 *DAF*

A William IV canted glass dish, with crenelated rim and diamond-cut base, the step-cut sides etched with a crown, national emblems and royal cipher, rim chipped, 10¾in (27.5cm) wide.
£150–200 *DN*

A glass powder bowl, painted with roses, 1920s, 6¼in (16cm) diam.
£30–40 *SUS*

l. A lead crystal step-cut bowl, 1930s, 4¼in (11cm) high.
£70–80 *PSA*

A sepia glass finger bowl, with etched decoration and star-cut base, c1890, 5in (12.5cm) diam.
£80–100 *MJW*

A Lalique powder bowl, with mark, c1925, 5in (12.5cm) diam.
£450–550 *SHa*

Decanters

A glass decanter, with stopper, c1800, 11½in (29cm) high.
£160–190 *MJW*

A square glass decanter, with stopper, c1840, 10¼in (26cm) high.
£140–170 *MJW*

A glass decanter, with 3 neck rings above wheel-cut swags and leaf sprays, with fluted base, late 18thC, 10in (25.5cm) high.
£230–270 *JAd*

An engraved
glass sherry
decanter, c1860,
15¼in (39cm) high.
£235–265 *MJW*

A thistle pattern cut glass liqueur set,
by Edinburgh & Leith Co, engraved
with maker's name, mid-19thC,
decanter 8in (20.5cm) high.
£160–190 *HEI*

l. A facet-cut glass
decanter, c1840,
13¾in (35cm) high.
£120–150 *MJW*

Three late Victorian club-shaped
glass decanters, engraved with
festoons, in trefoil frame on
caryatid feet, with carrying
handle, 13¾in (35cm) high.
£375–425 *WL*

A Hollands gin
glass decanter,
c1860, 13½in
(34.5cm) high.
£235–265 *MJW*

l. A glass decanter,
with stopper, c1890,
12¾in (32.5cm) high.
£120–140 *MJW*

A glass claret jug,
in the style of
Pugh, engraved
with a deer in a
woodland setting,
late 19thC,
12½in (32cm) high.
£400–450 *JAd*

r. A glass decanter,
by Max Greger & Co,
London, inscribed 'By
Special Appointment
to Her Majesty', c1880,
11¼in (28.5cm) high.
£400–450 *MJW*

A French glass decanter,
with enamelled flower
decoration, c1920,
10in (25.5cm) high.
£160–200 *MJW*

A cut glass decanter,
with stopper
and hand-engraved
fish, c1938,
9¾in (25cm) high.
£75–85 *BKK*

Friggars and Curiosities

A friggar is an object created from 'end of day' glass to show off the glass blower's skill. In some regions they were made on Saturdays, when the factory was not working, and then paraded around the area on Sundays. The best pieces would be awarded prizes and the most popular put into production. Friggars included ships, pipes, bells, hats, musical instruments and a miscellany of other objects. This section also includes glass curiosities, many being mundane household or garden items, not normally associated with the medium of glass.

r. A Georgian glass bird feeder, 6in (15cm) high.
£45–55 *FD*

A Hydes pressed glass bird feeder, late 19thC, 4¼in (11cm) high.
£8–10 *FD*

A lacemaker's condensing globe, on pedestal foot, c1740, 10in (25.5cm) high.
£280–310 *FD*

A glass fly trap, early 19thC, 7¾in (20cm) high.
£45–55 *FD*

A glass bird feeder, with hollow and frilled knops, early 19thC, 7in (18cm) high.
£55–65 *FD*

Two French glass truffle bottles, mid-19thC, tallest 7¾in (20cm) high.
£10–16 each *FD*

A blown friggar of a crown, mid-19thC, 9in (23cm) diam.
£90–110 *FD*

Two glass top hats, with folded brims, late 19thC, largest 7in (18cm) wide.
£55–65 each *FD*

Five miniature glasses, possibly travellers samples, c1830, tallest 2in (5cm) high.
£170–200 *Som*

Three coloured glass rolling pins, c1860, 15¾in (40cm) long.
£80–100 each *Som*

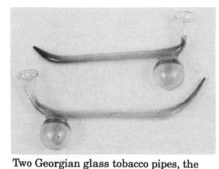

r. A green, blue and white glass pipe, possibly Nailsea, mid-19thC, 21in (53cm) long.
£120–140 *FD*

Two Georgian glass tobacco pipes, the bubbles used for cooling with water, 9½in (24cm) long.
£35–45 each *FD*

A glass three-masted ship and cutter, with glass dome, on round ebonised base, 19thC, 7¾in (20cm) high.
£165–185 *FD*

A vaseline glass bell, the clapper missing, 19thC, 10¼in (26cm) high.
£80–100 *TAC*

A wrythen glass bugle, early 19thC, 9¼in (23.5cm) high.
£55–65 *FD*

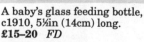

A baby's glass feeding bottle, c1910, 5½in (14cm) long.
£15–20 *FD*

These were called 'murder' bottles because they were so difficult to clean.

A white combed glass bellows on a stand, mid-19thC, 13¾in (35cm) high.
£180–220 *FD*

A pressed glass hollow pistol, c1910, 9¾in (25cm) long.
£25–35 *FD*

l. A glass axe and hammer, both with hollow handles, mid-19thC, 9¾in (25cm) long.
£120–125 each *FD*

Glasses

An ale glass, engraved with hops and barley, c1800, 4¾in (12cm) high.
£45–55 *CaL*

A wrythen ale glass, c1800, 5½in (14cm) high.
£45–55 *CaL*

Short Glossary of Drinking Glasses

Firing glass: A low drinking glass, with a short, thick stem and a thick foot, used on ceremonial occasions when, after toasting, the glass would be rapped on the table. Also known as a 'bumping glass'.

Knop: The bulge in the stem of a glass. Knops come in many styles, singly and in groups and may be hollow or solid.

Pontil mark: A mark in the centre of the base of a blown glass object, made from breaking off the pontil or iron rod used during glass manufacture.

Rummer: An English drinking glass usually in the form of a low goblet with a stemmed foot.

Syllabub glass: A vessel for drinking syllabub, a popular drink in the 17th and 18th centuries, made from cream whipped to a froth, with sherry, ratafia and spices.

Teardrop: An air bubble in the form of a teardrop encased in the stem of drinking glasses, or occasionally in a knop. Teardrops were originally produced accidentally but later became a popular form of decoration.

Thistle glass: A drinking glass in the form of a thistle.

A rummer, with petal-moulded base to the bowl and sharp pontil, c1810, 5½in (14cm) high.
£45–55 *CaL*

A rummer, with petal-moulded base to the bowl, c1810, 5¾in (14.5cm) high.
£45–55 *CaL*

A plain bucket-shaped rummer, with bladed knop, c1830, 6¼in (16cm) high.
£65–75 *CaL*

An ale glass, with petal-moulded bowl, c1820, 5in (12.5cm) high.
£25–35 *CaL*

l. & r. A pair of amethyst wine glasses, with conical bowls, on plain stems and feet, c1850, 5¼in (13.5cm) high. **£200–240**
c. A pair of amber wine glasses, with flute-cut trumpet bowls, on baluster stems and plain feet, c1850, 4¾in (12cm) high.
£100–120 *Som*

A rummer, with engraved border and petal-moulded bowl, early 19thC, 5in (13cm) high.
£70–80 *CaL*

A pair of early Victorian flake-cut ale glasses, 6¼in (16cm) high.
£55–60 *OBS*

A Victorian ale
glass, with
decorative cutting
and bladed knop,
5¾in (14.5cm) high.
£18–22 *CaL*

A pair of Bohemian
engraved glasses, 19thC,
5in (13cm) high.
£55–65 *PSA*

A Victorian thistle
glass, with teardrop,
6¾in (17cm) high.
£80–100 *OBS*

A rummer, with decorative
cutting to bowl, above
bladed knop, c1860,
6¼in (16cm) high.
£65–75 *CaL*

A Victorian
champagne flute,
with flared rim,
6in (15cm) high.
£30–40 *CaL*

A Victorian
champagne flute,
with bladed knop,
6¼in (16cm) high.
£35–45 *CaL*

A rummer, with bladed
and rounded knops,
c1860, 6¼in (16cm) high.
£65–75 *CaL*

A Victorian flake-cut
goblet, 5in (13cm) high.
£45–50 *OBS*

A set of 4 pale green wine glasses, with
flute-cut trumpet bowls and facet-cut
knopped stems, on plain feet, c1860,
5in (13cm) high.
£200–250 *Som*

A pair of wine glasses,
engraved with monkeys,
c1880, 5½in (14cm) high.
£240–270 *MJW*

A souvenir goblet
of the RMS *Mary*,
with box, 1967,
6½in (16.5cm) high.
£150–160 *OBS*

Italian Glass

A Venetian powdered gold glass bowl, 1930s, 12in (30.5cm) wide.
£60–70 *PSA*

A Venini handkerchief vase, with pale blue and white *latticino* decoration, etched 'Venini Murano Italia', small chip, c1955, 6in (15cm) high.
£225–275 *S(S)*

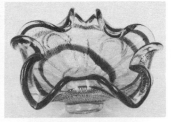

A Murano glass dish, with aubergine and gold decoration and curled edges, 1950s, 9½in (24cm) wide.
£25–35 *FD*

A Murano green glass dish, with silver leaf insert, 1950s, 5in (13cm) wide.
£15–20 *FD*

A Murano green glass dish, with gold leaf insert, 1950s, 5in (13cm) wide.
£20–25 *FD*

A Murano Sommerso technique glass dish, with red, white and gold layers, 1950s, 3¾in (9.5cm) diam.
£25–30 *FD*

Jugs

A Nailsea type bottle glass footed pitcher, with opaque white decoration, c1810, 9½in (24cm) high.
£250–300 *NWi*

A Nailsea type light green cream jug, with vertically ribbed baluster body, and white splash decoration, folded rim, applied foot ring and loop handle, c1810, 4½in (11.5cm) high.
£320–360 *Som*

A Victorian vaseline glass cream jug, 3¾in (9.5cm) high.
£50–60 *AnS*

l. A blue wrythen-moulded cream jug, with waisted body, folded rim and loop handle, c1820, 3in (7.5cm) high.
£80–100 *Som*

r. A Victorian cranberry glass jug, c1880, 6¼in (16cm) high.
£80–90 *AnS*

Paperweights

A magnum or dump paperweight, possibly by Kilner or J. Tower, 1860, 4¾in (12cm) diam.
£60–70 *TAC*

A Studio paperweight, by Isle of Wight Glass Co, 1960–70s, 4¾in (12cm) high.
£35–45 *TAC*

A Baccarat paperweight/ashtray, with nude figure, c1920, 4½in (11.5cm) long.
£100–135 *MJW*

A Strathearn large leaf green millefiori and latticino star weight, 1964–80, 3in (7.5cm) diam.
£35–45 *TAC*

A Whitefriars amber-bubbled paperweight, 1960s, 2¾in (7cm) diam.
£25–35 *TAC*

A faceted paperweight, with engraving of a ship's wheel and blue overlay, by Webb Corbett, 1960, 2¾in (7cm) diam.
£35–45 *TAC*

Wedgwood Glass

A Wedgwood brown and cream trout paperweight, 1970, 7½in (19cm) long.
£15–20 *SWB*

A Wedgwood paperweight, with bust of Lord Mountbatten of Burma, 1970, 3in (7.5cm) diam.
£55–65 *SWB*

A Wedgwood pink frog paperweight, 1970, 4½in (11.5cm) high.
£20–25 *SWB*

r. A Wedgwood elephant paperweight, 1967–83, 3½in (9cm) high.
£25–30 *SWB*

l. A Wedgwood jasper medallion paperweight, with a horse in lead crystal with star-cut base and fluted sides, 1970, 3in (7.5cm) diam.
£35–45 *SWB*

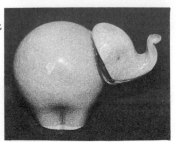

A Wedgwood jasper medallion paperweight, with the head of Julius Caesar in lead crystal, 1970, 3¼in (8.5cm) diam.
£55–65 *SWB*

A Wedgwood clear glass paperweight, with seagull, 1970, 4½in (11.5cm) high.
£15–20 *SWB*

A Wedgwood Christmas paperweight, 1984, 4in (10cm) high.
£25–30 *SWB*

A Wedgwood clear glass polar bear paperweight, 1970, 5in (12.5cm) long.
£20–25 *SWB*

Vases

A Wedgwood dog-shaped paperweight, 1970, 3½in (9cm) high.
£30–40 *SWB*

A Wedgwood green penguin paperweight, 1970, 4½in (11.5cm) high.
£25–35 *SWB*

A hand-painted cranberry glass flower vase, c1880, 8½in (20cm) high.
£45–65 *AnS*

A blue opalescent glass hyacinth vase, c1880, 6½in (16.5cm) high.
£40–50 *AnS*

A Victorian pink cased-glass posy vase, with butterfly decoration, c1880, 8¾in (22cm) high.
£345–385 *MJW*

A vaseline glass vase, with moulded decoration, c1890, 7½in (19cm) high.
£300–350 *MJW*

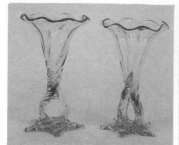

A pair of cranberry glass vases, 19thC, 5½in (14cm) high.
£120–160 *PSA*

A Victorian 'Jack in the pulpit' vase, 7in (18cm) high.
£35–45 *AnS*

l. A pink cranberry glass vase, c1880, 5½in (14cm) high.
£125–145 *AnS*

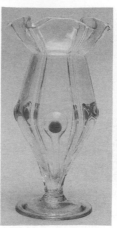

A Webb Peacock ware glass vase, with green spot decoration, c1900, 6½in (16.5cm) high.
£70–90 *MJW*

A glass hyacinth vase, with combed decoration, c1900, 7¾in (19.5cm) high.
£95–115 *MJW*

A Czechoslovakian amber pressed-glass flower trough, c1931, 8in (20.5cm) wide.
£10–15 *BKK*

Miller's is a price GUIDE not a price LIST

An amber glass hyacinth vase, c1910, 5in (12.5cm) high.
£12–16 *CaL*

A Czechoslovakian amber pressed-glass penguin bowl, with plinth, c1929, 13in (33cm) diam.
£65–75 *BKK*

A Jobling pale green glass vase, 1930s, 7¾in (20cm).
£85–95 *BEV*

A coral and clear glass bottle vase, signed, No.4420, 1995, 5¼in (13cm) high.
£35–40 *GLA*

A Gray-Stan purple and white glass vase, with everted rim, engraved signature, c1930, 12in (30.5cm) high.
£280–320 *CMO*

A Gray-Stan green glass vase, with engraved signature, 1930s, 11½in (30cm) high.
£250–300 *CMO*

GRAMOPHONES & TAPE RECORDERS

An Edison home phonograph, with Model C reproducer, 56in (142cm) long brass horn and original gilt floorstand, c1904.
£900–1,000 *BTA*

An Edison opera phonograph, No. 2763, with Model L reproducer, transversing mandrel, mahogany case and lid, part of horn, c1905.
£2,200–2,600 *P(Ba)*

A Colombia Type AA graphophone, with Colombia reproducer, black and brass 'witches hat' horn and Dulcetto retailer's transfer, c1904, 10½in (27cm) wide.
£280–350 *BTA*

An HMV Intermediate Monarch wind-up gramophone, with laminated wood horn and mahogany case, Reg No. 557674, c1910, 14in (35.5cm) square.
£1,400–1,600 *RBB*

A Gramophone and Typewriter Junior Monarch, with single spring motor, No. 5A soundbox, in oak case, with repainted blue morning glory horn, c1910, 18¼in (46.5cm).
£600–700 *P(Ba)*

An HMV Model IV, with oak case and horn, and exhibition soundbox, c1910, 30in (76cm) high.
£2,000–2,500 *BTA*

A Peter Pan folding portable gramophone, in the form of a box camera, with 4-spoke turntable, Peter Pan soundbox, in a black case, c1920.
£400–500 *P(Ba)*

A Symphony Victory Green Horn gramophone, with exhibition soundbox, single spring motor, and oak case, c1905.
£450–550 *P(Ba)*

A Peter Pan folding portable gramophone, in the form of a camera, with Peter Pan soundbox, c1926, 12in (30.5cm) wide.
£250–300 *BTA*

l. An HMV Model 193 gramophone, with No. 5 soundbox, exponential horn and oak case, c1927, 44¼in (112.5cm) high.
£2,800–3,500 *BTA*

r. An HMV Model 145 gramophone, with No. 5A soundbox, exponential horn and mahogany case, c1927, 34¼in (87cm) high.
£300–350 *BTA*

Three HMV portable gramophones, 2 Model 102, with 5B soundboxes and one Model 101 with No. 4 soundbox, c1930, 20in (51cm) high.
£120–150 each *BTA*

A Stuzzi battery tape recorder, Austrian, 1959, 10⅜in (27.5cm) wide.
£12–15 *JON*

A Clystal battery tape recorder, Japanese, 1960, 8¼in (21cm) wide.
£10–15 *JON*

A Miny tape recorder, Japanese, 1960s, 8in (20.5cm) wide.
£10–15 *JON*

A Steelman tape recorder, American, 1960s, 7in (18cm) wide.
£10–15 *JON*

An Aiwa TP30 battery tape recorder, Japanese, 1960, 9in (23cm) wide.
£5–10 *JON*

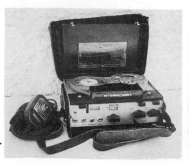

r. A Fi-Cord 202A battery tape recorder, 1966, 9in (23cm) wide.
£15–20 *JON*

A Western Electric Dynamic microphone, with reproduction BBC label, 1946, 3¼in (8cm) diam.
£90–100 *JON*

GUINNESS

These days Guinness certainly can be good for you, especially when it comes to collectables. At a recent auction at Christie's South Kensington devoted to Guinness memorabilia, prices reached double the original estimates and achieved a total of nearly £85,000. Guinness was first brewed over two hundred years ago at the St James's Gate Brewery in Dublin, the drink named after owner Arthur Guinness (1725–1803). It was not until 1928, however, that the firm began advertising and their subsequent campaigns were to produce some of the most distinctive advertising of the century.

The first Guinness advertisement was produced in the form of the poster, carrying the now famous slogan 'Guinness is Good for You'. Over the years Guinness were to employ many celebrated illustrators ranging from Ronald Searle, to H. M. Bateman to John Gilroy (1898–1985). Gilroy produced the first 'Man with the Girder' poster in 1934 and devised a number of brilliant, and highly collectable, posters using animal themes. In 1936 the toucan was introduced into Guinness promotions providing a famous image and another celebrated slogan, surprisingly created by Dorothy L. Sayers, better known as a crime novelist but then working for the advertising company S. H. Benson, 'How Grand to be a Toucan just think what Toucan do'.

In the 1950s Guinness commissioned Carlton to produce advertising ceramics, resulting in many items including toucan lamps and flying toucan wall plaques, the birds balancing pints of Guinness on their prodigious beaks. A huge variety of Guinness material has been produced over the years, encompassing many forms and media. While at the lower end of the market much is still available for under £20, early posters, unusual items and the best Carlton Ware ceramics can now fetch hundreds of pounds.

l. A Carlton Ware advertising lamp base, in the form of a toucan and a pint of Guinness, decorated in coloured enamels, on a titled oval mound base, printed mark in black and GA/2178, c1958, 9½in (24cm) high.
£340–380 *DN*

A Guinness's Extra Stout ashtray, 1930s, 5in (13cm) long.
£15–20 *OD*

Cross Reference
Colour Review

r. A wooden clothes brush, in the form of a Guinness Extra Stout bottle, 1950s, 8in (20.5cm) high.
£14–17 *HUX*

A tin tray, with multi-coloured picture of bandsmen playing horns, and Guinness for strength, 1950s, 10½in (27cm) diam.
£24–28 *BBR*

An oblong tin tray, with multi-coloured picture of a zoo keeper and kangaroo with a bottle of beer in its pouch, and My Goodness, My Guinness, 1950s, 16in (40.5cm) long.
£25–35 *BBR*

A Guinness Time electric clock, plastic with chrome metal top, 1950s, 17in (43cm) high.
£110–130 *BBR*

A Guinness Time pocket watch, the dial with subsidiary seconds and automated toucan, with keyless lever movement, signed Ingersoll, late 1950s.
£300–350 *Bea*

A Guinness calendar, from a campaign by Allen, Brady & Marsh, c1983.
£8–12 *DW*

An original gouache design, by John Gilroy, signed and dated '1947', 14½ x 11½in, (36.5 x 29cm), together with a copy of the printed advertisement.
£3,300–4,000 *CSK*

Posters & Signs

A lithograph poster in colours, by N. R. Price, printed by Wickham Displays Limited, London, minor creases, c1938, 30 x 20in (76 x 51cm).
£225–275 *CSK*

A lithograph poster in colours, by F. C. Harrison, printed by John Waddington Ltd, Leeds, minor damage, 1942, 59¾ x 40in (152 x 102cm).
£425–475 *CSK*

A lithograph poster in colours, printed by Sanders, Phillips & Co Ltd, London, minor damage, c1950, 30 x 40in (76 x 102cm).
£280–320 *CSK*

r. A lithograph poster in colours, by John Gilroy, printed by Mills & Rockleys (Production) Ltd, Ipswich, 1959, 30 x 20in (76 x 51cm).
£200–250 *CSK*

l. A plastic-covered multi-coloured tin sign, 1950s, 12 x 8in (30.5 x 20.5cm).
£85–100 *BBR*

A lithograph poster in colours, by R. Pepé, minor damage, c1962, 61 x 41in (155 x 104cm).
£240–280 *CSK*

A Guinness rubberoid bar-top figure, 1940s, 6½in (16.5cm) high.
£70–80 *HUX*

A poster, c1938, 30 x 20in (76 x 51cm).
£420–460 *CSK*

A poster, 1956, 60 x 40in (152 x 102cm).
£300–350 *CSK*

A poster, c1940, 60 x 40in (152 x 102cm).
£600–700 *CSK*

Three Carlton Ware wall plaques, modelled as flying toucans, printed factory marks, c1957, largest 9¼in (23.5cm) wide.
£750–850 *CSK*

A Carlton Ware Guinness mug, c1930, 3¾in (9.5cm) high. **£40–48** *BSA*

A lithograph poster, 1936, 60 x 40in (152 x 102cm).
£475–575 *CSK*

Under the spreading chestnut-tree
A glass of Guinness stood.
The smith, a mightier man is he—
His Guinness did him good.
And would it do the same for me?
My Guinness, yes it would!

A Guinness lithograph poster, backed on linen, 1938, 30 x 80in (76 x 203cm).
£440–500 *CSK*

r. A plastic walking pengiun, 1950s, 3in (7.5cm) high.
£25–30 *HUX*

A full set of Guinness buttons, 1940–50s, ½in (10mm) diam.
£58–68 *PSA*

A Carlton Ware toucan, 1940s, 4½in (11.5cm) high.
£35–45 *BGA*

A Guinness lighter, 1960s, 4in (10cm) high.
£20–25 *HUX*

A Guinness aneroid barometer, 1950s, 8in (20.5cm) diam.
£40–50 *OD*

A late Victorian 18ct gold oval locket, c1900, 1¾in (45mm) long.
£3,000–5,000 *PC*

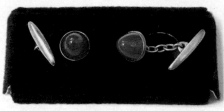

A pair of silver and cornelian cuff links, 1920s, ½in (10mm) diam.
£50–60 *JBB*

An American 'whimsy' brooch, 1920s, 2½in (65mm) wide.
£50–75 *PGH*

An enamel necklace, 1920s, 16in (40.5cm) long.
£100–125 *FMN*

An American brooch, set with rhinestones, 1920s, 2½in (65mm) wide.
£80–100 *BaH*

Two American Christmas brooches, 1930s, 1½in (40mm) wide.
£40–50 each *PGH*

A pair of American earrings and a brooch, signed 'Trifari', brooch 2½in (65mm) wide. **£120–150** *BaH*

An American enamel and gold-plated Christmas brooch, 1930s, 2¼in (55mm).
£50–60 *PGH*

An American rhinestone and gold-plated Christmas tree brooch, 1930s, 2¼in (55mm) wide.
£70–90 *BaH*

An American mother-of-pearl and rhinestone clip brooch, 1930s, 3in (75mm) long.
£120–150 *BaH*

An American fish brooch, set with rhinestones, 1930s, 2in (50mm) wide.
£50–60 *PGH*

A Lucite necklace, with pendants in the form of dice, 1930s, 18in (45.5cm) long.
£55–65 *TCF*

An American pin brooch, set with rhinestones, 1930s, 2½in (65mm) wide.
£50–65 *BaH*

An American bracelet, set with *faux* turquoise stones on a gilt mount, 1940s, 7in (18cm) long. **£70–90** *PGH*

An American bracelet, set with rhinestones, *faux* pearls, coral and turquoises, in gilt mount, 1950s, 7½in (19cm) long. **£90–110** *BaH*

Two American strawberry pin brooches, set with rhinestones on enamelled gilt mounts, 1940s, 1½in (40mm) long. **£40–60 each** *PGH*

An American brooch/pendant, signed 'Avon', 1950s, 2¼in (60mm) diam. **£50–60** *BaH*

An American Art Deco enamel on gilt bird brooch, 1930s, 3in (75mm) high. **£50–75** *BaH*

A pair of pink and green plastic bead earrings, 1950s, 1½in (40mm) long. **£12–16** *PSA*

A pair of plastic earrings, 1950s, 2¾in (70mm) long. **£12–15** *PSA*

An American brooch and pair of earrings, set with glass and rhinestones on gold-plated mounts, 1950s, brooch 3in (75mm) wide. **£90–120** *PGH*

A sterling silver brooch, set with Roman glass fragments, c1990, 2¼in (55mm) wide. **£100–130** *JFG*

An American gold-plated necklace, signed 'Napier', 1960s, 17in (43cm) long. **£85–110** *PGH*

A gold-plated Christmas tree brooch, with *faux* stones, 1960s, 2in (50mm) high. **£35–50** *PGH*

A sugar tin, 1930s,
6in (15cm) high.
£10–12 *AL*

A kettle on stand, 1930s,
11in (28cm) high.
£80–95 *TAC*

An enamel Willow pattern teapot,
1920s, 7in (18cm) high.
£55–65 *Ber*

A ceramic toast rack, 1950s,
6in (15cm) long.
£6–8 *TAC*

Two ceramic shakers, for flour and
sugar, 1920s, 5½in (14cm) high.
£15–20 each *AL*

A Cornish Kitchen Ware
flour jar, black shield mark,
8in (20.5cm) high.
£40–45 *AL*

Four Cornish Kitchen Ware storage jars,
black shield marks, 1930s, 5in (12.5cm) high.
£30–35 *AL*

A Cornish Kitchen Ware rolling pin, with
wooden handles, 1930s, 18in (45.5cm) long.
£25–30 *AL*

A ceramic sugar shaker,
1920s, 5½in (14cm) high.
£16–18 *AL*

A Cornish Kitchen Ware catalogue and
price list, 1936–37, 24in (61cm) wide.
£15–20 *PC*

A milk bottle carrier, c1970,
9½in (24cm) wide.
£6–8 *BGA(R)*

A Victorian brass binnacle lamp, 5¼in (13cm) high.
£70–90 *PC*

A Victorian candle sconce, with original mirror, 19thC, 11in (28cm) high.
£100–125 *LIB*

A Victorian glass night light, 7in (18cm) high.
£100–120 *ML*

A Webb's Burmese ware glass night light, c1880, 9½in (24cm) high.
£1,000–1,200 *PC*

A Victorian bronzed-brass ceiling light, with original shade, 14in (35.5cm) high.
£210–260 *ML*

A brass swan neck wall lamp, with glass shade, c1890, 15in (38cm) wide.
£100–125 *LIB*

A French brass hanging oil lamp, with matching shade fount and smoke bell, 19thC, 24in (61cm) high.
£250–300 *LIB*

A pair of gilded-spelter ceiling lights, c1880, 11in (28cm) high.
£500–600 *ML*

A French electric lamp, in the form of a copper-gilt bowl with glass fruit, c1890, 15in (38cm) wide.
£850–1,200 *PC*

A Baccarat glass millefiori boudoir lamp, c1890, 11in (28cm) high.
£1,000–1,500 *PC*

A French illuminated hanging lamp, modelled as a bunch of grapes, c1910, 8½in (21.5cm) long.
£120–140 *ML*

Two green glass oil lamps, 1920s, 4½in (11.5cm) high.
£8–10 each *ML*

A table lamp, with matching shade, 1930s, 11½in (29cm) high.
£48–58 *ML*

An Oriental porcelain table lamp, c1910, 16¼in (41.5cm) high.
£150–200 *ML*

A stained glass lantern, 1930s, 9in (23cm) high.
£90–110 *LIB*

A pair of oak lamps, c1930, with Victorian hand-painted shades, 10in (25.5cm) high.
£115–135 *ML*

l. A pair of Oriental pierced brass wall shades, 1930s, 11in (28cm) high.
£60–75 *LIB*

An Art Nouveau brass table lamp, with beaded shade, c1920, 24in (61cm) high.
£300–360 *ML*

A crackle glass globe ceiling light, with chrome fitting, 1930s, 8½in (21.5cm) high.
£60–80 *ML*

A Glasform iridescent lamp-shade, c1995, 8in (20.5cm) high.
£25–30 *GLA*

A travelling iron, in leather case, c1910, 4¾in (12cm) wide.
£40–48 *WAB*

A naval hat tin, printed with name of original owner and period travel and hotel labels, c1900, 17in (43cm) wide.
£100–135 *RIS*

A leather hat case, c1920, with labels, 24in (61cm) wide.
£75–95 *AXT*

A canvas case, with original airline and cruise labels, 1950s, 21in (53.5cm) wide.
£40–45 *RIS*

A canvas and leather hat box, with brass fittings, and Cunard Line *Queen Elizabeth* label, 1920s, 18in (45.5cm) wide.
£100–125 *RIS*

A picnic hamper, with original fittings, c1920, 21in (53.5cm) wide. **£80–100** *AL*

A French enamel lunch tin, 1950s, 6in (15cm) wide.
£15–18 *TaB*

A shaving set, in Bakelite box, c1930–40s, 3½in (9cm) wide.
£12–15 *FAM*

A gentleman's razor, in tin box, 1940s, 3in (7.5cm) wide.
£4–6 *FAM*

l. A Gillette razor, with original box, 1940s, 3½in (9cm) wide.
£6–8 *FAM*

r. Five razor blade packets, with contents, 1940s, 2in (5cm) long.
40–50p each *FAM*

A Victorian embossed-brass cutlery box,
registration mark for 22nd November, 1878
on each panel, 15½in (40cm) long.
£200–225 *PSA*

Three Victorian butter knives, *top* silver-
plated. **£12–15** *c.* silver with mother-of-pearl
handle, Birmingham 1873. **£40–50** *bottom*
silver-plated with ivory handle. **£17–20** *TAC*

A set of silver teaspoons and sugar nips,
Sheffield 1902, box 10¼in (26cm) wide.
£90–110 *ABr*

A set of 6 Victorian silver and
gilt Apostle spoons, tongs and
tea strainer, London 1896,
box 6¼in (16cm) wide.
£155–185 *HEI*

A set of 6 silver Apostle
spoons, with twist stems,
Birmingham 1900,
3¾in (9.5cm) long.
£55–65 *PSA*

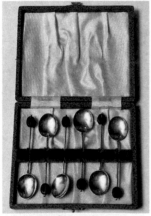

A set of 6 silver coffee spoons,
Birmingham 1938, 3½in (9cm) long.
£50–60 *ABr*

A silver-plated jam
spoon, 1920s,
6in (15cm) long.
£12–15 *FMN*

A brass hot water can, 19thC,
11in (28cm) high.
£45–55 *BSA*

l. A silver-plated
muffin dish, design by
C. R. Ashbee, c1900,
9in (23cm) diam.
£1,000–1,250 *SHa*

r. A silver teapot, with
inscription, 1882,
5in (12.5cm) high.
£300–400 *PC*

A Victorian silver-backed hair brush, Birmingham 1894, 9½in (24cm) long.
£24–28 *ABr*

A silver-backed dressing table hand mirror, Birmingham 1902, 11in (28cm) long.
£75–85 *ABr*

A pair of Victorian hair curling tongs, with brass handles, 9½in (24cm) long.
£10–15 *OD*

A silver-backed crumb brush, Birmingham 1904, 12½in (32cm) long.
£25–30 *OBS*

A pair of silver-backed clothes brushes, Birmingham 1932, 6in (15cm) long.
£30–40 *ABr*

An oval brass photograph frame, late 19thC, 4¾in (12cm) high.
£80–100 *MSB*

A pair of W. A. S. Benson copper and brass candlesticks, c1880, 7½in (19cm) high.
£550–650 *SHa*

A pair of fireplace ornaments, modelled as buttoned boots, c1890, 5½in (14cm) high.
£22–30 *OD*

A brass paperweight/ card holder, 1900s, 2½in (6.5cm) long.
£80–90 *OD*

A Liberty pewter biscuit box, design by Archibald Knox, c1905, 6in (15cm) high.
£450–500 *NCA*

A Mauchline type money box, German, late 19thC, 3½in (9cm) high.
£25–35 *IW*

A book-shaped tin money bank, by Chad Valley, 1930s, 5¾in (14.5cm) high.
£65–85 *MSB*

A tin money bank, in the form of a soldier firing at a bottle, 1950s, 8½in (21.5cm) long. **£55–65** *MSB*

A tin money bank, in the form of a cash register, by World Metal Stamping Co, USA, 1930–40s, 3in (7.5cm) high.
£65–85 *MSB*

A tin money bank, by Louis Marx & Co, 1940s, 4in (10cm) high. **£60–80** *MSB*

l. A bank note jigsaw puzzle, 1994, 26¾ x 18¾in (68 x 48.5cm).
£8–10 *WP*

A steel and copper bank money shovel, with wooden handle, 1930s, 12in (30.5cm) long.
£18–22 *WAB*

A Bank of England sealing wax box, with original wax, 1930s, 12in (30.5cm) long.
£8–10 *WP*

A Bradbury first type ten shillings note, 1914.
£150–200 *WP*

A Britannia lion and key five pounds note, issued 1957. **£20–22** *WP*

A Nanking cargo soup dish, decorated with Three Pavilions pattern, c1750, 9in (23cm) diam.
£350–400 *RBA*

A Chinese Imari pattern tea caddy, 18thC, 4in (10cm) high.
£80–90 *PC*

A Diana cargo blue and white bowl, c1816, 6½in (16.5cm) diam.
£140–190 *RBA*

A pair of Chinese bamboo brush pots, 19thC, 7in (18cm) high.
£100–150 *ORI*

A Nanking cargo Fence pattern tureen, c1750, 10¼in (26cm) high.
£5,000–6,000 *RBA*

A Chinese birdcage, c1920, 14in (35.5cm) high.
£100–150 *PC*

A French electric pig shocker amusement machine, 1898, 29in (73.5cm) high.
£15,000–17,000 *PC*

A ceramic money box, Mr Pig, by Ellgreave, England, 1920s, 9in (23cm) high,
£85–95 *GEM*

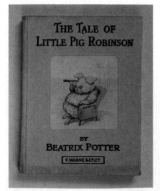

Beatrix Potter, *The Tale of Little Pig Robinson*, published by F. Warne & Co Ltd, 1964.
£15–20 *NW*

A Loetz glass posy holder, in the shape of a pig, c1900, 7½in (19cm) long.
£800–900 *JES*

A Wade Heath jug, depicting Walt Disney's Three Little Pigs, 1934, 10½in (26.5cm) high.
£400–500 *TOY*

Two Goebels ceramic pigs, 1960s, largest 2in (5cm) high.
£12–14 each *TAC*

r. A complete set of Wade money boxes, given away by National Westminster bank when a child opened an account and at various savings targets, c1982, Sir Nathaniel, 7½in (19cm) high. **£40–50** Woody (in nappy). **£15–20** Others. **£25–40 each** *PC*

A tin decorated with a pig, c1900, 2in (5cm) long.
£25–30 *YC*

A Marutomo ware child's tea set, Japanese, 1920–30s, teapot 3½in (9cm) high.
£75–85 *BEV*

P. G. Wodehouse, *Pigs Have Wings,* published by Herbert Jenkins, first edition, 1952.
£60–80 *NW*

A Medina mushroom paperweight, signed, 1950–90s, 3½in (9cm) high. **£12–15** *TAC*

A Glasform peacock's eye paperweight, signed by John Ditchfield, 1982, 3½in (9cm) diam. **£90–100** *GLA*

A Strathearn millefiori and latticinio paperweight, 1964–80, 2¾in (7cm) diam. **£35–45** *TAC*

Four sets of Glasform decorative glass apple paperweights, 1995, largest 6½in (16.5cm) high. **£8–28 each set** *GLA*

A Wedgwood glass paperweight, in the form of a dolphin, 1970, 7in (18cm) long. **£30–35** *SWB*

A French Punchinello puppet,
19thC, original silk costume,
24in (61cm) high.
£400–500 *CWA*

A ventriloquist's dummy,
c1910, 43in (109cm) high.
£120–150 *AXT*

A fairground rod puppet,
with a bell in her head,
c1900, 20in (51cm) high.
£150–200 *PaM*

A Pelham string
puppet, from Pinky
and Perky, 1970s,
9in (23cm) high.
£35–45 *PaM*

A Pelham guitarist
string puppet, 1970s,
12in (30.5cm) high,
original yellow box.
£45–55 *PaM*

A Pelham Huckleberry
Hound string puppet,
1970s, 9in (23cm) high,
original yellow box.
£60–70 *PaM*

A Pelham wolf string
puppet, 1970s, 14in
(35.5cm) high, no box.
£45–55 *PaM*

A Pelham string puppet,
c1950, 13in (33cm) high,
original box.
£30–40 *ARo*

A Pelham Thunderbirds
puppet, 1970s,
12in (30.5cm) high.
£25–30 *HUX*

A Pelham baby dragon string
puppet, 1970–80s, 9in (23cm)
high, no box.
£45–55 *PaM*

A GEC Home Broadcaster, unused, 1930s, 8in (20.5cm) wide. **£60–80** *ET*

A Murphy A122 valve radio, 1948, 22in (56cm) wide. **£40–80** *GM*

A GEC BC4940 Bakelite valve radio, 1948, 16in (41cm) wide. **£70–120** *GM*

A Roberts Model RT–8 radio, c1961, 9½in (24cm) high. **£25–30** *PC*

A Perdio Carnival radio, c1962, 7in (18cm) high. **£30–35** *PC*

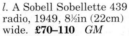

l. A Sobell Sobellette 439 radio, 1949, 8½in (22cm) wide. **£70–110** *GM*

An Internet Model S–100 radio, with box, 1960s, 4½in (11.5cm) high. **£15–20** *PC*

An Ekco portable radio, in red case, c1960, 6½in (16.5cm) high. **£20–30** *PC*

A Gaiety radio, with box and accessories, c1965, 4in (10cm) high. **£15–25** *PC*

A Cossor valve battery portable radio, 1956, 10¼in (26cm) wide. **£30–50** *GM*

A '57 Chevy radio/cassette player, c1975, 9in (23cm) high. **£50–70** *PC*

A Roberts Model R200 radio, 1961, 4in (10cm) high.
£25–40 *PC*

A Hacker Herald transistor radio, c1965, 11¼in (29cm) wide.
£25–50 *GM*

A National Mickey Mouse radio, c1975, 3in (7.5cm) high.
£25–40 *PC*

An RGD Model R100 radio, c1975, 4in (10cm) high.
£10–15 *PC*

A Philips Moving Sound portable cassette player, 1980s, 6in (15cm) high.
£15–20 *PC*

A National Panasonic bangle radio, 1970s.
£45–65 *Bon*

A 'Hamburger' novelty radio, with controls on the side, 1980s, 5in (13cm) diam.
£10–20 *PC*

A Systral radio, modelled as the word 'RADIO', 1970s, 9in (23cm) wide.
£75–95 *Bon*

A Tomy radio robot, Mr DJ, 1990s, 7in (18cm) high.
£30–40 *PC*

A Bush clock radio, c1975, 14in (35.5cm) high.
£20–30 *PC*
Produced as a kitchen wall clock.

A Ekco TMB 272 battery/mains portable televison, 1956, 13¾in (35cm) high.
£40–100 *GM*

A selection of televison screen magnifiers, c1950, largest 16in (40.5cm) wide.
£10–40 each *ET*

JEWELLERY

Much of the following section focuses on costume jewellery. From the 1920s–30s onwards manufacture of costume jewellery flourished in the USA. Hollywood was an important influence and the fact that movies showed stars bedecked in fabulous fakes helped costume jewellery become acceptable even for the most elegant of women. Film stars wore costume jewellery on as well as off the screen; fashion luminaries such as Diana Vreeland, editor of *Harpers* and *Queen*, then *Vogue*, formed major collections of fashion jewellery, whilst an eminent fan in the 1950s was First Lady 'Mamie' Eisenhower who wore a simulated pearl choker by the American firm of Trifari for the President's Inaugural Ball in 1953.

With the best costume jewellery, though the stones might have been imitation, standards of manufacture were often extremely high. Many of the designers – often émigrés to the USA – had trained with 'real' jewellers, such as Cartier or Van Cleef & Arpels. Top quality rhinestones were used, labour-intensive processes were developed to give pearls their lustre and diamanté its glitter. Pieces were even set in sterling silver, especially during WWII when there was a ban on employing metals that could be used in the war industry.

Today there is a developing market for costume jewellery ranging from the fantasies of the Art Deco period, to the plastic creations of the 1970s. Signed works by major names command a premium (check necklace clasps, earring backs and the reverse of brooches), though many good quality pieces can also be unmarked.

Bracelets

A gold bracelet, set with 133 garnets, c1860, 6½in (16.5cm) long.
£1,000–1,200 *PC*

A Danish bracelet and matching earrings, by From, marked, 20thC, bracelet 7in (18.5cm) long.
£200–250 *P*

A René Lalique red glass bracelet, Poussins, with 15 plaques each moulded with chicks heads, linked by elasticated cord, signed twice on edge, c1920.
£2,200–2,500 *P*

A Murrle Bennet enamelled bracelet, with 7 plaques each cast as a Viking ship decorated with green and blue enamelling, stamped with M B & Co monogram and No. 950, c1900.
£475–550 *P*

A white rhinestone bracelet, with rhodium setting, unsigned, 1930s, 8in (20.5cm) long.
£60–80 *PGH*

An American bracelet, set with blue rhinestones and foil-backed composite stones on rhodium, 1940s, 8in (20.5cm) long.
£120–180 *PGH*

An American bracelet, with gilded flowers on silver-plated rhodium, signed 'Linc', 1940s, 3in (7.5cm) wide.
£60–80 *PGH*

An American Art Deco sterling silver bracelet, with copper lilies, signed 'Nye', 1930s, 2½in (65mm) wide.
£80–120 *PGH*

An American bracelet, set with blue stones on fine mesh gilded chains, 1950s, 7½in (19cm) long.
£85–110 *PGH*

An American bracelet, set with enamel on gilt leaves, signed 'Trifari', 1950s, 7½in (19cm) long.
£75–90 *PGH*

A silver charm bracelet, with 6 charms including 2 opening caravans, 1950s–60s.
£30–40 *BGA*

Five silver charms, for fitting to a bracelet, 20thC, largest ¾in (20mm) high.
£8–10 each *TAC*

Three onyx and cornelian bangles, 1960s, 3½in (9cm) diam.
£50–75 each *PGH*

l. An American bracelet, with composite bars on gilded setting, signed 'Monet', 1960s, 7in (18cm) long.
£65–80 *PGH*

Brooches

r. Three silver name brooches, Annie, Pollie and Eliza, c1880, 1½in (35mm) diam.
£45–65 each *FMN*

l. A Guild of Handicraft Ltd brooch, with large faceted amethyst, c1900, 1¼in (30mm) wide.
£425–475 *P*

r. A Ruskin turquoise ceramic brooch, set in pewter, early 20thC, 1¾in (45mm) wide.
£30–40 *SnA*

A Victorian silver name brooch, Kate, 1¾in (45mm) wide.
£65–75 *FMN*

Brooches with names that are still popular today, ie, Kate, Anne or Rose, fetch higher prices than those showing names that have fallen from fashion, ie, Mildred or Agnes.

An Arts & Crafts cornelian and silver brooch, c1900, 1¼in (30mm) wide.
£40–60 *GOO*

A George Hunt Arts & Crafts brooch, depicting a bridge, river and trees in naturalistic colours, within a wirework mount, signed 'G.H.' and dated '1920', 1½in (40mm) wide.
£525–600 *P*

An Arts & Crafts brooch, designed and made by Edgar Simpson, with abalone plaques, marked, late 19th/early 20thC, 3¾in (9.5cm) wide.
£950–1,100 *P*

r. An Unger Brothers Art Nouveau brooch, depicting the head of a girl in high relief, stamped 'Sterling', c1900, 3in (7.5cm) long, with fitted box.
£450–550 *P*

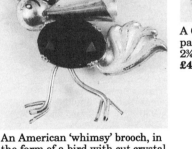

An American 'whimsy' brooch, in the form of a bird with cut crystal body on enamelled copper, 1920s, 2½in (65mm) wide.
£50–75 *PGH*

r. An American floral brooch, with green rhinestones on enamelled florets and stem, 1920s, 2¾in (70mm) high.
£45–60 *PGH*

A Liberty & Co oval brooch, probably designed by Jessie M. King, unmarked, and an oval moonstone brooch, possibly retailed through Liberty & Co, unmarked, c1900, 1¼in (30mm) wide.
£130–160 *P*

A Czechoslovakian filigree and paste pin brooch, early 1900s, 2¾in (70mm) wide.
£40–50 *SnA*

A silver-plated name brooch, Janey, 1920s, 2in (50mm) wide.
£20–25 *FMN*

Two Spratts brooches, Nelson Products, Birmingham, 1920s, 1½in (40mm) wide.
£10–15 each *REN*

A Bakelite flower brooch,
1920s, 2in (50mm) diam.
£35–50 *PGH*

An American Art Deco brooch, set with
pink rhinestones and cut lavender
stones, 1930s, 2½in (65mm) high.
£80–100 *PGH*

An American brooch, by
Weiss, with amber and ruby
rhinestones, set with *faux*
pearls, with crown and fleche
rhodium mount, 1930s,
2in (50mm) wide.
£90–150 *PGH*

An American clip
brooch, with pink
and blue crystals in
hand-worked brass
setting, 1920s,
2½in (65mm) long.
£75–100 *BaH*

An American butterfly pin
brooch, with white
rhinestones set on a rhodium
metal setting, unsigned,
1930s, 1¼in (30mm) wide.
£40–60 *PGH*

An American brooch, in the form
of a minstrel with 'jelly belly'
face, rhinestones and Lucite on
copper, 1930s, 3½in (9cm) high.
£150–200 *PGH*

l. An American
leaf brooch, set
with amber
rhinestones on a
gold-plated
setting, 1930s,
2¼in (55mm) wide.
£45–60 *PGH*

An American brooch, set with
white glass stones, rhinestones
and cut crystals on a rhodium
setting, 1930s, 2½in (65mm) wide.
£75–90 *PGH*

An American pin
brooch, with enamel
flowers on a gilt
setting, 1930s,
3½in (9cm) high.
£50–60 *BaH*

l. An American pin brooch, set as
entwined coils with turquoises
and auror borrealis rhinestones,
1940s, 2in (50mm) diam.
£45–65 *BaH*

An American pin brooch, set with azure crystals, rhinestones, and agate gemstones on gilt, 1940s, 2½in (65mm) high.
£80–120 *BaH*

An American brooch and earrings set, by Botticelli, hand-crafted from rhodium metal in the form of leaves, 1940s, brooch 3½in (9cm) long.
£80–100 *PGH*

A floral silver-plated brooch, with amethyst and clear rhinestones, 1940s, 2in (50mm) high.
£50–60 *PGH*

An American flower pin brooch, set with blue rhinestones and crystal leaves on a gilded mount, 1940s, 2¾in (70mm) high.
£50–75 *BaH*

Miller's is a price GUIDE not a price LIST

An American turtle brooch, with cut crystal body and eyes on gold-plated setting, 1940s, 3in (7.5cm) wide.
£90–120 *PGH*

A Balle enamelled brooch, embossed with scrolls, heightened with areas of colour enamels, possibly Scandinavian, marked 'Balle' and '925S', 1950s.
£100–120 *P*

Christmas Brooches

Two American gold-plated Christmas brooches, modelled as reindeer, with ruby rhinestones, 1920s, 2½in (65mm) high.
£60–75 each *BaH*

An American Christmas tree brooch, with rhinestones on a rhodium setting, 1930s, 3in (7.5cm) high.
£70–80 *PGH*

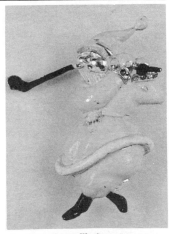

An American Christmas Santa brooch, enamel on gold-plated setting, 1930s, 2½in (65mm) high.
£70–80 *PGH*

Crown Jewels

A tiara, with *faux* diamonds, coloured stones and imitation pearls, 1924, 6in (15cm) diam.
£300–350 *JBB*

A tiara, with *faux* diamonds, 1924, 5½in (14cm) diam.
£550–600 *JBB*

In 1924 Christie's sold a collection of Russian crown jewels. These copies were made for display and to publicise the sale.

A tiara, with *faux* diamonds, imitation rubies and baroque pearls, 1924, 6¼in (16cm) diam.
£350–400 *JBB*

Cuff Links

A pair of 9ct gold cuff links Chester, c1888, ¾in (20mm) long.
£45–65 *TAC*

A pair of 9ct gold cuff links, Chester 1868, ¾in (20mm) long.
£22–38 *TAC*

A pair of 9ct gold cuff links, Birmingham 1852, ½in (15mm) wide.
£45–65 *TAC*

Cuff links first appeared in the Victorian era when white shirts with long sleeves and starched cuffs were worn.

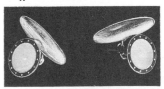

A pair of 9ct gold cuff links, Chester, c1923, ¾in (20mm) wide.
£50–60 *TAC*

A pair of 15ct gold, enamel and mother-of-pearl cuff links, c1900, ½in (15mm) diam.
£120–140 *JBB*

A pair of 14ct gold cuff links, with diamond centres, 1940s, ¾in (20mm) wide.
£125–150 *JBB*

A pair of silver hand-painted cuff links, depicting pin-up girls, 1950s, ¾in (20mm) wide.
£175–225 *JBB*

A pair of American gold-plated silver nugget cuff links, 1970s, ¾in (20mm) wide.
£28–32 *JBB*

A pair of 9ct gold cuff links, c1904, ¾in (20mm) long.
£50–60 *TAC*

The term 'pin-up' derives from WWII when servicemen would 'pin up' girlie pictures in their quarters. Pin-up material, especially from the 1940s–50s, is highly collectable today and the more unusual items such as these cuff links can fetch high prices.

Earrings

A pair of American clip earrings, each with single black rhinestone mounted on pewtered metal, signed 'Carnegie', 1930s, 2½in (65mm) long.
£80–120 *PGH*

A pair of American screw earrings, with blue crystals and rhinestones on gold-plated mounts, 1930s, 1¼in (30mm) diam.
£60–80 *PGH*

A pair of American clip earrings, with beehive drops, set with clear rhinestones on rhodium settings, 1940, 2in (50mm) long.
£75–100 *BaH*

A pair of American clip earrings, set with opals in gold-plated mounts, 1950s, 2in (50mm) long.
£60–70 *PGH*

A pair of American earrings, with green and amber crystals and rhinestones on rhodium, 1930s, 1½in (40mm) diam.
£65–90 *BaH*

A pair of American clip earrings, with amber rhinestones on spiral rhodium settings, unsigned, 1930s, 1in (25mm) diam.
£45–65 *PGH*

A pair of American earrings, set with aquamarine cut crystals and rhinestones on rhodium, 1940s, 1in (25mm) long.
£50–60 *BaH*

A pair of American clip earrings, set with green crystal and rhinestones on gold-plated settings, signed 'Sarah Coventry', 1950s, 1½in (40mm) long.
£50–60 *PGH*

A pair of American clip earrings, with composite flowers on gilt, signed 'Weiss', 1950s, 1¼in (30mm) diam.
£40–60 *PGH*

A pair of American Christmas tree earrings, with rhinestones on gold-plated setting, 1930s, 1¼in (30mm) long.
£70–90 *BaH*

A pair of American clip earrings, by Saks of Fifth Avenue, with white rhinestones and unusual double drops on rhoduim settings, 1940s, 2½in (65mm) long.
£100–150 *PGH*

A pair of American clip earrings, with blue crystals and gemstones on pierced settings, 1940s, 1in (25mm) long.
£60–75 *BaH*

A pair of earrings, set with Roman glass in gold mounts, c1990, 1in (25mm) long.
£210–250 *JFG*

Necklaces & Pendants

An Arts & Crafts pendant,
set with Swiss lapis cabochons,
c1900, 1¾in (45mm) diam.
£150–200 *P*

An Arts & Crafts
silver pendant,
enamelled with a
sailing ship, c1900,
2¼in (55mm) long.
£100–140 *GOO*

A Murrle Bennet
pendant, with
hammer-textured
surface, scrolled top
and pierced sides,
with central wood opal
cabochon and drop,
marked with mono-
gram and '950', c1900,
1¾in (45mm) long.
£225–275 *P*

A Murrle Bennet
pendant, with
central turquoise
and half-pearls
and pearl drop,
marked with
monogram
and '15ct',
2in (50mm) long.
£400–500 *P*

A Georg Jensen part necklace, with foliate and floral plaques set
with labradorite cabochons linked by oval loops, marked and
'830', c1920, 8in (20.5cm) long.
£300–400 *P*

An enamelled plaque, designed
and made by Harold and Phoebe
Stabler, depicting a playful faun
cavorting between flowering
stems against a blue background,
signed and dated 'London 1916',
3in (8cm) wide.
£950–1,150 *P*

A pearl and amethyst glass
necklace and earrings, 1920s.
£55–75 *TCF*

A blue bugle glass
multi-stranded
necklace, with
gilt and beaded
clasp, 1930s,
20in (51cm) long.
£70–90 *PGH*

An American necklace
and earrings, set with
rhinestones, pearls,
enamel leaves on
gold-plated mounts,
1930s, necklace
16in (40.5cm) long.
£120–150 *BaH*

An American necklace,
set with clear rhine-
stones on rhodium
setting, 1930s,
16in (40.5cm) long.
£60–70 *BaH*

An American necklace, set with baguette cut amethyst crystals and clear rhinestones on gold-plated setting, 1930s, 16½in (32cm) long.
£90–120 *PGH*

A silver chain with bird-shaped penknife pendant, 1940s, 9½in (24cm) long.
£22–26 *PSA*

l. A diamanté necklace, 1940s.
£75–95 *TCF*

A gilt-metal necklace, 1940s, 15in (38cm) long.
£20–25 *PSA*

An Art Deco style necklace, with red and black enamelling and gilt-brass chain, maker's mark, 1940s, 16in (40.5cm) long.
£80–100 *PGH*

A gilt-metal choker, 1940s, 14in (35.5cm) long.
£35–45 *PSA*

A pink necklace, with gut wire and plastic bobbles, 1940s, 16in (40cm) long.
£30–40 *SnA*

An American necklace, bracelet and earrings, by Kramer, set with kingfisher blue rhinestones and gilt settings, 1950s, 16in (40.5cm) long.
£200–250 *PGH*

A gold-plated necklace, 1970s, 10in (25.5cm) long.
£65–75 *SnA*

l. An American mesh scarf, by Whiting & Davis, 1940s–50s, 8½in (22cm) square.
£50–60 *SnA*

KITCHENWARE

Two servants' bells, c1850,
7in (18cm) high overall.
£25–35 each *LIB*

A pair of galvanised
sausage makers, c1910.
£40–55 each *OLM*

A skimmer, with
brass pan and iron
handle, c1800,
24in (61cm) long.
£65–85 *LIB*

*l. Mrs Beeton's Book of
Household Manage-
ment*, published by
Ward Lock and Co,
New Edition, c1900,
8½in (21.5cm) high.
£25–30 *AL*

An Italian clockwork spit,
c1880, 13in (33cm) high.
£100–120 *ET*

An American tin cookie cutter,
in the shape of an anchor,
c1905, 3½in (9cm) wide.
£90–110 *MSB*

r. A clothes
beater, c1900,
24in (61cm) long.
£40–50 *ByI*

l. An American tin
cookie cutter, in the
shape of a goose,
c1910, 2¾in (7cm) high.
£40–50 *MSB*

Two horn mugs, c1900,
tallest 4in (10cm) high.
£8–11 each *AL*

A pine sink, c1900, 21½in (55cm) wide.
£20–25 *AL*

A pine dough bin, c1900, 29in (73.5cm) wide.
£45–65 *OLM*

A maid's tin box, c1920, 9in (23cm) high. **£20–25** *AL*

A washing dolly, c1900, 35½in (90cm) high. **£30–40** *ASP*

A pair of chromium-plated egg coddlers, with felt-lined covers, c1948, 4in (10cm) high. **£8–10** *BKK*

A Black Forest carved wooden nut-cracker, c1910, 7in (18cm) high. **£30–50** *ET*

l. A tin patty pan, c1920, 12in (30.5cm) wide. **£3–4** *AL*

r. A Tala cook's measure, c1950, 6in (15cm) high. **£6–8** *AL*

A bull's-head iron tin opener, c1910, 6½in (16.5cm) long. **£8–9** *WAB*

A brass nutcracker, in the shape of a crocodile 1930s, 10in (25.5cm) long. **£9–12** *WAB*

Three cake decorations, a bisque rabbit, a snow-baby and a polar bear, c1925, the baby 1½in (3.5cm) high. **£12–18 each** *PSA*

Ceramics

A ceramic foot warmer, c1890, 14in (35.5cm) long.
£10–15 *AL*

A turtle soup jar, glazed, impressed and with a coat-of-arms, c1890, 4½in (11.5cm) high.
£60–70 *BBR*

A ceramic ham stand, late 19thC, 7½in (29cm) high.
£40–48 *NO7*

A ham stand was an essential item for large scale entertaining and would also have been used in a grocer's shop when carving a ham by hand.

A Victorian cress dish, with gilt decoration, on 3 feet, 8in (20.5cm) diam.
£24–28 *TAC*

A ceramic bowl colander, c1920, 10in (25.5cm) diam.
£20–25 *NO7*

A Fortnum & Mason Ltd Stilton cheese jar, with black transfer, 1920s, 6½in (16.5cm) high.
£20–25 *BBR*

A Fielding's cress dish, with gilt decoration, on 3 feet, c1920, 8¼in (21cm) diam.
£30–35 *TAC*

A SylvaC sauce pot, No.4754, inscribed 'Parsley Sauce', c1950s, 5in (12.5cm) diam.
£20–25 *JDC*

FURTHER READING
Christina Bishop,
Collecting Kitchenware
Miller's Publications 1995

A set of 4 Watcombe Pottery Torquay egg cups on a plate, c1950, 6in (15cm) diam.
£18–22 *AL*

r. A Crowan stoneware cruet set, designed by Harry and May Davis, 1946–62, 2⅜in (6cm) high.
£24–28 *SnA*

Cream & Milk Pots

A two-handled milk pail, with deal cover, inscribed, some damage, 19thC.
£240–280 *HOLL*

Two cream pots and a jug, c1920, tallest 4in (10cm) high.
£2–3 each *AL*

A Broughty Ferry cream jar, with black transfer, some damage, c1910, 4¾in (12cm) high.
£50–60 *BBR*

A Stranraer cream jar, with transfer to both sides, good condition, c1910, 3¾in (9.5cm) high.
£45–55 *BBR*

Toast Racks

A two-slice toast rack, with bamboo design, c1910, 4¼in (10.5cm) long.
£10–15 *TAC*

A four-slice toast rack, with shell design, 1920s, 6½in (16.5cm) long.
£7–9 *TAC*

A two-slice toast rack, black with white spots, 1960s, 3¾in (9.5cm) long.
£4–6 *TAC*

r. A Royal Winton four-slice toast rack, 1930s, 8in (20.5cm) long.
£7–8 *TAC*

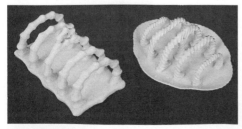

Two four-slice toast racks, 1920s, longest 6in (15cm).
£15–22 each *TAC*

Three toast racks, 1920–30s, longest 6½in (16.5cm).
£8–10 each *TAC*

Cornish Kitchen Ware

Cornish Kitchen Ware has been attracting a growing band of collectors. In spite of its name this distinctive blue and white striped china was not made in Cornwall but Derbyshire. In 1864 Thomas Green, a builder, decided to change career and purchased a small pottery in Church Gresley, South Derbyshire. T. G. Green & Co specialised in tableware and as the factory expanded, they diversified manufacture to produce a range of blue and white striped kitchen china. The new line needed a name. According to legend, T. G. Green's south of England representative, John Fanshawe, had just returned from a trip to Cornwall. The colours of the china reminded him of the blue of the Cornish skies and the white crests of the waves. 'Let's call it Cornish Kitchen Ware,' he suggested and the name stuck.

In the twenties and thirties Cornish Kitchen Ware became enormously successful. Its clean and modern lines appealing greatly to the new generation of housewives, many of whom were learning to cope without the assistance of full time cooks and who,

because they were spending more time in their kitchens, wanted items that looked attractive as well as being practical.

In addition to the classic blue and white Cornish Kitchen Ware, T. G. Green also produced a limited amount of yellow, gold and even red and white striped ceramics, these colours being highly collectable today because of their rarity. Also fetching high prices are the more unusual blue and white items such as jelly moulds and Cornish Kitchen Ware rolling pins, which were not a success at the time, since the ridged stripes left lines on the pastry!

Though other firms manufactured blue and white striped pottery and similarly styled ware, T. G. Green's Cornish Kitchen Ware can be identified by its backstamps and by touch. The stripes on traditional Cornish Kitchen Ware are raised. Blue and white striped ceramics remain in production today (T. G. Green was sold to Cloverleaf in 1987 – part of the Tootal organisation), but on modern products the stripes are flat, painted on the surface, rather than being a distinguishing part of the pottery.

A yellow and white cup and saucer, with green shield mark, cup 3¼in (8cm) high.
£30–35 *TAC*

A cheese dish, with green shield mark, 8½in (21.5cm) diam.
£40–48 *TAC*

A soup bowl, with green shield mark, 9in (23cm) diam.
£8–10 *AL*

A teapot, with green shield mark, 4¼in (11cm) high.
£65–75 *TAC*

A pudding basin, with green shield mark, 3¾in (9.5cm) high.
£10–15 *AL*

A cup and saucer, with green shield mark, cup 3in (7.5cm) high.
£10–15 *AL*

l. Five spice jars, with black shield marks, 3½in (9cm) high.
£18–22 each *AL*

Cornish Kitchen Ware Marks

Green Shield Mark

Black Shield Mark

Green Church Mark

Target Mark

Over the decades T. G. Green & Co has used a number of different marks. The shield mark (which appears in both black and green) and the green church mark, showing the church at Church Gresley, were both used from the late twenties until the early sixties. The round target mark distinguishing a new range of shapes designed by Judith Onions, dates from the late sixties.

A sugar shaker, with black shield mark, 5¼in (13cm) high. **£20–30** *AL*

A meal storage jar, with green church mark, 6½in (16.5cm) high. **£30–40** *AL*

An egg separator, with green church mark, 4in (10cm) diam. **£20–25** *AL*

A jug, with green church mark, 5¾in (14.5cm) high. **£20–25** *AL*

Two mugs, with black target mark, 3½in (9cm) high. **£6–8 each** *AL*

FURTHER READING

Paul Atterbury, *Cornish Ware*, Richard Dennis Publications, London, 1996

A globe teapot and cup and saucer, 1950s, cup 4½in (11.5cm) high. Teapot **£45–50** Cup and saucer **£15–18** *SMI*

Related Ware

Two storage jars, banded white on white, c1900, 6½in (16.5cm) high. **£20–25** *AL*

A green and white striped sugar storage jar, c1920, 6in (15cm) high. **£20–25** *AL*

A Price Bros blue and white striped mixing bowl with lip, c1920, 9¾in (25cm) diam. **£20–25** *AL*

Glass

A 'penny lick' glass,
c1880, 3⅜in (9.5cm) high.
£8–9 *WAB*

Used for ice-cream.

A glass pestle and mortar,
19thC, bowl 4¼in (11cm) diam.
£20–25 *FD*

A glass comport, c1890,
6in (15cm) high.
£10–12 *AL*

A glass sundae dish, c1920,
4in (10cm) high.
£5–10 *AL*

A glass cake stand, c1900,
5in (12.5cm) high.
£10–15 *AL*

A glass cake stand, c1890,
5in (12.5cm) high.
£15–20 *AL*

Kettles & Coffee Makers

Whereas Victorian copper kettles have long
been collectable, interest in design technology,
particularly among younger collectors, has
stimulated demand for stainless steel and
electric kettles from the twentieth century.
In good condition classic designs can fetch
what might seem to be surprisingly high
prices. As the century draws to a close there
is a growing interest in post-war domestic
products, ranging from fifties American-
style refrigerators to period espresso
machines, grandparents of the consumer
products that we all take for granted today.

A batchelor's brass
picnic kettle, on stand,
with brass and copper
spirit burner, c1920,
7¼in (18.5cm) high.
£55–65 *TAC*

A French Cadillac
Submersible kettle, c1957,
12in (30.5cm) high.
£40–50 *DGP*

A brass hot water kettle,
with iron slug for
maintaining the heat,
c1850, 16in (40.5cm) high.
£300–350 *ET*

l. A Sunbeam
Coffeemaster,
by Sunbeam
Corporation,
Chicago, USA,
1940s, 14in
(35.5cm) high.
£80–100 *DGP*

A Canadian Krups kettle,
c1959, 11in (28cm) wide.
£60–70 *DGP*

Moulds

A three-piece tin ice-cream mould, with fluted sides and fruit-moulded cover, by Jos Matauschek, Wien, late 19thC, 5½in (14cm) high.
£80–100 *MSB*

A Victorian Britannia metal ice-cream mould, 6½in (16.5cm) diam.
£100–120 *PC*

A set of 6 melon-shaped confectionery moulds, c1900.
£8–10 *IW*

A boxed set of metal conical moulds, 2 missing, c1900, 6¾in (17cm) long.
£10–15 *IW*

Three aluminium jelly moulds, c1930, largest 8in (20cm) long.
£3–5 each *AL*

A two-piece tin chocolate mould, in the shape of a swan, c1900, 8in (20.5cm) wide.
£130–150 *MSB*

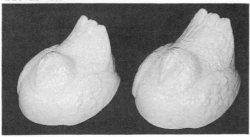

Two Shelley ceramic moulds, in the shape of chickens, 1930s, 8in (20.5) wide.
£275–300 each *BEV*

Three aluminium jelly moulds, c1930, largest 5¼in (13cm) long.
£2–3 each *AL*

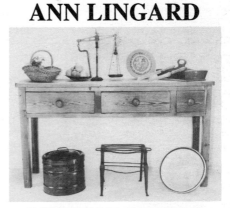

Tin & Metal Containers

An enamel bread bin, c1920,
11½in (29cm) high.
£20–25 *OPH*

A tortoiseshell-coloured tin sugar
container, 7in (18cm) high.
£15–20 *AL*

A Chivers tin custard
container, c1930,
5¾in (14.5cm) high.
£8–10 *AL*

A pair of red and white
aluminium storage tins, c1950,
largest 8in (20.5cm) high.
£10–13 each *AL*

A tin pastry cutter container,
c1950, 3½in (9cm) high.
£10–15 *AL*

Wooden Containers

A pine knife tray, c1890,
14¾in (37.5cm) long.
£15–25 *OPH*

A pine salt or candle box,
with original green paint,
c1870, 15in (38cm) high.
£120–140 *WLD*

A Hungarian salt
box, with original
paint, c1860,
12in (30.5cm) high.
£110–130 *WLD*

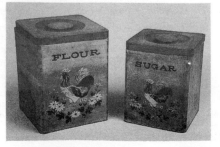

r. Two wooden storage
canisters, c1950, largest
6½in (16.5cm) high.
£15–20 each *AL*

A miniature flour barrel,
1938, 5¼in (13cm) high.
£40–45 *WAB*

LIGHTING

This section covers lighting from candlesticks to oil lamps to electric lights, with examples ranging from the sixteenth to the twentieth centuries. Since most collectors buy these objects to use and not just to look at, a major attraction is the quality of illumination that early lights can provide. 'Old electric lamps for example give a wonderfully soft glow because of their shades and the fact that they were designed for low wattage bulbs,' explains dealer and specialist Josie Marsden. 'You can use 40 or even 60, but I prefer 25 watt. You don't need strong lights to see well just good directional lighting, which is much more effective than a single, glaring multi-functional light hanging in the centre of the room.' To conform with safety regulations, all electric lamps should be earthed and

table and standard lamps connected to a 3-pin plug with a 3 amp fuse. Oil lamps also require careful use and equally careful checking before purchase.

'If the reservoir (the part containing the oil) is cracked, the lamp will leak,' warns Marsden. 'If the glass funnel or any other bits are broken or missing, they can be expensive if not impossible to replace. You can think you've found a bargain at a flea market, when all you have purchased is an unusable, or worse still a dangerous light.' As Josie Marsden notes, a living flame should never be left unattended. Candles should always be extinguished, oil lamps not turned up too high and need to be stood in a safe place, not immediately under shelves or cupboards, and out of the reach of small children.

Candlesticks

A pair of brass candlesticks, with twist ejectors, 18thC, 7in (18cm) high.
£380–450 *BSA*

A brass candle sconce, 19thC, 10in (25.5cm) high.
£80–90 *LIB*

r. A Victorian brass spring-loaded student's candle lamp, 12½in (32cm) high.
£80–100 *ML*

Popular with scholars, the student's lamp had a metal hood that reflected the light onto the book being read. An internal spring mechanism pushed the candle up as it melted, ensuring that it always remained at the same height.

A Victorian candlestick, with Greek design and gilt decoration, 5in (13cm) high.
£20–30 *ML*

A pair of black wood candlesticks, in the form of feet, age unknown, 3½in (9cm) long.
£8–10 *OD*

r. Two miners' cap copper candle holders, c1890, 5½in (14cm) long.
£100–120 *PC*

A pair of silver-plated chambersticks, c1900, 5in (13cm) diam.
£45–55 *PSA*

Ceiling Lamps

A naval bronze hanging lamp,
c1900, 18½in (47cm) wide.
£650–800 *PC*

FURTHER READING
Marsden, Josie A.,
Lamps and Lighting
Guinness Publishing 1990

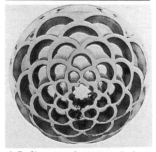

A Lalique amber tinted glass
ceiling light, Rinceaux,
moulded in bold relief with
fan-shaped panels, some
damage, etched mark, 1920s,
14¾in (37.5cm) diam.
£250–300 *DN*

An Art Deco glass and chrome
hexagonal hanging lamp,
c1930, 14½in (37cm) wide.
£120–140 *ML*

A three-light brass chandelier,
with original reeded glass shades,
c1905, 20in (51cm) high.
£270–320 *LIB*

An Art Deco hanging
Holophane lamp, with brass
gallery and frosted shade,
1920s, 16in (40.5cm) long.
£150–175 *LIB*

An Art Deco ceiling light,
with copper gallery and
decorative frosted shade,
1920s, 10in (25.5cm) high.
£120–150 *LIB*

A ceiling light, with decorative
brass gallery and cut glass
shade, c1910, 9in (23cm) diam.
£190–225 *LIB*

A German five-arm crystal
chandelier, with coloured beads,
c1920, 20in (51cm) high.
£400–500 *ML*

A pair of French iron and glass
ceiling lights, with transfer-
printed milk glass shades,
c1920, 9½in (24cm) high.
£80–100 *ML*

Lamps & Lanterns

A tin candle lantern, with 3 windows, 18thC, 12in (30.5cm) high.
£150–180 ET

A miner's brass lamp, c1815, 12½in (32cm) high.
£250–300 ET

A Victorian iron farm candle lantern, 8in (20.5cm) high.
£35–45 ML

An early Victorian copper binnacle lamp, c1860, 5in (13cm) high.
£100–120 PC

A late Victorian brass binnacle lamp, 7in (18cm) high.
£50–70 PC

A Victorian brass and iron blow lamp, 5½in (14cm) high.
£70–90 PC

A marine brass honeymoon lamp, 1880s, 6¼in (16cm) high.
£40–50 PC

A tinplate miner's carbide lamp, c1880, 9½in (24cm) high.
£60–70 PC

A disposable carbide lamp, unused, c1900, 6in (15cm) high.
£60–70 PC

A brass binnacle lamp, 1920s, 10in (25cm) high.
£60–70 PC

Oil Lamps

A bronze crusie lamp,
16thC, 9½in (24cm) high.
£150–180 *PC*

*A crusie lamp consisted
of a simple iron bowl
containing oil and a
floating wick of moss
or wool. It was in use
from the Iron Age until
the early part of the
20thC. The crusie was
introduced to America
by European settlers
where it became
known as the Betty or
Phoebe lamp.*

A double pan crusie lamp,
c1700, 6¼in (16cm) high.
£150–160 *PC*

A showman's oil lamp,
by J. Hickey, 1860–70,
35in (89cm) high.
£60–90 *ET*

A gimbal saloon oil
lamp, with cut glass
font and glass knop
with opal shade, c1820,
14in (35.5cm) high.
£400–500 *PC*

A brass and glass gimbal
paraffin lamp, c1870,
13in (33cm) high.
£150–200 *PC*

A Victorian oil lamp,
with hand-painted
and enamelled glass
reservoir, with silver-
plated base, French,
18½in (47cm) high.
£95–115 *ML*

A pair of brass gimbal
paraffin lamps, c1895,
8½in (22cm) high.
£150–200 *PC*

r. A brass and glass
gimbal paraffin lamp,
c1870, 8in (20cm) high.
£125–175 *PC*

A Venetian oil lamp, with
pedestal stem, 19thC,
7½in (19cm) high.
£75–85 *FD*

A German oil lamp,
in the form of an
owl, attributed to
Volkstedt, c1850,
18in (45.5cm) high.
£120–140 *LIB*

A pair of brass gimbal paraffin lamps, c1895, 11¾in (30cm) high.
£220–280 *PC*

A glass smoke bowl, c1900, 10¼in (26cm) high.
£25–30 *WAB*

Smoke bowls were hung from the ceiling above oil lamps to prevent smoke damage.

An oil lamp, with blue base, c1910, 16in (40.5cm) high.
£20–25 *AL*

A pair of French enamel and brass oil lamps, 1920s, 10in (25.5cm) high.
£40–48 *LIB*

Two nursery bedside oil lamps, 1920s, 5¼in (13cm) high.
£7–8 each *TAC*

Two Continental nursery bedside oil lamps, one with Ostende crest, 1920s, 5½in (14cm) high.
£10–15 each *TAC*

A Victorian brass oil lamp, with patterned glass globe, 21½in (54.5cm) high.
£70–80 *HEM*

A French opaline glass oil lamp, decorated with flowers, 1930s, 8in (20.5cm) high.
£15–20 *LIB*

A brass chamberstick oil lamp, 1930s, 7¼in (18.5cm) high.
£20–22 *ML*

l. A brass oil lamp, with glass funnel and opal glass shade, 1920s, 21½in (54.5cm) high.
£60–70 *Gam*

Table & Desk Lamps

A Victorian spelter
gas light, with
flambeau glass shade,
converted to electricity,
22in (56cm) high.
£175–225 *ML*

A painted spelter
table lamp, with
original painted glass
flambeau shade, c1900,
22in (56cm) high.
£250–300 *ML*

A multi-coloured peg
lamp, with brass
stand, early 19thC,
8½in (21.5cm) high.
£18–22 *FD*

A silver Arts & Crafts
style table lamp, by
James Dixon & Sons,
inscribed and dated
'1889–1914', Sheffield
1913, 13¼in (33.5cm) high.
£550–650 *DN*

r. A spelter and onyx
cherub table lamp, 1920s,
16in (40.5cm) high.
£150–200 *ML*

An Art Nouveau brass
table lamp, with
transfer-printed glass
shade, 1910–20s,
21in (54cm) high.
£120–140 *ML*

A pair of American
brass and painted
spelter three-light
table lamps, 1910–20,
29in (74cm) high.
£550–650 *ML*

A brass table lamp,
with reeded stem and
marbled decorative
shade, 1920s,
19in (48cm) high.
£130–150 *LIB*

r. A carved Oriental
figure lamp, with
shade, c1920,
19½in (50cm) high.
£140–170 *ML*

An Art Nouveau table lamp, with beaded shade, c1920, 27in (68.5cm) high.
£240–280 *ML*

A French Art Nouveau iron and copper table lamp, with etched cut frosted glass shade, 1920s, 20½in (52cm) high.
£160–200 *ML*

A brass adjustable desk lamp, with original pull, 1920s, 23in (58.5cm) high.
£250–300 *LIB*

A brass fully adjustable table lamp, 1920s, 16in (40.5cm) high.
£200–250 *LIB*

r. A child's painted plaster bedside light, with a figure of Miss Muffet, 1930s, 10in (25.5cm) high.
£55–65 *ML*

A brass multi-adjustable desk lamp, 1930s, 17½in (44.5cm) high.
£200–230 *ML*

A bendy desk lamp, with brass shade, 1920s, 17in (43cm) high.
£100–120 *LIB*

A French Art Deco iron desk lamp, with original glass shade, 1930s, 19in (48cm) high.
£100–125 *ML*

A Glasform pink iridescent glass lamp, 1993, 18in (45.5cm) high.
£200–240 *GLA*

Wall Lights

A pair of Victorian brass and copper gas lights, with replica glass shades, converted to electricity, c1860, 15½in (40cm) high.
£325–375 *ML*

A brass elbow gas wall light, converted to electricity, c1900, 22in (56cm) wide extended.
£150–175 *LIB*

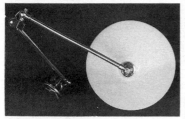

A pair of brass swan neck gas wall lights, with marbled glass globe shades, converted to electricity, c1900, 10in (25.5cm) wide.
£200–240 *LIB*

A brass adjustable picture light, 1940s, 10in (25.5cm) wide.
£75–85 *LIB*

A brass gimbal spring-loaded candle holder, c1860, 12in (30cm) high.
£130–175 *PC*

A gimbal is the term used for a jointed metal lampshade carrier.

A pair of brass wall lights, with frosted glass shades, 1900–1910, 7in (18cm) high.
£125–145 *ML*

These were original samples from an Edwardian salesman's stock.

A set of 4 iron candle lamps, wired for electricity, 1920s, 6½in (16.5cm) high.
£230–270 *ML*

A Victorian brass wall light, with original milk glass shade, c1900, 15½in (40cm) wide.
£140–170 *ML*

An Edwardian brass wall light, with glass globe, 11in (28cm) wide.
£120–140 *ML*

A set of 4 iron wall candle lights, with glass crystal drops, 1910–20, 10in (25.5cm) high.
£500–580 *ML*

A pair of brass swivelling gas wall lights, with etched frosted glass shades, c1910, 12½in (32cm) wide.
£200–250 *ML*

LUGGAGE

A leather Gladstone bag, with brass fittings, 19thC, 14½in (37cm) wide.
£80–85 *RIS*

The Gladstone bag, a leather portmanteau made in various sizes, was named after the great Victorian statesman William Ewart Gladstone (1809–98). He served a total of 60 years in parliament and was Prime Minister 4 times.

Two wicker hampers, c1900, largest 13in (33cm) wide.
£20–25 each *AL*

A tin trunk, c1905, 9¾in (25cm) wide.
£70–75 *RIS*

A leather portmanteau, with brass fittings, 1920s, 18in (45.5cm) wide.
£45–55 *WAB*

A Victorian canvas travelling case, with leather and brass fittings, 14in (35.5cm) wide.
£125–145 *RIS*

A tin hatbox, c1900, 10in (25.5cm) high.
£70–75 *RIS*

A canvas case, trimmed with leather, c1910, 17in (43cm) wide.
£55–65 *WAB*

A leather map case, with brass fittings, 1920s, 13in (33cm) wide.
£50–55 *RIS*

A brown leather Gladstone bag, with brass fittings, late 19thC, 10in (25.5cm) wide.
£70–75 *RIS*

A German leather and brass Thermos flask, in a leather case, c1905, 12in (30.5cm) high.
£30–50 *MSh*

A green crocodile skin travelling case, by John Round & Co, with ivory, silver-topped and leather fittings, c1912, 21¾in (55.5cm) wide, together with canvas outer case.
£550–650 *Bri*

A leather case, 1920s, 16in (40.5cm) wide.
£30–40 *WAB*

A leather suitcase, with reinforced corners and brass locks, 1920s, 16½in (42cm) wide.
£45–55 *WAB*

A leather travelling bag, with a label for Hotel New York, 1920–30s, 25in (63.5cm) wide.
£175–195 *RIS*

A travel label of this period can add interest to luggage.

A French canvas case, with leather trimming and brass locks, with 2 hotel labels, 1920–30s, 19in (48.5cm) wide.
£100–135 *RIS*

A canvas hatbox, with leather trimming and brass fittings, with original labels, 1920s, 15in (38cm) wide.
£100–125 *RIS*

A leather briefcase, with brass fittings, 1960s, 20in (51cm) wide.
£40–45 *RIS*

A leather collar box, c1930, 6in (15cm) diam.
£15–20 *AXT*

MEDALS

Medals have been struck to commemorate every conceivable subject, ranging from great historical occasions, to local livestock shows, from the building of mighty monuments, to a child's proficiency in arithmetic. As dealer Christopher Eimer explains, medal collecting inspires a correspondingly wide range of individuals. 'Unlike coins or stamps where enthusiasts tend to specialise solely in those fields, people collect medals through an interest in a particular personage, event or hobby.' As such, again unlike many other areas of the antiques market, what the medal represents tends to be more important in terms of value, than who it is by, though many fine sculptors were involved in the designing of medals.

Whilst at the top of the range, rare pieces celebrating significant events can fetch many hundreds of pounds, this section includes examples valued at around £5, whilst many medals over a hundred years old can still be purchased for under £50. 'In some ways medal collecting is a forgotten field,' says Christopher Eimer. 'Its heyday was the eighteenth and nineteenth centuries, when gentlemen formed great cabinet collections in their libraries. It was a very popular hobby with men of the cloth and a fine collection was a sign of good education and an interest in history and antiquity.' History remains the main attraction with enthusiasts today and this selection includes one of the most famous events in British history, a medal from 1605 marking the Gunpowder Plot.

A marriage of Princess Mary and William of Orange, silver medal, 1641, by J. Blum, 2¾in (70mm) diam.
£750–850 *BAL*

A Duke of Monmouth beheaded, silver medal, 1685, unsigned, showing the head of the Duke spouting blood, 1½in (40mm) diam.
£180–220 *EIM*

r. A Gunpowder Plot silver medal, 1605, unsigned, showing snake of sedition gliding among lilies and roses, inscription on reverse, 1¼in (30mm) diam.
£100–120 *EIM*

A Treaty of Utrecht, cast and chased copper gilt medal, 1713, by John O'Brisset, 2in (50mm) diam.
£115–135 *BAL*

A birth of Prince Charles, 31st December, 1720, copper medal, by Ermenegildo Hamerani, showing busts of James III and Clementina, Providence, 1½in (40mm) diam.
£65–75 *BAL*

l. A George II and Caroline of Ansbach, silver medal, 1732, by John Croker and John Tanner, 2¾in (70mm) diam.
£650–750 *BAL*

A Capture of Portobello, brass medal, 1739, unsigned, showing bust of Admiral Vernon, ships in the harbour on reverse, 1½in (40mm) diam.
£30–50 *EIM*

An accession of King George III silver medal, 1760, signed by T. Pingo, figures dancing around an oak tree on reverse, 2in (50mm) diam.
£200–250 *EIM*

A Carib War, St Vincent's Rebellion, cast-silver presentation medal, 1773, by G. M. Moser, with bust of George III, Britannia offers an olive branch to defeated native on reverse, 2¼in (55mm) diam.
£400–500 *BAL*

A Newcastle Volunteers, silver prize medal, 1801, showing a lion with banner on top of a tower, inscription on reverse, 2in (50mm) diam.
£345–385 *BAL*

The Parthenon, bronze medal, 1820, unsigned, Royal arms on reverse, 2in (50mm) diam.
£60–80 *EIM*

One of 48 medals in a series of the Elgin Marbles.

A London Christ's Hospital, silver gilt prize, 1833, inscribed 'The Second Proficient in Arithmetic, 13 Dec, 1833', 1½in (35mm) diam.
£75–85 *BAL*

A Worshipful Company of Distillers, silver medal, 1835, unsigned, 2in (50mm) diam.
£60–80 *EIM*

A Coronation of Queen Victoria, bronze medal, 1838, 2in (50mm) diam.
£35–45 *BAL*

The *Fighting Temeraire*, bronze medal, 1876, signed by L. C. Wyon, issued by the Art Union of London, bust of J. M. W. Turner on reverse, 2in (50mm) diam.
£60–80 *EIM*

A completion of the Thames Tunnel, bronze medal, 1842, by J. Davis, showing head of Sir Marc Isambard Brunel, view of the twin tunnels on reverse, 2½in (65mm) diam.
£75–85 *BAL*

A Cambridge University Bicycle Club, bronze medal, 1876, by Peters & Munsey, showing a Penny Farthing bicycle within a wreath, with engraved case, 2in (50mm) diam.
£100–125 *BAL*

A Queen Victoria Golden Jubilee, bronze medal, 1887, signed by Pinches, view of Stockton-on-Tees bridge on reverse, 1½in (35mm) diam.
£12–15 *EIM*

l. A Forth Bridge Opened, bronze medal, 1890, by L. C. Lauer, inscribed with legend on reverse, 2½in (65mm) diam.
£135–165 *BAL*

r. A Dog Exhibition, silver prize medal, 1890, signed T. O., inscribed with recipient's name on reverse, 1½in (40mm) diam.
£40–60 *EIM*

A London Olympics Judge's badge, silvered, bronze and blue enamel, 1908, by Vaughton and Sons, very good condition, 2¼in (55mm) diam.
£400–500 *BAL*

A Save *The Victory* fund, bronze medal, 1923, unsigned, inscribed on reverse, 1¼in (30mm) diam.
£4–6 *EIM*
This medal was struck with metal from the ship.

An Armistice Anniversary, bronze medal, 1918–28, signed by C. L. Doman, 3in (7.5cm) diam.
£25–30 *EIM*

A Launching of the R101 Airship, aluminium medal, 1929, signed by J. R. Gaunt, 1½in (40mm) diam.
£30–40 *EIM*

A London Olympic Games, bronze medal, 1948, unsigned, chariot and horses on reverse, 2in (50mm) diam.
£40–60 *EIM*

A King George VI Coronation, silver medal, 1937, signed by P. Metcalfe, Queen Elizabeth, the Queen Mother on reverse, 1in (25mm) diam.
£4–6 *EIM*

l. An International Golf Show, gold medal, 1986, engraved 'For outstanding services to golf/ Henry Cotton M.B.E., 5th February 1986', 1¾in (45mm) diam, together with a badge of St Andrew.
£350–450 *S*

MEN'S TOILETRIES

A cut-throat razor, with box, c1900, 6¾in (17cm) long.
£4–6 *JEN*

A Victorian gentleman's toilet mirror, 21in (53cm) high.
£100–120 *AXT*

A penknife, with razor and comb attachments, c1900, 3¾in (9.5cm) long when closed.
£18–22 *WAB*

A travelling razor, in box, 1940s, 3½in (9cm) long.
£6–8 *JEN*

An Ever-Ready razor, in Bakelite box, 1930s, 4½in (11.5cm) long.
£14–16 *FAM*

A metal razor, with decorated handle, 1930s, 3½in (9cm) long.
£2–3 *FAM*

An Ever-Ready razor, in Bakelite box, 1930s, 4in (10cm) long.
£12–14 *FAM*

r. A Bakelite Rolls Razor Imperial blade holder, 1930s, 2in (50mm) high.
50p–£1 *FAM*

A German travelling razor, in box, 1930s, 1¾in (45mm) wide.
£10–12 *JEN*

A Rolls Razor Super blade, hollow ground steel, 1930s, 2in (50mm) wide.
£1–2 *FAM*

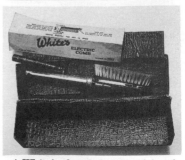

A White's electric hairbrush/comb, c1940, 9½in (24cm) long.
£20–30 *ET*

A Gillette boxed shaving set,
1940s, 13¼in (34cm) long.
£4–5 *FAM*

A 7 o'clock razor, in Bakelite
box, 1940s, 3¾in (9.5cm) long.
£3–4 *FAM*

A metal razor, 1950s,
3½in (9cm) long.
£1–2 *FAM*

A shaving brush, 1940s,
4in (10cm) high.
£3–4 *FAM*

A Gillette razor set, in Bakelite
box, 1940s, 4in (10cm) long.
£3–4 *FAM*

A Boots Bakelite shaving
stick container, 1940–50s,
3½in (9cm) high.
£3–4 *FAM*

r. An Eclipse
Model BB
razor, in
Bakelite box,
1940s, 4in
(10cm) long.
£7–9 *FAM*

A packet of Gillette blue razor
blades, 1940s, 2in (50mm) long.
£2–3 *FAM*

Two plastic razors, 1940–50s,
3in (7.5cm) long.
£4–5 each *FAM*

A badger and hair shaving brush, 1950s,
3½in (9cm) high.
£5–6 *FAM*

A pure badger hair shaving brush, 1950s,
4½in (11.5cm) high.
£4–5 *FAM*

r. Two tins of
Ultrex Platinum
condoms, 1950s.
£15–20 each *HUX*

l. A Culmak
Senior shaving
brush, 1950–60s,
3½in (9cm) high.
£4–5 *FAM*

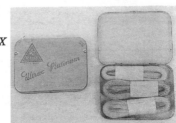

METALWARE

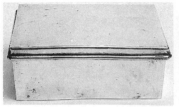

A copper casket, 19thC,
5¼in (13cm) wide.
£30–35 *SnA*

A 'Go to Bed' cast iron match
striker, c1880, 4in (10cm) high.
£55–65 *WAB*

A hand bell, with a leather handle,
engraved 'W. D. Dunn, 2 Castle
Street, Bloomsbury', on one side,
'Rich'd Smith, King's Head, North
Hide', on the other, c1831,
5½in (14cm) high.
£75–85 *WAB*

An electroplated Britannia
metal teapot, by James
Dixon & Sons, c1890,
9¼in (23.5cm) high.
£80–120 *PC*

A WMF Arts & Crafts
two-handled vase, c1890,
6in (15cm) high.
£35–45 *AnS*

An Arts & Crafts silver-plated
inkwell, by Hukin & Heath,
1880s, 5in (12.5cm) square.
£200–250 *SHa*

A brass sun dial, c1910,
7in (18cm) diam.
£75–85 *LIB*

A pair of French bronze
jugs, signed St Peron, c1915,
6½in (16.5cm) high.
£450–550 *AnS*

Two Christopher Dresser
style chrome sauce dishes,
c1930, 7½in (19cm) high.
£30–40 *ATI*

A bronze figure of a naked
female, on a black marble
base, stamped 'J. G.' foundry
mark, signed, dated '1985',
10¾in (27.5cm) high.
£240–280 *P(Ba)*

Door Furniture, Locks & Security Items

A Victorian cast iron door stop, in the form of a lion, 9in (23cm) wide.
£75–85 *PSA*

A Victorian cast iron door stop, modelled as a musician, 11in (28cm) high.
£30–40 *WAB*

A Victorian painted cast iron door stop, modelled as St George and The Dragon, 7in (18cm) wide.
£65–75 *PSA*

Three brass door knockers, modelled as John Peel, an Indian and William Wordsworth, c1925, largest 4in (10cm) high.
£12–25 each *ML*

Three brass pixie door knockers, c1925, largest 4in (10cm) high.
£12–18 each *ML*

A 25-Lever delector lock, together with 4 keys, 19thC, 8in (20.5cm) high.
£1,400–1,600 *ET*

Weighing an impressive 8½lbs this lock is massive, finely engraved, complex in mechanism and comes complete with 4 differently numbered keys. Its price reflects its rarity, though such an item would only appeal to a select number of collectors.

A collection of brass padlocks and keys, c1920, cycle lock 2in (5cm) wide.
£18–28 each *WAB*

Three brass door knockers, in the form of a Clovelly donkey, a Pekingese dog and a fox, c1930, largest 6¼in (16cm) high.
£15–25 each *ML*

A bunch of servants' keys, by Smith & Sons, Birmingham, c1912, 3½in (9cm) long.
£65–75 *WAB*

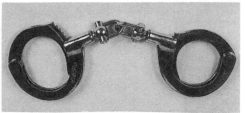

r. A pair of chromed-steel handcuffs, by H. & R. Arms Co, Worcester, Massachusetts, USA, key missing, 1930s, 10in (25.5cm) long.
£25–35 *WAB*

Dressing Table Items

Victorian and Edwardian dressing tables were set with a large variety of silverware ranging from hairbrushes to shoehorns. In London, Sheffield and Birmingham elaborate dressing table sets were produced in solid silver or even gold for the wealthy, and thin die stamped or electroplated silver for the less well off. For women the most basic sets consisted of a hand-mirror, hairbrush, comb and clothes brush. Larger vanity sets, often originally housed in handsome wooden boxes or leather travelling cases, could contain up to twenty or thirty items, including silver-topped bottles for scent and cosmetics, trinket boxes, bonnet brushes, glove stretchers and buttonhooks, (an essential accessory for coping with the endless array of tiny buttons affixed to everything from dresses to boots).

A single set might have been produced by several different makers, each one specialising in a certain accessory. Smaller boxes were also produced to contain manicure sets. Decoration tended to be ornate and pretty – flowers, shells, scrolls and cherubs, with cartouches left free for the engraving.

From the turn of the century sets were being produced in the Art Nouveau style, superseded after WWI by Art Deco patterns. Men's dressing sets, though somewhat smaller than women's, could also contain a surprisingly large number of items ranging from handleless hair brushes (supplied in pairs) to cologne bottles, moustache curlers and shaving equipment. Styles tended to be simpler with restrained decoration or plain tops bearing nothing but their owner's initials. Whilst an historically important crest or monogram can add interest to a piece, someone else's initials are not necessarily a desirable addition, and when the silver is thin, these cannot be removed without damaging the item.

Most of the following pieces would have originally come from large sets. While complete cases command a premium, individual items can still be assembled comparatively cheaply.

A Victorian silver shoehorn, c1884, 7½in (19cm) long.
£18–20 *OBS*

An Art Nouveau silver button hook, c1900, 8¼in (21cm) long.
£18–20 *OBS*

A silver-backed clothes brush, London 1910, 7in (18cm) long.
£20–30 *ABr*

A silver eyebrow brush, Birmingham 1913, 4in (10cm) long.
£20–25 *ABr*

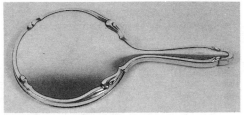

A WMF silver-plated hand-mirror, c1910, 10½in (26.5cm) long.
£30–40 *PSA*

A gold and tortoiseshell-mounted green leather travelling case, by Asprey & Co, fitted with a bedside timepiece, bottles, brushes, a tray, writing and other implements, the 18ct gold mounts London 1912, 12in (30.5cm) wide, with canvas outer case.
£1,600–1,800 *Bea*

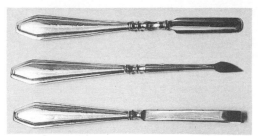

A set of 3 manicure tools, with silver handles, Birmingham 1917, 4¾in (12cm) long.
£10–12 each *ABr*

A silver nail file, with decorated handle, Birmingham 1919, 6in (15cm) long.
£18–22 *ABr*

A silver-backed clothes brush, Birmingham 1930, 5¼in (13cm) long.
£20–25 *ABr*

A silver-backed clothes brush, Birmingham 1932, 5¼in (13cm) long.
£20–25 *ABr*

A silver-backed clothes brush, by Walker & Hall, Sheffield 1955, 6¼in (16cm) long.
£24–28 *ABr*

A silver-backed tortoiseshell comb, by Walker & Hall, Sheffield 1955, 6¾in (17.5cm) long.
£30–40 *ABr*

A silver nail buff with handle, Birmingham 1919, 3½in (9cm) long.
£25–30 *ABr*

An engine-turned silver comb and holder, Birmingham 1927, 3½in (9cm) long.
£30–35 *ABr*

An engine-turned silver nail buff, Birmingham 1930, 4in (10cm) long.
£24–28 *ABr*

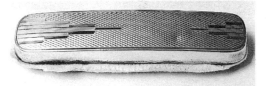

An engine-turned silver nail buff, with Art Deco design, Birmingham 1934, 3½in (9cm) long.
£22–26 *ABr*

A silver-backed hairbrush, Birmingham 1933, 9½in (24cm) long.
£10–15 *ABr*

r. A silver hand-mirror, depicting The Reynolds Angels, Birmingham 1955, 9in (23cm) long.
£60–70 *PSA*

Serving Cutlery

A Georgian silver punch ladle, with twisted
whalebone handle, probably Scottish,
7½in (19cm) long.
£75–85 *TAC*

Two Victorian silver-plated bread forks,
ivory handle 8½in (21.5cm) long, ebony
handle 9¾in (25cm) long.
£35–45 each *TAC*

Two Victorian silver-plated pickle forks, with
mother-of-pearl handles, longest 7½in (19cm).
£12–28 each *TAC*

Two Victorian pickle forks, with ivory handles:
Silver, Sheffield 1898, 7in (18cm) long.
Silver-plated, 8in (20.5cm) long.
£25–35 each *TAC*

Two pickle forks:
Victorian silver-plated, with engraved handle,
7¼in (18.5cm) long.
Silver-handled, Sheffield 1917, 7½in (19cm) long.
£10–22 each *TAC*

Two Edwardian silver-plated pickle forks,
one with bone handle, the other horn,
longest 8¾in (22cm) long.
£14–24 each *TAC*

A Victorian silver-plated flan slice, with ivory
handle, 7¼in (18.5cm) long.
£15–20 *TAC*

Two Victorian silver-plated spoons, for
cranberries and preserves, 6in (15cm) long.
£15–20 each *TAC*

A silver-plated jam spoon, c1910,
6½in (16.5cm) long.
£12–15 *FMN*

A silver cranberry spoon, with ivory handle,
Sheffield 1918, 7¼in (18.5cm) long.
£20–24 *TAC*

l. A silver-plated jam spoon, by Walker & Hall,
c1920, 6¼in (16cm) long.
£15–18 *FMN*

Silver
Cruets

A pair of silver cruets, c1888, 6in (15cm) high.
£300–350 *OBS*

A silver cruet with cut glass bottles, by George Angel, London 1853, 10¾in (27cm) high.
£1,500–1,600 *WAC*

A silver-topped mustard pot, by George Angel, hallmarked, c1850, 5¼in (13cm) high.
£75–85 *ML*

A silver three-piece condiment set with salt spoon, by Aide Bros, Birmingham 1932, pepper pot 3¼in (8cm) high.
£155–185 *SnA*

Cutlery

An early Victorian silver spoon, c1841, 9in (23cm) long.
£30–35 *SnA*

r. A set of 6 tea knives, with silver handles, Sheffield 1909, boxed 7½in (19cm) wide.
£80–100 *ABr*

l. An American silver dessert fork, by Ball Black & Co, USA, c1880.
£10–15 *PC*

Sugar Tongs

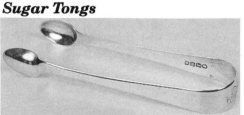

A pair of silver sugar tongs, London 1793–4, 3½in (9cm) long.
£20–30 *PC*

A pair of silver sugar tongs, with maker's mark SR, c1781, 3½in (9cm) long.
£20–30 *PC*

A pair of silver sugar tongs, London 1828, 3½in (9cm) long.
£20–30 *PC*

A pair of silver sugar tongs, Birmingham 1890, 3½in (9cm) long.
£20–30 *PC*

Tableware

A silver sauce boat, Birmingham 1911, 6¾in (17cm) wide.
£95–115 *SnA*

A silver bowl and spoon, c1885, bowl 5in (12.5cm) diam, cased.
£200–250 *PC*

A silver christening mug, with Georgian style handle, hallmarked 1924, 8in (20.5cm) high.
£80–90 *SnA*

A silver dessert bowl, with 3 feet, London 1929, 12¼in (31cm) diam.
£115–135 *SnA*

Writing Accessories

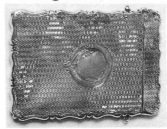

A silver card case, Birmingham 1871, 4in (10cm) wide.
£70–80 *SnA*

An enamelled silver notebook sleeve, by Liberty & Co, with Knox design motif, marked 'L & Co', Birmingham 1903, 2¾in (7cm) wide.
£200–220 *P*

A penknife for trimming quills, with silver mount and mother-of-pearl handle, c1890, 6¼in (16cm) long.
£18–22 *WAB*

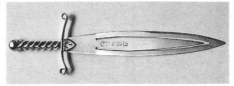

A Victorian silver page marker, Birmingham 1894, 3½in (9cm) long.
£55–65 *ABr*

An inkstand with 2 cut-glass and silver-mounted bottles, base probably originally a snuffer's tray, marked, c1890, 8¾in (22cm) wide.
£275–325 *L*

A silver 'Yard-O-Led' pencil, 1952, 4¾in (12cm) long.
£60–70 *ABr*

A silver 'Yard-O-Led' Diplomat pencil, London 1948, 4¾in (12cm) long.
£60–70 *ABr*

A Lady's 'Yard-O-Lette', 1955, 4in (10cm) long.
£40–50 *ABr*

Toast Racks

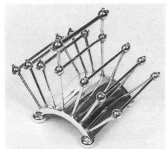

An EPNS toast/letter rack, by
Hukin & Heath, attributed to
Christopher Dresser, c1880,
5½in (14cm) high.
£300–360 *NCA*

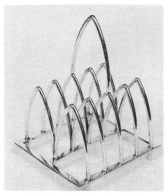

An EPNS toast rack, by Dixon &
Sons, attributed to Christopher
Dresser, c1884, 7in (18cm) high.
£1,000–1,250 *NCA*

> **Cross Reference**
> Ceramics

An EPNS toast rack, by Atkin
Bros, c1885, 4½in (11.5cm) long.
£100–120 *NCA*

*This is a copy of a Christopher
Dresser design.*

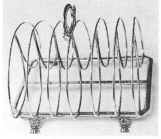

A George III silver toast rack,
by W. Summers, London 1816,
6in (15cm) wide.
£380–430 *SnA*

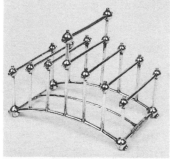

An EPNS toast rack, by Hukins &
Heath, attributed to Christopher
Dresser, c1885, 7in (18cm) long.
£400–500 *NCA*

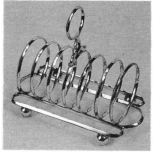

A silver-plated 6-slice toast
rack, on ball supports, c1900,
6¾in (17.5cm) wide.
£35–40 *PSA*

An EPNS toast rack, by
Atkin Bros, Sheffield, in the
style of Christopher Dresser,
c1880, 7in (18cm) long.
£100–120 *NCA*

An EPNS toast rack, by Hukin
& Heath, design attributed to
Christopher Dresser, c1883,
7in (18cm) long.
£650–750 *NCA*

A silver-plated 4-slice toast
rack, 1920s, 3¼in (8cm) wide.
£25–35 *PSA*

l. A silver-plated toast rack, by
Harrods, c1930, 3½in (9cm) wide.
£35–45 *ABr*

MILITARIA
Armour & Uniform

An Indian mail and lamellar shirt, with steel plates and shaped finials to buckles, the outside engraved with Islamic inscription, the inside with Devanagri inscription, good condition, 17thC, weight 16½lbs (7.5kgs).
£600–700 *WAL*

From a group of shirts taken at the Siege of Adoni in 1689.

A one-piece cabasset, with pear stalk finial to crown, acid cleaned overall, rosettes missing, brim pierced with small mounting hole, c1600.
£225–275 *WAL*

A pair of articulated gauntlets for a German harness, in the black and white style, finger plate leathers replaced slight damage, excellent condition, c1600.
£400–480 *ASB*

A Danish cavalry officer's blue cloth shako, the gilt star plate with leaf garter supporting royal crown and shield of Royal Danish coat-of-arms, with gold wire pompon and silver royal cipher, leather-backed gilt chinchain, very good condition, c1870.
£340–380 *ASB*

A major's full dress scarlet tunic of the Border Regiment, good condition, post-1902.
£100–120 *WAL*

An other ranks full dress scarlet tunic of the 1st (Brighton) Sussex Rifle Volunteers, contemporary ink inscription on silk lining 'F. Vickers, 1288, 1st S.R.V. 1869', very good condition.
£325–375 *WAL*

An English pikeman's breastplate, with central ridge, some pitting, good condition, mid-17thC, 18in (45.5cm) overall.
£550–650 *ASB*

A pair of Imperial Prussian officer's dress epaulettes of a captain in the 85th Infantry Regiment, with copper half-moons and gilt numerals, good condition, c1900.
£70–90 *WAL*

An African heart-shaped multi-coloured beaded pectoral or gorget, the beads arranged in geometric patterns around 2 stars made from cowrie shells, the centre with 6 brass plates, complete with cord suspension strap, slight damage, 19thC.
£200–250 *ASB*

An officer's blue cloth spiked helmet of The Buffs, velvet-backed chinchain and ear rosettes, gilt and silver-plated helmet plate, leather and silk lining, good condition, post-1902.
£500–600 *WAL*

Cap Badges

An Army Cyclist Corps
brass cap badge, 1914–19,
2in (50mm) high.
£10–12 *PC*

A Berkshire Imperial
Yeomanry brass cap badge,
1902–08, 2in (50mm) high.
£20–25 *PC*

A Lancashire Fusiliers bimetal
cap badge, 1898–1958,
2in (50mm) high.
£6–8 *PC*

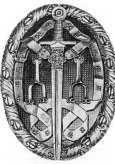

A Knight Bachelor's
silver gilt and
enamel cap badge,
hallmarked London
1926, 3in (7.5cm)
high, in fitted case.
£120–140 *WAL*

A Montgomeryshire Imperial
Yeomanry white metal cap badge,
1902–08, 2in (50mm) high.
£20–25 *PC*

A Northamptonshire Regiment
bimetal cap badge, 1921–58,
2in (50mm) high.
£6–8 *PC*

An 1874 pattern other
ranks white metal
glengarry cap badge of
the 92nd (Gordon
Highlanders) Regiment,
3in (7.5cm) high.
£120–140 *WAL*

A Portsmouth
Volunteers Training
Corps bronze cap
badge, 1914,
2in (50mm) high.
£110–130 *WAL*

A Royal Army Jewish
Chaplain's bronze cap
badge, 1945,
2in (50mm) high.
£10–12 *PC*

A North Devon
Hussars bronze
cap badge, 1914–24,
2in (50mm) high.
£20–25 *PC*

A Parachute Regiment white
metal cap badge, 1943–53,
2in (50mm) high.
£8–10 *PC*

Badges

It is quite difficult to date a badge exactly
as they remained constant over long
periods. The only changes were from
Victorian crown to King's crown to Queen's
crown. It is also not normal to use bronze
for other ranks' badges. Bronze is usually
reserved for officers badges.

A Royal Naval Division Hood Battalion brass cap badge, 1914–18, 2in (50mm) high.
£35–40 PC

A Royal Observer Corps white metal cap badge, 1945, 2in (50mm) high.
£6–8 PC

r. A West Riding Regiment bimetal cap badge, 1897–1958, 2in (50mm) high.
£8–9 PC

A Royal Naval Division Machine Gun Battalion brass cap badge, 1914–18, 2in (50mm) high.
£20–25 PC

A Royal Army Church of England Chaplain's bimetal cap badge, 1945, 2in (50mm) high.
£10–12 PC

A Victorian Royal Fusiliers officer's embroidered forage cap badge, 2in (50mm) high.
£35–45 WAL

A Westmorland & Cumberland Yeomanry brass cap badge, 1908–22, 2in (50mm) high.
£18–20 PC

A Royal Scots Dragoon Guards bimetal cap badge, post-1971, 2in (50mm) high.
£8–10 PC

Edged Weapons

A European trade tomahawk head, 18thC, mounted on hanging wall plaque, 6in (15cm) wide overall.
£180–220 *ASB*
Found at Crown Point, New York State, USA.

An African iron dagger, with hardwood hilt, good condition, 19thC, blade 12in (30.5cm) long.
£120–140 *ASB*

l. A French silver-hilted hunting sword, with double-edged blade, the hilt signed 'Janisset, Paris', c1850, blade 18¼in (46.5cm).
£8,000–10,000 *S(S)*

The presentation inscription reads: 'I.H.A., K.D.Gds., The Gift of His Father'. Janisset is last recorded as an active silversmith in the Paris directories of 1822.

A Georgian officer's hanger, with curved bi-fullered single-edged blade, copper-gilt stirrup hilt, good condition, blade 24in (61cm) long.
£180–200 *WAL*

A steel sword, in original steel-mounted leather scabbard, some damage, c1855, blade 31¾in (81cm).
£140–160 *ASB*

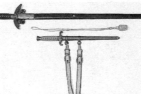

Two Nazi German weapons, c1940:
top A Nazi Luftwaffe officer's second pattern sword, by Paul Weyersberg & Co, Solingen, 38⅞in (98.5cm) long overall. **£400–500**
below A Nazi army officer's dagger, marked 'Original Eickhorn Solingen', 15¾in (40cm) long overall.
£200–400 *MCA*

r. A Russian cavalry trooper's sabre, with curved blade, brass guard, engraved with double bravery inscriptions in Cyrillic script, c1850, blade 31in (78.5cm).
£350–400 *WAL*

Powder & Ammunition

A priming horn, probably Eastern European with brass stopper, very good condition, 19thC, overall 6in (15cm) long.
£140–160 *ASB*

A shotgun cartridge extractor and dog whistle, c1930, 2¼in (55mm) long.
£25–30 *WAB*

A leather cartridge case, with brass lock, c1900, 15½in (39.5cm) wide.
£300–325 *RIS*

MONEY BOXES

A Mauchline ware money box, with a print of Holyrood Palace, Edinburgh, c1880, 4¾in (12cm) wide.
£30–40 *IW*

A Victorian cast iron money box, in the form of a bear, 6½in (16.5cm) high.
£75–85 *AnS*

A German tin and glass Stollwerck Savings Bank chocolate dispenser, c1900, 6in (15cm) high.
£200–230 *MSB*

The New Century Eureka Bank tin stove, No. 410, c1910, 5¼in (13cm) high.
£75–85 *MSB*

An American tin Commonwealth Three Coin Registering Savings Bank, 1905, 5in (12.5cm) high.
£70–90 *MSB*

A tin money box, 1932, 5½in (14cm) high.
£150–180 *CSK*

r. An American Champion tin Cash Register money box, c1925, 3½in (9cm) high.
£70–80 *MSB*

l. A wooden money box, in the form of St Mary-of-the-Song School, c1925, 4in (10cm) high.
£75–85 *MSB*

A tin money box, by Burnett Ltd, 1930s, 5¾in (14.5cm) wide.
£70–80 *MSB*

A Yorkshire Penny Bank, 1930s, 3¼in (8cm) diam.
£8–12 *WAB*

A Birmingham Municipal Bank money box, 1930s, 2¾in (70mm) high.
£8–12 *WAB*

An American Dime Register Bank tin money box, by J. Chien, c1945, 2in (50mm) high.
£40–50 *MSB*

Two American tin money boxes, with coffee labels, 1950s, 4in (10cm) high.
£20–25 each *MSB*

A tin Play-Store Register money box, 1930s, 3½in (9cm) wide.
£75–85 *MSB*

Two American wood and tin barrel money boxes, 1930s–1950s, tallest 3¾in (9.5cm) high.
£15–35 each *MSB*

A Yorkshire Electricity Board Savings Bank money box, 1950s, 4½ x 3in (11.5 x 7.5cm).
£2–3 *WAB*

> **Cross Reference**
> Advertising & Packaging

A Manchester & County Bank Ltd money box, 1950s, 4in (10cm) wide, with original box.
£8–12 *WAB*

A Queen's dolls' house money box, by Chubb & Sons, 1930s, 4¼in (11cm) high.
£24–28 *WAB*

A Get Rich Quick Bank tin money box, by Louis Marx & Co, 1940s, 3½in (9cm) high.
£70–80 *MSB*

A Vim tin money box, c1945, 2¾in (70mm) high.
£45–55 *BBR*

MUSIC

A six-bells musical box, No. 11962, playing 10 airs, in grained case with rosewood lid and inlay tune sheet, late 19thC, cylinder 11in (28cm).
£550–650 *P(Ba)*

La Danse a l'Opéra de Paris, by Léandre Vaillat, published by Amiot-Dumont, Paris, 1870, 12 x 9½in (30.5 x 24cm).
£50–60 *HB*

A musical box, No. 29814, by Ernst Holzweissig Nachfolger, playing 10 airs, with zither attachment and a tune sheet, in grained case, c1890.
£800–900 *P(Ba)*

l. A West African wooden and leather drum, probably Gambia region, c1910, 15½in (39.5cm) high.
£250–300 *LHB*

An Indonesian Mandurah wooden slit gong, c1925, 28½in (72.5cm) long.
£100–120 *LHB*

A Weber pianola, Model 50, c1921, 59in (150cm) wide.
£4,000–4,500 *PIA*

A Boyd-London Autoplayer, with oak case, unrestored, c1926, 61½in (156cm) wide.
£550–650 *PIA*

ORIENTAL

In 1986 public imagination was caught by the auctioning of the Nanking cargo in Amsterdam. This 18th century Chinese porcelain had been salvaged from the wreck of a Dutch ship sunk in the South China Sea and the romantic story, combined with expertly handled publicity, attracted enthusiastic prices. This section includes ceramics from the Nanking collection as well as Oriental ware rescued from the vessels carrying the Vung Tau Cargo (foundered c1690) and the Diana Cargo (lost c1816).

Ceramics

A Chinese blue and white tea caddy, 18thC, 10¾in (27.5cm) high.
£100–120 *PC*

A Japanese Kutani bottle-necked vase, 19thC, 7¼in (18.5cm) high.
£30–40 *PSA*

A pair of Chinese vases, some damage, 19thC, 7in (18cm) high.
£45–55 *PSA*

A Chinese celadon porcelain baluster-shaped vase, with fluted design, 1900s, 15in (38cm) high.
£225–265 *PSA*

A Japanese enamelled and hand-painted plate, c1910, 8½in (21.5cm) diam.
£30–35 *BGA(K)*

Diana Cargo

Three brown glazed storage jars, c1816, 6in (15cm) high.
£80–100 each *RBA*

l. An encrusted glass port bottle, c1816, 10in (25.5cm) high.
£140–170 *RBA*

A brown glazed storage jar, c1750, 15¾in (40cm) high.
£400–500 *RBA*

For a further selection of Diana Cargo items please refer to *Miller's Collectables Price Guide 1996–97*, page 277.

A blue and white Starburst dish, c1816, 11in (28cm) diam.
£150–180 *CFA*

A collection of blue and white conical bowls, c1816, 5½in (14cm) diam.
£115–125 each *RBA*

Nanking Cargo

A selection of *blanc de chine* figures of Immortals, c1750, 4¼in (11cm) high.
£120–140 *RBA*

A blue and white soup dish, Three Pavilions pattern, c1750, 9in (23cm) diam.
£350–380 *RBA*

A blue and white underglazed bowl, with trellis pattern border, c1750, 7½in (19cm) diam.
£350–400 *RBA*

A provincial blue and white Dragon plate, c1750, 7¾in (20cm) diam.
£110–130 *RBA*

An Imari blue and white beer mug, c1750, 5½in (14cm) high.
£650–750 *RBA*

An Imari overglazed teapot and cover, c1750, 9in (23cm) high.
£425–475 *RBA*

A blue and white tea bowl and saucer, c1750, tea bowl 3in (7.5cm) diam.
£165–175 *ORI*

Vung Tau Cargo

A blue and white octagonal bowl and saucer, c1690, saucer 5½in (14cm) diam.
£400–450 *RBA*

r. A blue and white vase with cover, c1690, 5in (12.5cm) high.
£450–500 *RBA*

Costume & Textiles

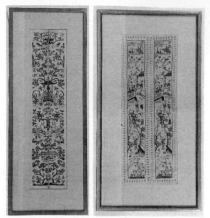

Two Chinese sleeve panels, c1890, largest 22 x 5¼in (56 x 13cm), framed.
£200–250 each *PC*

A pair of Chinese blue silk sleeve panels, decorated with vases of flowers in gold couching, c1890, 20 x 4½in (51 x 11.5cm), framed.
£165–185 *PBr*

A Chinese hand-embroidered tunic, 1940s.
£100–120 *TCF*

Netsuke & Carvings

A Chinese silver two-piece clasp, 1930s, 2¾in (7cm) square.
£65–75 *JBB*

A bone netsuke, in the form of a bat, c1850, 1½in (3.5cm) wide.
£350–400 *AnS*

r. A bone netsuke, in the form of Sennin, 18thC, 3½in (9cm) high.
£750–850 *AnS*

An ivory *okimono*, c1870, 2½in (6.5cm) high.
£200–250 *AnS*

An okimono is a small carved ornament worn by the Japanese.

A Manchurian anthracite figure, 1930s, 5in (12.5cm) high.
£70–80 *AnS*

A pair of dogs of Fo, c1900, 11½in (29cm) high.
£350–400 *AnS*

PAPER MONEY
British Isles

A Monmouthshire Bank five guineas note, 1791.
£350–400 *P*

A Fisher United Kingdom of Great Britain and Ireland, ten shillings note, second issue, c1922.
£60–80 *WP*

A Union Bank of Scotland one pound note, 1903.
£200–250 *NAR*

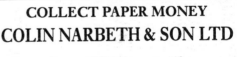

A States of Guernsey WWII occupation sixpence note, dated '16th October 1941'.
£100–120 *NAR*

A Bradbury one pound note, first-type, signed by John Bradbury, 1914.
£200–250 *WP*

A Belfast Banking Co Ltd five pounds note, dated '2nd October 1942'.
£25–30 *WP*

r. A British Linen Bank twenty pounds note, dated '15th November 1957'.
£50–60 *WP*

A Bank of England one pound note, c1940–45.
£5–8 *NAR*

A Black Sheep Company of Wales 50p 'Fantasy' note, c1960.
£10–15 *WP*

A States of Jersey one pound
note, c1963.
£12–14 *WP*

A States of Jersey ten pounds
note, c1965.
£20–25 *WP*

A States of Guernsey five pounds
note, signed by Hodder, c1970.
£15–20 *WP*

Foreign

A French ten livres note, c1720.
£180–200 *NAR*

A French Louis XVI five
hundred livres note, 1790.
£80–100 *NAR*

An Italian Siege of Venice one
hundred lire note, 1848.
£50–70 *NAR*

A Latvian twenty latu note, 1936.
£30–40 *NAR*

An Israeli
ten pound
note, 1952.
£60–100 *NAR*

A Sudanese Siege of Khartoum
one hundred piastros note, 1884.
£200–250 *NAR*

A Charas Bank one yuan note, 1937.
£375–400 *P*

A Polish twenty zlotych note, issued by
a government in exile, 1939.
£100–150 *NAR*

PHOTOGRAPHS

A sixth-plate hand-tinted daguerreotype, Jenny Lind, by Jessie H. Whitehurst, cased, 1850s.
£620–700 *S(NY)*

A cabinet card, by Lafayette, London, c1880, 5½ x 4in (14 x 10cm).
£5–8 *HEG*

Lafayette had studios in Paris from 1865 and in the British Isles from the 1880s. His photographs are among the most collectable of the late 19thC.

An ambrotype, in a case, 1880s, 3¼ x 2¾in (8.5 x 7cm).
£30–40 *HEG*

A stereoscopic daguerreotype, by W. E. Kilburn, 1850s,
£400–600 *HEG*

A stereoscopic daguerreotype, Town Square with Hoche Monument, by Jules Duboscq, 1850s, 3½ x 7in (9 x 18cm).
£1,400–1,600 *S(NY)*

An ambrotype, in a union case, possibly American, 1880s, 2½ x 2in (6.5 x 5cm).
£30–40 *HEG*

Ambrotype is the American name given to a photograph on glass, with lights given by the silver and shades created by a dark background showing through.

Cross Reference
Ephemera

An album of sporting memorabilia photographs, 1880s, albumen prints 8¾ x 11in (22 x 28cm).
£30–50 *HEG*

A stereoscopic daguerreotype, Le Pompe Notre-Dame, by Jules Duboscq, 1850s, 3½ x 7in (9 x 18cm).
£2,200–£2,800 *S(NY)*

A stereoscopic daguerreotype, by Claudet, with original viewing case and collapsible lenses, 1850s.
£2,500–2,700 *HEG*

A Victorian album of *cartes de visite* and cabinet cards, 11 x 9in (28 x 23cm).
£65–85 *HEG*

A late Victorian album of photographs taken in Egypt, albumen prints 8¾ x 11in (22 x 28cm).
£200–300 *HEG*

The value of an album depends on the quantity of photographs, quality, subject, date, album condition and photographer – in this case Zangakis and Arnoux.

A late Victorian album of 24 photographs of Newmarket, some damage to album, albumen prints 6 x 7¾in (15 x 20cm).
£350–400 DW

An album of *cartes de visite*, 1900s, 11 x 9in (28 x 23cm).
£35–45 HEG

A cabinet card, c1900, 6½ x 4¼in (16.5 x 10.5cm).
£4–5 HEG

A photograph, On The Line, by William Hart, signed, 1950s.
£1,000–1,200 S(NY)

A collection of 5 photogravures, by Alfred Stieglitz, from the Picturesque Bits portfolio, 1897, largest 6 x 11¼in (15 x 28.5cm).
£4,800–5,200 S(NY)

A ferrotype, by Jacques-Henri Lartigue, c1911, 7¼ x 9½in (18.5 x 24cm).
£1,400–1,600 S(NY)

Two photographs, Selected Images, by Jacques-Henri Lartigue, c1908, 9½ x 13½in (24 x 34cm).
£2,400–2,800 S(NY)

A ferrotype of a woman with a dog, by André Kertész, c1938, 9¼ x 7¾in (23 x 20cm).
£1,200–1,500 S(NY)

A *carte de visite* and cabinet card album, 1900s, 10 x 8in (25.5 x 20.5cm).
£35–45 HEG

A satinwood frame, containing a photograph of two young ladies, 1920s, 4½ x 3½in (11.5 x 9cm).
£35–45 PSA

A matt photograph, Virginia Creeper at Green Cove, by O. Winston Link, signed, framed, 1956, 3¾ x 4¾in (9.5 x 12cm).
£2,000–2,400 S(NY)

A matt photograph of a man with his horse, by Josef Koudelka, signed, 1968, 8¼ x 12½in (21 x 32cm).
£1,200–1,400 S(NY)

PIGS

People often focus a collection around a favourite subject. Animals are certainly one of the best-loved themes and this year Miller's have centred their attention on the pig.

Many stories and customs have been attached to this round-bodied, short-legged, omnivorous mammal. In mythology, Jupiter was said to have been suckled by a sow. The pig was sacred and consequently sacrificed to Ceres, goddess of fertility, 'because it taught men to turn up the earth.' An unclean animal according to Mosaic law, in the middle ages the pig was portrayed in Western art as a symbol of lust and greed, whilst according to the Gospel (Mark V: 11–15) the five dark marks on the inner-

side of a pig's forelegs were left by the devil as he entered the animal's body.

More recent stories have, with some notable exceptions, been kinder to this rotund and clever creature. Famous pigs in literature include Beatrix Potter's Pigling Bland, Piglet – friend of Winnie the Pooh – Wilbur in *Charlotte's Web*, the dreaded Napoleon from George Orwell's *Animal Farm* and the Three Little Pigs. Porcine successes on film and TV include *Pinky and Perky*, *The Muppets'* Miss Piggy and the movie of *Babe*, who is perhaps the only pig who has ever been tipped for an Oscar nomination. The following selection of decorative pigs dates from the 19th century.

A Dennis's Pig Powders tin sign, slight damage, 1930s, 12¼ x 18in (31 x 45.5cm).
£150–170 *BBR*

A pair of bronze pig candlesticks, c1920, 5in (12.5cm) high.
£150–200 *HIK*

A silver pincushion, in the form of a pig, c1905, 3¼in (8cm) long.
£350–375 *HAN*

A white metal pin-cushion, in the form of a pig, c1910, 5½in (14cm) high.
£90–110 *HIK*

A gold brooch, in the form of a pig with sapphire eyes, c1950, 1¼in (3cm) long.
£250–300 *JES*

Books

P. G. Wodehouse, *Service with a Smile*, first edition, 1961, 7½ x 5in (19 x 12.5cm).
£35–45 *NW*

E. B. White, *Charlotte's Web*, published by Harper & Row, New York and Evanston, 1980, 9 x 6in (23 x 15cm).
£8–10 *PC*

Famous People's Pigs, published by The Forum Press, first edition, 1943, 7 x 5in (18 x 12.5cm).
£10–15 *NW*

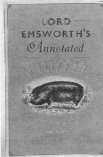

l. Augustus Whiffle, *The Care of the Pig*, Lord Emsworth's annotated copy, edited by James Hogg, first US edition, 1992, 8¾ x 5½in (22 x 14cm).
£10–14 *NW*

A 1952 first edition of this American children's book (with an identical cover to the example shown) fetched £530 when sold recently by California Book Auctions, USA.

Ceramics

Two Wemyss pigs, painted mark to bases,
restored, c1900, 6½in (16.5cm) high:
l. £420–500
r. £280–320 *GAK*

A Royal Doulton pig, 1922–46,
4¼in (11cm) long.
£125–145 *TP*

A Samson pig, c1870,
5in (12.5cm) long.
£160–170 *AnA*

A pottery pig with Poole crest,
c1920, 2¾in (7cm) long.
£12–15 *BCO*

A pair of Aynsley bisque pigs,
1920–30, 2½in (6.5cm) high.
£30–35 *ML*

An underglazed pig, possibly
by Denby, marked 'Wilag',
c1950, 15in (38cm) long.
£100–125 *KES*

An inkwell/pin holder, in
the form of a pig, c1970,
3in (7.5cm) long.
£5–6 *TAC*

A bisque pig, with 2 piglets,
c1950, 4¾in (12cm) high.
£8–9 *KNG*

A Rye Pottery Sussex Pig, 1950s, 5in (12.5cm) long,
together with box.
£100–125 *NCA*

*The Sussex Pig was traditionally used at country
weddings to drink the health of the bride and
bridegroom. The head is removable and stands on
its snout as a mug. From this the guests could drink
the traditional 'hogshead of beer'. The body stands
independently and can be used as a jug. The pig
carries the motto:*
*'And you can pook, and you can shove,
But a Sussex pig he wun't be druv'.*

A Royal Doulton pig, on a wooden plinth,
c1970, 6in (15cm) long.
£24–28 *TAC*

Beswick

A Beswick pig, c1910,
5¾in (14.5cm) long.
£85–95 *GAS*

A Beswick pig, 1940–71,
1½in (3.5cm) long.
£30–40 *TP*

A Beswick figure, Pigling
Bland, from the Beatrix Potter
series, first version, 1955–72,
4½in (11.5cm) high.
£200–225 *TP*

Two Beswick English Country
Folk figures, The Lady Pig and
Gentleman Pig, 1993–present,
5½in (14cm) high.
£18–23 each *TP*

l. A Beswick figure, Little Pig
Robinson Spying, from the
Beatrix Potter series, 1987–93,
3¾in (9.5cm) high.
£140–160 *TP*

A Beswick Wall Queen Pig,
1980s, 6in (15cm) long.
£18–22 *TAC*

A collection of Beswick Pig Promenade figures:
Andrew the cymbal player, Gloucester Old Spot,
David the flute player, Tamworth, Daniel the
violinist, Saddleback, James the triangle player,
Tamworth piglet, 1993–96, tallest 5¼in (13cm) high.
£28–30 each *TP*

Piggy Banks

A cast iron pig money bank,
c1880, 8½in (21.5cm) long.
£140–160 *HIK*

A SylvaC pig money bank,
c1930–82, 4in (10cm) long.
£25–30 *TAC*

A cast iron pig money bank,
painted to appear old, c1996,
6in (15cm) long.
£30–50 *YC*

PLASTICS

A phenolic sugar box, 1920s,
5¼in (13cm) high.
£16–18 *REN*

Two Dunlop Punch and Judy
hot water bottles, 1920s,
largest 15½in (40cm) high.
£16–18 each *WAB*

An ivorine mini cruet,
1920s–30s, 2in (5cm) high.
£12–15 *REN*

l. A Bakelite
perpetual
calendar, 1920s,
3in (7.5cm) wide.
£24–28 *TAC*

A plastic flat fish brooch,
1920s, 2in (5cm) wide.
£18–22 *SnA*

A speckled Bakelite cup and
saucer, British made, 1920s,
5½in (14cm) high.
£10–12 *REN*

A Bakelite inkstand, 1930s, 11in (28cm) wide.
£55–65 *WAB*

A speckled Bakelite string or
wool ball, 4in (10cm) diam, and
a darning mushroom, 1920s.
£9–12 each *REN*

A Bakelite lemon squeezer,
1930s, 5½in (14cm) diam.
£10–12 *REN*

A set of Bandalasta beakers,
contained in a leather case,
1930s, 4¼in (11cm) high.
£15–18 *WAB*

Select Glossary

Bakelite: Trade name for
plastics by the Bakelite
company, also generic name
for phenolic plastics.

Bandalasta: Marbled plastic
ware, popular 1920s–30s.

Ivorine: Plastic imitating ivory.

Lucite: Trade name for acrylic
plastic, its strength and
clarity make it a substitute
for glass. Also known under
the trade names Perspex
and Plexiglas.

Melamine: Tough, glossy
plastic, popular from the
1950s for tableware.

Phenolic: Shortened version
of phenol formaldehyde,
can be clear or coloured,
and was used for jewellery
and domestic items.

A selection of Bakelite egg cups, 1930s, 1¾in (4.5cm) high.
£3–4 each *REN*

A Stewart's Bakelite hair dryer, 1930s, 8in (20.5cm) long.
£30–40 *WAB*

A Bakelite egg cup, 1936, 1¾in (4.5cm) high.
£4–6 *BKK*

An American smoky plastic transparent handbag, studded with rhinestones, with green detachable lining, 1940s, 5½in (14cm) wide.
£30–40 *SnA*

A green plastic The Velos ash barrel non-smoker ashtray, c1940, 3¼in (8cm) high.
£7–9 *REN*

A plastic egg timer, 1950s, 4in (10cm) high.
£8–12 *WAB*

A transparent plastic bangle with yellow trails, early 1960s, 3½in (9cm) diam.
£35–45 *SnA*

Andy Capp, an Avon talcum powder plastic container, 1969, 9in (23cm) high.
£30–35 *WAB*

A Beetleware pale blue Melamine salt cellar, 1950s, 2¾in (7cm) high.
£1–2 *REN*

A Lucite pepper and salt set, 1950s, 3½in (9cm) high.
£20–25 *BEV*

Three orange Melaware cups and saucers, 1960s–70s, saucer 6in (15cm) diam.
£12–15 *BEV*

r. A pair of fluorescent plastic ear clips and a bangle, 1970s, 3in (7.5cm) diam.
£40–50 *SnA*

PUPPETS

Many of the puppets in the following section were produced by Pelham, perhaps the most famous of all British puppet companies. The firm was launched by Bob Pelham in 1947, employing disabled war veterans to create his hand-painted wooden puppets and remained in operation until 1992. Subjects ranged from traditional fairytale characters, such as witches and pirates, to film and TV favourites beginning with *Muffin the Mule* in the 1950s, moving on to include Disney characters and subsequent television heroes from *Magic Roundabout* figures to the Wombles. Puppets were well made and

easy to operate with the black stringing eventually being replaced by colour-coded string to avoid confusion and the ever present threat of tangling. Known as 'Pelpop', Bob Pelham's greatest wish was to encourage children to take up puppetry and at its peak, his 'Pelpup Club' had a membership of thousands of children. It is these children, now grown-up, who are returning to collect the puppets. Old and rare examples are becoming increasingly desirable and the value is enhanced by the presence of the original box, which can also be helpful in dating the puppet.

A carved wood Burmese tiger puppet, cloth between neck and shoulders and waist for flexibility, 1930s, 16in (40.5cm) long.
£240–270 *PaM*

A ventriloquist's dummy, dressed as a sailor, with eye, mouth, top lip and independent moving eyebrow movements, c1910, 35in (89cm) high.
£750–850 *PaM*

A Pelham puppet, Muffin the Mule, c1950s, 5½in (14cm) high.
£40–60 *RAR*

A pair of dancing figures, with papier mâché heads and wooden hands, loose on rod for dancing movement, used in cabaret, 1940s, 25in (63.5cm) high.
£100–125 *PaM*

A Richard Barr puppet, with eye and mouth movements, c1940s–50s, 18in (45.5cm) high.
£125–155 *PaM*

Richard Barr, the boy magician and professional puppeteer, made this puppet for performance use.

l. A Thomas the Tank Engine professional puppet, used in children's theatre, the engine driver's moustache moves and Thomas has eye and mouth movement, 1950s, 14in (35.5cm) high.
£110–130 *PaM*

r. A set of Pelham glove puppets, Punch, Judy, clown and dog, good condition, retailed by Harrods, 1950s, 13in (33cm) high.
£95–115 *CMF*

A Pelham golly string puppet, unboxed, 1950s, 12in (30.5cm) high.
£45–55 *CMF*

A Pelham string puppet, Fritzi, c1960, 12½in (32cm) high.
£20–30 *ARo*

Two Walt Disney puppets, Pinocchio and Goofy, 1960s, 7½in (19cm) high.
£15–20 each *TAR*

A Pelham guitarist puppet, unboxed, 1960s, 12in (30.5cm) high.
£30–40 *CMF*

l. A Pelham puppet, Oz the Ostrich, boxed, 1960s, 8in (20.5cm) high.
£30–40 *CMF*

A Pelham puppet, The Girl, c1966, 13in (33cm) high.
£30–40 *CMF*

A Pelham puppet, Rupert Bear, boxed, 1971, 10½in (26.5cm) high.
£45–55 *CMF*

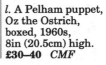

l. A Pelham puppet, Donald Duck, unboxed, 1970s, 9in (23cm) high.
£45–55 *PaM*

A Pelham puppet, Mickey Mouse, unboxed, 1970s, 11in (28cm) high.
£35–45 *PaM*

A Pelham puppet, McBoozle, the whisky-drinking Scotsman, mint condition, blue box, 1970s, 12in (30.5cm) high.
£45–55 *PaM*

A Pelham puppet, Mickey Mouse, 1970s, 10¾in (27.5cm) high.
£30–40 *ARo*

A Pelham puppet, Pinocchio, 1970s, 11½in (29cm) high.
£25–30 *HUX*

A Pelham green faced witch string puppet, with black dress and cloak with red lining, unboxed, 1970s, 12in (30.5cm) high.
£45–55 *PaM*

A Pelham Womble puppet, Orinoco, boxed, 1975, 9in (23cm) high.
£30–40 *CMF*

r. A Pelham Rotundan, with blue head and orange limbs, yellow box, mint condition, 1970s, 7in (18cm) high.
£45–55 *PaM*

The Beatles, 'Hello Goodbye', 7in single, US Capitol, 1967.
£35–40 *TOT*

A poster for The Beatles concert at Widnes, 1962, 29½ x 20 (75 x 51cm).
£2,300–2,600 *S*

A hand-painted poster for The Beatles concert at the Kaiserkeller, Hamburg, 1960, 42½ x 28½in (108 x 72.5cm).
£18,000–20,000 *S*

A peaked motorcycle helmet, with hand-painted designs of the yellow submarine, signed by John Lennon and Paul McCartney, 1960s.
£2,400–2,800 *CSK*

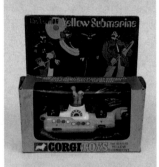

A Corgi Toys The Beatles Yellow Submarine, 1960s, 7in (17.5cm) wide.
£250–300 *NTM*

The Beatles, 'Sgt Peppers Lonely Hearts Club Band', picture disc, US Capitol, 1977.
£15–20 *TOT*

The Blues Project, 'Best of the Blues Project', US Verve, 1970.
£12–15 *TOT*

The Champs, 'Go Champs Go', LP, London Records, 1958.
£15–20 *TOT*

l. A Parisian Ambassador alto saxophone, signed by Bill Clinton, accompanied by a Sheraton Washington Hotel Inauguration room keycard, an Inauguration Day pin badge and *The Washington Post*, January 20, 1993.
£2,500–3,000 *CSK*

Roger Daltrey's chamois leather stage jumpsuit, early 1970s, some wear.
£3,000–3,500 *S*

The Detroit Spinners, UK album, mono, Tamla-Motown label, 1968.
£30–40 *CTO*

The Dixie Cups, 'Riding High', stereo LP, ABC Paramount, Canada, 1965.
£20–25 *TOT*

Jimi Hendrix's 'Afghan' jacket, signed and inscribed on the left sleeve 'To Jools Stay free', dated '1968'.
£11,500–12,500 *S*

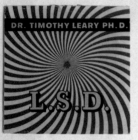

Dr Timothy Leary PH.D., 'L.S.D.', LP, US Dixie, 1966.
£40–100 *TOT*

A pair of Freddie Mercury's PVC stage trousers, with letter from the Queen Official International Fan Club and colour photocopies of Freddie, 1982.
£2,400–2,800 *CSK*

Various artists, 'Robin and the 7 Hoods', LP, Reprise UK, 1964.
£15–20 *TOT*

The Rolling Stones, 'Jumpin' Jack Flash, 7in single, London US, 1968.
£10–15 *TOT*

l. Xray Spex, 'Germfree Adolescents', LP, with lyric inner sleeve, EMI, 1978.
£5–20 *CTO*
The value of a record is dependent upon condition.

Keith Richards' 'Crazy Joe' Stratocaster model guitar, signed in gold marker, 1989.
£3,700–4,200 *S*

A Wurlitzer Lyric Hi-Fi Stereo jukebox, 1960s, 54in (137cm) high.
£600–800 *SWO*

A brass surveying level, by
H. Barrow & Co, London, with
mahogany transit case, 19thC,
15¾in (40cm) wide.
£400–475 *BSA*

A mahogany cased Sykes
hydrometer, with brass float and
weights, by J. Long, London,
c1900, 8in (20.5cm) wide.
£75–95 *BSA*

A Hearson's Patent
Strophometer, 19thC,
9in (24cm) high.
£100–150 *BSA*

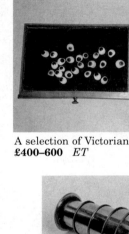

A brass microscope,
rack-and pinion focusing,
with 3-stage object lens,
c1890, 9½in (24cm) high.
£150–200 *BSA*

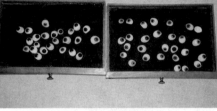

A selection of Victorian glass eyes.
£400–600 *ET*

A brass veterinary syringe,
by Maw & Sons, c1900,
10¼in (26cm) long.
£14–18 *WAB*

A gilt-brass and ivory seven-draw
monocular, 18thC, 5in (12.5cm) diam.
£250–300 *BSA*

A pair of gilt-brass and pierced
ivory opera glasses, with
leather travelling pouch,
c1920, 4¼in (11cm) long.
£75–95 *BSA*

r. A brass electric fan, c1920,
11in (28cm) diam.
£90–110 *HHa*

A Western Electric/Hawthorn
fan, with 'vane' oscillator
American, c1912,
12in (30.5cm) diam.
£200–250 *MRo*

A thuya wood sewing
casket, with fittings,
c1800, 9in (23cm) wide.
£450–550 *COT*

A pewter inlaid rosewood sewing
box, c1830, 6in (15cm) wide.
£150–200 *MB*

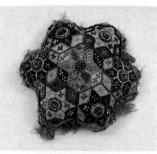

A velvet patchwork and
beaded pincushion, c1884,
9in (23cm) diam.
£150–200 *LB*

A doll needle case,
attributed to Alt, Beck &
Gottschalck, c1900,
4½in (11.5cm) high.
£180–220 *PSA*

A purple leather sewing
case, the tools with
mother-of-pearl handles,
1920s, 6in (15cm) long.
£30–40 *WAB*

A Dewhurst's Sylko Machine Twist
haberdashers wooden counter dispenser,
c1920, 20½in (52cm) wide.
£90–110 *OTS*

r. A hand-embroidered
silk velvet sewing
bag, with wooden
handles, 1920s,
14½in (37cm) wide.
£15–20 *SUS*

A crêpe sewing bag,
1920s–30s, 10in (25.5cm) high.
£18–20 *SUS*

A wicker sewing basket, with raffia
decoration, 1920s, 11in (28cm) wide.
£20–30 *SUS*

A handmade felt sewing
bag, 1930s, 11in (28cm) wide.
£15–20 *SUS*

A model ship, hand-built by
a seaman who had sailed in
the original vessel, c1931,
27in (69cm) long.
£120–140 *AXT*

A Bowman Aquaplane model
yacht, c1935, 20in (51cm) long.
£35–45 *OTS*

A Sestrel ship's barometer,
c1950, 8in (20cm) diam.
£90–100 *BSA*

A pair of copper double
masthead electric lamps,
1960s, 34in (87cm) high.
£200–250 *GWA*

A Victorian shell work
picture frame, with
picture depicting
Grace Darling,
18in (45.5cm) high.
£40–50 *BSA*

A modern reproduction
Titanic poster, 1990s,
33½ x 23½in (85 x 60cm).
£10–15 *MAP*

A ship in a bottle, with
coastal scene, c1930,
10½in (27cm) long.
£35–45 *BSA*

A share certificate for The Channel Tubular
Railway Preliminary Company Ltd,
for 5 shares, dated '19th May, 1892'.
£200–250 *GKR*

A certificate for Mossley
Spinning & Manufacturing
Co Ltd, dated '1875'.
£15–20 *GKR*

A certificate for
Mines D'Or De La
France, dated '1898'.
£35–45 *GKR*

A horn snuff mull, with silver
mounts, c1773, 6¼in (16cm) long.
£200–240 *MB*

A Scottish painted sycamore snuff
box, c1800, 4in (10cm) wide.
£250–300 *MB*

A brass cigarette case,
c1900, 4in (10cm) long.
£10–15 *PC*

A John Bull cigar and
cigarette vending machine,
c1900, 36in (19cm) high.
£3,000–4,000 *PC*

A carved wood pipe,
possibly German,
c1910, 7in (18cm) long.
£18–20 *OD*

Two Muratti's After Lunch Cigarettes
tins, 1920s–30s, 3½in (9cm) wide.
£24–28 each *WAB*

A smoking set, with playing
card decoration, 1940–50s,
2½in (6.4cm) high.
£18–22 *FAM*

A German match striker,
c1910, 5¼in (13cm) high.
£40–50 *ML*

A Junior Shell tin,
inscribed 'For Cleaning and
Automatic Lighters', 1930s,
3¾in (9.5cm) high.
£14–18 *WAB*

A table lighter in the form of a
roulette wheel, fully operational,
possibly Japanese, 1950s,
5in (12.5cm) diam.
£75–85 *FAM*

A chrome and enamel
table lighter, possibly
Japanese, 1950s,
3in (7.5cm) high.
£40–50 *FAM*

An American cotton gaberdine
bowling shirt, 1950s.
£125–150 *TCR*

*The figure of Snoopy on the back makes
this shirt particularly collectable.*

A Mattel Snoopy musical
box, 1969, 5½in (14cm) high.
£15–20 *PC*

A plastic chirping Woodstock,
c1977, 6in (15cm) high.
£8–15 *PC*

A selection of Snoopy fruit-shaped
money boxes, 1976, 4¾in (12cm) high.
£8–15 each *PC*

A Snoopy die-cast car,
in original box, 1977,
6in (15cm) wide.
£15–20 *PC*

Two Pelham puppets,
Snoopy and Peanuts, 1979,
10¼in (26cm) high.
£20–30 *PC*

A Snoopy burger money
box, 1979, 4in (10cm) diam.
£2–3 *BGA(B)*

A Snoopy Mother's Day plate,
1980, 7¾in (19.5cm) diam.
£15–20 *PC*

A pair of Snoopy rubber book ends, 1981,
4¼in (11cm) high.
£10–15 *PC*

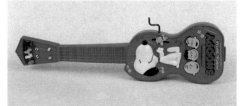

A Snoopy musical guitar,
1980, 16in (41cm) long.
£15–20 *PC*

Two Snoopy die-cast bi-planes, mid-1980s,
smallest 2in (5cm) high.
£5–10 each *PC*

A straw-filled archery target, inscribed 'Jacques, London', 1950s, 20in (50.5cm) diam.
£25–35 *WAB*

A cricket ball trophy, inscribed 'Ripon C.C., 1958, D. Drake, 122 Wickets', 7in (18cm) wide.
£20–30 *WAB*

A 2½in polished brass crank-wind fishing reel, with bone handle, 19thC.
£40–50 *BSA*

A Hardy Silex Major fishing reel, 1930, 4½in (11.5cm) diam.
£75–95 *WAB*

A Royal Doulton golfer character jug, 1970, 3in (7.5cm) high.
£35–45 *PSA*

Two Carlton Ware golfing figures, 1980s, 3½in (9cm) high.
£14–18 each *TAC*

A copper and brass hunting horn, by Gallow & Sons, Park Lane, London, c1800, 9in (23cm) long.
£80–85 *TAR*

A tennis racket and press, 1930s, 27in (68cm) long.
£20–25 *WAB*

A boxed set of 6 Slazenger lawn tennis balls, c1935, 8in (20.5cm) wide.
£30–50 *MSh*

A Coalport commemorative plate for the Commonwealth Games, 1986, 28in (71cm) diam.
£25–50 *TAR*

A Sèvres vase, for the Paris Olympics, 1924, 13¼in (33.5cm) high.
£1,000–1,200 *SUC*

RADIOS & TELEVISIONS

Radio values are determined both by the external design and the internal mechanism. 'Technical interest is important and anything novel in design, outrageous in styling or of superlative quality will always be collectable,' says dealer Philip Knighton.

The production of domestic radios took off in Britain in the 1920s, coinciding with the birth of the BBC. Many innovative sets were created and these earlier models can be highly desirable, especially for the academic collector with historical and technical interest in the field.

The 1930s was a golden age for radio design and the Art Deco extravaganzas from this period appeal not only to the wireless buff but the growing band of collectors seeking a period set to suit a particular decor. Good looks can be more important than technical innovation. 'Ekco radios from the early thirties have been fetching enormous sums,' explains

Knighton, 'inside they might not be very interesting, but the round case was a breakaway design only rendered possible through Bakelite and they epitomise the spirit of the period.'

Production of radios was extremely curtailed during the war, leading to shortages once hostilities had ceased. Manufacture flourished again in the late 1940s, and collectable radios from this and the following decade include midget and miniature sets and the first transistor radios that appeared in the 1950s and revolutionised popular listening. 'The market for fifties radios is currently very strong, particularly with people who grew up in the sixties,' says Knighton. 'Collectors are looking for extravagant, typically fifties' designs, the more over-the-top the better.' Post-1960, novelty and unusually designed radios are among the most desirable items, and contemporary novelty radios could be a good bet for collectables of the future.

An AJS Symphony Five radio, in mahogany case with sloping pull-down front panel, with bracket feet, c1926, 22in (56cm) wide.
£350–400 *P(Ba)*

A Spartan Bluebird type 558 console radio, with AM/SW dial, blue mirror and chrome trim design, some damage, 1933, 48in (122cm) high.
£1,450–1,650 *P(Ba)*

A BTH horn speaker, 1927, 21½in (55cm) high.
£50–100 *GM*

An Amplion battery valve radio, 1930, 20½in (52cm) high.
£120–180 *GM*

An Ekco type A22 mains receiver, with black Bakelite cabinet, chrome trim and circular dial, 1930s, 14in (35.5cm) high.
£700–800 *P(Ba)*

A Sterling wireless loudspeaker, with original box, 1927, 16½in (42cm) high.
£120–180 *ET*

l. A Ekco AD65 Bakelite radio, with walnut finish and original Ekco beechwood framed radio stand, stamped under shelf 'Ekco Registered Design No. 794465', c1934, 41in (104cm) high.
£800–1,000 *BTA*

A Cossor Melody Maker radio, 1930, 8in (20.5cm) high.
£60–100 *GM*

A Mullard MA3 valve radio, with wooden case, 1935, 19in (48cm) high.
£50–100 *GM*

An Emerson Snow White and the Seven Dwarfs radio, in painted cream case with imitation painted wood front, 1936, 9in (23cm) high.
£950–1,000 *P(Ba)*

A Pye AC4D radio, 1930, 19¾in (50cm) high.
£140–200 *GM*

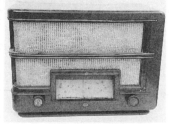

A Mullard MAS90 radio, with brown Bakelite case and brass trim, 1939, 12½in (32cm) high.
£70–120 *GM*

A Mullard MAS6 valve radio, with Bakelite case, 1937, 12½in (32cm) high.
£60–100 *GM*

An His Master's Voice 496 radio, with wooden case and aircraft dial, 1938, 19¾in (50cm) high.
£50–100 *GM*

A GEC 4040 valve radio, with brown Bakelite case, 1939, 11in (28cm) high.
£70–120 *GM*

l. A GEC BC4650 valve radio, with Bakelite case, 1946, 13½in (34cm) high.
£50–100 *GM*

A Ferranti 146 radio, with black Bakelite case and white sprayed fret, 1946, 11¾in (29cm) high.
£40–100 *GM*

A GEC BC4750 valve radio, with wooden case, 1947, 13¼in (34cm) high.
£80–120 *GM*

A Marconi C10A corner console radio, 1947, 30¼in (77cm) high.
£100–180 *GM*

A Bush DAC90 valve radio, with ivory Bakelite case, 1947, 9in (23cm) high.
£70–120 *GM*

An Ekco U143 valve radio, with Bakelite case, 1949, 13in (33cm) high.
£30–70 *GM*

A Cossor Melody Maker valve radio, with Bakelite case, 1949, 10¼in (26cm) high.
£30–70 *GM*

A Philips type 462 radio, with Bakelite cabinet, 1948, 13in (33cm) high.
£60–120 *GM*

A Bush DAC10 radio, with brown Bakelite case, 1950, 13in (33cm) wide.
£180–220 *AAV*

A Bush DAC90A radio, with brown Bakelite case, c1950, 13in (33cm) wide.
£110–130 *AAV*

An Ekco U215 valve radio, with thermo-plastic case, 1950, 9½in (24cm) high.
£50–100 *GM*

A Ivalek crystal set, 1950, 3½in (9cm) high.
£30–70 *GM*

l. A GEC BC5243 valve radio, with brown Bakelite case, 1950, 10¼in (26cm) high.
£40–100 *GM*

A Stella ST239U valve radio, with burgundy Bakelite case, 1956, 9in (23cm) high.
£30–50 *GM*

A PAM transistor radio, c1956, 10in (25cm) high.
£60–80 *PC*

This rare model was the first British transistor radio to be marketed.

A Bush VHF 61 valve radio, with Bakelite case and gold trim, 1956, 11¼in (29cm) high.
£30–60 *GM*

An Ever Ready Sky Casket valve battery portable radio, 1957, 7in (18cm) high.
£25–40 *GM*

A Bush TR82B all-transistor radio, c1959, 10in (25cm) high.
£35–45 *PC*

A Cossor all-transistor radio, with bentwood cabinet, c1958, 8in (20.5cm) high.
£20–30 *PC*

A Decca portable radio, c1958, 9in (23cm) high.
£20–30 *PC*

A Telefunken Opus 2004 stereo radio, 1959, 15¼in (39cm) high.
£50–120 *GM*

A Bush transistor radio, with folding lid over the tuning dial, 1960s, 9½in (24cm) high.
£20–25 *PC*

A Perdio Continental PR73 radio, the control knobs orbit around the central tuning dial, 1959, 9in (23cm) high.
£30–40 *PC*

A Berec Pioneer kit valve radio, with blue sprayed metal case, 1959, 8in (20.5cm) high.
£20–40 *GM*

A Bush TR 91 transistor radio, c1960, 7½in (19.5cm) high.
£35–50 *PC*

An HMV radio, c1960, 9in (23cm) high.
£20–30 *PC*

A Fleetwood 6 globe radio, with gold oceans and silver continents, the top knob operating side slide tuning, c1961, 7in (18cm) diam.
£70–110 PC

A Channel Master 6505 cordless radio, Japanese, 1962, 5in (13cm) high.
£30–35 PC

A Civic Model 730 miniature pocket radio, with back-stand and box, c1963, 4in (10cm) high.
£15–25 PC

A Sony TR7120 radio, c1961, 7in (18cm) high.
£25–40 PC
This radio was produced in the Republic of Ireland to avoid tax.

A Westinghouse Holiday sub-miniature six-transistor pocket radio, with original box and earpiece, c1962, 4in (10cm) high.
£35–45 PC

l. A Philco T160 radio, American, c1965, 4in (10cm) high.
£15–20 PC

A Philips Reverbeo stereo radio, 1962, 9½in (24cm) high.
£50–100 GM

A Sanyo cordless transistor table top radio, c1964, 6½in (16.5cm) high.
£30–40 PC

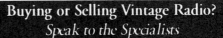

A Ferguson Fieldfare radio, with unusual tuning dials, c1965, 6½in (16cm) high.
£20–35 *PC*

A Roberts R303 radio, c1965, 6in (15cm) high.
£20–30 *PC*

This model was made in a range of colours, the brightest being the most desirable.

A Decca TPW70 wall radio, c1967, 10in (25.5cm) diam.
£45–70 *PC*

This model was intended for mounting on the wall of a kitchen or bathroom.

A National Panasonic Vostok radio, c1970, 4½in (11.5cm) diam.
£30–40 *PC*

This radio was intended to represent Yuri Gagarin's spacecraft.

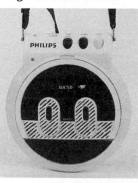

l. A Philips Moving Sound portable cassette player, with speaker and headphones, c1980s, 6in (15cm) high.
£15–20 *PC*

r. A novelty radio, 1970s, 14in (35.5cm) high.
£50–75 *ET*

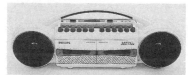

A Philips Moving Sound Roller radio-cassette, c1985, 8in (20.5cm) high.
£20–30 *PC*

An Ekco Elf radio, c1972, 2½in (6.5cm) high.
£15–20 *PC*

Televisions

A selection of internal TV aerials, 1950–60s, largest 36in (91cm) long.
£10–100 each *ET*

A Bush Type TV 12AM table model television, with 9in (23cm) screen, in brown Bakelite case, with 4 controls to front and Perspex magnifying lens, 15½in (40cm) wide.
£300–400 *S*

An HMV Model 901 console television, with 12in (30.5cm) screen, mirror lid and speaker grille, contained in a walnut veneered cabinet, 1936, 23¾in (60cm) wide.
£1,400–1,600 *S*

RAILWAYANA

The disappearance of steam engines in the second half of the 1960s stimulated the foundation of preservation groups such as the Bluebell and the Watercress lines, and enhanced the desirability of railwayana which today attracts a devoted band of enthusiasts. Among the most collectable items are nameplates. 'These are scarce because there were comparatively few named engines,' explains dealer and railwayana specialist Alan Tonks. 'Big express locomotives might have carried names, but freight engines on local routes would have simply had a running number.' Rare nameplates and crests can command large sums of money. Included in the following section is a Battle of Britain Class RAF crest dating from just after the war, when Southern Railway named some thirty locomotives after Battle of Britain squadrons. The value reflects the rarity of the crest and is enhanced by the fact that it has not been restored.

Other sought-after objects covered this year range from posters to totem station signs, familiarly known because of their shape, as 'hot-dogs'. 'Value for these depends on condition, name of the station and rarity,' says Alan Tonks. 'Larger stations would have had a number of signs, smaller stations only a few and condition depends on whether these were placed in an exposed position or protected under a station awning. Prices vary from region to region, with northern names often fetching higher prices than southern examples.'

A George Stephenson Centenary gold medal, 1781–1881, signed by T. P. Chapman, with bust of Stephenson on reverse, 2in (5cm) diam.
£700–900 *EIM*

A LB & SCR pay tin, the hinged lid with brass plate and No. 785, c1900, 2½in (6.5cm) diam.
£15–25 *SOL*

A Victorian oil lantern, 19½in (49.5cm) high.
£65–75 *ML*

A toilet seat from a train, with BR signs attached, 1950s, 11in (28cm) diam.
£30–35 *WAB*

l. A SR, Wickham to Knowle Junction, fibre tablet, c1935, 4¼in (11cm) diam.
£40–50 *SOL*

r. A GNR cast iron luggage rack bracket, with company initials in serif, c1890, 8in (20cm) long.
£30–70 *SOL*

Boards & Signs

ELDERSLIE №̲ 2

A G & SWR wooden signal box board, Elderslie No. 2, with metal letters, restored, c1925, 67in (170cm) long.
£80–90 *SRA*

URMSTON STATION

A BR (Midland) maroon enamel signal box sign, Urmston Station, 1950s, 48in (122cm) long.
£340–380 *SRA*

PANGBOURNE

WHITCHURCH

Two BR enamel totem station signs, 1950s, 36in (91.5cm) long.
£250–380 each *SOL*

Name, Numberplates & Crests

A MR cast iron bridge number-plate, c1880, 15in (38cm) wide.
£20–25 *SOL*

An L & NWR engraved brass on polished wood nameplate, Atalanta, 1906, 55½in (141cm) long.
£5,750–6,500 *SRA*

An LMS Jubilee Class nameplate, 1930s, in original condition, 38in (96.5cm) long.
£5,200–6,000 *SRA*

FRANCIS

A nameplate, Francis, as carried by a Peckett Type R2 0-4-0ST engine, face restored, c1927, 28in (71cm) long.
£350–400 *SRA*

l. A SR Battle of Britain Class RAF crest, City of Glasgow 602 Squadron, brass moulding with gun metal vitreous enamel, c1947, 28in (71cm) high.
£5,500–6,500 *SOL*

FORMIDABLE
WARSHIP CLASS

A BR Warship Class nameplate, worksplate and shedplate, Formidable, c1958, 48in (122cm) long.
£2,200–2,500 *SRA*

Posters

A SR linen poster, *Visitez l'Angleterre*, by Maurice Foussaint, c1932, excellent condition, 40¼ x 25¼in (102 x 64cm).
£300–350 *SRA*

A LNER poster, Giants Refreshed, c1947, 40¼ x 50in (102 x 127cm).
£1,400–1,600 *SRA*

A LNER poster, St Andrews, very good condition, 1939, 40¼ x 50in (102 x 127cm).
£2,400–2,800 *SRA*

l. A LMS poster on linen, Scotland by LMS, McCorquodale Studio, very good condition, 1930s, 40¼ x 50in (102 x 127cm).
£550–750 *SRA*

A LMS/LNER Great Yarmouth & Gorleston on Sea, by Septimus Scott, some folds, 1930s, 40¼ x 50in (102 x 127cm).
£650–850 *SRA*

A LNER poster, Dunoon, by Frank Mason, minor damage, 1940, 40¼ x 50in (102 x 127cm).
£550–600 *SRA*

Steam Engines – Models

A live steam locomotive, mainly brass, with cylinder below the body, adjustable front wheels, c1880, 6in (15cm) long.
£120–150 *RAR*

A horizontal stationary steam engine, by Mersey Model Co Ltd, Liverpool, 1950s, 7in (18cm) long.
£50–60 *RAR*

An Astra gauge 1 SR Schools Class live steam locomotive, Winchester, 1979, 22⅜in (58cm) long, together with original box and instructions.
£1,700–2,000 *OT*

ROCK & POP
Memorabilia

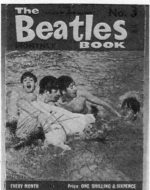

The Beatles Book, the cover signed in blue ballpoint pen by all 4 Beatles, slight wear, 1963.
£1,900–2,200 *S*

A colour photograph of The Beatles, on the set of the television show *Around The Beatles*, by Tommy Hanley, 1964, 15¾ x 11¾in (40 x 30cm).
£175–225 *CSK*

A set of autographs of The Beatles, on a blue album page, collected at the ABC Theatre, Blackpool, 1960s.
£1,000–1,400 *Bon*

Cross Reference
Ephemera/Posters

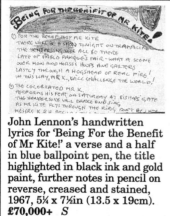

John Lennon's handwritten lyrics for 'Being For the Benefit of Mr Kite!' a verse and a half in blue ballpoint pen, the title highlighted in black ink and gold paint, further notes in pencil on reverse, creased and stained, 1967, 5¼ x 7½in (13.5 x 19cm).
£70,000+ *S*

The Beatles are probably the most collectable of all bands with particularly high prices being reserved for original material referring to the composition of famous songs.

Paul McCartney's recording notes for 'Hey Jude', black felt pen on lined paper, with notes on structure, instrumentation and arrangement, with doodles, creased, 1968, 12¾ x 8in (32.5 x 20.5cm).
£25,000–30,000 *S*

At just over 7 minutes this was The Beatles' longest single and the first on the Apple label. It topped the charts both in the UK and the United States, maintaining No. 1 for 9 weeks, and selling more than eight million copies around the world.

A pair of sunglasses believed to have been worn by John Lennon on an American tour, the metal frames with non-prescription mirrored lenses and plastic ear-pieces, together with a copy of a statement of provenance, 1960s.
£2,700–4,000 *S*

These glasses were left at the Cleveland Sheraton Hotel where they later became the possession of the catering manager who thirty years later decided to sell them at auction.

An American Beatles four-speed phonograph Model 1000, the turntable complete with mat, in blue vinyl-covered case, 1960s, 17½in (44.5cm) wide.
£5,200–5,700 *S*

Bono's 'Fly' sunglasses, worn by him as McPhisto on the U2 Zooropa tour, one-piece wrap-around style in dark green plastic, together with documents of provenance, 1993.
£1,000–1,200 *S*

Billy Fury's sweater, together with a colour xerox of the EP cover 'Forget Him' showing Fury wearing the sweater.
£350–400 *CSK*

Buddy Holly's sunglasses, worn by him at Junior High School, non-prescription, green-tinted lenses, with tortoiseshell and metal frames, in brown leather case stamped, 1950s, with certificates of authenticity.
£900–1,100 *S*

Nine unpublished black and white photographs of the Jimi Hendrix Experience, taken in the Hotel Opalen, Gothenburg, before the Experience's concert at the Lorensberg Cirkus, 1968, 3½in (9cm) square.
£1,300–1,600 *S*

After the concert Jimi Hendrix and Mitch Mitchell went out and returned to the hotel at around 2am. Jimi became agitated and caused damage to Mitch's room, the police were called and Jimi was arrested. He was treated in hospital for an injured hand.

A white Gibson Flying V electric guitar, with gold hardware, signed in gold pen by Albert King, 1960s.
£950–1,200 *Bon*

l. A pair of Madonna's stage-worn gloves, in black stretch fabric, the left signed by her in gold marker, c1988.
£750–850 *S*

A tee-shirt worn by Freddie Mercury during Queen's 'Magic' tour, with Betty Boop cartoon, 1986, together with 2 letters of authenticity from The Official International Queen Fan Club.
£1,200–1,500 *S*

An original costume design for Frank'n'Furter in *The Rocky Horror Show*, by Sue Blane, water-colour, ink, pencil and glitter, signed and titled in pencil, c1973, 16 x 10¼in (40.5 x 26cm), framed and glazed.
£600–800 *S*

A Weather King Ambassador Batter drumskin, signed by The Rolling Stones, in blue and black marker pens, 1994, 14in (35.5cm) diam.
£450–550 *S*

An Electra plastic toy four-string Rolling Stones guitar, 1960s, 22in (56cm) long.
£125–175 *NTM*

A black and white machine-print photograph of The Rolling Stones, signed in 3 different coloured inks by all 5 members of the group, c1964, 9¼ x 13½in (23.5 x 34.5cm).
£350–400 *CSK*

A Sex Pistols white cotton tee-shirt, screen printed on the front, signed in pink fluorescent pen by Johnny Rotten, Paul Cook and Steve Jones and in black felt pen by Sid Vicious, c1977, in common mount with 2 Sex Pistols' pin badges, 16in (40.5cm) square, and a colour xerox of a photograph showing the group standing outside a clothing shop named Suecide in Stockholm attached to the reverse.
£1,100–1,400 *CSK*

According to Thomas Dellert, the owner of Suecide, this shirt was a one-off made by him for the Sex Pistols and signed by them during their visit to his shop in 1977.

The Sex Pistols, Great Rock 'N' Roll Swindle, Sid Vicious with a chain, an animation cel, gouache on a multi-cel set-up applied to a mixed media production background, 1979, image 3¾ x 7in (9.5 x 18cm).
£850–1,000 *CSK*

A Sid Vicious/Vivien Westwood/Malcolm McLaren cheesecloth bondage shirt, with print of Sid on the front, c1980.
£450–550 *Bon*

l. The Yardbirds, an early colour machine-print photograph, c1965, signed by all members of the group, 8¼ x 13in (21 x 33cm).
£400–500 *CSK*

The Who, a cibachrome colour portrait photograph of the group, c1965, printed later, 24in (61cm) square, laminated on board.
£175–225 *CSK*

A Wurlitzer 1050 jukebox, for playing 45rpm records, in perfect working order, 1973.
£2,000–3,000 *Bon*

This jukebox is one of only 1,900 produced.

Records

The Beach Boys, 'Fun, Fun, Fun', 45rpm single, UK Capitol demonstration, 1964.
£50–60 *TOT*

The Beatles, album cover, 'Sgt Pepper's Lonely Hearts Club Band', signed recently by Paul McCartney, George Harrison and Ringo Starr, framed.
£475–600 *CSK*

Kate Bush, 'The Red Shoes' promotion box containing, record, video, fountain pen and 35mm colour slide, 1993.
£200–250 *TOT*

r. Dave Brubeck Quartet, 'When You're Smiling', EP, Philips, 1959.
£5–6 *ED*

The Beatles, 'A Hard Day's Night', EP, first issue, Parlophone, 1964.
£5–8 *CTO*

The Beatles 'Let It Be', jukebox special, Italian white label promotion, Apple, 1970.
£10–15 *TOT*

Brubeck & Rushing, EP, Fontana label, 1960.
£4–5 *ED*

The Beatles, 'Do You Want to Know a Secret', and 'Thank You Girl', 45rpm, VJ Records, 1960s.
£25–35 *CTO*

A selection of Beatles Japanese 3in (7.5cm) CD singles, 1980s.
£6–10 each *TOT*

Bix Beiderbecke, 'Bix and His Gang', EP, Fontana, 1960.
£5–6 *ED*

Records

With records, it is not only artist, recording and the rarity of label that counts, but condition, both of the vinyl and its cover. Using £1,000 as the top figure the following chart illustrates how much prices, for the same record, can vary depending on condition.

Cover	Record	£
Mint	Mint	1,000
Excellent	Excellent	800
Near/Ex.	Near/Ex.	500
Very Good	Very Good	250
Good	Good	100
Poor	Poor	25

The Doors, 'L.A. Woman', LP, window sleeve with crucifixion insert, UK Elektra, 1971.
£10–15 *TOT*

Jimi Hendrix Experience, 'Hey Joe' and 'Stone Free', signed by all 3 members of the group, 45rpm single, Polydor label, 1966, framed.
£1,200–1,500 *CSK*

Glastonbury Fayre, triple album, with outer cover foldout, inner sleeves, pyramid and booklets, Revelation label, 1972.
£80–100 *CTO*

The Jam, 'The Eton Rifles', 45rpm, Japanese Polydor label, 1979.
£10–15 *TOT*

Gene Krupa, 'Sounds of Jazz',
EP, Fontana label, 1960.
£5–6 *ED*

The Mothers of Invention,
'Burnt Weeny Sandwich', first
issue LP, Reprise label, 1969.
£15–20 *CTO*

Pink Floyd, 'Apples and
Oranges', 45rpm, UK Columbia
demonstration record, 1967.
£40–50 *TOT*

Little Richard, 'Jenny, Jenny',
45rpm single, one-sided
demonstration record,
London label, 1957.
£20–30 *TOT*

'The Original Gerry
Mulligan Quartet', EP,
Fontana label, 1960.
£5–6 *ED*

Elvis Presley, 'Heartbreak
Hotel' and 'Blue Suede Shoes',
2 single-sided 78rpm records,
HMV label, 1950s.
£600–700 *S*

r. Queen, 'Radio Ga Ga', signed
by all band members, 12in, 1984.
£180–220 *Bon*

l. Prince, 'Lovesexy', signed on
the cover, Park Records, 1988.
£130–160 *CSK*

Madonna, 'Something to
Remember' and 'Bedtime
Stories', 2 CD's, both signed on
the front, Maverick Recording
Company, 1995 and 1994.
£175–225 *CSK*

'In Beat Sandy Nelson', LP,
Imperial label, 1966.
£10–15 *TOT*

Django Reinhardt, 'Django', EP, Oriole label, 1957.
£6–7 *ED*

The Rolling Stones, 'Five By Five', EP, Decca label, signed, c1964.
£300–350 *Bon*

Sam & Dave, 'Born Again' and 'Get It', 7in Italian pressing of Atlantic label, 1969.
£6–10 *CTO*

Stone Roses, 'So Young', first single, Twin Line Production, 1985.
£40–50 *TOT*

One of only 1,200 produced.

The Shadows, 'Foot Tapping With The Shadows', EP, Columbia label, 1963.
£10–12 *ED*

Dinah Washington, 'Queen Dinah', EP, Mercury label, 1959.
£4–5 *ED*

'Josh White Stories', EP, HMV label, 1957.
£5–6 *ED*

Billy Williams Quartet, 'Stepping Out Tonight', 45rpm, Coral label, 1958.
£30–50 *TOT*

The presence of the original tri-centre is an important factor in determining value.

l. York Pop Music Project, 'All Day', LP, York University Pressing, 1973.
£300–350 *TOT*

SCENT BOTTLES

A Bohemian cut glass scent bottle, c1800, 3¼in (8.5cm) high.
£200–220 *LBr*

A Swiss glass scent bottle, with gold top, 3¼in (8.5cm) long, c1840, in original shagreen case.
£400–450 *LBr*

A Pratt ware scent flask, c1800, 3in (7.5cm) high.
£150–180 *LBr*

A glass scent bottle, with blue and white double overlay on a waisted clear body, embossed silver mount, c1860, 4in (10cm) high.
£340–380 *Som*

A cut glass scent bottle, with gold top, possibly Dutch, c1840, 4in (10cm) high.
£150–170 *LBr*

A set of 3 gilt-metal scent bottles, possibly Swiss or French, c1840, 4½in (11.5cm) high.
£400–450 *LBr*

A French 18ct gold friendship finger chain and scent bottle, mid-19thC, bottle 2in (5cm) long.
£1,400–1,600 *LBr*

l. An oval double-ended scent bottle, with diamond and prism cutting, notched edges, unmarked gold caps, c1800, 5½in (14cm) long.
£550–650
r. A disc-shaped clear glass scent bottle, with panels of cut diamonds, silver-gilt cap, c1820, 3¼in (8cm) long.
£180–220 *Som*

A rock crystal scent bottle, c1840, 1½in (4cm) high.
£140–160 *LBr*

r. A blue glass diamond cut barrel-shaped scent bottle, with embossed silver mounts, c1860, 3¼in (8.5cm) long.
£300–350 *Som*

l. A green overlay glass scent bottle, with embossed silver mount, c1860, 3½in (9cm) long.
£350–400
r. A brick-red Lithyalin scent bottle, with silver mount, c1850, 2¾in (7cm) long.
£400–500 *Som*

A lime-green double-ended scent bottle, with engine-turned silver mounts, c1870, 5½in (14cm) long. **£300–360** *Som*

l. A dark blue double-ended scent bottle, with flute cut body, plain silver mounts, c1870, 5¼in (13.5cm) long.
c. An opaque pea-green double-ended scent bottle, flute cut with plain gilt-brass mounts, c1860, 5¼in (13.5cm) long.
r. An amber double-ended scent bottle, flute cut with gilt-brass mounts, c1860, 5¾in (14.5cm) long.
£100–150 each *Som*

Double-ended scent bottles were designed to hold scent at one end and smelling salts at the other. The scent end usually has a screw top, whilst the other end often has a hinged lid with a spring-loaded fastener.

A glass scent bottle, with red body and cut white overlay decoration, embossed silver mount, c1860, 3¾in (9.5cm) high. **£340–380** *Som*

Two double-ended scent bottles,
l. Clear waisted body with green overlay, embossed silver mounts, c1870, 5½in (14cm) long.
r. Clear glass engraved overall with floral sprays, a printy cut band round the centre, one silver-gilt plain cap engraved '18 March 1880', monogram on the other, c1880, 5in (13cm) long.
£400–450 each *Som*

An amethyst shaded glass toilet water bottle, with diamond and fan-cut decoration, silver mount marked Birmingham, c1880, 6¾in (17cm) high. **£500–600** *Som*

A French yellow glass scent bottle, with white overlay, c1880, 3in (7.5cm) long. **£180–200** *LBr*

A French porcelain scent bottle, with red and gilt decoration, c1880, 5½in (14cm) diam. **£100–130** *LBr*

A light blue horn effect scent bottle, with a band of enamel floral decoration, gilt-brass finger ring and chain, c1880, 3¼in (8.5cm) long.
£300–350 *Som*

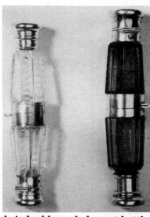

l. A double-ended scent bottle, the clear tapered body with diamond cut panels, with hinged vinaigrette compartment in centre, silver-gilt mounts, c1860, 5¼in (3.5cm) long.
r. A double-ended flute cut red scent bottle, with picture frame inside hinged compartment, plain silver-gilt mounts, c1880, 5¼in (13cm) long.
£150–180 each *Som*

The vinaigrette compartment in the clear glass bottle would have contained a sponge soaked with either liquid ammonia or aromatic vinegars, and would be secured by a pierced grille.

An alabaster scent bottle, c1880, 2¼in (5.5cm) high.
£140–160 *LBr*

A Worcester porcelain scent bottle, c1880, 3½in (9cm) high.
£150–200 *LBr*

r. A pair of cut glass scent bottles, c1910, 7¼in (18.5cm) high.
£120–140 *LBr*

A Venetian scent bottle, with finger chain, c1880, 2¼in (5.5cm) long.
£180–220 *LBr*

A Samson porcelain scent bottle, c1880, 4in (10cm) high.
£280–320 *LBr*

Two glass scent bottles, signed J. Ditchfield, *l.* pearl with feathering *r.* blue with pearl lily trail, 1995, largest 4¼in (11cm) diam.
£40–50 each *GLA*

A double-ended scent bottle, with clear wrythen-moulded body, wrythen-cast silver mounts, hallmarked Samson Mordan 1883, 4½in (11.5cm) long.
£340–380 *Som*

Four Venetian miniature scent bottles, c1890, 1¼in (3.5cm) long.
£60–150 each *LBr*

SCIENTIFIC INSTRUMENTS

A pocket sundial, incorporating a small compass, known as an equatorial compass, in a brass-lidded case, 1820, 2½in (6.5cm) diam.
£200–250 *GWA*

A pocket microscope, with folding magnifier and ivory handle, adjustable specimen holder and original morocco leather case, 19thC, 11in (28cm) wide.
£325–375 *BSA*

A surveyor's standard brass level, made by Troughton Simms, with original mahogany case, c1865, 12in (30.5cm) side.
£280–300 *GWA*

A polished brass dissecting microscope, by E. Leitz Wetzlar, with rack-and-pinion focusing, c1900, 18in (45.5cm) high.
£135–155 *BSA*

The Brical Money Calculating Machine, 1910, 5¼in (13.5cm) diam.
£70–80 *ET*

A Castella sun recorder, c1910, 10in (25.5cm) wide.
£150–200 *ET*

A Fowler's double-sided long scale calculator, in an aluminium outer case, and a Fowler's watch style textile calculator type E1, c1920, both 2½in (6.5cm) diam.
£45–60 each *MRT*

Electrical Equipment

A generator torch, 1920–30, 3¼in (8.5cm) high.
£25–30 *WAB*

Three electric motors:
top. c1910, 6in (15cm) wide.
l. A boat motor, c1905, 7½in (19cm) long.
r. Avery bi-polar motor, c1900, 8in (20.5cm) long.
£25–70 each *ET*

A Siemens battery, 1930s, 8in (20.5cm) wide.
£10–20 *ET*

Electric Fans

A Knapp fan, with brass pizza style blades, exposed power terminals and brush motor for AC/DC, on a wooden base, American, 1890–1902, blades 9in (23cm) diam.
£200–250 *MRo*

A G.E. coin-operated/ 'prepayment' fan, with locking door at rear, American, 1905, brass blades 12in (30.5cm) diam.
£150–200 *MRo*

This type of fan was used in hotels and 5 cents bought one hour's use.

An Emerson fan, with brass 'Bulwinkle'/moose horn blades, guard and arms, 'yoke' motor mount, ornate pattern on motor and base, American, 1906, blades 12in (30.5cm) diam.
£125–150 *MRo*

A Fort Wayne fan, with brass housing, base, blades and guard, American, 1916–20, blades 8in (20.5cm) diam.
£80–100 *MRo*

A Westinghouse all-brass fan, with pizza style blades, no front ring on guard, American, 1915–20, blades 8in (20.5cm) diam.
£100–125 *MRo*

l. A C.A. fan, with brass blades and guard, AC/DC brush motor, 1918–20, blades 8in (20.5cm) diam.
£55–65 *MRo*

The guard has an odd number of wires, ie. 7, with no outer ring.

A Gilbert Polar Cub Type D fan, with painted steel blades and guard, American, 1916–25, blades 6in (15cm) diam.
£25–35 *MRo*

The badge in the centre has a picture of a polar bear.

r. An electric fan, with brass blades and guard, 1920, blades 13in (33cm) diam.
£100–125 *HHa*

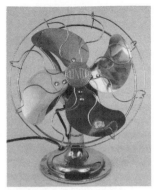

A Gilbert fan and pen set, with round steel blades, on a cast base, American, 1920s, blades 4in (10cm) diam.
£80–100 *MRo*

These fans were given away by salesmen to retail merchants.

An electric fan, by Limit Engineering Co Ltd, 1920, blades 12½in (32cm) diam.
£100–125 *HHa*

An electric fan, by Limit Engineering Co Ltd, 1920, blades 15in (38cm) diam.
£110–135 *HHa*

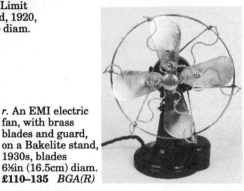

r. An EMI electric fan, with brass blades and guard, on a Bakelite stand, 1930s, blades 6½in (16.5cm) diam.
£110–135 *BGA(R)*

An Art Deco Fitzgerald Star Rite lightweight tin fan, with octagonal guard, brass blades, American, 1925, blades 10in (25.5cm) diam.
£25–30 *MRo*

A Frost three-bladed stationary fan, with tin motor, gold-painted steel blades, on a cast base, 1925–35, blades 10in (25.5cm) diam.
£25–35 *MRo*

A Singer Ribbonaire fan, with cloth ribbon blades, Bakelite base and housing, American, 1920s, 12in (30.5cm) high.
£25–30 *MRo*

This fan was advertised as 'safe for children'.

A Westinghouse fan, with overlapping blades for 'quiet air', with a heavy solid case, American, 1940s, blades 12in (30.5cm) diam.
£55–65 *MRo*

This was also known as the 'Power Aire' fan.

Medical Collectables

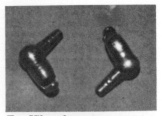

A late George III mahogany apothecary's chest, with caddy moulding, with fitted interior, drawer to base, the reverse with a sliding panel containing various glass bottles, 13in (33cm) wide.
£450–550 *L*

A red-painted box containing electro-magnetic medical apparatus, by Griggs, with 3 original Smee cells, silver, platinised cathodes, 1855, 11 x 8in (28 x 20.5cm).
£400–500 *ET*

Two Vibraphone ear wells hearing aids, 1860, 1in (2cm) wide.
£130–160 *ET*

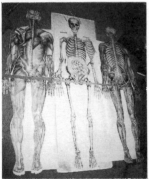

A Phillip's anatomical chart, 1900, 65 x 64in (165 x 162.5cm).
£450–600 *ET*

Four battery-operated hearing aids, 1930–40, largest 6½in (16.5cm) long.
£10–60 each *ET*

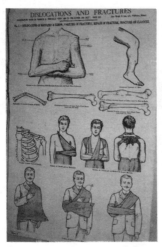

Six medical charts, on a hanger, c1920, 39 x 26in (99 x 66cm).
£50–70 *ET*

r. A Veritable Irrigateur du Docteur Iguisilr, 1930s, 9in (23cm) high.
£34–38 *WAB*

A Ritter dental X-Ray machine, 1910, 75in (190.5cm) high.
£600–800 *ET*

Opera Glasses

A pair of Carl Zeiss Jena prismatic opera glasses, gilt-metal and abalone with detachable telescope handle, late 19thC, 7in (18cm) wide.
£175–200 *BSA*

A single opera glass, with a suede case, c1900, 3¾in (9.5cm) high.
£55–65 *PSA*

Optical Equipment

An optometer, used for sight testing, 1850, 10½in (26.5cm) long.
£150–200 *ET*

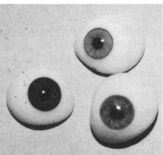

Three Victorian glass eyes.
£10–15 each *ET*

A blue eye bath, c1960, 2½in (6.5cm) high.
£10–12 *WAB*

Telescopes

A gentleman's brass pocket telescope, c1870, 4in (10cm) long, closed.
£80–100 *GWA*

Telescopes are either refracting, in which the image is produced by a lens, or reflecting in which it is produced by a mirror. Small, hand-held telescopes used by sailors, soldiers, hunters and others are refracting.

A brass and leather four-draw telescope with variable magnification settings, The Target, by Aitchison of London, c1910, 22in (56cm) long, open.
£235–265 *BSA*

A silver-plated and blacked four-draw presentation telescope, by J. P. Sutton Cutts & Sons, Opticians to Her Majesty, Sheffield and London, 19thC, 30in (76cm) long, open.
£200–235 *BSA*

A brass horizontal telescope level, by C. J. Gowland Ltd, with internal split view mirror to view level bubble and horizon, c1900, 16in (40.5cm) long.
£65–75 *BSA*

A brass three-draw telescope, by Stanley, London, c1920, 15¾in (40cm) long.
£85–95 *BSA*

Veterinary Instruments

Three veterinary pumps:
top c1820, 27in (68.5cm) long.
£200–250
centre c1890, 27in (68.5cm) long.
£80–120
bottom c1890. 24in (61cm) long.
£70–110 *ET*

An horn-handled fleame, used for bleeding animals, late 19thC, 3¼in (8.5cm) long, closed.
£24–28 *WAB*

A selection of instruments for animal pedicare, contained in two fitted drawers, c1850, case 11 x 12in (28 x 30.5cm).
£600–700 *ET*

SCRIPOPHILY

Scripophily is the collecting of bond and share certificates. The subject has international market coverage, appealing predominantly to business men and women and those involved in the legal and financial professions. A major attraction is history. Through bonds you can follow the building of bridges, the digging of mines, the establishing of great railroad companies across the globe. The more interesting the history, the more attractive an item. Collectors often concentrate on particular themes ranging from popular subjects such as railways and shipping, to more esoteric areas such as zoos and aquaria. As well as subject the physical appearance of a bond is important. Many examples can be extremely decorative. As in other areas of the market, dealers tend to advise buying for pleasure rather than investment, although very occasionally if the certificate has not been cancelled there could be extra hidden value. In certain rare and exceptional cases, old bonds have been proven to be still valid, transforming their owners from collectors of historical ephemera into present-day shareholders.

China

A Railway Equipment £20 loan bond of the Government of the Chinese Republic, blue/black with red chop, 1922.
£10–15 *SCR*

A Honan Railway £100 bond certificate of the Chinese Imperial Government, multi-coloured with yellow underprint, 1905.
£75–85 *SCR*

A Hukuang Railway £100 bond certificate of the Imperial Chinese Government, red/black, 1911.
£100–125 *SCR*

This was the last foreign bond issue raised by the Manchus and thus the last to be termed 'Imperial'.

A share certificate of the Société Viticole et Vinicole d'Egypte, dark green/light green, dated '1938–44'.
£35–45 *GKR*

Egypt

A share certificate of the Youssef & Ahmed El-Gammal, for 10 Egyptian pounds, yellow/black, issued in Alexandria, 1924.
£15–18 *SCR*

A share certificate of the Credit Agricole d'Egypte, for 25 shares, light/dark green, dated '1934'.
£15–20 *SCR*

France

A share certificate of the Stadium de Paris, for 100 shares, c1896.
£24–28 *GKR*

Great Britain

A share certificate of The South Staffordshire Railway Company, for £12, green, red seal, dated '1846'.
£50–60 *SCR*

A share certificate of The Channel Tubular Railway Preliminary Company Ltd, dated '1892'.
£225–245 *SCR*

Plans for a tunnel connecting England with France have been under discussion for well over 100 years. The end of the last century saw the formation of at least 3 companies, one involving a bridge, one a tunnel and this one – a tubular railway. Most plans were scuppered by the British Government on the grounds of the country's security. This is regarded as one of the classic pieces of scripophily.

A share certificate of the Middleton & Tonge Cotton Mill Ltd, black/white, dated '1875'.
£65–75 *SCR*

A share certificate of the Yarmouth Aquarium Society Ltd, brown/cream, dated '1877'.
£40–45 *SCR*

A share certificate of the Bessemer Saloon Steamboat Company Ltd, for £50, purple/white, dated '1873'.
£30–35 *GKR*

Sir Henry Bessemer (1813–98) invented the process of making steel, and later he also invented a steamship saloon which did not rock. This saloon was hung on an arrangement of hydraulic rams which kept it upright even under the worst conditions. On its first public voyage in May 1875 the Bessemer crashed into Calais harbour destroying 20 yards of the Eastern pier – the Bessemer Saloon Steamboat Company Ltd was sued for damages. In 1879 the steamboat was sold for scrap with her saloon being re-erected as a billiard room in a house in Kent.

Hungary

A Banque Commerciale Hongroise de Pest 4% loan bond, light green/dark green, dated '1911'.
£10–15 *GKR*

A City of Budapest 4% loan bond, FF420, beige/blue, 1911.
£12–16 *GKR*

South America

A bond certificate of the Republic of Peru, for £10, green/black, 1920.
£20–25 *SCR*

A bond certificate of the Buenos Ayres Lacroze Tramways Company, for £100, green/black, dated '1910'.
£30–35 *SCR*

Spain

A share certificate of Islas del Guadalquivir SA, pale orange/grey, 1896.
£15–18 *GKR*

A share certificate of the Compania de las Hulleras de Ujo-Mieres, turquoise/blue/black, dated '1904'.
£40–45 *GKR*

USA & Canada

l. An Atlantic & Pacific Railroad Company bond certificate, for $1,000, brown/black with coupons, dated '1880'.
£20–25 *SCR*

A Beech Creek Railroad Company bond certificate, for $1,000, brown/black, dated '1892'.
£25–30 *SCR*

A Cleveland, Cincinnati, Chicago & St Louis Railway Company bond certificate, red/black, for $1,000, dated '1891'.
£20–25 *SCR*

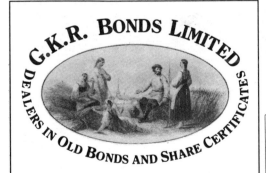

Four share certificates for Dominion Stores Ltd, green, brown, red and orange, 1920s–30s.
£50–60 *GKR*

A share certificate for The Mary Murphy Gold Mining Company, red/black, dated '1909'.
£15–18 *SCR*

r. A share certificate for Canadian Mortgage Association, brown/blue/beige, dated '1910'.
£45–55 *SCR*

SEWING & HANDICRAFTS

A French silver bright needle
holder, 18thC, 3¾in (9.5cm) long.
£125–150 *GLN*

A French mulberry sewing box,
with fitted interior, early
19thC, 7¼in (18.5cm) wide.
£300–350 *WAC*

A Little Wanzer sewing
machine, together with wooden
case and instructions, c1867,
13in (33cm) wide.
£80–120 *ET*

An all-bisque doll pincushion,
c1890, 2in (5cm) high.
£40–50 *PSA*

A boxwood bobbin stand,
mid-19thC, 5in (12.5cm) high.
£75–85 *COT*

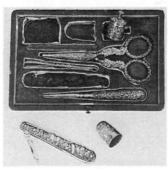

A *nécessaire*, including 6 silver
coloured metal pieces, later
thimble, fitted in a red leather
box, 19thC, 5¼in (13cm) wide.
£325–375 *L*

l. A beaded velvet pincushion,
embroidered as a sampler,
dated '1884', 9in (23cm) diam.
£150–200 *LB*

A walnut-veneered sewing box,
inlaid with mother-of-pearl,
mid-19thC, 11in (28cm) wide.
£200–250 *COT*

A Mauchline ware tape
measure, depicting
Stirling Castle, late
19thC, 2in (5cm) high.
£40–60 *IW*

A walnut sewing cabinet, with
fitted interior and brass handles,
c1880, 10⅞in (27.5cm) wide.
£320–370 *MB*

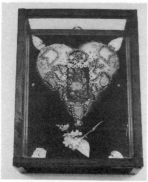

A heart-shaped beadwork
pincushion, cased, c1900,
2½in (6.5cm) high.
£140–160 *LB*

A heart-shaped beadwork
pincushion, c1900,
8in (20.5cm) high
£80–100 *LB*

A Middle Eastern spinning
wheel, c1900, 32in (81.5cm) long.
£18–22 *WCA*

A shaped yard measure, with brass fitting, c1910,
36in (91.5cm) long.
£25–30 *WAB*

*A tailor's trouser measure, sometimes described as a curved
measure, is used for taking measurements before making
bespoke suits or trousers.*

A bone tape measure,
c1900, 2in (5cm) high.
£40–50 *PC*

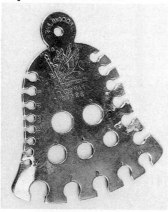

l. A bell-shaped
brass knitting
needle gauge,
1920s, 2½in
(6.5cm) high.
£15–20 *BS*

r. An umbrella
knitting needle
case, 1930s, 12in
(30.5cm) long.
£28–32 *WAB*

A handmade sewing bag,
with wooden handles, 1930s,
22in (56cm) wide.
£20–25 *SUS*

A needlepoint work bag,
with wooden handles,
1930s, 11¾in (30cm) wide.
£40–50 *SUS*

A fabric-covered sewing box,
1930s, 11in (28cm) wide.
£40–50 *SUS*

A turned serpentine stone pin
dish, c1940, 3in (7.5cm) wide.
£3–5 *OD*

SHIPPING

A ship's brass hand-lantern, with original oil burner, c1860, 18in (45.5cm) high.
£160–200 *GWA*

> **Cross Reference**
> Scientific Instruments

An 8-day platform movement ship's clock, with enamel dial, c1940, 8in (20.5cm) diam.
£140–160 *GWA*

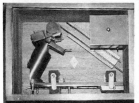

A brass azimuth sight, in mint condition, c1950, 10in (25.5cm) long.
£60–80 *GWA*

A bosun's call, with broad arrow stamp, c1920, 4¼in (11cm) long.
£35–45 *BSA*

A wooden water-breaker, c1870, 30in (76cm) long.
£175–200 *GWA*

Used for carrying water from land to ship.

A lignum vitae fid, 19thC, 15¾in (40cm) long.
£35–45 *BSA*

Used for rope splicing.

A Siebe Gorman 12-stud diver's helmet, with original tinning and matching part numbers, c1940.
£1,500–1,700 *TEM*

A willow boat fender, c1870, 22in (56cm) wide.
£40–50 *GRP*

A serving mallet, 19thC, 8¼in (21cm) long.
£35–45 *BSA*

Used for rigging work.

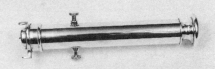

A ship's gimbal candle light, without bracket, 19thC, 9in (23cm) high.
£40–50 *BSA*

A copper ship's anchor electric lamp, c1960, 18in (45.5cm) high.
£100–125 *GWA*

A ship's glass telegraph plate, mounted and framed, c1950, 12in (30.5cm) diam.
£15–20 *GWA*

A Sestrel ship's standard binnacle, fitted with original compass and compensators, c1950, 54in (137cm) high.
£1,000–1,200 *GWA*

A pair of 'Not Under Command' electric lamps, c1960, 34in (86.cm) high.
£200–250 *GWA*

Compasses

- Early compasses often came in fitted wooden boxes
- The rose could be made of paper, silvered brass or even mother-of-pearl
- Instruments were often signed by their maker and these can carry a premium

A pair of *Queen Mary* salt and pepper pots, c1970, 4in (10cm) high.
£10–15 *TAC*

r. A mahogany dry card compass, by Wright of Bristol, c1780, 5in (12.5cm) square.
£200–250 *GWA*

An American brass lifeboat's compass, with oil lamp and bevelled glass front, 1930s, 8in (20.5cm) high.
£180–200 *GWA*

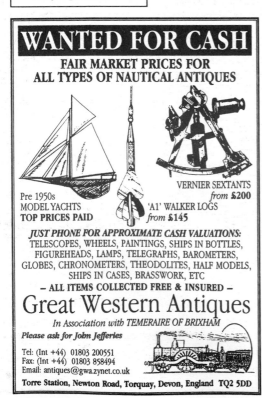

A Sestrel hand-bearing compass, fitted in an oak carrying case, c1980, 8in (20.5cm) high.
£45–80 *GWA*

A Magnapole Series II marching compass, with rotating bezel and directional disc, with lid, c1930, 5in (12.5cm) diam.
£60–70 *BSA*

Model Ships & Yachts

A seaman's wooden model of the *Jane Filey*, cased, c1860, 11in (28cm) long.
£100–120 GWA

A wooden five-masted half-model of a brig, in full sail, original wooden frame, c1900, 20in (51cm) wide.
£550–620 MR

r. A wooden scale model of a pond yacht, with cloth sails, 1920s, 30in (76cm) long.
£420–470 MR

Sextants & Octants

An ebony and brass octant, with bone scale, stamped 'J. Hemsley & Son, Tower Hill, London', c1800, 11¾in (30cm) high.
£550–600 BSA

A diamond framed vernier sextant, with additional lenses, with wedge-shaped case, c1820, 12in (30.5cm) radius.
£500–600 GWA

An ebony framed octant, with ivory scale, with original oak case, c1820, 10in (25.5cm) radius.
£450–500 GWA

A lacquered-brass ladder framed sextant, by Heath of Crayford, with fitted mahogany case and additional telescopes, c1890, 10in (25.5cm) radius.
£500–600 GWA

A plastic model of the *Cutty Sark*, in display case, 1990s, 48in (122cm) long.
£180–200 GWA

Sextant: An astrological instrument with a graduated arc equal to a sixth part of a circle used for measuring angular distances, especially the altitudes of celestial objects for ascertaining latitude at sea.
Octant: In the form of an eighth of a circle.
Quadrant: A quarter-circle.

SMOKING & SNUFF TAKING

Smoking might have become less and less acceptable but tobacco paraphernalia, ranging from pipes to snuff boxes, continues to attract collectors. Perhaps the most popular of all smoking accessories are lighters, to which we devote a special feature in this year's guide.

As cigars then cigarettes gradually took over from snuff taking, so the lighter came into its own. An enormous variety of designs have been produced in the twentieth century, ranging from Art Deco extravaganzas, in the form of bartenders and ballerinas, to the classic simplicity of the Zippo lighter, from 1950s table lighters shaped like rockets to modern-day plastic disposable lighters, emblazoned with advertising and produced every conceivable colour. Major names include the long-established British firm of Dunhill, whose elegant accessories can command extremely high prices, and Ronson, founded in New York in 1896 by Louis V. Aronson. One hundred years later Ronson's centenary was celebrated by an auction in London devoted to their lighters, examples from which are featured in the following section. Prices for lighters depend on maker, material and shape. Novelty designs command a premium and many serious collectors prefer to focus on petrol rather than gas lighters. Condition is important, dents can lower the value of a piece and missing parts such as screws can be very difficult to replace.

A miniature bisque pipe, c1890, 2¼in (5.5cm) long.
£24–28 *PSA*

A Boer hand-carved wood pipe, c1900, 6in (15cm) long.
£110–130 *OD*

A Dutch pottery pipe, inscribed 'It's a Shame to take the Money', c1860, 5in (12.5cm) long.
£30–35 *JO*

A wooden cigar mould, c1900, 22in (56cm) long.
£30–40 *ByI*

A brass cigarette box, 1920s, 3½in (9cm) wide.
£25–30 *PC*

A cigar cutter and striker, 1920s, 6in (15cm) high.
£60–70 *FAM*

A silver vesta case, by Walker & Hall, 1920s, 2¼in (5.5cm) high.
£45–55 *FMN*

A collage of Player's Navy Cut cigarette packets, 1930–40s, 9½in (24cm) diam.
£10–15 *AnS*

The New Wunup one-hand Bakelite cigarette case, inscribed 'Doctors' Special', 1930s, 3½in (9cm) wide.
£20–25 *REN*

Lighters

A silver regimental table lighter, with horn handle, by Joseph Braham, engraved with the cipher of the Royal Artillery Regt and presentation inscription, 1905, 2½in (6.5cm) long.
£320–360 *DN*

A Dunhill silver and black enamel bridge-top lighter, with a clock, import marks for London 1929, 2in (5cm) high.
£1,300–1,600 *AAV*

A Ronson penguin Picacig combined table lighter and cigarette box, chrome-plated, enamelled-brass and spelter, wand missing, 1930s, 5½in (14cm) high.
£750–850 *SAS*

A Ronson monkey Picacig combined table lighter and cigarette box, chrome-plated, enamelled-brass and spelter, wand missing, 1930s, 5½in (14cm) high.
£650–750 *SAS*

A Ronson bartender combined table cigarette box and petrol/flint lighter, chrome-plated and enamel-decorated brass, wand and baseplate missing, 1930s, 7in (17.5cm) high.
£500–600 *SAS*

A Ronson elephant table lighter, chromed-brass with plastic tusks, marked and dated '1935', 5in (12.5cm) high.
£140–180 *SAS*

A Ronson Rondelight ballerina, petrol/flint lighter, chromed-brass with black enamel decoration, on spelter base, 1930s, 6in (15.5cm) high.
£500–600 *SAS*

A Ronson hound/dog chrome-plated brass petrol striker lighter, modelled as a stylised seated dog, on painted spelter base, tip of wand missing, 1935, 4½in (11cm) high.
£110–140 *SAS*

l. A Rowenta silver-cased pocket lighter, German, 1930–40s, 2in (5cm) high.
£50–60 *FAM*

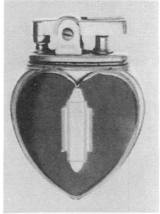

A Ronson heart petrol/flint pocket lighter, chromed-brass decorated with brown enamel, marked, c1940, 2¼in (6cm) high.
£300–350 *SAS*

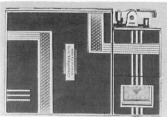

A Ronson king case combined cigarette case, watch and petrol/flint lighter, the brass body with engine-turned chrome decoration and tortoiseshell finish, with inscription to the central escutcheon, c1938, 4¼in (11cm) high.
£600–700 *SAS*

A classic leather-covered 'jumbo' table lighter, 1940s, 3in (7.5cm) high.
£60–70 *FAM*

A boxed lighter and cigarette case, with one pound note decoration, 1940–50s, box 6½in (16.5cm) wide.
£40–50 *FAM*

Two cigarette lighters, in the form of cameras, by KKW, 1940–60, 4in (10cm) high.
£30–40 each *FAM*

Lighters like these would fetch a higher price if manufactured in occupied Japan.

An Augusta patent table lighter, German, 1950s, 2½in (6.5cm) high.
£65–75 *FAM*

A Colibri silver cigarette case with lighter, 1950s, 5in (12.5cm) long.
£40–50 *FAM*

A Presto chrome-plated table lighter, with 2 buttons, the red to light and black to close, 1950s, 4in (10cm) wide.
£15–20 *FAM*

A Ronson Lotus table lighter, with black and chrome finish, 1950s, 3in (7.5cm) wide.
£50–60 *FAM*

A Ronson standard petrol/flint pocket lighter, finished in chromed-brass with engraved silvered-metal slip, marked, c1950, 2in (5cm) high.
£30–40 *SAS*

A Parker silver lighter, advertising Esso, with velvet case and box, 1950s, 2in (5cm) long.
£50–70 *FAM*

A Myon leather-bound table lighter, with box, French, 1950s, 3½in (9cm) wide.
£30–40 *FAM*

An Aircraft chrome-plated lighter/cigarette case with watch, 1950s, 5in (12.5cm) long. **£65–75** *FAM*

A Ronson Juno silver-plated brass petrol/flint table lighter, in the form of an urn, marked, 1950s, 6¼in (16cm) high. **£80–90** *SAS*

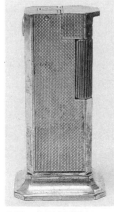

A rocket table lighter, 1950s, 11in (28cm) high. **£100–125** *FAM*

A Dunhill silver lighter, in the form of a tankard, 1950s, 4in (10cm) high. **£75–85** *FAM*

A Ronson Royalty chromed-brass petrol /flint table lighter, with Wedgwood blue jasper ware slip case applied with portraits of HRH the Queen and Prince Philip, the base with impressed marks and dated '1953', 2¾in (7cm) high. **£30–40** *SAS*

These lighters were produced to commemorate the coronation of Queen Elizabeth II, on 2 June 1953.

A chrome-plated aeroplane table lighter, 1950s, 9in (23cm) wide. **£100–125** *FAM*

A Ronson Varaflame Princess set, pocket lighter with gas/flint mechanism, lipstick and cigarette case, gold-plated brass with green hammered enamel decoration, c1960, cigarette case 4in (10cm) wide, with original fitted case. **£35–45** *SAS*

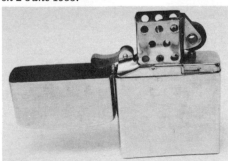

A Zippo style lighter, possibly Japanese, 1960s, 6¾in (17cm) high. **£30–40** *FAM*

The Zippo lighter was created by American George Grant Blaisdel in 1932. The long chimney protected the flame from wind and the lighter was designed to light at the first flick. The case was restyled in 1937, becoming shorter and losing its sharp corners. Solid, functional and timeless, the Zippo remains in production today.

A Dunhill tallboy silver-plated butane gas lighter, 1960s, 3in (7.5cm) high. **£100–125** *FAM*

A Dupont gold-plated cigarette lighter, 1970s, 3in (7.5cm) high. **£90–110** *TAC*

Tobacco Tins

A Sheffield plate, copper and brass tobacco tin, late 18thC, 3½in (9cm) wide.
£70–90 *PC*

A brass tobacco tin, in the form of a book, c1780, 2¼in (5.5cm) wide.
£70–90 *PC*

An engraved brass tobacco tin, c1800, 2in (5cm) wide.
£90–100 *PC*

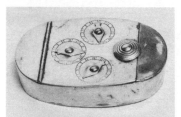

A brass three clock combination tobacco tin, c1800, 3¼in (8cm) wide.
£300–400 *PC*

A brass and silver tobacco tin, in the form of a bible, c1830, 2¾in (7cm) wide.
£90–115 *PC*

A Crimean lead commemorative tobacco box, c1856, 6in (15cm) wide.
£300–350 *MB*

A nickel plated tobacco tin, with engraved inscription 'J. Horton, 1st March 1870', 3¼in (8cm) wide.
£45–60 *PC*

An Edgeworth tobacco tin, 1930s, 3¼in (8cm) wide.
£5–6 *FAM*

A Mahogany tobacco tin, 1950s, 3in (7.5cm) diam.
£2–3 *FAM*

Snuff Boxes

Two snuff boxes, with painted scenes on the lids, c1850, 2¼in (5.5cm) wide.
£45–55 each *PSA*

A hand-painted papier mâché snuff box, c1820, 3¾in (9.5cm) wide.
£200–235 *MB*

SNOOPY & PEANUTS

Written and illustrated by Charles M. Schulz (b1922), 'Peanuts' was a newspaper cartoon strip that first appeared in the US in 1950. The main protagonists were a little boy, Charlie Brown, and his dog Snoopy, the beagle that was to launch a marketing revolution. Other main characters include Lucy, the tough elder sister, blanket-sucking, insecure Linus, Schroeder, top pianist and Beethoven fan, and Woodstock, the bird.

Merchandising began in the 1950s in the hopes of popularising the cartoon strip and has become a major industry. Today Peanuts is known across the world. Its figures, familiar through comics, film and TV, have been translated into innumerable toys and other products, ranging from salt and pepper cruets to radio sets. Snoopy is the most reproduced of all the characters and a candidate for the most popular cartoon dog of all time. In the US there are already Peanuts collectors clubs and, as the following section shows, the subject is also popular in Britain, where for some, to coin Schulz's famous bumper-sticker phrase 'Happiness is . . . a Peanuts Collection'.

A pack of Snoopy playing cards, 1952, and a soft toy, 1958, cards 3½in (9cm) high.
£3–4 each *CMF*

A Snoopy canvas and plastic shopping bag, 1958, 10½ x 9½in (26.5 x 24cm).
£5–7 *CMF*

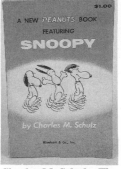

Charles M. Schulz, The New Peanuts Book, published by Rinehart & Co Inc, 1958, 8 x 5½in (20.5 x 14cm).
£3–5 *CMF*

r. Two papier mâché figure scenes, c1972, tallest 5in (13cm) high.
£20–30 *PC*

A Snoopy bottle, 1958, 8½in (21.5cm) long.
£10–12 *CMF*

Four Snoopy planters, c1975, tallest 5½in (14cm) high.
£10–25 each *PC*

A Snoopy soft toy, 1968, 10in (25.5cm) high.
£10–12 *CMF*

A leather Snoopy, 1950–70s, 6in (15cm) high.
£10–12 *CMF*

Two Snoopy vases, 1970, 7½in (19cm) high.
£15–20 each *PC*

A Snoopy pottery money box, 1970, 6in (15cm) high.
£5–7 *CMF*

A Snoopy soft toy, 1970s,
8in (20.5cm) high.
£5-7 *CMF*

Two Snoopy paperweights,
c1975, 3in (7.5cm) diam.
£8-10 each *PC*

A pottery Snoopy swing musical
box, 1974, 6¼in (16cm) high.
£40-50 *PC*

A selection of Snoopy clockwork walkers,
1975, 3½in (9cm) high.
£2-5 each *PC*

Three Snoopy transport money boxes, 1977,
4in (10cm) wide.
£10-15 *PC*

Two Snoopy junk food series money boxes,
1979, hot dog 5in (12cm) high.
£10-20 *PC*

A selection of Snoopy rubber figures,
1970–80s, 2½in (6.5cm) high.
£2-5 each *PC*

A Snoopy music box, Christmas
1981, 7½in (19cm) high.
£60-70 *PC*

A Snoopy bubble bath bucket,
1979, 5½in (14cm) high.
£10-15 *PC*

Snoopy ceramic salt and pepper pots,
c1975, tallest 4¾in (12cm) high.
£15-20 *PC*

SPORT

A pitch pine sauna box, 1880, 54in (137cm) high.
£200–400 *MSh*

A 'Juvenile' hockey stick, 1920s, 29in (73cm) long.
£10–15 *WAB*

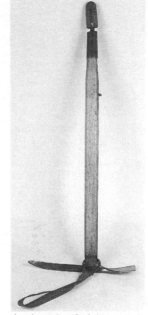

An Austrian lady's ice-pick, 1930s, 25⅞in (65.5cm) long.
£30–40 *WAB*

A pair of leather skating boots and skates, 1930s, 11in (28cm) long.
£15–18 *WAB*

A French épée, c1880, 34½in (88cm) long.
£15–18 *WAB*

A lacrosse stick, c1930, 42½in (108cm) long.
£15–20 *AXT*

A 'Dignus' ashtray, The New Champ, 1935, 4¼in (10.5cm) wide.
£20–30 *GL*

A pair of unworn cycling shoes, 1930s, size 8.
£25–30 *WAB*

A kendo leather and wire mesh fencing mask, by the Wilkinson Sword Co, 1930s, 15in (38cm) high.
£35–45 *WAB*

A Stadia medicine ball, 1930, 9in (23cm) diam.
£35–45 *WAB*

A glass paperweight, advertising Burroughes & Watts billiard tables, 1930s, 2½in (6.5cm) diam.
£40–50 *BRA*

Two snooker and billiards
rules booklets, 1935,
5½ x 8½in (14 x 21.5cm).
£15–20 each *BRA*

Three silver-plated
trophies, 1930–70s,
largest 6in (15cm) high.
£20–30 each *WAB*

A pair of leather boxing gloves,
1960s, 11in (28cm) long.
£15–20 *WAB*

A Wedgwood plate,
commemorating the 1972
Olympics, 6¼in (16cm) diam.
£25–30 *TAR*

Olympia 1936, 2 volumes,
summer and winter
editions, with extra
postcard pictures, 1936,
12½ x 9½in (32 x 24cm).
£50–60 *NW*

A Burroughes & Watts
snooker league winner's
certificate, 1962,
17¼ x 11½in (44 x 29cm).
£30–50 *BRA*

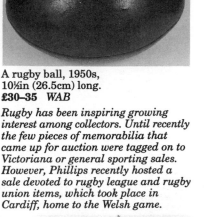

A rugby ball, 1950s,
10½in (26.5cm) long.
£30–35 *WAB*

*Rugby has been inspiring growing
interest among collectors. Until recently
the few pieces of memorabilia that
came up for auction were tagged on to
Victoriana or general sporting sales.
However, Phillips recently hosted a
sale devoted to rugby league and rugby
union items, which took place in
Cardiff, home to the Welsh game.*

*Billiards & Snooker Teasers
Explained*, published by
Burroughes & Watts Ltd, and
Notes on the Game of Snooker,
published by Thurston & Co Ltd,
c1956, 5¼ x 8½in (13.5 x 21.5cm).
£15–20 each *BRA*

Baseball

r. A Phillies
display baseball,
American, 1960s,
11in (28cm) high.
£25–30 *TAR*

l. A soft ball,
catching mitt
and baseball bat,
1960s, bat 33½in
(85cm) long.
£15–25 each *WAB*

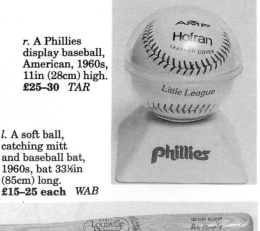

A 'Louisville Slugger' baseball bat, 1950–60s, 26½in (67cm) long.
£35–40 *RIS*

Cricket

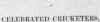

FREDERICK LILLYWHITE'S

CRICKET SCORES

AND

BIOGRAPHIES

OF

CELEBRATED CRICKETERS,

FROM

1746 to 1826.

VOL. I.

LONDON:
PUBLISHED BY FREDERICK LILLYWHITE,
THE OVAL, KENNINGTON, SURREY.
1862.

Cricket Scores and Biographies of Celebrated Cricketers from 1746 to 1826, Vol 1, published by Frederick Lillywhite, recent half calf gilt, *ex libris* G. B. Buckley, with his annotations, 1862, octavo.
£110–150 DW

A late Victorian coloured print of W. G. Grace, advertising Colman's Mustard, framed and glazed, 23 x 15in (58.5 x 38cm).
£80–100 DA

l. A Warwickshire County Cricket Club County Champions plate, by Royal Grafton, limited edition of 1,000, Stoke-on-Trent, 1994, 10¾in (27.5cm) diam.
£40–45 NuP

F. S. Ashley-Cooper, *Curiosities of First-Class Cricket*, original gilt decorated cloth, limited signed edition, No. 18 of 100, *ex libris* Edmund Blunden, with pencilled note to front endpaper, 1901, octavo.
£400–500 DW

l. A chain for measuring a cricket pitch, 1930s, 23in (58.5cm) wide.
£18–22 WAB

A cricket bat, 1890, 34in (86.5cm) long.
£40–50 WAB

Croquet

CROQUÊT:

THE

LAWS AND REGULATIONS OF THE GAME,

WITH

A DESCRIPTION OF THE IMPLEMENTS,
ETC. ETC.

ILLUSTRATED WITH DIAGRAMS AND ENGRAVINGS.

BY JOHN JAQUES.

NEW EDITION, THOROUGHLY REVISED

LONDON:
JAQUES AND SON, 102, HATTON GARDEN,
AND SOLD BY
LONGMAN, GREEN, LONGMAN, ROBERTS, AND GREEN.
1865.

[The Right of Translation is reserved.]

John Jaques, *Croquêt: The Laws and Regulations of the Game*, with black and white illustrations, 1865, octavo.
£200–225 DW

A croquet mallet, 1920s, 38½in (98cm) long.
£24–28 WAB

Fishing

In 1996 at Angling Auctions, West London, a world record of £17,000 was set, and another world record was set for an 1891 Hardy Perfect fishing reel, more than doubling the previous British record for a reel. Fishing is a worldwide sport and has a long tradition of attracting wealthy enthusiasts. In the Victorian and Edwardian eras, fishing along with hunting and shooting was the pastime of the aristocracy and the landed gentry. A host of manufacturers emerged to cater for their angling needs, and celebrated makers include Hardy of Alnwick, Northumberland, (probably the most famous name in the field), Charles Farlow, based in the Strand, London, and the Redditch firm of Samuel Allcock & Co. Because they were supplying an affluent clientele, the objects created by these makers were often expensive, extremely high in quality and built to last. 'Take the example of Samuel Allcock's aerial centre pin reels,' says dealer Richard Dowson, 'they might be well over fifty years old, yet they were so precisely engineered that if you spin one with

your finger it can carry on turning for up to a minute. The engineering was superlative and these reels are highly sought-after today.'

It is not just reels that collectors want. From the mid-19th century onwards, well over a thousand patents were taken out for fishing tackle of every possible description ranging from bizarre line winding machines to customised fishermen's bicycles, and as well as looking for tackle by named and respected makers there is also demand for angling oddities and rarities.

Collectors tend to fall into three main categories: serious enthusiasts, fascinated by the history of the sport and the precise academic details of its objects; nostalgic fishermen, attracted by the quality and engineering of period tackle, who often enjoy using their purchases; and those simply buying for decorative purposes, looking for a pretty item to put on the shelf. 'The most important thing is to buy the best you can afford,' concludes Dowson. 'It is better to buy one good piece for £100 than ten indifferent items for £10.'

General Tackle

A folding line winder, 1920–30, 15in (38cm) long. **£75–85** *AnS*

A saleman's wallet, for W. Bartleet & Sons, containing a selection of fish hooks, 1890–1932, 8¾in (22cm) high. **£600–700** *PC*

A Farlow carved wooden half-block hen salmon, weighing 33lbs, caught by H. St George, 17th November 1917, 17 x 50in (43 x 127cm). **£2,500–3,000** *AGA*

A Recorde 5 brass extending gaff, with cork handle, point guard and belt clip, c1920, 48in (122cm) long.
£65–75 *BSA*

A Hardy's Unique salmon fly cabinet, with leather carrying case, 1930, cabinet 9¾in (25cm) wide.
£6,500–7,000 *AGA*

A Hardy Bros brass Zephyr dry fly oil bottle, c1920, 2¾in (7cm) long.
£80–140 *OTB*

r. A wicker fishing creel, c1920, 13in (33cm) wide.
£75–85 *AnS*

l. The Forrest salmon fly scale, c1930, 4¼in (11cm) long.
£10–15 *PC*

A dry fly dryer and oiler, c1921, 1¾in (4.5cm) diam.
£70–80 *PC*

A selection of Hardy drinking cups, with a leather wallet, 1930s, 3¼in (8.5cm) high.
£150–200 *PC*

Four Land em Loach style lures, probably by Milwards, fins stamped 'Made in England', c1940, largest 3½in (9cm) long.
£5–8 each *OTB*

An Allcock's aluminium fly case, with a selection of dry and wet flies, c1930, 4in (10cm) square.
£25–30 *AnS*

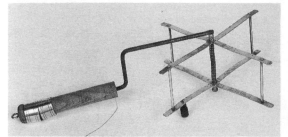

A line winder, the wooden handle with brass rings, 1950s, 17in (43cm) long.
£24–28 *WAB*

Three Hardy wooden tackle releasers, 1930–60, 12¾in (32.5cm) long.
£10–30 each *PC*

Our Founder, Jamie Maxtone Graham, c 1924, with a 4¾" All brass Hardy Perfect

We are keen to buy the very best reels and rods, particularly those made by Hardy before 1939. Other desired piscatoriana: ingenious fly boxes and cabinets, books and catalogues; line driers, and all the fishing gadgets - including all modern tackle.

Jamie Maxtone Graham's three books - Best of Hardy's Anglers' guides, 210pp paperback (being reprinted, price on application); To Catch a Fisherman (Patents) 275pp hardback £25; Fishing Tackle of Yesterday - A Collector's Guide, 226pp paperback £25 - are obtainable direct from Timeless Tackle.

Send £3 for our exhaustive catalogue
Write or call:
Rob Maxtone Graham's Timeless Tackle
1 Blackwood Crescent, Edinburgh, EH9 1QZ

**TEL: 0131 667 1407 or 0370 234997
FAX: 0131 662 4215**

Reels

A 3in brass plate-wind fishing reel, with ratchet, bone handle, late 19thC.
£70–80 *BSA*

A Hardy Perfect 2½in all-brass reel, 1891.
£17,000–18,000 *AGA*

This reel is one of only two examples known to have been made in this unusually small size.

A Farlow & Co 4½in brass plate wind reel, late 19thC.
£100–125 *WAB*

r. A Hardy Perfect 4in brass-faced reel, with solid faceplate, 1898–1908.
£350–400 *ND*

l. A Seaton Nottingham 4in reel, with star back centre pin, c1900.
£45–55 *AnS*

A Hardy St. George 3in fly reel, made 1927–68.
£250–300 *PC*

A Malloch's 4in patent No. 1 polished brass rotating drum salmon spinning reel, with reversible spool, c1900.
£145–165 *BSA*

A Carter & Peek 4in brass and alloy salmon fly reel, with perforated brass drum, brass foot and pillars, alloy side plates, c1910.
£60–90 *OTB*

A Malloch 2½in bronze reel, 1920.
£35–40 *WAB*

An Allcock's 4in sea reel, with wooden centre pin, star back, c1920.
£40–50 *AnS*

A Hardy Perfect 4¼in brass-faced salmon fly reel, strapped tension screw with turk's head locking nut, early check, ivorine handle, unperforated drum and brass foot, early 1900s.
£320–360 *EP*

l. An Ogden Smith Exchequer 4in salmon fly reel, engraved 'D' on inner surface of backplate, for maker Walter Dingley, c1930.
£40–70 *OTB*

r. A Hardy 3½in 'Hardy-Wallis' bottom fishing reel, with unventilated drum, twin-tapered black handles, phosphor bronze bush, on/off rim lever check and grooved brass foot, 1930s.
£130–160 *EP*

An Allcock's Aerialite
3¼in reel, with Bakelite
handle, 1930–40.
£25–30 *AnS*

A 5in ebonite sea reel, by Eton
Sun, Scarborough, 1950s.
£25–30 *WAB*

An Ambidex 4½in fixed spool reel,
by J. W. Young & Sons, c1947.
£15–25 *OTB*

*This was the first model with a
black finish, half-bale arm and
'Patents Pending' marks.*

A Farlow's Cobra 3½in fly
reel, 1950–60.
£40–50 *AnS*

A Mitchell Match auto reel,
with spare spool, 1950–60,
6in (15cm) long.
£20–30 *AnS*

A Mitchell Cap reel, 1950s,
4in (10cm) wide.
£15–20 *AnS*

A Mitchell 300
reel, 1950–60,
5in (12.5cm) wide.
£20–25 *AnS*

A Hardy Tournament
H.J.S. 2in casting
reel, 1952.
£2,400–2,800 *AGA*

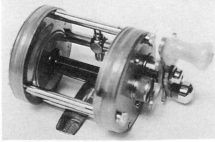

An Ambassador 6000 reel, c1959,
4½in (11.5cm) wide.
£70–90 *AnS*

Football

Famous Footballers, edited by C.W. Alcock & Rowland Hill, some damage, 1895–96, 10 x 7in (25.5 x 18cm).
£220–300 *DW*

An official home programme of Tottenham Hotspur v. Everton, 8th January 1910, torn, 9½ x 7in (24 x18cm).
£60–70 *VS*

An official programme of the FA Cup Final, Bolton Wanderers v. Manchester City, 1926, some damage, 9 x 6in (23 x 15cm).
£300–360 *VS*

An official away programme of Tottenham Hotspur v. Chelsea, 15th September 1934, folds, 9½ x 7in (24 x 18cm).
£30–40 *VS*

A spelter figure of a goalkeeper, on a marble stand, 1940–50, 15in (38cm) high.
£200–250 *MSh*

r. A leather laced football, 1950s, 7½in (19cm) diam.
£25–30 *WAB*

A leather football, c1930.
£20–25 *AXT*

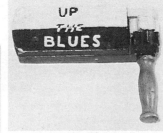

A bird scarer/football rattle, painted blue and white and inscribed, 1950s, 4¼in (11cm) wide.
£15–18 *TAN*

A pair of leather studded football boots, c1950.
£30–35 *WAB*

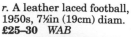

A football pools forecaster, 1950s, 6in (15cm) long.
£8–10 *OD*

Golf

Included in this section are items from the sale of the Sir Henry Cotton Golfing archive, offered by Sotheby's recently. Sir Henry Cotton MBE (1907–87) was one of the leading British golfers of the century – three times Open Champion, journalist and author of many books, course designer and an influential teacher. Despite his fame in Europe he was not greatly known in America, and the lack of US interest in the sale was responsible for many lots selling below the auction house's estimates. In general the golfing market, which has seen such enormous prices in recent years, has now stabilised. Collectors are becoming increasingly discriminating, prepared only to pay top prices for items of the highest quality and rarity.

Two golf balls, c1885.
£100–200 each *PC*

A Copeland Spode three-handled tyg or loving cup, decorated with scenes of golfers in white relief over a green glaze, c1890, 5½in (14cm) high.
£400–500 *MSh*

A silver-plated cut-glass cruet set, the stand in the form of a golf ball and clubs, c1890, 3½in (9cm) high.
£120–140 *MSh*

A chrome bottle opener, in the form of a golf club, 1950s, 6in (15cm) high.
£3–5 *OD*

A Springvale Kite Golf Ball advertising card, with red lettering on blue background, c1890, 10 x 15in (25.5 x 38cm).
£100–120 *BBR*

r. A collection of 32 Masters Tournament Winners' autographed golf balls.
£1,800–2,000 *CNY*

A silver golfing spoon, inscribed 'Coxmoor 1969', 4½in (11.5cm) long.
£15–18 *WAB*

Golf Clubs

A collection of 7 golf clubs,
l.–r.: A Tom Morris wooden-headed putter,
£400–450;
A brass-headed putter, by Halley & Co; a
socket-headed fairway wood, by J. H. Taylor;
a hickory-shafted rut iron, by Nicholl; a
socket-headed fairway wood, by C. Millar; a
hickory-shafted putter, by Spalding; a socket-
headed fairway wood, by T. Stewart, c1905,
largest 40in (101.5cm) long.
£25–90 each *MR*

A putter, with spliced and
whipped joint, by Gibson
of Kinghorn, c1915,
34in (86.5cm) long.
£100–120 *MSh*

A rut iron, c1880,
38in (96.5cm) long.
£200–300 *MSh*

Sir Henry Cotton Memorabilia

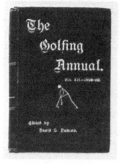

The Golfing Annual,
Volume XII, edited
by David & Duncan,
signed by Henry
Cotton, cloth bound,
1898–99, octavo.
£800–900 *S*

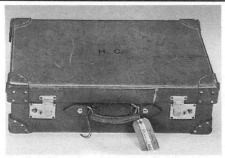

A tan leather travelling case, gilt stamped
with presentation inscription to Henry
Cotton, dated 'December 17th, 1932',
27in (68.5cm) wide.
£550–650 *S*

A set of 5 Dunlop 65 golf
balls, in fitted velvet-
lined mahogany case,
the lid inset with brass
plaque engraved
'Presented to Henry
Cotton OBE, To celebrate
the 50th Anniversary of
his participation in the
Open Championship',
balls dating 1935–75,
13½in (34cm) wide.
£2,200–2,500 *S*

r. A silver trophy,
entitled 'The Cotton
Grip', with facsimile
signature, hallmarked
Birmingham 1970,
17¼in (44cm) high.
£13,000–14,000 *S*

A Ryder Cup souvenir
photo album, 48 whole
plate photographs of
the players for the
matches played 1st &
2nd November, 1947,
oblong quarto.
£750–850 *S*

A PGA life members'
red and blue enamelled
lapel badge, inscribed,
1960s, 1¼in (3cm) diam.
£240–280 *S*

Horses, Hunting & Shooting
Horses

A riding crop, with horn handle and silver collar, Birmingham 1902, 26½in (67cm) long.
£45–50 *TAR*

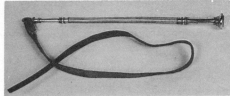

A wooden and brass whip, with leather lash, c1910, 17½in (44.5cm) long.
£40–50 *WAB*

A Regency mahogany jockey's weighing machine, marked 'Young & Son, maker, Bear Street' beneath a crown, 25in (63.5cm) wide.
£800–1,000 *B*

A wooden polo stick, 1960s, 49in (124.5cm) long.
£20–25 *WAB*

A leather saddle, c1930–60.
£30–35 *WAB*

A leather game bag, 1930s, 11½in (29cm) wide.
£20–25 *WAB*

Hunting & Shooting

A simulated bamboo tripod shooting stick, c1910, open 21in (53.5cm) high.
£240–300 *MSh*

A Hardy's shooting stick, with leather seat, c1930, 25in (63.5cm) high.
£90–110 *WAB*

r. A Rifle Club trophy, 1975, 9¼in (23.5cm) high.
£18–22 *WAB*

Rowing

An oak butler's tray, the stand shaped with 4 oars and the tray as a boat, c1890, 35in (89cm) high.
£600–700 *MSh*

A seat from a racing scull, 1960s, 25in (63.5cm) long.
£20–25 *WAB*

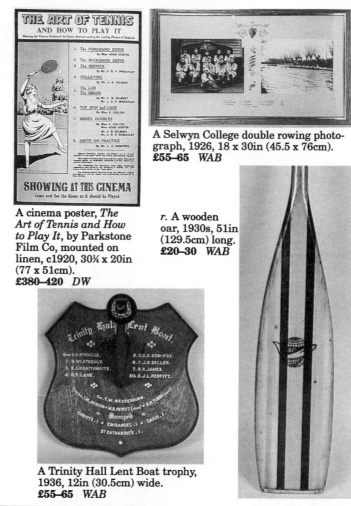

A cinema poster, *The Art of Tennis and How to Play It*, by Parkstone Film Co, mounted on linen, c1920, 30¼ x 20in (77 x 51cm).
£380–420 *DW*

A Selwyn College double rowing photograph, 1926, 18 x 30in (45.5 x 76cm).
£55–65 *WAB*

r. A wooden oar, 1930s, 51in (129.5cm) long.
£20–30 *WAB*

A Trinity Hall Lent Boat trophy, 1936, 12in (30.5cm) wide.
£55–65 *WAB*

Tennis

An oak and silver-plated three-handled trophy, engraved 'Cheltenham Lawn Tennis Tournament', c1884, 8in (20.5cm) high.
£120–150 *MSh*

Two Dayton steel rackets, with wooden handles, American, c1920, 27in (68.5cm) long.
£75–95 each *MSh*

Albert de Luze, *A History of The Royal Game of Tennis*, published by Roundwood Press, signed by translator, limited edition, 1979, octavo.
£460–500 *DW*

TEDDY BEARS & SOFT TOYS

A Strunz rod bear, with golden mohair, black boot button eyes, pronounced snout, brown stitched nose and mouth, swivel head, long jointed shaped limbs, felt pads, rod jointing and button in ear, some wear, c1904, 19in (48cm) high.
£2,200–2,500 *CSK*

Although little is known about Strunz, they were clearly influenced by Steiff and produced copies of Steiff products adopting the similar trademark of a button in the left ear. Steiff took legal action against the company and patented the button in the left ear as their own trademark.

A Steiff teddy bear, with gold mohair plush, centre seam, wide apart ears, pronounced clipped muzzle, black boot button eyes, excelsior filled body with swivel joints, elongated arms and large cotton covered pads, pads recovered, some stitching missing, Steiff button to ear, early 20thC, 21in (54cm) high.
£4,000–4,500 *P(Ba)*

Teddy Bears

- Pre-WWI bear manufacture was dominated by Germany. Early bears had long limbs, pointed muzzles and often humped backs. They were made from mohair plush, with felt pads and boot button eyes.
- From the 1920s arms became shorter and glass eyes replaced the boot buttons. The war stimulated European countries to develop their own toy industries. British bears had flatter faces than their German rivals, the hump disappeared and velveteen or cotton was often used instead of felt for pads.
- During WWII production was severely restricted as manufacturers contributed to the war effort – firms such as Merrythought produced fleecy linings for helmets rather than soft toys.
- The post war period saw the introduction of new synthetic materials – eyes were made of plastic, fur of nylon and the machine-washable bear was born.

A Steiff blue pocket bear, 1918, 3½in (9cm) high.
A Schuco fully-jointed teddy bear, 1930s, 2½in (6.5cm) high.
£200–250 *CMF*

Pocket bears were used as mascots by airmen and soldiers.

A French black bear, with beige pads, 1920s, 12in (30.5cm) high.
£250–300 *CMF*

r. A British teddy bear, with long fur, 1920s, 20in (51cm) high.
£400–450 *PC*

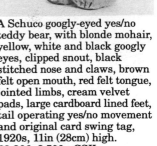

A Schuco googly-eyed yes/no teddy bear, with blonde mohair, yellow, white and black googly eyes, clipped snout, black stitched nose and claws, brown felt open mouth, red felt tongue, jointed limbs, cream velvet pads, large cardboard lined feet, tail operating yes/no movement and original card swing tag, 1920s, 11in (28cm) high.
£2,200–2,500 *CSK*

A teddy bear, 1930s,
28in (71cm) high.
£650–750 *AnS*

*This bear was probably
made for a department
store and would
originally have been
a pale gold colour.*

An English musical
teddy bear, plays a
lullaby, pre-WWII,
14in (35.5cm) high.
£145–165 *AnS*

An English blue
bear, 1930s, 23in
(58.5cm) high.
£145–165 *CMF*

A German brown-tipped
mohair bear, 1930s,
15in (38cm) high.
£155–175 *B&F*

A Chiltern fully-jointed
mohair teddy bear, c1935,
20in (51cm) high.
£175–195 *B&F*

A Chad Valley teddy bear,
1935, 18in (46cm) high.
£150–175 *CSA*

A German clockwork
walking brown bear,
1940s, 5in (12.5cm) long.
£55–65 *CMF*

A Merrythought tan mohair teddy
bear, with glass eyes, stitched nose
and mouth, swivel head, felt pads,
stitched label, Dutch, repaired,
c1938, 12in (30.5cm) high.
£425–475 *CSK*

A Chiltern mohair teddy bear,
c1935, 13½in (34cm) high.
£325–375 *B&F*

A Chad Valley nightdress case,
c1940, 14in (35.5cm) high.
£175–200 *CMF*

A homemade teddy bear, made
from an old camel-hair coat,
c1940, 13in (33cm) high, and a
teddy bear nightdress case,
made from an old coat and
apron, c1940, 19in (48.5cm) high.
£40–45 each *CMF*

An Australian musical koala,
1950s, 9in (23cm) high.
£24–28
A small koala, 1950s,
6in (15cm) high.
£10–12 *CMF*

A Chiltern musical teddy
bear, with long blonde fur,
black and amber glass eyes,
moulded plastic snout and
stitched mouth, moving limbs
with felt pads, kapok and
excelsior filled, with
musical movement
playing a Brahms
lullaby, printed label,
c1950, 16in (31cm) high.
£350–400 *P(HSS)*

A Dutch cotton plush
teddy bear, c1950,
18in (45.5cm) high.
£55–65 *CMF*

> **Cross Reference**
> Colour Review

r. A Chad Valley
teddy bear, 1950s,
14in (35.5cm) high.
£150–200 *CMF*

A Dean's fully-jointed
teddy bear, original
Childsplay label, 1950s,
13½in (34.5cm) high.
£95–115 *B&F*

A Pedigree mohair
teddy bear, with
fully-jointed limbs,
original label, 1950s,
18in (45.5cm) high.
£125–145 *B&F*

A Schuco teddy bear,
1950s, 29in (74cm) high.
£325–375 *CMF*

l. A Sooty bear, 1950s,
10in (25.5cm) high.
£75–95 *CMF*

A Chiltern teddy bear, remains of original label, c1960, 13in (33cm) high.
£120–140 B&F

A Wendy Boston teddy bear, 1960s, 14in (35.5cm) high.
£55–65 AnS

This bear was the first bear produced that could be put into a washing machine.

A flannel Winnie-the-Pooh, 1960s, 13in (33cm) high.
£30–40
A *Winnie-the-Pooh and Tigger* book, 1970s.
£5–7 CMF

Soft Toys

A Steiff ride-on camel, with beige tipped brown curly mohair neck and front legs, beige felt face, body and lower legs, large black boot button eyes, on metal wheels, worn, some repairs, c1908, 41in (104cm) long.
£475–525 CSK

A Dean's Mickey Mouse rag toy, play worn, 1933, 8½in (21.5cm) high.
£100–150 PC

A seated fox, possibly Farnell, with golden mohair and white mohair chest and tip of tail, brown and black glass eyes backed on black felt, pronounced clipped snout, black stitched nose and mouth and swivel head, c1930s, 13in (33cm) high.
£260–300 CSK

A golly, with floral shirt and blue trousers, 1940s, 20in (51cm) high.
£20–30 OD

A soft toy, with tail, c1960, 10½in (25.5cm) high.
£12–18 OD

Two Steiff squirrels, 1950–60s, largest 4½in (11.5cm) high.
£28–32 each CMF

TELEPHONES

Most old telephones are purchased by people who either have an old house or have decorated in a particular style and feel that a modern telephone would look out of place. Many are bought for nostalgic reasons – the heavy handset, the dial, the traditional ring or simply because it is like the one owned by their parents or grandparents.

In the USA the open market led to a wide choice of models, and telephone collecting is now a well-established hobby. In the UK, because the GPO had a general monopoly, the range of designs produced, particularly since the 1920s, was comparatively limited. As such, telephones have never had the same appeal as gramophones or radios, and telephone collecting is still in its infancy in Britain.

There are signs, however, that this area of collecting is beginning to grow. 'Old telephones are much harder to source than they were five years ago,' admits dealer Gavin Payne. 'The 200 and 300 Bakelites of the 1930s to 1960s used to be really common. Now they are much more difficult to find, especially in good condition, and prices have doubled in three years.'

Early candlestick and wooden wall telephones can command very high prices, and because of their decorative/historical qualities have always been attractive to collectors. Recently, however, there has also been an upsurge of interest in the 700 series telephones from the 1960s–80s. 'They are being bought by people who want a basic telephone with a bell and a dial, and who are attracted by the wide range of models and colours, and the currently low prices,' explains Payne. 'Vast numbers of these phones are being shipped abroad to Third World countries, so now is a good time to start collecting.'

Prices depend not only on model, rarity and provenance, but also on what type of guarantee is offered with a telephone, as well as the standard of restoration.

An L. M. Ericsson skeleton magneto telephone, c1898, 13in (33cm) high.
£650–800 *OTC*

A 121 wall telephone, on a blackboard with writing slope, 1927, 18in (45.5cm) high.
£400–500 *OTC*

A mahogany or walnut 1a bell set, 1924, 9in (23cm) high.
£100–150 *OTC*

A Danish magneto telephone, 1920, 13in (33cm) high.
£200–250 *OTC*

A black Bakelite and chrome telephone, 1920s, 9in (23cm) wide.
£125–150 *HHa*

A 354 Siemens wall telephone, c1936, 8in (20.5cm) high.
£160–180 *OTC*

A magneto switchboard, 1930–50, 12in (30.5cm) high.
£100–150 *OTC*

A 232 black Bakelite telephone, with original handset, cord, and alphabet dial, mounted on a bell set type 26, 1930s, 7½in (19cm) high.
£220–270 *OTC*

A black Bakelite telephone, with plain number dial and no drawer, 1950s, 6in (15cm) high.
£100–120 *OTC*

A black Bakelite Gecophone, 1939, 7in (18cm) high.
£200–250 *OTC*

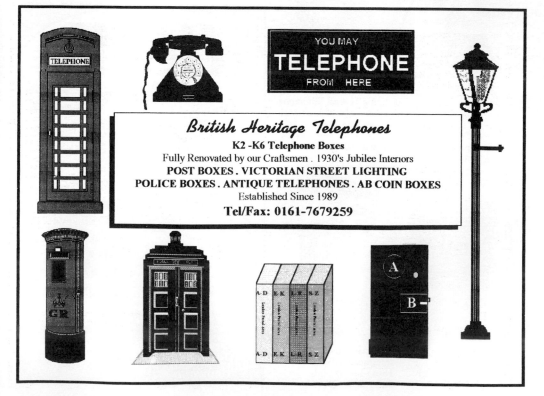

A 232 ivory acrylic telephone, with original handset, cord, alphabet dial and drawer, with bell set 64d, 1950s, 6in (15cm) high.
£450–500 *OTC*

An American standard 500 black desk telephone, 1950–70, 4¾in (12cm) high.
£50–60 *OTC*

This telephone was available in various colours.

A standard 700 series desk telephone, 1960–80, 4in (10cm) high.
£40–75 *OTC*

A GEC 1000 black Bakelite telephone, early 1960s, 5in (12.5cm) high.
£75–90 *OTC*

A black telephone, produced for HRH Queen Elizabeth II's Silver Jubilee, 1977, 4in (10cm) high.
£140–160 *OTC*

A Danish black Bakelite desk telephone, 1960s, 5in (12.5cm) high.
£100–120 *OTC*

TEXTILES & COSTUME
Textiles

A mid-Victorian Berlin woolwork panel, worked with a frieze of flowers and blossom, on an opalescent beadwork ground, braided border, 176 x 8in (447 x 20.5cm).
£220–260 *DN*

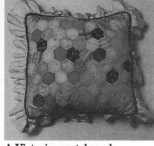

A Victorian patchwork and linen cushion, 17¾in (45cm) square.
£40–50 *SUS*

A Victorian beadwork lobed panel, based on a Roman mosaic design depicting 2 reed buntings and sedges on a bright blue sky ground, flanked by flowers and geometric borders, 28½ x 20½in (72.5 x 52cm).
£170–200 *DN*

A pair of firescreens, with panels of Aubusson tapestry, c1905, 37¾ x 35in (96 x 89cm).
£1,400–1,600 *CSK*

A set of 12 Chinese silk hand-painted mats, 1900, each 5in (12.5cm) square.
£35–55 *LB*

A Welsh hand-stitched double-sided quilt, 1910, 35 x 38½in (90 x 98cm).
£180–200 *SUS*

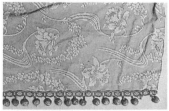

A French pair of curtains, with fringe, 1910, 118 x 157in (300 x 400cm).
£165–185 *SUS*

A silk and lace cushion cover, embroidered 'Souvenir de France', 1910, 19in (48.5cm) square.
£30–40 *LB*

Cushion covers such as this were made during WWI, and sent by soldiers to their loved ones.

l. A cushion cover, made with floral fabric with blue striped border, 1920s, 17¾in (45cm) square.
£30–40 *SUS*

A set of 4 American abstract patterned cotton curtains, interwoven with gold thread, 1950s, each 76in (193cm) long.
£200–250 *TCR*

Costume

A French jet bead dress, 1920s.
£185–275 *TCF*

A diamanté, pearl and bugle beads, on a heavy gauze dress, 1920s.
£250–350 *TCF*

A flower-patterned chiffon dress and jacket, 1930s.
£95–120 *TCF*

A black silk velvet evening dress, 1930s.
£65–95 *TCF*

A black *Dévoré* jacket, 1930s.
£95–120 *TCF*

A pair of American cotton pedal pushers, with matching blue floral top, made by Casino, almost unworn, 1950s.
£35–45 *SPS*

r. A blue shot-silk evening dress, with boned bodice, net underskirt, bow to rear, 1950s.
£55–65 *SBT*

An American deerskin jacket, in very good condition, 1950s.
£100–150 TCR

An American Western-style man's jacket, by Mac Murray of California, cotton gabardine with square pearl buttons, 1950s.
£200–250 TCR

A pair of Hawaiian lady's shorts, 1950s.
£25–35 TCR

r. A chain mail sleeveless top, set with clear glass beads, early 1970s.
£130–160 CSK

l. A gentleman's black velvet jacket, with high buttoned roll neck, lined with psychedelic printed silk, labelled 'Peculiar to Mr Fish, 17 Clifford Street, London, W1', late 1960s.
£450–500 CSK

A pink organza evening cape, appliquéd with pink silk rose petals and silk leaf feathers, probably by Givenchy, 1960s.
£320–360 CSK

A short black lace evening dress, the skirts hooped with black satin ribbons, the underskirt labelled 'Balenciaga, 10 Avenue George V, Paris', the reverse with canvas tag inscribed '56.190', c1960.
£320–360 CSK

A black and royal blue jersey dress, labelled 'Exclusively Designed by Pierre Cardin, Paris', 1970s.
£350–400 CSK

Two Merrythought soft toys, Tom and Jerry, 1960s, Jerry 6¼in (16cm) high. **£25–30 each** *TAR*

A Chiltern musical bear, 1950s, 11¾in (30cm high). **£180–220** *P(B)*

A Chiltern bear, c1945, 16½in (42cm) high. **£225–265** *B&F*

Three Winnie the Pooh characters, 1950–60s, Pooh 13in (33cm) high. **£20–40 each** *CMF*

A roly-poly jingle bear, 1950s, 9in (23cm) high. **£40–50** *CMF*

An American nylon fur bear, 1970s, 12in (30.5cm) high. **£30–40** *CMF*

A green Bakelite telephone,
No. 232, with original handset,
cord, alphabet dial and drawer,
with GPO crest engraved in red,
1930s, 9in (23cm) wide.
£650–750 *OTC*

A black Bakelite telephone,
c1920, 9in (23cm) wide.
£100–120 *HHa*

A tinplate musical telephone
cigarette lighter, dispenses
cigarettes when dial
is turned, 1940s,
5in (12.5cm) wide.
£120–150 *FAM*

A Belgian wall telephone,
1940s–60s, 9in (23cm) high.
£130–150 *OTC*

A green acrylic telephone,
No. 332, with original
handset, cord and alphabet
dial, 1950s, 9in (23cm) wide.
£450–550 *OTC*

A red acrylic telephone,
No. 232, with original handset,
cord, alphabet dial and drawer,
1950s, 9in (23cm) wide.
£500–600 *OTC*

An L. M. Ericsson & Co ivory
Bakelite telephone, 1960s,
9in (23cm) wide. **£170–250** *OTC*

A BT telephone,
depicting Snoopy and
Woodstock, c1981,
13¾in (35cm) high.
£65–75 *PC*

A GEC loudspeaker telephone,
Type 2B, c1962, 14½in (37cm) wide.
£80–100 *OTC*

r. A set of 5 *X Files*
telephone cards,
first limited edition,
in presentation
pack, 1996.
£40–45 *PC*

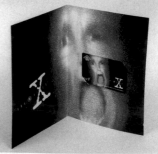

A French silk and lace embroidered cushion cover, c1910, 25in (63.5cm) square.
£30–40 *LB*

A pair of tapestry stools, c1880, 11in (28cm) diam.
£150–200 *PSA*

A rosewood and tapestry prayer stool, c1880, 9½in (24cm) wide.
£180–200 *TAR*

A Victorian beadwork footstool, 11in (28cm) diam.
£80–100 *PSA*

A length of printed velvet, 1920s, 30in (75cm) wide.
£150–170 *SUS*

A length of printed velvet, 1920s, 28in (71cm) wide.
£160–180 *SUS*

A hand-embroidered silk picture, 1920s, 16¾in (17cm) high.
£70–80 *SUS*

A hand-embroidered silk picture, 1930s, 11½in (29cm) wide.
£40–50 *SUS*

A hand-stitched patchwork quilt, c1920, 98in (249cm) long.
£100–120 *SUS*

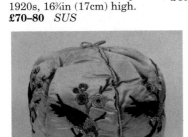

An Edwardian embroidered silk tea cosy, 8in (20cm) high.
£75–85 *PSA*

A French beaded handbag, c1900, 8in (20cm) high.
£50–60 *TAR*

A petit point handbag, 1940s, 14¼in (36cm) wide.
£40–50 *SUS*

An 18thC style theatrical
frock coat, c1900.
£80–120 *AXT*

A Chinese silk embroidered
tunic, c1900.
£95–120 *TCF*

A black and gold lamé
dress, c1910.
£150–175 *TCF*

A Haileybury school
blazer, c1936.
£30–40 *AXT*

A floral patterned parasol, 1930s,
28in (72cm) diam.
£30–40 *SUS*

A silk velvet opera coat,
with large collar, 1930s.
£120–175 *TCF*

A hand-crocheted silk brassiere,
with silk straps, 1920s.
£15–20 *REN*

*Undergarments from this period
are comparatively rare and
surviving examples are often
beautfully handmade.*

l. A cut velvet shift style dress,
with floral pattern, 1930s.
£120–150 *TCF*

A gold sequinned long
sleeved jacket, 1920s.
£75–95 *TCF*

A floral and net hat, by Sonni, 1950s.
£35–55 *TCF*

A poppy hat, made from silk petals, 1920s.
£15–20 *SUS*

A selection of 4 American gentlemen's ties, 1950s.
£10–25 each *TCR*

A floral patterned cotton showerproof rain coat, 1960s.
£18–25 *TCF*

A House of Shamhouse Sportswear cotton gabardine zip-up man's jacket, Rockability style, 1950s.
£100–150 *TCR*

A French scouting/hiking cotton triangular scarf, 1950s.
£25–30 *REN*

A sequinned long waistcoat, 1960s.
£30–35 *TCR*

A pair of Nike trainers, made in Japan, worn, c1971, US size 9.
£300–350 *ROK*

A Levi ringspun denim jacket, capital 'E', with yellow stitching, pre-1973, size 38.
£300–350 *ROK*

A pair of GWG 'Cowboy King' denim jeans, pre-1940s.
£1,000–1,250 *ROK*

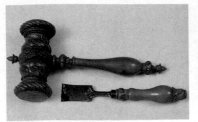

A turned and carved boxwood ceremonial set, consisting of mallet and chisel for a ship's keel, c1850, mallet 9in (23cm) long.
£250–300 *MRT*

A beech and boxwood mitre plane, by Hathersich, Manchester, c1820, 13in (33cm) long.
£80–100 *MRT*

A boxwood and brass clinometer, by Stanley, 1890, 6in (15cm) wide.
£180–200 *MRT*

A beech and boxwood straw plait mill, with grooved rollers for fancy plaiting, late 19thC, 16in (40.5cm) long.
£70–90 *MRT*

A pair of steel grips or pincers, with wooden handles and brass ferrules, c1900, 6in (15cm) long.
£18–25 *BS*

A Millington & Mills utensil for removing light bulbs, 1930s, 8in (20cm) high.
£15–20 *WAB*

A nickel plated shoulder plane, by Ed. Preston, 1¼ x 8in (3 x 20cm).
£55–70 *MRT*

A galvanised watering can, with copper rose, 1930s, 25½in (65cm) high.
£25–30 *SUS*

A wooden fire bucket, with hand-painted crest, copper rings and brass fittings, rope and leather handle c1910, 12in (25.5cm) high.
£85–95 *WAB*

A selection of garden sprayers, 1920s–40s, longest 26in (66cm).
£20–45 each *ET*

l. A brass wagon wheel hub cap, engraved with maker's name, c1900, 3½in (9cm) diam.
£15–20 *BS*

A mahogany fitted games box, c1880, 12½in (32cm) wide.
£150–175 *MB*

A Waddington's Totopoly board game, 1949, 20in (51cm) wide.
£15–18 *OTS*

A BBC *Muffin the Mule* card game, by Pepys, 1949, 3½ x 2¾in (9 x 7cm).
£20–25 *OTS*

A Waddington's Go board game, an international travel game, 1960, 20in (51cm) wide.
£12–15 *OTS*

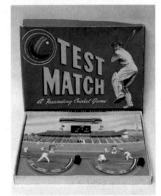

A Waddington's Test Match cricket game, 1960, 15¼in (59cm) wide.
£15–18 *OTS*

An Inspector Morse 550-piece jigsaw puzzle game, The King's Men, 1994, 9¼in (23.5cm) wide.
£9–12 *NW*

A Chad Valley clockwork ladybird, 1950s, 3in (7.5cm) long.
£10–15 *OD*

A Triang United Dairies pull-along milk float, 1950s, 22in (56cm) long.
£40–60 *RAR*

A Chad Valley humming top, 1960s, 8in (20.5cm) diam.
£10–12 *OD*

l. A child's tin bucket, 1960s, 6in (15cm) high.
£12–16 *WAB*

r. A Schuco tinplate clockwork submarine, with adjustable diving vanes and rudder, 1950s, 12in (30.5cm) long.
£90–120 *RAR*

A Lehmann clockwork tinplate baulky mule, early version, c1900, 8in (20cm) long.
£275–325 *OTS*

A Tipp & Co articulated truck, with adjustable steering and removable canopy, 1937, 13in (33cm) long.
£950–1,150 *HOB*

A Valnikem yellow tinplate tractor and yellow and green trailer, in original box, Swedish, 1950, 13in (33cm) long.
£50–70 *HOB*

A Bandai battery-operated tinplate tug boat, Neptune, Japanese, 1958, 14in (36cm) long.
£100–125 *HOB*

r. A set of Abtotpacca tinplate cars and circuit, original box, Russian, 1950, 9½in (24cm) long.
£40–50 *HOB*

A German clockwork tinplate motorcyclist, c1950, 8¼in (21cm) high.
£45–50 *TAR*

A German clockwork tinplate clown, 1950s–60s, 5in (12.5cm) high.
£85–95 *MSB*

An Italian clockwork tinplate tank, c1970s, 5in (12.5cm) long.
£8–12 *OD*

A Japanese battery-operated monkey, c1930, 10¼in (26cm) high.
£85–100 *TAR*

A Schuco clockwork dancing mouse, 1935, 4¾in (12cm) high.
£125–150 *OTS*

A pair of nodding dachshunds, c1950, 6¼in (16cm) long.
£35–40 *TAR*

A set of 4 Timpo model knights in armour, from the MGM movie, 1950, 3¼in (8cm) high.
£40–50 each *OTS*

A Britains model of Knights of Agincourt, mint condition, with original box, 1954, 4in (10cm) high.
£100–120 *OTS*

A sponge Donald Duck toy, 1950s, 8½in (21.5cm) high.
£5–10 *OD*

A Corgi No. 852 Magic Roundabout musical carousel, boxed, 1960s, 12in (30.5cm) high.
£250–300 *TMA*

A Julip model of Queen Elizabeth II and her horse, handmade from latex rubber on wire, 1977, 6¼in (16cm) high.
£50–60 *JLo*

l. A mucking-out set for Julip horses, 1985–95, barrow 4¾in (12cm) wide.
£6–7 *JLo*

r. A Stevenson Brothers replica of a G. & J. Lines rocking horse, c1985, 46in (117cm) high.
£2,000–2,500 *STE*

A Dinky Toys filling station,
with set of petrol pumps and 2 cars,
1930s, station 19in (48.5cm) wide.
Station **£150–200**
Pumps set **£75–85**
Cars **£100–150 each** *NTM*

A Dinky Supertoys Guy van,
No. 919, 'Golden Shred',
1950s, 15in (38cm) wide.
£600–800 *NTM*

A Dinky No. 236 Connaught
Racing Car, mint, boxed,
1956, 3¾in (9.5cm) wide.
£60–70 *OTS*

A Dinky Toys No. 25 refuse
wagon, mint, unboxed, 1950s,
4in (10cm) wide.
£30–35 *NTM*

A Dinky Toys No. 419 Leyland
Cement Wagon, mint, boxed,
1956, 5½in (14.5cm) long.
£125–150 *OTS*

A Dinky Toys No. 274
AA Mini Van, 1960s,
3¼in (8.5cm) long.
£100–125 *NTM*

A Dinky Supertoys No. 935 Leyland
Octopus Flat Truck, with chains,
1960s, 8in (20.5cm) long.
£1,100–1,300 *NTM*
*This model is rare as it was
produced for a short period.*

A Corgi Toys BRM Formula 1
Racing Car, mint, boxed, 1958,
3½in (9cm) long.
£60–70 *OTS*

A Corgi No. 1505 Vanwall
Formula 1 Racing Car,
mint, boxed, 1961, 3½in
(9cm) long. **£50–60** *OTS*

A Corgi Toys No. 309 Aston
Martin, mint, boxed, 1962,
3¾in (9.5cm) long.
£80–90 *OTS*

A Dinky Toys 200 Matra
630, mint, boxed, 1971,
4in (10cm) long.
£30–35 *OTS*

A Corgi Toys Chipperfield's Circus
set, No. 23, first version, 1960s,
16in (41cm) long.
£400–500 *NTM*

A Hornby 1st Series Shell Motor Spirit tanker, 1922, 5½in (14cm) long.
£150–180 *HOB*

A Hornby 4-4-4 Great Western No. 2 tank locomotive, green livery, with original box, 1927, 11in (28cm) long.
£850–950 *HOB*

A Meccano open coal wagon, c1935, 6in (15cm) long.
£125–150 *HOB*

A Hornby LNER 201 Bramham Moor locomotive No. 3 and tender, 1937, 14½in (37cm) long.
£600–750 *HOB*

A Märklin locomotive No. 3027, mint, original box, 1958, 11in (28cm) long.
£250–300 *OTS*

A set of Dinky Toys figures for Gauge O model railways, 1952, 1½in (4cm) high.
£70–80 *OTS*

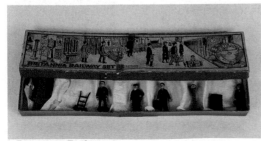

A Britannia Railway Set, 1935, box 15¾in (40cm) long.
£90–110 *HOB*

A set of Dinky Toys No. 053 Miniature Figures for Model Gauge OO Railways, Passengers, 1960, figures 1in (2.5cm) high.
£25–30 *OTS*

A Batmobile, with Batman and Robin, Robin lacking costume, 1974, 13in (33cm) long.
£35–45 *CBP*

Three Batman ceramic mugs, by Applause, c1995, 5½in (14cm) high.
£15–22 *ALI*

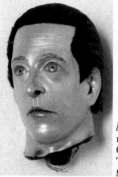

l. A life-sized model head of Lt Cdr Data of Star Trek, c1995.
£200–250 *ALI*

Star Trek socks, distributed by Skansen Tee Shirt Co, c1996.
£5–6 per pair *ALI*

Two Star Wars Return of the Jedi figures, 1983, 9 x 6in (23 x 15cm).
£20–22 each *CMF*

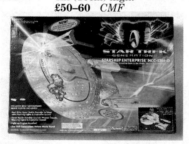

Star Wars Sy Snootles and the Rebo Band, c1979, 4in (10cm) high.
£50–60 *CMF*

Star Trek Star Ship Enterprise, c1994, 17in (43cm) wide.
£35–45 *ALI*

An X Files illuminating clock, c1996, 8½in (21.5cm) diam.
£18–25 *ALI*

Lumat and Yak Face Star Wars figures, c1979, 3–4in (7.5–10cm) high.
l. **£30–35** *r.* **£70–75** *CMF*

Red and Blue Snaggletooth Star Wars figures, c1979, 3–4in (7.5–10cm) high.
l. **£8–10** *r.* **£100–115** *CMF*

Star Trek Star Ship Enterprise, featuring voice of William Shatner, 1994, 8in (20.5cm) wide.
£40–60 *ALI*

An X Files light key chain, c1996, 4in (10cm) long.
£8–10 *ALI*

A selection of watchmaker's wooden items, 19thC:
A glass-topped movement cover. **£15–20**
A set of 9 graduated movement stands. **£18–24**
A three-part oiler with agate inserts. **£15–20**
A watch case stake. **£8–12**
A set of polishing plates. **£15–18** *MRT*

A Tunbridge ware cribbage board, with pegs,
19thC, 9¼in (23.5cm) long.
£75–95 *PSA*

A Tunbridge ware rosewood desk inkstand,
c1840, 10in (25.5cm) wide.
£400–460 *MB*

A mahogany piqué shoe snuff, c1810,
4in (10cm) long.
£190–230 *MB*

r. A boxwood and silver
pipe tamper, in the form
of a greyhound, 18thC,
4½in (11.5cm) high.
£850–950 *AEF*

A Tunbridge ware walnut box,
c1870, 11in (27.5cm) wide.
£120–140 *MB*

A Victorian Mauchline ware
snuff box, 3in (7.5cm) diam.
£60–70 *MB*

A Rob Roy tartan snuff box,
c1870, 3in (7.5cm) long.
£150–175 *EUR*

A Tunbridge ware paperweight,
by Barton, 19thC, 5in (12.5cm) wide.
£275–335 *PSA*

Two Tartan ware egg cups,
c1900, 3¼in (8.5cm) high.
£45–60 each *MRW*

A brass-inlaid rosewood writing slope, c1820, 12in (30cm) wide.
£200–235 *MB*

A walnut-inlaid writing slope, c1850, 20in (50cm) wide.
£275–325 *MB*

A Victorian bronze inkstand, in the form of a recumbent camel, the nutshell body containing the inkwell, 4¼in (11cm) wide.
£300–350 *TMA*

Two brass letter clips, on wooden bases, c1900, largest 5½in (14cm) long.
£30–40 each *WAB*

A selection of miniature pen nib tins, c1900, largest 2in (5cm) wide.
£14–18 each *WAB*

A silver desk set, with pen wipe and dip pen and inkwell, Chester 1910, inkwell 1½in (4cm) high.
£100–130 *ABr*

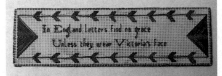

A hand-embroidered stamp case, with verse, 19thC, 6in (15cm) long.
£25–30 *ABr*

r. An Austrian painted hardwood sectional writing cane, c1890, 35in (89cm) long.
£150–200 *MGe*

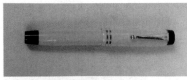

A Parker Duofold Steamline Junior, c1929, 4½in (11.5cm) long.
£200–240 *RUS*

A Conway Stewart No. 84 red-mottled fountain pen, with gold vein pattern, c1952, 4½in (11.5cm) long.
£40–50 *RUS*

A Parker Duofold 'Lucky Curve' lady's pen, c1931, 4½in (11.5cm) long.
£75–85 *RUS*

A gold pencil, c1950, 3¾in (9.5cm) long.
£50–55 *ABr*

A rolled-gold Yard-O-Led pencil, with original box, c1950, 5½in (14cm) long.
£38–42 *ABr*

Six celluloid Scottie dog buttons, 1920s, 1½in (4cm) long.
75p–£1 each *REN*

A Roman coin, dating from the time of Emperor Nero, 54–68 AD. **£2–3** *PC*

Mimi, The Snappy Bubble Dancer, made for the American market, late 1930s, 4in (10cm) high.
£3–4 *ARo*

A Boots Home First Aid case, 1940s, 7in (18cm) wide.
£4–5 *FAM*

A Victory wooden jigsaw puzzle, 1950s, Teddy Bears Wash Day, 4½in (11.5cm) high.
£2–3 *CMF*

Boy's Own Paper, Vol. 68, No. 12, September 1946, 7½ x 5in (19 x 12.5cm).
£2–4 *PC*

Ella Fitzgerald, 'Sings Gershwin', No. 2, stereo EP, HMV, 1960.
£4–5 *ED*

A Korean Olympics 1988 mascot, 1in (2.5cm) high.
£2–3 *JBB*

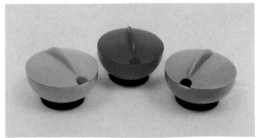

Three Beetleware Melmex melamine mustard pots, designed by A. H. Woodfull, early 1950s, 2¼in (5.5cm) diam.
£2–3 each *REN*

Two Womble pencil tops, 1970s, 2¼in (6cm) high.
£2–3 each *TAR*

Two sporting memorabilia items. Football figures. **£2 each** *WOO* Scale Model. **£50** *GPL*

Sport themed collectables are inspiring growing interest.

Two first edition magazines, Nov 1996. **£1.50–3.50 each** *PC*

First issues of illustrated magazines can fetch high prices. Any free gifts should be preserved intact.

A Coalport porcelain figure, Lady Sylvia from the English Roses collection, hand-decorated and modelled by J. Bromley, No.68 of a limited edition of 1,000, 1996, 10in (25.5cm) high. **£195** *Hs*

Coalport produces new ceramic figures every year. Demand seems to be endless for such nostalgic items.

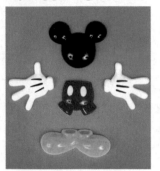

A Mickey Mouse fridge magnet, with separate magnetic body parts, 1996. **£6–8** *PC*

A section of miniature scent bottles. **Free** *PC*

Miniature scent bottles are often distributed free with a full-size flask. Packaging and other promotional material should be preserved.

A 1948 Irish sixpence and a 1959 halfpenny, enamelled and mounted as pendants. **£40–45 each** *LM*

A good way to transform an old item into a collectable of the future.

A Wallace & Gromit T-shirt, in original packaging, 1996, 11½in (29cm) square. **£10**
A card with fridge magnet, 1996, 7 x 5in (18 x 12.5cm). **£2** *CtC*

Created by Nick Park, Wallace and Gromit appear in the 1993 animated film A Close Shave. *Since then these Plasticine British characters have become superstars, their Oscar-winning films appealing to children and adults across the world. Their success has spawned an avalanche of merchandise.*

Wallace and Gromit are Miller's top tip for this year's collectable of the future.

Two flashing musical badges, mounted on original cards. **£3** *CtC*

Denim

Most of us have a favourite pair of old jeans, but anybody with a pair of trousers in vintage denim could be literally sitting on a fortune. Levi's jackets and jeans from the 1950s can fetch hundreds of pounds, whilst examples from the thirties or earlier can be worth four-figure sums. 'You have to understand that these items are extremely rare,' explains Patricia Penrose, founder of vintage clothing store, Roket. 'Until comparatively recently jeans were just work clothes, people wore them till they fell apart and then threw them away. Period examples in good condition are harder to find than the most precious antiques.' The man who started the blue revolution was Levi Strauss. The Bavarian émigré arrived in San Francisco at the height of the Gold Rush in 1953 intending to make tents for miners. He soon diversified into work pants importing *'serge de Nîmes'* from France (hence the name denim) and giving this hard-wearing material the lot number '501' in the firm's warehouse. His product was a huge success, and as rivals began to produce denim overalls Levi introduced the features that were to turn his utilitarian

jeans into a symbol of America: buttons embossed with the company name, copper rivets to reinforce stress points, a double line of stitching on the back pockets, known as the 'arcuate' and modelled on the American eagle, and a leather patch on the waistband. The red pocket tab, Levi's other famous symbol, was introduced in 1936.

Since most of these still appear on current Levi's products how do you spot collectable garments? Jeans and jackets start becoming vintage before 1971, the year that the company changed the writing of its name on the red pocket tab from LEVIS to Levis. Collectors refer to these items as Capital E's. Another important element is 'selvedge', a white edge marked with faint red lines on the inner trouser seams, which shows that the jeans have not been made on modern looms. Weight and colour of the denim is important, lemon as opposed to orange stitching denotes age, as do a host of small, now long vanished details, such as the martingale found on the back of pre-WWII models. As this section shows other old brands apart from Levi's can also be collectable.

A Levis 'No. 1' 506XX blouse, 1930s, chest 48in (122cm).
£1,000–1,250 *ROK*

Known as a blouse this was Levi's first jacket, designed in 1905 and remaining in production, with some modifications, until the 1950s. Distinguishing features include the single pocket, the martingale or waist-cincher on the back, rivets on the arms and the pockets and the Capital E red pocket tab. This is an extremely rare example.

A GWG Cowboy King jacket, 1930s, chest 40in (101.5cm).
£1,600–1,800 *ROK*

> **Cross Reference**
> Colour Review

A Buckaroo jacket, by Big Smith, 1940s, chest 42in (106.5cm).
£300–350 *ROK*

A Levis 'No. 2' 507XX jacket, 1950s, chest 40in (101.5cm).
£650–750 *ROK*

Designed in 1953, this jacket featured two pockets, with bar tacks instead of rivets, the waist-cincher on the back replaced by buttoned side straps, and Capital E red pocket tab.

A Lee Storm Rider jacket, with brass buttons on the back, 1970s, chest 44in (112cm).
£45–55 *ROK*

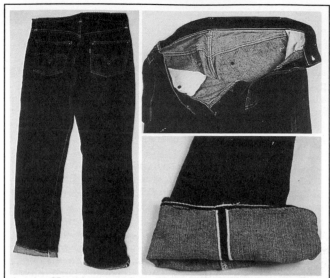

A pair of Levi jeans, with studded inside back pocket, selvedge seam on outside leg seam, yellow stitching, ringspun denim, late 1940s–late 50s.
£650–750 *ROK*

A pair of Turner Togs denim dungarettes, unworn, American, 1950s.
£25–30 *SPS*

A Levis 557XX jacket, the 2 front pockets with pointed flaps, no side pockets, Capital E red pocket tab, 1960s.
£150–200 *TCR*

Also known as the Trucker Jacket.

A GWG engineer's jacket, 1950s.
£150–185 *ROK*

A pair of Lee women's Cowboy jeans, 1950s, waist 28in (71cm).
£65–75 *ROK*

l. A pair of Levi jeans, with selvedge seam on outside leg, ringspun denim, Capital E red pocket tab, late 1960s, waist 31in (78.5cm).
£300–350 *ROK*

A Lee jacket, with brass buttons on front and cuffs, black buttons on back waist straps, 1950s–60s, chest 46in (117cm).
£400–450 *ROK*

Embroidered Pictures & Samplers

A silk embroidery, depicting a pair of bullfinches with a nest containing 5 speckled eggs, worked in long and short stitch on ivory satin, late 18thC, 10½in (25.5cm) diam, framed.
£375–425 *P*

A felt appliqué picture, possibly depicting Little Miss Muffet, with embroidered highlights, c1800, 21 x 20in (53 x 51cm), framed and glazed.
£950–1,100 *CSK*

A silkwork sampler, the verse within a border of flowers, by Sophia Becroft, aged 11, November 1803, 11in (28cm) square.
£240–280 *DN*

A black cross-stitch map sampler, by H. Bower, the boundaries marked in chain stitch, early 19thC, 21 x 20in (53 x 51cm).
£275–325 *DN*

A silkwork sampler, by Jessy Dun, worked mainly in cross-stitch, early 19thC, 14¼ x 13¾in (36 x 35cm), framed and glazed.
£1,000–1,200 *CSK*

A silk cross-stitch sampler, by Matilda Willis, August 1814, 11½ x 11in (29 x 28cm).
£225–275 *DN*

A Victorian tapestry, in original frame, 34¼ x 26¾in (87 x 68cm).
£350–400 *TAR*

A silk cross-stitch sampler, by Priscilla Smart, the verse within a border of carnations, April 4, 1826, mounted as a firescreen, 16½ x 12½in (42 x 32cm).
£320–360 *DN*

A silk embroidered picture, depicting a coastal scene, 1930s, 9 x 7¾in (23 x 20cm).
£40–50 *SUS*

Hats

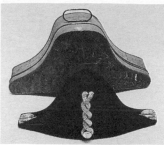

A naval officer's hat and box,
c1900, 19in (48cm) wide.
£100–150 *COB*

A straw hat, decorated with
fabric flowers, 1930s.
£30–40 *SUS*

Two topis:
l. white, c1950.
r. khaki, war issue 1942.
£30–40 each *AXT*

A black silk top hat, by
Lock & Co, St James's
Street, London, with an
original box, 1910, size 7.
£40–50 *AXT*

A collection of millinery
flowers, 1920s–1930s.
£2–3 each *SUS*

A straw boater, c1920.
£25–30 *AXT*

A black bowler hat, by Lock
& Co, St James's Street,
London, with an original box,
1950s, size 6⅞.
£15–25 *AXT*

Handbags

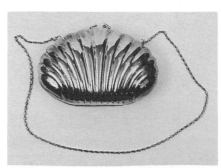

A silver-plated shell-shaped handbag,
1970s, 7½in (19cm) wide.
£25–35 *SnA*

A handmade needlepoint
handbag, 1920s,
13in (33cm) square.
£30–40 *SUS*

A beaded handbag,
with imitation tortoise-
shell frame, c1900,
10¾ x 7½in (27 x 19cm).
£60–65 *TAR*

Linen & Lace

A Victorian lace and silk wedding dress.
£200–250 *LB*

An Edwardian cotton nightdress.
£45–55 *TCF*

A Victorian christening gown, with insertions of Valencia lace, with slip, c1890, 42in (106.5cm) long.
£100–150 *LB*

A lawn christening gown, with daisies embroidered to hem, with slip, c1900, 40in (101.5cm) long.
£65–85 *LB*

An Edwardian child's dress, lawn with cutwork flowers, c1910, 22in (56cm) long.
£30–35 *LB*

An Irish crocheted collar, c1900.
£18–25 *LB*

l. A lawn and lace bib, c1900, 8in (20.5cm) wide.
£15–20 *LB*

A child's crocheted collar, Irish, c1920, 8in (20.5cm) long.
£15–18 *LB*

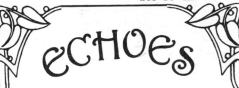

Shoes

A pair of gentleman's leather riding boots, with wooden trees, c1960.
£50–60 *AXT*

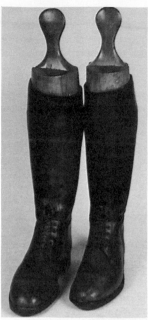

A pair of gentleman's leather riding boots, c1920, 16in (40.5cm) high.
£100–120 *WAB*

Two pairs of lady's shoes, c1925:
l. black satin, with inlaid diamanté heel.
r. cream satin, with inlaid mirrors.
£60–75 each *AXT*

A pair of Victorian handmade leather clogs, Yorkshire, c1880, 3½in (9cm) long.
£50–55 *FMN*

Trainers

A pair of Adidas suede trainers, with leather uppers, 1970s, US size 6.
£25–35 *ROK*

As every parent knows, trainers can be expensive items. Nevertheless, consolation can be gained from the fact that they are fast becoming the latest in collectable footwear. Aficionados are seeking out brands and styles from the 1970s and 80s, with popular names including Nike, Puma and Adidas. Condition can be surprisingly good, since style-conscious owners might only have worn a pair of trainers for a short period of time until fashions changed and they were replaced by a trendier design.

l. A pair of Nike trainers, 1975, US size 7.
£45–55 *ROK*

Cross Reference
Colour Review

r. A pair of Adidas 'Old Skool' trainers, with leather uppers, 1970s, US size 10.
£55–65 *ROK*

A pair of Puma trainers, 1970s, US size 7.
£55–65 *ROK*

A pair of Nike high top trainers, 1970s.
£65–75 *ROK*

TILES

A Minton tile, with a gold
leaf floral design, c1870,
6in (15cm) square.
£20–25 *BAS*

A set of ceramic tiles, with
continuous design for the
surround of a fireplace or
washstand, c1880, each
6in (15cm) square.
£6–8 each *LIB*

A set of eight Dutch Delft tiles,
painted in manganese with
2 seated cats, 18thC,
10 x 21in (25.5 x 53cm).
£750–850 *SWO*

Four Minton tiles, designed by
Christopher Dresser, c1875,
each 6in (15cm) square.
£100–120 each *APO*

A green tile, with a daisy
design, marked 'England B',
c1900, 6in (15cm) square.
£15–20 *BAS*

A set of 4 Minton and Hollins
Seasons tiles, framed, late
19thC, 9½in (24cm) square.
£50–60 each *PC*

A tile commemorating WWI,
by Craven Dunnill & Co Ltd,
Jackfield, Shropshire, used
as a teapot stand, 1914–18,
6in (15cm) square.
£20–30 *OD*

l. A ceramic tile, used for
the surround of a fireplace
or washstand, c1905,
6in (15cm) square.
£6–8 *LIB*

A set of 4 Desvres tiles,
French, c1910, overall
9in (23cm) square.
£15–20 *LIB*

TOOLS

Old tools are collected for their decorative appearance, as examples of technological history, and for practical purposes. Collectors like working with old tools both for nostalgic reasons and because the range of hand tools was broader and more varied in the past than in the present. Craftmanship has today been largely superseded by mechanisation and many traditional tools are no longer produced. Tools were manufactured by individual craftsmen as well as by commercial companies. The value depends on rarity, function, maker and condition. Specific areas worth looking out for in the present market include early moulding planes and measuring items, which are currently attracting considerable interest.

A pair of farrier's pincers, forged from old rasps, c1810, 14in (35.5cm) long.
£12–15 *MRT*

A gunstocker's 'float', with beechwood handle, by Buck, c1860, 9in (23cm) long.
£15–18 *MRT*

l. A set of mid-Victorian tools/toys, possibly carved by a prisoner of war, 3½in (9cm) long.
£65–75 *WAB*

A beech brace, with boxwood head and brass chuck, c1870, 14in (35.5cm) long.
£35–45 *MRT*

A steel screw gauge, 19thC, 10¾in (27cm) long.
£20–25 *BS*

A War Department brass and steel in-and-out vernier calliper, c1850, 18in (45.5cm) high.
£100–125 *MRT*

A Victorian adjustable ruler, with brass fittings, 12in (30.5cm) long.
£24–28 *WAB*

An ironmonger's four-fold boxwood and brass calliper rule, by Sampson Aston, Birmingham, marked with extensive tables, c1850, 24in (61cm) long.
£50–65 *MRT*

A Victorian brass gas horsehair singer, 11½in (29cm) long.
£40–45 *TAR*

A pocket sash chisel, with boxwood handle, by Ward & Payne, c1880, 11in (28cm) long.
£15–18 *MRT*

A dovetailed steel panel plane, by Spiers, Ayr, c1880, 20½in (52cm) long.
£275–325 *MRT*

A pair of boxwood-handled draw bore pins, by Hearnshaw Bros, c1880, 16in (40.5cm) long.
£15–18 *MRT*

Three saddler's tools, c1880, largest 6½in (16.5cm) long.
£10–30 each *MRT*

A selection of draughtsman's tools, c1870, scales 6in (15cm) long.
£20–60 each *MRT*

Three pattern maker's paring gouges, c1900, longest 19in (48cm)
£10–20 each *MRT*

top. A boxwood, brass and ivory slide rule for gauging, by Dring & Fage, c1870, 10in (25.5cm) long.
£40–50
below. A Ewarts boxwood and ivory cattle gauge slide rule, c1870, 8½in (21.5cm) long.
£80–100 *MRT*

A Blusta saw-setter, c1920, 7in (18cm) long.
£15–18 *WAB*

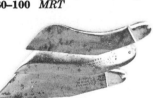

Three farrier's steel knives, with brass end grips, c1900, 5in (12.5cm) long.
£20–25 each *BS*

A selection of watchmaker's tools, c1900:
A nickel-silver glass dome gauge, a screw plate, by Stubs, and in-and-out callipers, by Stubs, screw plate 6in (15cm) long.
£8–20 each *MRT*

Three nickel-plated spoke-shaves, by Ed. Preston, c1910, largest 10in (25.5cm) wide.
£20–30 each *MRT*

FURTHER READING
Rees J. & M., *Tools, A Guide for Collectors*, published by Ray Arnold, 1996.

An oak Home Companion Tool Set, with drawer, c1950, 15½in (39.5cm) wide.
£55–65 *OPH*

r. A foot measure for shoe sizes, 1930s, 14½in (37cm) long extended.
£24–28 *WAB*

TOYS

A Victorian child's iron hoop, 22½in (57cm) diam.
£35–40 *OBS*

A push-along horse, by Lines Bros, c1920, 28in (71cm) long.
£250–300 *STE*

A Structo heavy steel tractor, with 2 trailers, American, 1935, 25¼in (64cm) long.
£80–90 *HOB*

A wooden car, with opening roof, 1940s, 9½in (24cm) long.
£15–20 *OD*

During WWII toy manufacturers had to turn their attention to the war effort, and many toys were homemade or hand-crafted.

l. A Bendy Toys figure of a Walt Disney Mickey Mouse, 1960s, 10in (25.5cm) high.
£35–45 *RAR*
In original box.

Dougal, from *The Magic Roundabout*, with long orange nylon fur, c1966, 13in (33cm) long.
£35–40 *CMF*

The generation who watched The Magic Roundabout has now grown up, and there is increasing interest in toys and other spin-offs from the series.

Corgi Toys

Corgi Toys was started in 1956, in direct competition to Dinky. Cars were advertised as 'the ones with the windows'. Plastic windows were one of many innovations that the firm introduced to attract children. Other extras included jewelled headlights, spring suspension and opening bonnets, boots and doors. Corgi's technical expertise reached its peak in the 1960s with the creation of film and TV vehicles such as the Batmobile and James Bond's Aston Martin, one of the most popular cars of all time.

A Corgi Toys No. 224 Bentley Continental Sports Saloon, mint and boxed, 1961, 4¼in (11cm) long.
£50–60 *OTS*

A Corgi Toys No. 151 Lotus Mark Eleven Le Mans racing car, mint and boxed, 1958, 3¼in (8.5cm) long.
£60–70 *OTS*

A Corgi Toys No. 150 Vanwall Formula 1 Grand Prix racing car, mint and boxed, 1957, 3½in (9cm) long.
£60–70 *OTS*

A Corgi Toys No. 151A Lotus Mark Eleven Le Mans racing car, mint and boxed, 1961, 3¼in (8.5cm) long.
£30–40 *OTS*

A Corgi Toys No. 315 Simca 1000, with plated finish, mint and boxed, 1964, 3½in (9cm) long.
£30–40 *OTS*

r. A Corgi Toys No. 3045 Mercedes-Benz 300SL, with plated finish, mint and boxed, 1961, 3¾in (9.5cm) long.
£50–60 *OTS*

A Corgi Toys No. 327 MGB GT, mint and boxed, 1967, 3½in (9cm) long.
£70–80 *OTS*

A Corgi Toys No. 158 Lotus-Climax F/1, mint and boxed, 1969, 3½in (9cm) long.
£25–35 *OTS*

l. A Corgi Toys No. 256 Volkswagen 1200, in East African safari trim, with rhinoceros, mint and boxed, c1972, 5½in (14cm) long.
£120–140 *RAR*

Dinky Toys

Frank Hornby (1863–1936) was one of Britain's most influential toy makers. His Meccano company, founded in Liverpool in 1901, was responsible for the metal construction kits for Hornby trains, made from c1920, and for Dinky toys. Hornby designed the first vehicles in 1933, initially as a supplement to railway layouts. The new line was a success in its own right and from 1934 became known as Dinky Toys, the name inspired by the Scottish word 'dink', meaning neat or small.

From the 1930s until the end of production in 1979, Dinky produced a vast range of cars and other toys. Currently popular with collectors are models from the 50s and early 60s, the so-called golden age of Dinky production. 'Nostalgia is a major influence,' explains dealer David Wells. 'People often want the vehicles that they played with as children or a model of the real car that they used to drive. Other diecast favourites include racing cars, film and TV-related products and commercial vehicles.'

Prices depend on rarity, condition and the presence of the original boxes. Once upon a time these pocket-sized cars sold for shillings. Today, prices can run into hundreds of pounds and more.

A Dinky Toys Foden truck, 1947, 7¼in (18.5cm) long.
£40–50 *OTS*

r. A Dinky Toys No. 42 police set, 1930s, box 7½in (19cm) long.
£250–300 *NTM*

A Dinky Supertoys No. 514 Guy Van, 1949, 5¼in (13.5cm) long.
£145–165 *OTS*

Three Dinky Toys double-decker buses, 1950s, 7in (18cm) long.
£175–200 *NTM*

A Dinky Toys No. 12c Telephone Call Box, 1950s, 5in (13cm) long.
£45–55 *NTM*

A selection of Dinky Toys 23 Series Formula 1 cars, 1952–58, 4in (10cm) long.
Mint and boxed **£70–80 each**
Unboxed **£25–35 each** *OTS*

A Dinky Toys Jaguar XK120 Coupé, mint and boxed, 1954, 3¾in (9.5cm) long.
£90–100 *OTS*

A Dinky Toys 238 Jaguar Type D Racing Car, 1957, 3½in (9cm) long.
£90–100 *OTS*

A Dublo Dinky Toys No. 069 Massey Harris-Ferguson tractor, mint and boxed, 1959, 1½in (4cm) long.
£25–35 *OTS*

A Dublo Dinky Toys No. 062 Singer Roadster, mint and boxed, 1958, 2in (5cm) long.
£45–55 *OTS*

A Dinky Toys No. 135 promotional Triumph 2000, mint condition, mid-1960s, 3¼in (8.5cm) long.
£950–1,100 *WAL*

l. A Dinky Toys Ford Fairlane police car, mint, no box, 1960s, 4¼in (11cm) long.
£25–35 *NTM*

A Dinky Toys No. 620 Berliet Missile Launcher, 1960s, 5¾in (14.5cm) long.
£85–95 *NTM*

A Dinky Toys No. 293 Leyland Atlantean Bus, 1960s, 4¾in (12cm) long.
£75–85 *NTM*

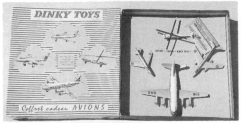

A French Dinky Toys No. 60 aircraft gift set, 1960s, box 9in (23cm) square.
£375–425 *RAR*

Julip Horses

Julip horses were first produced in 1945, in a little workshop in Beauchamp Place, Knightsbridge, London, that still serves as the company store. These one-twelfth scale models of horses are handmade of latex rubber. They come complete with riders, accompanying animals and miniature tack. Until the 1990s, all horses were handmade – since then, less expensive models in injection-moulded plastic have also been produced, alongside the original models.

A Julip latex rubber and hand-painted Shetland pony, 1985–95, 5½in (14cm) long.
£30–40 *JLo*

The mane and tail were long to enable children to plait or cut and trim them.

A Julip latex rubber and hand-painted horse with dressage rider, with leather harness, 1945–65, 7in (18cm) long.
£45–55 *JLo*

The joints bend, and the mouth also opens.

A Julip Welsh pony and rider, 1945–65, 6½in (16.5cm) long.
£30–40 *JLo*

A Julip piebald New Forest pony and rider, with leather saddle and bridle, 1985–95, 5½in (14cm) long.
£45–55 *JLo*

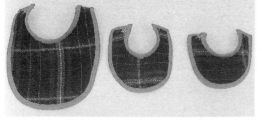

Three Julip tartan wool horse rugs, 1985–95, largest 5in (12.5cm) long.
£3–5 each *JLo*

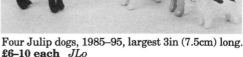

Four Julip dogs, 1985–95, largest 3in (7.5cm) long.
£6–10 each *JLo*

A Julip cat, 1985–95, 1½in (4cm) high.
£6–8 *JLo*

A Julip blanket-spotted Appaloosa horse and foal, 1985–95, horse 6in (15cm) high.
Horse **£30–40**
Foal **£18–25** *JLo*

Two Julip painted wood jumps, the wall with removable bricks, 1985–95, 7¼in (18.5cm) wide.
£7–8 each *JLo*

Military Vehicles

A Britains No. 1512 Army Ambulance, with driver, wounded man and stretcher, mint and boxed, 1946, 6in (15cm) long.
£110–130 *OTS*

A Tri-ang Minic Push and Go Armoured Assault Group presentation set, c1950, 15in (38cm) wide.
£110–130 *RAR*

A Tri-ang Minic Armoured Brigade HQ Squadron M117 rocket-firing tank, c1950, 8in (20cm) wide.
£35–45 *RAR*

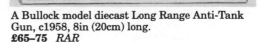

A Britains No. 433 RAF monoplane, unboxed, c1937, 5in (13cm) wide.
£410–450 *RAR*

A Bullock model diecast Long Range Anti-Tank Gun, c1958, 8in (20cm) long.
£65–75 *RAR*

Model Soldiers & Figures

A Britains set No. 203 Pontoon Section RE, Light Harness, unboxed, 1920, 13in (33cm) long.
£680–520 *RAR*

A set of Britains Hunting Series lead huntsmen, whippers-in, horses, riders, hounds and fox, c1920, fox 1½in (4cm) long.
£345–375 *AnS*

A Britains set No. 258 British Infantry in gas masks, mint, in original Fred Whisstock box, 1927, figures 2¼in (5.5cm) high.
£125–150 *OTS*

FURTHER READING

Hugo Marsh, *Toys & Games Antiques Checklist* Miller's Publications 1995

A Britains figure of King Henry VIII, Souvenir of Madame Tussaud's, mint, original box, 1938, 3¼in (8.5cm) high.
£40–50 *OTS*

Two Britains Gauge 1 figures, of a porter and a passenger, 1933, largest 5in (12.5cm) high.
£8–10 each *HOB*

A collection of Britains anti-aircraft guns and equipment, c1950, figures 2in (5cm) high.
£160–180 *RAR*

A Britains set No. 1308 Knights of the Middle Ages, mint and boxed, 1933, figures 2in (5cm) high.
£125–150 *OTS*

A collection of Britains Hunting Series huntsmen, horses, riders, whippers-in and hounds, c1950, hounds 1¾in (4.5cm) long.
£260–280 *RAR*

A Britains set No. 1258, Knights in Armour (Tournament), with herald and marshal, mint, original box, 1950, figures 2¼in (5.5cm) high.
£220–250 *OTS*

Two Timpo figures from the MGM film *Knights of the Round Table*, mid-1950s, 3¼in (8cm) high.
£40–50 each *OTS*

Noddy

Noddy was the creation of Enid Mary Blyton (1897–1968), one of the most successful children's writers of the century. Blyton trained as a teacher, studying the Froebel and Montessori methods, gaining experience that was to resurface in her remarkable literary career. Her first book, *Child's Whispers*, appeared in 1922 and by the time of her death she had published more than 400 different titles, still read by children across the world. Hugely prolific, Blyton could produce up to 10,000 words a day, and was known to complete a book in a five-day week. She became well-known with the *Famous Five* and *Secret Seven* stories in the 1940s, but it was Noddy, conceived in 1949, that made her famous. A publisher showed Blyton some puppet drawings by Dutch artist Harmsen van der Beek. She immediately gave the figures names and wove them into stories, creating Little Noddy, Big Ears, Mr Plod the policeman, and all the other characters of Toyland.

The Noddy books were a huge success, selling millions of copies, and spawning innumerable related products from toys to toothpaste. The earliest toys shown here date from the 1950s. Although the original stories might have been changed somewhat in the cause of political correctness, Noddy and his Toyland friends remain popular today, stimulating the interest and desirability of merchandising from the past.

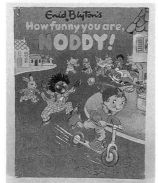

Enid Blyton, *How funny you are, Noddy!*, 1954, 10 x 7½in (25.5 x 19cm).
£3.50–4.50   *CMF*

A Noddy and Big Ears wooden money box, 1960s, 3½in (9cm) wide.
£10–12   *CMF*

Two Noddy puppets, 1950s, largest 10in (25.5cm) high.
£15–18 each   *CMF*

A tinplate car, with Noddy, Big Ears and Golly, 1969, 3½in (9cm) long.
£60–65   *CMF*

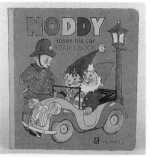

r. Noddy loses his Car, a board book, published by Purnell, 1970, 7½ x 7in (19 x 18cm).
£1.50–2.50   *CMF*

Three rubber figures of Noddy, Big Ears and PC Plod, by Combex, 1950s, largest 5½in (14cm) high.
£15–25 each   *CLW*

A rubber Noddy and car, by Bendy Toys, 1970s, 16in (40.5cm) long.
£14–16   *CMF*

Two plastic egg cups in the form of Noddy and Big Ears, 1970s, 3½in (9cm) high.
£6.50–8.50 each   *CMF*

Rocking Horses

A Caledonian three-seater rocking horse, by G. & J. Lines, unrestored, c1800, 69in (175.5cm) long.
£1,000–1,300 *STE*

In restored condition this rocking horse would be worth between £2,500–3,000.

A Victorian dapple grey rocking horse, c1860, 48in (122cm) long.
£650–750 *HOA*

A rocking horse, on bow rocker, unrestored, c1840, 56in (142cm) long.
£850–1,000 *SPU*

A rocking horse, possibly Kain, on bow rocker, unrestored, c1810, 77in (195.5cm) long.
£3,000–4,000 *STE*

A dapple grey rocking horse, by F. H. Ayres, on original bow rocker, c1860, 52in (132cm) long.
£4,000–4,500 *STE*

A dapple grey rocking horse, by F. H. Ayres, on spring rocker, in original condition, c1885, 53in (134.5cm) long.
£4,000–5,000 *STE*

A dapple grey rocking horse, by F. H. Ayres, with extra carving, in original condition, c1890, 57in (145cm) long. **£3,000–3,500** *STE*

A dapple grey rocking horse, by F. H. Ayres, 1880s, 68in (172.5cm) long. **£3,000–3,500** *SPU*

A carved wood and polychrome-decorated rocking horse, with original leatherwork and stirrups, mounted on a frame, later painted red, c1900, 58in (147.5cm) long. **£450–550** *L&E*

A silver painted rocking horse, by F. H. Ayres, on red and green painted rocker, c1900, 48in (122cm) long. Restored **£1,900–2,000** *STE*

A dapple grey Jubilee rocking horse, by G. & J. Lines, unrestored, c1910, 39in (99cm) long. **£1,000–1,200** *STE*

A Baby Carriages dapple grey rocking horse, on natural wood rocker, in original condition, c1910, 33in (84cm) long. **£650–780** *SPU*

l. A Liverpool Toy Industry rocking horse, c1920, 56in (142cm) long. **£900–1,400** *STE*

A Collinson rocking horse, on natural wood rocker, c1920, 36in (91.5cm) long. **£350–420** *SPU*

A German calf-skin rocking horse, on painted wooden rocker, c1930, 57in (145cm) long.
£500–600 *STE*

A Tri-ang 'Bronco Buster' rocking horse, by G. & J. Lines, c1955, 34in (86.5cm) long.
£150–200 *STE*

A Stevenson Brothers dapple grey limited edition miniature rocking horse, on bow rocker, 1996, 29in (74cm) long.
£600–680 *STE*

One of only 250 produced.

Miller's is a price GUIDE not a price LIST

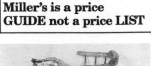

A Stevenson Brothers rocking chair, 1996, 45in (114.5cm) long.
£440–450 *STE*

A late Victorian painted elm carousel horse, 40in (101.5cm) long.
£800–1,000 *SPU*

A carousel horse, 'American racer', c1890, 74in (188cm) long.
£2,800–3,000 *SPU*

Sci-Fi Toys & Collectables

Sci-Fi toys and collectables are one of the fastest growing areas of the market attracting a huge international audience. In the 1940s and 50s interest in science fiction took off like a rocket, reflecting period fascination with space, and manifesting itself in film, television, magazines and toys. Heroes such as Batman, Superman, Buck Rogers and Dan Dare inspired spin-off products that are highly collectable today. The 1960s saw the appearance of cult TV series such as *Dr Who* and *Thunderbirds*. Not only are the related toys desirable, but enthusiasts are prepared to spend large sums on original props, like the Dalek shown below.

1966 marked the first TV transmission in the USA of *Star Trek*. Perhaps surprisingly, the space series was not a huge hit and was cancelled in 1969. It was not until the following decade that re-runs of the programme attracted a fanatical following.

'Trekkies' held conventions across the world and interest expanded still further with the release of *Star Trek: The Motion Picture* in 1979. The same decade also saw the birth of *Star Wars* (1977), the first of the trilogy of classic films, chronicling Luke Skywalker's battle with the evil empire, and including *The Empire Strikes Back* (1980) and *Return of the Jedi* (1983). The merchandising was more powerful than 'The Force' itself, and between 1977 and 1984 the toy manufacturers Kenna and MPC sold 300 million *Star Wars* toys. *Star Wars* and *Star Trek* are established leaders in the Sci-Fi field. As each film and TV series bring a new range of merchandising, so the previous generation of toys and products becomes collectable. Modern manufacturers have also capitalised on adult interest by producing limited edition and collectors' series toys designed for the adult market.

Four Thunderbirds plastic push-and-go models, Nos. 1, 2, and 3, and battery-operated No. 5, 1960s, largest 9in (23cm) long.
£140–150 *RAR*

A silver and red painted wood and fibreglass Dalek, from the BBC production of the series *Dr Who*, with fibreglass base and rubber skirting, some pieces missing, c1960, 66½in (169cm) high.
£4,000–5,000 *P(Ba)*

A Tardis playhouse, from the BBC series *Dr Who*, by Dekkertoys, mint, boxed, 1960s, 48in (122cm) high.
£55–65 *RAR*

A Meccano Space 1999 Eagle Transporter display model, constructed from silver, yellow, blue and red parts, c1976, 34in (86.5cm) long.
£240–260 *CSK*

An original Aspen Beer can, from the film *Alien*, with specially printed label inscribed 'Weylan Yutani – Aspen Beer – Extra Strong', 1979, 6in (15cm) high.
£370–420 *P(Ba)*

A gold coloured plaster figure, made for *Raiders of the Lost Ark*, the base impressed '2', 1981, 8in (20.5cm) high.
£1,900–2,200 *S*

Star Trek

A collection of *Star Trek* badges, by Dufort & Sons, c1995, 1¼ x 1½in (3 x 4cm).
£1–2 each *ALI*

A model of the Enterprise B, c1995, 6in (15cm) wide.
£10–15 *ALI*

This is from a limited edition of 2,400, and was the first model ever produced.

A collection of *Star Trek* miniature models, limited editions, by Applause, 1996, 5in (13cm) high.
£20–30 each *ALI*

A *Star Trek* The Next Generation Borg Ship, c1996, 7 x 10in (18 x 25.5cm).
£30–35 *ALI*

l. A film poster, for *Star Trek VI – The Undiscovered Country*, full colour, signed in blue marker by members of the cast, 1991, 38½ x 26in (98 x 66cm), framed.
£1,200–1,400 *S*

A Classic *Star Trek* Starfleet Phaser, c1996, 7 x 10in (18 x 25.5cm).
£17–25 *ALI*

Star Wars

l. A *Star Wars* pop-up book, illustrations by Wayne Douglas Barlowe, 1978, 8 x 6in (20.5 x 15cm).
£15–20 *Ada*

Three *Star Wars* models, c1979, 4in (10cm) high: Anakin Skywalker,
£18–22
Luke Skywalker and Imperial Gunner.
£50–75 each *CMF*

A *Star Wars* model
figure of Han Solo in
carbonite chamber,
c1979, 4in (10cm) high.
£50–60 *CMF*

A *Star Wars* model
figure of Jawa, c1979,
8in (20.5cm) high.
£55–65 *CMF*

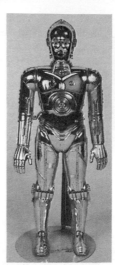

A *Star Wars* model
figure of C3P0, c1979,
12in (30.5cm) high.
£24–28 *CMF*

A *Star Wars* model figure
of Chewbacca, c1979,
16in (40.5cm) high.
£24–28 *CMF*

A *Star Wars*
model figure of
Darth Vader, c1980,
16in (40.5cm) high.
£24–28 *CMF*

Two *Star Wars* model
figures of Lando
Calrissian, one with
mouth closed and the
other open, c1983,
4½in (11.5cm) high.
£8–18 each *CMF*

A *Return of the Jedi*
X-wing Fighter
Vehicle, c1983,
13in (33cm) wide.
£35–45 *CMF*

A *Return of the Jedi*
sticker album, c1983,
10in (25.5cm) square.
£20–30 *Ada*

A *Return of the Jedi* INT-4
Interceptor vehicle, c1983,
4in (10cm) wide.
£10–12 *CMF*

X Files

An *X Files* mug, 1996,
4in (10cm) high.
£6–7 *ALI*

X Files *is a comparatively new
contender in the Science Fiction
field. With the international
cult success of the US TV series,*
X Files *memorabilia and
merchandising could well
become collectables of the future.*

Two *X Files* magazines,
published by Manga, c1996,
11½ x 8¼in (29 x 21cm).
£1–1.25 each *PC*

A set of *X Files* photographs 1996,
8 x 10in (20.5 x 25.5cm).
£16–20 *PC*

Tinplate

A Carette clockwork '50' four-seater open touring car, lithographed in red, cream and gold, some damage, c1912, 8½in (21.5cm) long.
£2,000–2,400 *CSK*

A Japanese wind-up tinplate dog with wagging tail, 1960s, 4in (10cm) long.
£60–70 *MSB*

A Schuco clockwork tinplate plush tumbling mouse, 1935, 4¾in (12cm) high.
£80–90 *OTS*

A clockwork tinplate bird/butterfly, c1960, 7½in (19cm) wide.
£10–15 *OD*

A Schuco Curvo 1000 tinpate motorbike, made in US zone of Germany, c1950, mint condition, 4in (10cm) long.
£375–425 *RAR*

l. A Schuco Electro Construction fire engine, 6080, c1961, 12in (30.5cm) long, boxed.
£1,000–1,200 *AAV*

A Burnett clockwork tinplate Green Line coach, with electric headlamps, c1930, 11in (28cm) long.
£170–200 *RAR*

A Triang Minic racing car, 1950s, 5in (12.5cm) long.
£35–40 *OD*

Trains

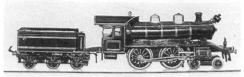

A Bing clockwork 4-4-0 Bavarian locomotive and tender, hand-painted in green, red and gold, some damage, c1914.
£550–650 *CSK*

A Bassett-Lowke LMS brake/luggage van, by Märklin, finished in maroon, c1920, 9½in (24cm) long.
£100–150 *HOB*

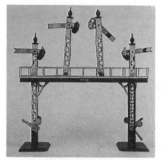

A set of Hornby gantry signals, with blue painted base, good condition, 1935, 13½in (34cm) high.
£250–300 *HOB*

A Hornby breakdown van and crane, good condition, 1924, 11¾in (30cm) long, with original box.
£140–160 *HOB*

A Hornby CR open wagon, fair condition, 1926, 5½in (14cm) long.
£250–350 *HOB*

A Märklin LMS 2-6-4 locomotive, No. 2526, 1928, 13in (33cm) long.
£4,500–4,700 *HOB*

This is an extremely rare model and is in mint condition.

A Bowman GWR railway carriage, 10152, finished in cream and chocolate, fair condition, 1930, 17in (43cm) long.
£80–90 *HOB*

A Märklin 01 steam-fired 4-6-2 Pacific locomotive and tender, finished in dark green and red, some damage, in original wooden box, c1930,
£3,300–3,600 *CSK*

A Hornby No. 3 locomotive and tender, No. 6100, finished in red, boxed, mint condition, 1937, 11in (28cm) long.
£375–450 *HOB*

A Märklin locomotive, No. 3013, mint condition, 1957, 6½in (16.5cm) long, with original box.
£240–280 *OTS*

A Märklin locomotive, No. 3031, mint condition, 1959, 5¼in (13cm) long, with original box.
£65–75 *OTS*

A Leeds LNER 0 gauge Nettle steam railcar, with electric motor, c1940, 12in (30.5cm) long.
£35–45 *RAR*

A Märklin locomotive, No. 3048, mint condition, 1961, 11in (28cm) long, with original box.
£100–120 *OTS*

A Mill's LSWR 0 gauge clockwork 0-4-4 tank locomotive, c1950, 8in (20.5cm) long.
£60–75 *RAR*

A Meccano Deltic mechanised locomotive, No. 9024, finished in yellow, silver and blue, 1970s, 68in (172.5cm) long.
£650–750 *P(HSS)*

A Märklin HO locomotive, No. 3102, mint condition, 1979, 12½in (31.5cm) long, with original box.
£120–140 *OTS*

TREEN & WOODEN COLLECTABLES

A carved wooden shoe, c1810, 3½in (9cm) long.
£18–22 *PSA*

A lignum vitae string box, c1800, 6in (15cm) high.
£120–150 *MB*

An ebony pipe tamper, in the form of a hand, dated '1827', 2½in (6.5cm) high.
£450–500 *AEF*

A wooden spoon, with a carved handle in the form of a sailor, 19thC, 9¾in (25cm) long.
£280–320 *AEF*

An ivory and ebony pipe tamper, in the form of a truncheon, 19thC, 3in (7.5cm) high.
£250–300 *AEF*

Tunbridge Ware, Tartan & Mauchline Ware

A Tunbridge ware box, 19thC, 3½in (9cm) wide.
£80–90 *BGA(K)*

A Tunbridge ware string box, 19thC, 3½in (9cm) diam.
£135–155 *PSA*

Mauchline ware: Wooden souvenirs, usually varnished sycamore, transfer printed with popular views
Tunbridge ware: Wooden objects, mainly produced in Tunbridge Wells, Kent, decorated with a mosaic image, formed by glueing together rods of various coloured woods and slicing the block crossways to obtain a number of patterns
Tartan ware: Wooden ware covered with tartan printed paper

A Tunbridge ware sliding book rack, with Battle Abbey decoration on one end, 19thC, 11½in (29cm) long.
£280–320 *PSA*

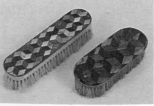

Two Tunbridge ware clothes brushes, with cube patterned decoration, c1870, longest 6¼in (16cm).
£50–80 each *PSA*

A Tunbridge ware box, inlaid with specimen wood decoration, c1850, 3in (7.5cm) square.
£100–120 *MB*

A Tunbridge ware inlaid
walnut box, c1870,
12in (30.5cm) wide.
£130–150 *MB*

A Tunbridge ware tray, 19thC,
5in (12.5cm) wide.
£115–135 *PSA*

A Tunbridge ware box, inlaid
with flower decoration, 19thC,
2½in (6.5cm) square.
£85–95 *PSA*

A Tunbridge ware rosewood box,
inlaid with mosaic decoration,
c1880, 6in (15cm) wide.
£60–80 *MB*

A Tunbridge ware glove
box, with key, 19thC,
10½in (26.5cm) long.
£280–320 *PSA*

A Tartan ware snuff box,
c1837, 3in (7.5cm) wide.
£160–180 *EUR*

A Tartan ware nib wiper,
good condition, c1850,
2½in (6.5cm) long.
£220–250 *EUR*

A Tartan ware gold-
edged needlecase,
with velvet lining,
c1845, 2in (5cm) high.
£200–225 *EUR*

A Mauchline ware
sycamore pot pourri,
with print of
St Margaret's Church,
Lowestoft, c1880,
4in (10cm) diam.
£60–70 *MB*

r. A Mauchline ware sycamore
thermometer, with print of the
Prince of Wales Terrace, Deal,
c1870, 6½in (16.5cm) high.
£100–120 *MB*

WALKING STICKS

Men have used sticks to lean on since the dawn of time. When Tutankhamen's tomb was excavated many types of staves and walking sticks were discovered, but the earliest examples shown here date from the seventeenth and eighteenth centuries. 'During this period fine canes were a sign of rank and the preserve of the upper classes,' explains dealer Michael German. 'They were often handsomely decorated with ivory or gold. It was not until the Industrial Revolution that everyone carried walking sticks from the ordinary man in the street to the nobleman.'

From the second half of the nineteenth century until 1914, the walking stick was a standard male accessory, a mark of fashion rather than infirmity. 'It was like a hat, you just didn't go out without one,' says Michael German. A gentleman needed at least three sticks, a malacca cane for daytime use, an ebonised model for the evening and a sturdy wooden stick for the country. Many would own a dozen or more, since they were popular gifts and can often

be found today complete with engraved presentation plaques. Handles came in innumerable shapes and materials and dual purpose sticks were created to meet every need. For the smoker, there were sticks that held lighters, matches or pipes. For the sportsman there were some canes that would measure the height of a dog or a horse and others containing a brandy flask for keeping a warming nip. Doctor's sticks were designed for medical instruments, scientific examples came complete with a telescope or compass. Because cities could be dangerous places men carried defence sticks concealing swords, daggers or even pistols. These were usually very plain and undecorated canes, because they weren't meant to attract attention.

By 1900 there were 60 cane shops in the London area alone. 'Only a couple survive now,' notes Michael German sadly, 'the golden age of the cane, came to an end with the first world war.' The value of sticks today depends on quality, rarity, condition and novelty.

A French malacca walking cane, with two-tone chased gold tau handle, c1780, 39in (99cm) long.
£2,600–2,900 *MGe*

A malacca walking stick, the ivory and silver *piqué* handle with crossed 'Cs' design, with silver collar, c1690, 38in (96.5cm) high.
£850–950 *MGe*

r. A silver-capped walking stick, formed from the end section of a narwhal tusk, c1850, 35in (89cm) long.
£1,400–1,600 *MGe*

A malacca silver-handled walking stick, Continental, c1790, 38in (96.5cm) long.
£600–700 *MGe*

A whalebone walking cane, the handle carved with a sailor's knot and barley-twist shaft, c1840, 35in (89cm) long.
£900–1,100 *MGe*

A Folk Art painted wood walking cane, with 2 entwined snakes, c1850, 35in (89cm) long.
£280–320 *MGe*

A pump action airgun/walking stick, c1850, 36in (91.5cm) long.
£350–400 *ET*

A Victorian metal-handled walking stick, with silver collar, containing a clay pipe, c1860, 35in (89cm) long.
£340–380 *MGe*

An Anglo-Indian ebonised walking stick, the silver crutch handle embossed overall with scenes of Indian rural life, 19thC, 37in (94cm) long.
£240–280 *MGe*

A hardwood walking stick, with ivory-handle, in the form of a snarling dog's head, with glass eyes, c1870, 36½in (92.5cm) long.
£380–420 *MGe*

An ebonised walking stick, with silver-plated handle in the form of a dog's head, c1870, 36in (91.5cm) long.
£150–180 *MGe*

A Folk Art walking cane, with carved serpent handle and silver collar, c1860, 36in (91.5cm) long.
£440–480 *MGe*

A Victorian tiger's-eye walking cane, with silver neck ring, 35½in (90cm) long.
£100–125 *SPU*

A Victorian whalebone walking cane, with a horn handle, 35in (89cm) long.
£150–200 *WeH*

A bamboo walking stick, with a polished horn handle, c1880, 35in (89cm) long.
£50–55 *WeH*

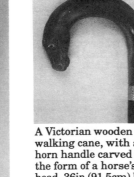

A Victorian wooden walking cane, with a horn handle carved in the form of a horse's head, 36in (91.5cm) long.
£75–95 *WeH*

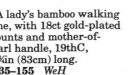

l. A lady's bamboo walking cane, with 18ct gold-plated mounts and mother-of-pearl handle, 19thC, 32¾in (83cm) long.
£135–155 *WeH*

A partridge wood walking stick, the carved handle in the form of Mr Punch's head, with silver buttons, c1880, 35in (89cm) long.
£360–400 *MGe*

An ebonised walking stick, the carved wooden handle in the form of a dog's head, with metal collar, c1880, 36in (91.5cm) long.
£150–170 *MGe*

A WWI officer's wristwatch, 1914–18.
£200–250 *BWC*

An A.E.F. lever 9ct gold gentleman's wristwatch, 1918.
£80–100 *BSA*

Wristwatches

Wristwatches did not come into general use until the early 20th century. In 1904, Cartier designed a wristwatch for the aviator Alberto Santos Dumont, who found a fob watch difficult to use. In Britain the late Victorian period saw the introduction of a pocket watch contained inside a leather flap worn round the wrist. In 1906, Alfred E. Pearson, a saddler, had the bright idea of fixing wire loops to the watch case and attaching straps. The wristwatch became popular during WWI, when soldiers discovered that it was far more practical than a pocket watch hidden inside the uniform which was difficult to extract.

A platinum and diamond wristwatch, with original grosgrain strap, 1920s, ¾in (20mm) long.
£325–375 *AnS*

A silver pocket watch, by James Walker of London, 1920s, 2in (50mm) diam.
£75–100 *BWC*

A lady's silver bracelet watch, with WWI inscription to rear, 1919.
£120–140 *BSA*

A lady's 18ct gold, diamond and sapphire wristwatch, import marks for London 1919, cased.
£900–1,100 *CSK*

A J. W. Benson 9ct gold half-hunter pocket watch, hallmark 1928.
£200–300 *PC*

l. An 18ct gold wristwatch, the winder with cabochon sapphire with grosgrain strap, 1920s, ¾in (20mm) long.
£165–185 *AnS*

r. A silver lurex wristwatch, Chester hallmark, c1930.
£120–140 *BWC*

An Art Deco 9ct
gold tonneau-
cased gentleman's
wristwatch, 1931.
£90–110 *BSA*

A 9ct gold
wristwatch, 1940s.
£125–150 *BWC*

l. A Jaeger leCoultre gold
cocktail wristwatch, the dial
concealed beneath a hinged
cover decorated with rubies
and diamonds, case marked
No. '6042' and 9ct gold mark
for London 1954.
£750–850 *P*

An Avia 9ct gold brooch watch,
1950s, 1½in (40mm) diam.
£250–300 *AnS*

A pocket watch,
by Smith & Son,
Trafalgar Square,
London, c1950,
2¼in (55mm) diam.
£20–30 *BGA*

*These watches were
mass-produced and
sold for 5 shillings.*

A Hopalong Cassidy
wristwatch, 'Good Luck
from Oppy' engraved
on reverse, c1950,
8in (20.5cm) long.
£85–100 *SPU*

*By US Time, which
became Ingersol.*

r. An Accurist 9ct gold
wristwatch with silver-
gilt wrist band set with
2 red stones and
ropetwist decoration,
21-jewel Swiss movement
No. F-4122, 1960s, dial
1in (25mm) diam.
£5,800–6,200 *S*

*This was John Lennon's
watch, originally in the
collection of the former
transport managers for
Apple, 1967–70.*

A commemorative
Coronation pocket watch,
1953, 2in (50mm) diam.
£30–40 *BGA*

A Movado gentleman's pink
gold automatic wristwatch,
American, 1959.
£650–750 *BSA*

An Invicta 17-jewel
wristwatch, c1970.
£50–75 *BWC*

WRITING

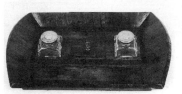

A Regency rosewood inkstand, c1820, 14in (35.5cm) wide.
£150–200 *TMi*

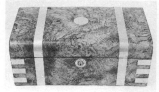

A burr walnut writing slope, with brass bands and coromandel interior, socket drawers, c1850, 7in (18cm) high.
£425–465 *MB*

A Regency rosewood and brass-mounted inkstand, with 2 cut glass pots, the drawer with brass leaf-chased handle, on brass bun feet, 12¾in (32cm) wide.
£400–450 *DN*

A Viennese cold-painted bronze pen wipe, in the form of an otter with a fish, c1870, 7in (18cm) wide.
£500–600 *CB*

A Victorian cast iron pen holder, c1890, 5¼in (13cm) wide.
£25–35 *ABr*

A papier mâché blotter, 19thC, 12 x 9¼in (30.5 x 23.5cm).
£110–130 *PSA*

A Mignon black typewriter, c1900, 12in (30.5cm) wide.
£70–80 *AUC*

A pair of brass postal scales, c1900, 6in (15cm) wide.
£70–80 *CSA*

Pens & Pencils

A Watermans 51V ripple pattern fountain pen, with nickel clip and lever, 1928, 4¼in (10.5cm) long.
£65–75 *RUS*

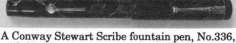

A Conway Stewart Scribe fountain pen, No.336, with blue/black mottled pearl vein pattern, steel clip and lever, c1935, 5in (12.5cm) long.
£40–45 *RUS*

A Conway Stewart fountain pen, No. 60, with 'cracked-ice' pattern, Duro nib, c1950, 5in (12.5cm) long.
£125–135 *RUS*

A rolled gold Yard-O-led pencil, 1941, 5in (12.5cm) long.
£36–42 *ABr*

r. A Conway Stewart fountain pen, No. 100, with Duro nib, 1962, 5½in (14cm) long.
£80–100 *RUS*

DIRECTORY OF SPECIALISTS

If you require a valuation for an item, it is advisable to check whether the dealer or specialist will carry out this service and if there is a charge. Please mention Miller's when making an enquiry. Having found a specialist who will carry out your valuation it is best to send a description and photograph of the item to the specialist together with a stamped addressed envelope for the reply. A valuation by telephone is not possible. Most dealers are only too happy to help you with your enquiry, however, they are very busy people and consideration of the above points would be welcomed.

London

Frank Andrews,
10 Vincent Road, N22 6NA
Tel: 0181 881 0658
Glass

Angling Auctions,
PO Box 2095, W12 8RU
Tel: 0181 749 4175
Fishing Tackle

Animation Art & Disney,
Wonderful World of
Animation, 30 Bramham
Gardens, SW5 0HF
Tel: 0171 370 4859
(001 212 888 3718 USA)
(by appointment only)

Antigo, Alfies Antique
Market, Unit S012,
13-25 Church Street,
Marylebone, NW8 8DT
Tel: 0958 283623
Art Deco, Metalware

Arenski, 185 Westbourne
Grove, W11 2SB
Tel: 0171 727 8599
Glass, Decorative Arts

A. H. Baldwin & Sons Ltd,
11 Adelphi Terrace,
WC2N 6BJ
Tel: 0171 930 6879
*Coins, Commemorative,
Medals*

Linda Bee, Art Deco,
Stand J20-21, Grays
Antique Market, W1Y 1AR
Tel: 0171 629 5921
Costume, Perfume Bottles

Beth, GO 43-44,
Alfies Antique Market,
13-25 Church Street,
Marylebone, NW8 8DT
Tel: 0171 723 5613
Art Deco

Beverley, 30 Church
Street, NW8 8EP
Tel: 0171 262 1576
Art Deco

Christina Bishop
Kitchenware, Portobello
Road Market, W11 2QB
Tel: 0171 221 4688
Kitchenware

Bloomsbury Book Auctions,
3-4 Hardwick Street, Off
Rosebery Avenue, EC1R 4RY
Tel: 0171 833 2636
Book Auctioneers

Books For Cooks,
4 Blenheim Crescent,
W11 1NN
Tel: 0171 221 1992/8102
Books

Nicolaus Boston,
Kensington Church Street,
Antiques Centre, W8 4DB
Tel: 0171 376 0425
Pottery

Christine Bridge Antiques,
78 Castelnau, SW13 9EX
Tel: 0181 741 5501
Glass

British Collectables,
9 Georgian Village, Camden
Passage, Islington, N1 8DU
Tel: 0171 359 4560
*Commemorative, Goss &
Crested China*

Button Queen, 19 Marylebone
Lane, W1M 5FF
Tel: 0171 935 1505
Buttons

Jasmin Cameron,
J6 Antiquarius, 131-141
King's Road, SW3 5ST
Tel: 0171 351 4154
Writing, Glass

Jack Casimir Ltd, The
Brass Shop, 23 Pembridge
Road, W11 3HG
Tel: 0171 727 8643
Metalware

Cekay Antiques,
Gray's Antique Market,
Davies Street, W1Y 1LB
Tel: 0171 629 5130
Walking Sticks

Circle, Alfies Antique
Market, 13-25 Church
Street, NW8 8DT

Classic Collection,
Pied Bull Yard, Bury Place,
WC1A 2JR
Tel: 0171 831 6000
Cameras

The Collector,
Tom & Annette Power,
9 Church Street, NW8 8EE
Tel: 0171 706 4586
Pottery, Ceramics, Pendelfins

Collectors World,
Alfies Antique Market,
Stand G143, 13-25 Church
Street, NW8 8DT
Tel: 0171 286 1255

Comic Book Postal
Auctions Ltd,
40-42 Osnaburgh Street,
NW1 3ND
Tel: 0171 586 3007

Pierre de Fresne,
'Beaux Bijoux',
Q9/10 Antiquarius,
135 King's Road, SW3 5ST
Tel: 0171 352 8882
Art Deco Jewellery

Decodence, Gad Sassower,
Shop 13, The Mall,
Camden Passage, N1 8DU
Tel: 0171 354 4473/
0181 458 4665
Art Deco, Bakelite

Didier Antiques,
58-60 Kensington Church
Street, W8 4DB
Tel: 0171 938 2537/
0836 232634
Jewellery, Silver

Dodo, Liz Farrow,
Stand F037, Alfie's Antique
Market, 13-25 Church
Street, NW8 8DT
Tel: 0171 706 1545
Posters

Donay Antiques, 35 Camden
Passage, N1 8EA
Tel: 0171 359 1880
Games

Eastgate Antiques,
Alfies Antique Market,
13-25 Church Street,
NW8 8DT
Tel: 0171 724 5650
Glass, Cameras

Christopher Eimer,
PO Box 352, NW11 7RF
Tel: 0181 458 9933
Medals

Eureka Antiques,
Geoffrey Vanns Arcade,
105 Portobello Road,
W11 2QB
(Saturdays) *Tartanware,
Card Cases, Jewellery*

Flying Duck,
320/322 Creek Road,
Greenwich, SE10 9SW
Tel: 0181 858 1964

Francis Joseph Publications,
15 St Swithuns Road,
SE13 6RW
Tel: 0181 318 9580

Rob Gee, The Fleamarket,
Pierrepont Row,
Camden Passage, N1 8DU
Tel: 0171 226 6627
(Wed & Sat)
Bottles, Pot Lids

Michael C. German,
38B Kensington Church St,
W8 8EP
Tel: 0171 937 2771
*Arms & Armour,
Walking Sticks*

Richard Gibbon, Alfies
Antique Market, 13-25
Church Street, NW8 8DT
Tel: 0171 723 0449
Costume Jewellery

Gosh Comics, 39 Great
Russell Street, WC1B 3PH
Tel: 0171 636 1011
Comics

Grand Prix Legends,
W10 6BR
Tel: 0171 229 7399
Grand Prix Memorabilia

Gregory, Bottley & Lloyd,
13 Seagrave Road, SW6 1RP
Tel: 0171 381 5522
Fossils, Minerals & Stones

Sarah Groombridge,
Stand 335, Grays Market,
58 Davies Street, W1Y 1LB
Tel: 0171 629 0225
Jewellery

Patricia Harbottle,
Geoffrey Vann Arcade,
107 Portobello Road,
W11 2QB
Tel: 0171 731 1972
(Saturdays)
Corkscrews, Bottles

Harrington Bros,
Chelsea Antique Market,
253 Kings Road, SW3 5EL
Tel: 0171 352 5689/1720
Books

Henry Hay,
Alfies Antique Market,
Stand S54,
13-25 Church Street,
Marylebone, NW8 8DT
Tel: 0171 723 6105
Electric Fans, Telephones

Jeanette Hayhurst Fine
Glass, 32a Kensington
Church Street, W8 4HA
Tel: 0171 938 1539
Glass

Hayloft Woodwork, 3 Bond St, Chiswick, W4 1QZ
Tel: 0181 747 3510
Boxes

Noel Hickey,
Stand F054, Alfies Antique Market, 13-25 Church St, Marylebone, NW8 8DT
Tel: 0171 723 0678
Decorative Collectables

David Hogg, S141 Gray's Antique Market,
Davies Street, W1Y 1LB
Tel: 0171 493 0208
Button Hooks, Tools

David Huxtable, Alfies Antique Market, Stand S03/05 (Top Floor), 13-25 Church Street, NW8 8DT
Tel: 0171 724 2200
Collectables

J. T. Antiques,
16 Christchurch House, Christchurch Road,
SW2 3UA
Tel: 0181 671 2354

Jafar Gallery,
24H Grays in the Mews, Davies Mews, W1Y 1AR
Tel: 0171 409 7919/
0181 300 2727
Glass, Jewellery

Jenies, Stand S57, Alfies Antique Market, 13-25 Church Street, NW8 8DT
Tel: 0171 723 2548
Collectables

John Jesse,
160 Kensington Church Street, W8 4BN
Tel: 0171 229 0312
Art Deco

Jessops, 65 Great Russell Street, WC1B 3BN
Tel: 0171 831 3640
Cameras

Keith, Old Advertising, Unit 14, 155a Northcote Road, Battersea, SW11 6QB
Tel: 0171 228 0741/6850
Tins & Metal Signs

King & Country,
Unit 46 Alfie's Antique Market, 13-25 Church Street, NW8 8DT
Tel: 0171 724 3439
Golfing

Lane Antiques,
40 Pittshanger Lane, Ealing, W5 1QY
Tel: 0181 810 8090

Marion Langham,
Tel: 0171 730 1002
Ceramics, Paperweights, Pottery

Enid Lawson Gallery,
36a Kensington Church Street, W8 4BX
Tel: 0171 937 8444
Glass, Ceramics

Julie Loughnam,
18 Beauchamp Place, Knightsbridge, SW3 1NP
Tel: 0171 589 0867
Julip Horses

Memories, 18 Bell Lane, Hendon, NW4 2AD
Tel: 0181 203 1772/
202 9080
Postcards

Murray Cards
(International) Ltd,
51 Watford Way,
Hendon Central, NW4 3JH
Tel: 0181 202 5688
Ephemera, Cigarette Cards

Colin Narbeth & Son Ltd,
20 Cecil Court, Leicester Square, WC2N 4HE
Tel: 0171 379 6975
Paper Money

New Century, 69 Kensington Church Street, W8 4DB
Tel: 0171 937 2410
Pottery, Textiles

Northcote Road Antiques,
155a Northcote Road, Battersea, SW11 6QB
Tel: 0171 228 6850
Collectables

Kenneth Norton-Grant,
Alfies Antique Market, 13-25 Church Street, Marylebone, NW8 8DT
Tel: 0171 723 1370
Decorative Arts

Old Amusement Machines,
Tel: 0181 889 2213 or
01782 680667/813621
Old Amusement Machines

Jacqueline Oosthuizen,
23 Cale Street,
Chelsea, SW3 3QR
Tel: 0171 352 6071
Staffordshire Pottery, Torquay Pottery

Pieter Oosthuizen,
De Verzamelaar, Georgian Village, Camden Passage,
N1 8DU
Tel: 0171 359 3322/
376 3852
Pottery, Commemoratives, Ceramics

Stevie Pearce,
G144 Alfies Antique Market, 13-25 Church St,
NW8 8DT
Tel: 0171 723 1513/
724 9319
Antique Costume Jewellery

Pieces of Time,
1-7 Davies Mews,
W1Y 1AR
Tel: 0171 629 2422
Watches

Pleasures of Past Times,
11 Cecil Court, WC2N 4EZ
Tel: 0171 836 1142
Books, Greetings Cards

Doug Poultney,
Tel: 0181 330 3472
Comics

Sylvia Powell Decorative Arts, 18 The Mall,
Camden Passage, N1 0PD
Tel: 0171 354 2977/
0181 458 4543
Ceramics, Pottery

John Rastall,
Stall GO47/8,
Alfies Antique Market, 13-25 Church Street,
NW8 8DT
Tel: 0171 723 0449
Collectables

The Reel Thing,
17 Royal Opera Arcade, Pall Mall, SW1Y 4UY
Tel: 0171 976 1830
Fishing Tackle, Sporting

Paul & Karen Rennie,
13 Rugby Street,
WC1N 3QT
Tel: 0171 405 0220

Reubens,
44 Honor Oak Park, Brockley, SE23 1DY
Tel: 0181 291 1786
Scientific & Medical Instruments

Risky Business,
44 Church Street, Marylebone, NW8 8DT
Tel: 0171 724 2194
Luggage, Sporting

Geoffrey Robinson,
Alfies Antique Market, 13-25 Church Street, Marylebone, NW8 8DT
Tel: 0171 723 0449

Rogers de Rin, 76 Royal Hospital Road, SW3 4HN
Tel: 0171 352 9007
Pottery, Boxes

Rokit Ltd, 225 Camden High Street, NW1 7BU
Tel: 0171 267 3046
Denim

Alvin Ross,
Alfies Antique Market, Stand G9-11, 13-25 Church Street, NW8 8DT
Tel: 0171 723 1513

Rumours, 10 The Mall, Upper Street, Camden Passage, Islington, N1 0PD
Tel: 01582 873561
Moorcroft Pottery

H. Samii Antiques,
S102/3 Alfies Antique Market, 13-25 Church Street, NW8 8DT
Tel: 0171 723 5731

Scripophily Shop,
Britannia Hotel,
Grosvenor Square,
W1A 3AN
Tel: 0171 495 0580
Scripophily

Shapiro & Co,
Stand 380, Grays Antique Market, 58 Davies Street,
W1Y 1LB
Tel: 0171 491 2710
Art Nouveau, Jewellery

Sparkle at the Stables,
Long Stables, Stables Market, Chalk Farm Road, Camden, NW1 8AH
Tel: 0181 809 3923
(Sat & Sun 10.30am-6.30pm)
Collectables

Sylvie Spectrum,
Stand 372, Gray's Market, 58 Davies Street, W1Y 1LB
Tel: 0171 629 3501
Jewellery

Steinberg & Tolkien
Vintage & Designer Clothing, 193 Kings Road,
SW3 5EB
Tel: 0171 376 3660
Textiles

Barbara Stone Rare Books, Antiquarius,
135 King's Rd, SW3 5ST
Tel: 0171 351 0963
Books

Susie Cooper Ceramics
GO70-4 Alfies Antique Market, 13-25 Church St,
NW8 8DT
Tel: 0171 723 0449
Art Deco Ceramics

The Talking Machine,
30 Watford Way, NW4 3AL
Tel: 0181 202 3473
Radios, Gramophones

Terrace Antiques,
10 & 12 South Ealing Rd, W5 4QA
Tel: 0181 567 5194/1223
Collectables

Totem, 168 Stoke Newington Church Street, N16 0JL
Tel: 0171 275 0234
Records

Trio (Theresa Clayton),
Gray's Mews, 1-7 Davies Mews, W1Y 1AR
Tel: 0171 629 1184
Perfume Bottles

Vintage Cameras Ltd,
256 Kirkdale, Sydenham, SE26 4NL
Tel: 0181 778 5416
Cameras

Catherine Wallis,
F058, Alfies Antique Market, 13-25 Church St, Marylebone, NW8 8DT
Decorative Arts

Warr & Peace Antiques,
No. 6, First Floor, Georgian Village, Camden Passage,
N1 8DU
Tel: 01206 212183
Glass, Militaria

Mark J. West,
Cobb Antiques Ltd,
39a High Street,
Wimbledon Village,
SW19 5YX
Tel: 0181 946 2811
Glass

John White,
Alfies Antique Market,
13-25 Church Street,
NW8 8DT
Tel: 0171 723 0449
Art Deco Ceramics

Nigel Williams,
Rare Books, 22 & 25 Cecil
Court, WC2N 4HE
Tel: 0171 836 7757
Books

Wynyards Antiques,
5 Ladbroke Road,
W11 3PA
Tel: 0171 221 7936
Treen

Yesterday Child, Angel
Arcade, 118 Islington High
Street, N1 8EG
Tel: 0171 354 1601
Dolls

Robert Young Antiques,
68 Battersea Bridge Road,
SW11 3AG
Tel: 0171 228 7847
*Pottery, Kitchenware,
Folk Art*

Zeitgeist, 58 Kensington
Church Street, W8 4DB
Tel & Fax: 0171 938 4817
Arts & Crafts, Art Nouveau

Avon

Dale Adams,
Fountain Antiques Market,
6 Bladud Buildings,
Bath, BA1 5LS
Tel: 01225 339104

Bath Dolls' Hospital,
2 Grosvenor Place, London
Road, Bath, BA1 6PT
Tel: 01225 319668
Dolls

Douglas Berryman,
Bartlett Street Antique
Centre, Bath, BA1 2QZ
Tel: 01225 446841
Watches

Lynda Brine,
Great Western Antique
Centre, Bartlett Street,
Bath, BA1 2QZ
Tel: 01225 837932
Perfume Bottles, Jewellery

Bristol Dolls' Hospital,
50-52 Alpha Road,
Southville, Bristol, BS3 1DH
Tel: 0117 966 4368
Dolls

Avril Brown, Gt Western
Antique Centre, Bartlett
Street, Bath, BA1 2QZ
Tel: 01225 428731

Peter & Sonia Cashman,
Bartlett Street Antique
Centre, Bath, BA1 2QZ
Tel: 01225 310457
Collectables

Collectable Costume,
Great Western Antique
Centre, Bartlett Street,
Bath, BA1 2QZ
Tel: 01225 428731
Costume

Ann Delores,
Bartlett Street Antique
Centre, Bath, BA1 2QZ
Silver

Frank Dux Antiques,
33 Belvedere,
Bath, BA1 5HR
Tel: 01225 312367
Glass

Glenville Antiques,
120 High Street,
Yatton, BS19 4DH
Tel: 01934 832284
*Collectables, Ceramics,
Silver, Sewing*

Glitterati, Great Western
Antique Centre, Bartlett
Street, Bath, BA1 2QZ
Tel: 01225 333294
Jewellery, Perfume Bottles

Great Western Toys,
Great Western Antique
Centre, Bartlett Street,
Bath, BA1 2QZ
Toys

Graham Hale, Gt Western
Antiques Centre, Bartlett
Street, Bath BA1 2QZ
Tel: 01225 446322
Collectables

Jessie's Button Box,
Great Western Antique
Centre, Bartlett Street,
Bath, BA1 2QZ
Tel: 01225 310388
Buttons

Linen & Lace, Great
Western Antiques Centre,
Bartlett St, Bath, BA1 2QZ
Tel: 01225 310388
Linen & Lace, Costume

Nick Marchant,
Bartlett St Antiques
Centre, Bartlett St,
Bath, BA1 2QZ
Tel: 01225 310457
(Wed & Sat only)
Metalware

Tim Millard Antiques,
Stand 31-32, Bartlett St
Antique Centre, Bartlett
Street, Bath, BA1 2QZ
Tel: 01225 469785
Boxes, Games

Nashers Music Store,
72 Walcot Street,
Bath, BA1 5DD
Tel: 01225 332298
Records

David Payne, Bartlett St
Antiques Market, Bath,
BA1 2QZ
Tel: 01225 330267
Smoking

Mark Rees Tools,
Tel: 01225 837031
Tools

Scott's, Bartlett St Antiques
Centre, Bath, BA1 2QZ
Tel: 01225 625335
Ceramics

Somervale Antiques,
6 Radstock Road,
Midsomer Norton,
Bath, BA3 2AJ
Tel: 01761 412686
Glass, Perfume Bottles

Susannah,
142/144 Walcot Street,
Bath, BA1 5BL
Tel: 01225 445069
Textiles

Bruce Tozer,
14a Margaret's Buildings,
Bath, BA1 2LP
Tel: 01225 420875
Textiles

Richard Twort,
Tel: 01934 641900
*Scientific & Medical
Instruments*

Walcot Reclamations,
108 Walcot Street,
Bath, BA1 5BG
Tel: 01225 444404
Architectural

Winstone Stamp Company,
S82 Great Western
Antiques Centre, Bartlett
Street, Bath, BA1 2QZ
Tel: 01225 310388
*Cigarette Cards,
Railwayana*

Bedfordshire

Something Old Antiques
& Collectables,
52a Shortmead Street,
Biggleswade, SG18 0AP
Tel: 01767 627564
Collectables

Christopher Sykes,
The Old Parsonage,
Woburn, Milton Keynes,
MK17 9QM
Tel: 01525 290259
*Corkscrews, Scientific &
Medical Instruments*

Berkshire

Below Stairs, 103 High St,
Hungerford, RG17 0NB
Tel: 01488 682317
*Kitchenware, Taxidermy,
Tools*

Mostly Boxes, 92 High
Street, Eton, SL4 6AF
Tel: 01753 858470
*Boxes, Inkwells,
Tunbridge Ware*

Special Auction Services,
The Coach House,
Midgham Park,
Reading, RG7 5UG
Tel: 0118 971 2949
*Auctioneers, Pottery,
Ceramics*

Buckinghamshire

Cottage Antiques,
Bakewell & Woburn
Antiques Centres,
Tel: 01283 562670
Treen

Ella's Button Box,
South View,
Twyford, MK18 4EG
Tel: 01296 730910
Buttons

A. & E. Foster,
Little Heysham,
Naphill, HP14 4SU
Tel: 01494 562024
Treen

Hannah,
Tel: 01844 237899/0831
800774

Mike Smith Motoring Past,
Chiltern House, Ashendon,
Aylesbury, HP18 0HB
Tel: 01296 651283
Automobilia

Cambridgeshire

Antique Amusement Co,
Mill Lane, Swaffham
Bulbeck, CB5 0NF
Tel: 01223 813041/0802
666755 mobile
Amusement Machines

Warboys Antiques,
Old Church School,
High Street, Warboys,
PE17 1NR
Tel: 01487 823686
Sporting Collectables

Cheshire

Avalon,
1 City Walls/Rufus Court,
Northgate Street,
Chester, CH1 2JG
Tel: 01244 318406
Postcards

Collector's Corner,
Tudor House,
29-31 Lower Bridge Street,
Chester, CH1 1RS
Tel: 01260 270429
Comics, Records, Rock & Pop

Dollectable,
53 Lower Bridge Street,
Chester, CH1 1RS
Tel: 01244 344888/679195
Dolls

Clifford Elmer, Books,
8 Balmoral Avenue,
Cheadle Hulme,
Cheadle, SK8 5EQ
Tel: 0161 485 7064
Crime Books

Legend Lane,
Albion Mill, London Road,
Macclesfield, SK11 7SQ
Tel: 01625 424661
Cottages

Nantwich Art Deco &
Decorative Arts, 87 Welsh
Row, Nantwich, CW5 5ET
Tel: 01270 624876
Art Deco

On The Air,
42 Bridge Street Row,
Chester, CH1 1NN
Tel: 01244 348468
Radios, TVs, Gramophones

Sweetbriar Gallery,
Robin Hood Lane,
Helsby, WA6 9NH
Tel: 01928 723851
Paperweights

Cornwall

Millcraft Rocking Horse Co,
Lower Trannack Mill,
Wendron,
Helston, TR13 0LT
Tel: 01326 573316
Toys, Rocking Horses

Cumbria

Banking Memorabilia,
PO Box 14,
Carlisle, CA3 8EW
Tel: 016974 76465
Paper Money

Domino Restorations,
129 Craig Walk,
Windermere, LA23 3AX
Tel: 015394 45751
Ceramic Restorers

Derbyshire

Spinning Wheel Garage,
Sheffield Road, Sheepbridge,
Chesterfield, S41 9EH
Tel: 01246 451772
Automobilia

Spurrier-Smith Antiques,
28, 39, 41 Church Street,
Ashbourne, DE6 1AJ
Tel: 01335 343669/342198
*Rocking Horses,
Collectables & Metalware*

Tanglewood Antiques,
Tanglewood Mills, Coke
Street, Derby, DE1 1NE
Tel: 01332 346005
Pine, Treen

What Now, Cavendish
Arcade, The Crescent,
Buxton, SK17 6BQ
Tel: 01298 27178/23417
Collectables

Devon

Bampton Telephone &
General Museum of
Communication and
Domestic History,
4 Brook Street, Bampton,
Tiverton, EX16 9LY
Telephones

Great Western Antiques,
Torre Station, Newton
Road, Torquay, TQ5 2DD
Tel: 01803 200551
Collectables, Shipping

Jonathan Hill,
2-4 Brook Street,
Bampton, EX16 9LY
Tel: 01398 331532
Radios

Shambles, 22 North Street,
Ashburton, TQ13 7QD
Tel: 01364 653848
Collectables

Brian Taylor Antiques,
24 Molesworth Road,
Plymouth, PL1 5LZ
Tel: 01752 569061
Gramophones

Dorset

Ancient & Gothic,
PO Box 356,
Christchurch, BH23 2YD
Tel: 01202 478592
Antiquities

Peter Bird,
811 Christchurch Road,
Boscombe, BH21 ITZ
Tel: 01202 429111
Ceramics

Books Afloat,
66 Park Street,
Weymouth, DT4 7DE
Tel: 01305 779774
Books, Shipping

Nautical Antiques,
Old Harbour Passage,
3a Hope Square
(opposite Brewers Quay),
Weymouth, DT4 8TR
Tel: 01305 777838/783180
Shipping

Old Button Shop,
Lytchett Minster,
Tel: 01202 622169
Buttons

Poole Pottery,
The Quay, Poole, BH15 1RF
Tel: 01202 666200
Poole Pottery

Vera Strange Antiques,
811 Christchurch Road,
Boscombe,
Bournemouth, BH7 6HP
Tel: 01202 429111
Pottery & Porcelain

Essex

GKR Bonds Ltd,
PO Box 1,
Kelvedon, CO5 9EH
Tel: 01376 571711
Scripophily

Old Telephone Company,
The Old Granary,
Battlesbridge Antiques
Centre,
Nr Wickford, SS11 7RF
Tel: 01245 400601
Telephones

R. F. Postcards,
17 Hilary Crescent,
Rayleigh, SS6 8NB
Tel: 01268 743222
Postcards

Gloucestershire

Acorn Antiques, Sheep
Street, Stow-on-the-Wold,
GL54 1AA
Tel: 01451 831519
Ceramics

Judi Bland, Durham House
Antique Centre, Sheep
Street, Stow-on-the-Wold,
GL54 1AA
Tel: 01451 870404/
01295 811292
Pottery

Christopher Clarke,
The Fosse Way, Stow-on-
the-Wold, GL54 1JS
Tel: 01451 830476
Animal collectables

Corinium Galleries,
25 Gloucester Street,
Cirencester, GL7 2DJ
Tel: 01285 659057
Auctioneer, Postcards

Judy & Brian Harden
Antiques
Tel: 01451 810684
Pottery, Boxes

Clive & Lynne Jackson,
Tel: 01242 254375
Mobile 0589 715275
Parian ware

Oriental Gallery
Tel: 01451 830944
Oriental

Park House Antiques,
Park Street,
Stow-on-the-Wold,
Cheltenham, GL54 1AQ
Tel: 01451 830159
*Dolls, Dolls House
Furniture, Teddy Bears*

Samarkand Galleries,
2 Brewery Yard, Sheep
Street, Stow-on-the-Wold,
GL54 1AA
Tel: 01451 832322
Rugs & Carpets

Telephone Lines Ltd,
339 High Street,
Cheltenham, GL50 3HS
Tel: 01242 583699
Telephones

The Trumpet,
West End,
Minchinhampton, GL6 9JA
Tel: 01453 883027
Collectables

Hampshire

Bona Arts Decorative,
19 Princes Mead Shopping
Centre, Farnborough,
GU14 7TJ
Tel: 01252 372188
Art Deco

Cobwebs,
78 Northam Road,
Southampton, SO2 0PB
Tel: 01703 227458
*Aeronautica, Automobilia,
Shipping*

Goss & Crested China Co,
62 Murray Road,
Horndean, PO8 9JL
Tel: 01705 597440
Goss & Crested china

Miller's of Chelsea
Antiques Ltd,
Netherbrook House,
86 Christchurch Road,
Ringwood, BH24 1DR
Tel: 01425 472062
Pottery, Kitchenware

The Old Toy Shop,
7 Monmouth Court,
Ringwood, BH24 1H8
Tel: 01425 476899
Toys

Romsey Medal Centre,
5 Bell Street,
Romsey, SO51 8GY
Tel: 01794 512069
Arms & Militaria

Solent Railwayana Auctions,
Community Centre,
Mill Lane, Wickham,
Fareham, PO17 5AL
Tel: 01489 578093
Railwayana

Lorraine Tarrant Antiques,
23 Market Place,
Ringwood, BH24 1AN
Tel: 01425 461123
Collectables, Automobilia

Toys Through Time
Tel: 01329 288678
Dolls

Hereford &
Worcester

BBM Jewellery & Coins
(W. V. Crook),
8-9 Lion Street,
Kidderminster, DY10 1PT
Tel: 01562 744118
Inkwells, Jewellery, Coins

The Button Museum,
Kyrle Street,
Ross-on-Wye,
HR9 7DB
Tel: 01989 66089
Buttons

Platform 6,
11A Davenport Drive,
The Willows,
Bromsgrove, B60 2DW
Tel: 01527 871000
Auctioneer, Toys

Hertfordshire

Ambeline Antiques,
By George Antique Centre,
St Albans, AL3 4ES
Tel: 01727 53032/
0181 449 8307
Hairdressing & Hat Pins

Forget Me Knot,
Over the Moon,
27 High Street, St Albans
Tel: 01727 848907/
01923 261172
Jewellery, Ceramics

Kohlberg Antiques,
By George Antique Centre,
23 George Street,
St Albans, AL3 4ES
Tel: 01727 853032

Magic Lanterns at By
George, 23 George Street,
St Albans, AL3 4ES
Tel: 01727 865680/853032
Lighting

Robby's Antiques,
23 George Street,
St Albans, AL3 4ES
Tel: 01727 853032
Collectables

Stateside Comics Plc,
125 East Barnet Road,
Barnet, EN4 8RF
Tel: 0181 449 5535
Comics

Humberside

Marine Art Posters,
71 Harbour Way,
Merchants Landing,
Victoria Dock,
Port of Hull, HU9 1PL
Tel: 01482 321173
Posters

Isle of Wight

Nostalgia Toy Museum,
High Street,
Godshill, PO38 3HZ
Tel: 01983 730055
Toys

Kent

Amelia Dolls, Pantiles Spa
Antiques, Tunbridge Wells,
TN4 8HE
Tel: 01892 541377/
01342 713223
Dolls

Amherst Antiques,
23 London Road,
Riverhead, Sevenoaks,
TN13 2BU
Tel: 01732 455047
Treen, Tunbridge Ware

B&B Military,
1 Kings Avenue,
Ashford, TN23 1LU
Tel: 01233 632923
Toys, Militaria

Bears Galore, 8 The
Fairings, High Street,
Tenterden, TN30 6QX
Tel: 01580 765233
Teddy Bears

Beatcity, PO Box 229,
Chatham, ME5 0PW
Tel: 01634 305383/
0370 650890
Beatles Memorabilia

Jon Bird,
Tel: 01227 273952
Tape Recorders, Microphones

Calamus, The Shambles,
Sevenoaks, TN13 1AL
Tel: 01732 740603
Jewellery

Candlestick & Bakelite,
PO Box 308,
Orpington, BR5 1TB
Tel: 0181 467 3743
Telephones

Canterbury Bookshop,
37 Northgate,
Canterbury, CT1 1BL
Tel: 01227 464773
Books

Collectables, PO Box 130,
Chatham, ME5 0DZ
Tel: 01634 828767
Collectables

David Wainwright,
Badgers Antiques
Tel: 01233 758337
Treen, Tunbridge Ware

Dragonlee Collectables,
Maidstone
Tel: 01622 202879
Collectables

Eaton and Jones,
120 High Street,
Tenterden, TN30 6HT
Tel: 01580 763357
Jewellery

Falstaff Antiques
(Motor Museum),
63-67 High Street,
Rolvenden, TN17 4LP
Tel: 01580 241234
Automobilia

Foxhole Antiques,
Swan & Foxhole, Albert
House, Stone Street,
Cranbrook
Tel: 01580 712720
Collectables, Kitchenware

Gem Antiques,
28 London Road,
Sevenoaks, TN13 1AP
Tel: 01732 743540
Jewellery, Clocks

Paul Haskell
Tel: 01634 669362
Jewellery

Stuart Heggie,
14 The Borough,
Northgate, Canterbury,
CT1 2DR
Tel: 01227 470422
*Cameras, Stereoscopes,
Photographs*

Hiscock & Hiscock Antiques,
47 High Street,
New Romney, TN28 8AH
Tel: 01797 364023
Teddy Bears, Pottery

J & D Collectables
Tel: 01227 452873
Ceramics, Pottery

J & M Collectables
Tel: 01580 891657
Ephemera, Plaques

Lace Basket,
116 High Street,
Tenterden, TN30 6HT
Tel: 01580 763923/763664
*Linen & Lace,
Hairdressing & Hat Pins,
Costumes*

Ian MacKenzie,
Tel: 01303 261220
Fishing Tackle

The Magpie's Nest,
14 Palace Street,
Canterbury, CT1 2DZ
Tel: 01227 764883
Dolls, Dolls House Furniture

The Old Mill, High Street,
Lamberhurst, TN3 8EQ
Tel: 01892 891196
Pine, Kitchenware

Old Tackle Box, PO Box 55,
Cranbrook, TN17 3ZU
Tel & Fax: 01580 713979
Fishing

Pantiles Spa Antiques,
4, 5, 6 Union House,
The Pantiles, Tunbridge
Wells, TN4 8HE
Tel: 01892 541377
*Pottery & Porcelain, Metal,
Watches, Collectables*

Paris, 42A High Street,
Tenterden, TN30 6AR
Tel: 01580 765328
Jewellery

Radio Memories &
Vintage Wireless,
203 Tankerton Road,
Whitstable, CT5 2AT
Tel: 01227 262491
Radios

Keith & Veronica Reeves,
Burgate Antiques,
10c Burgate, Canterbury,
CT1 2HG
Tel: 01227 456500/
01634 375098
Arms & Militaria

Roses, 60 King Street,
Sandwich, CT13 9BL
Tel: 01304 615303
Collectables

Serendipity, 168 High
Street, Deal, CT14 6BQ
Tel: 01304 369165/366536
*Ceramics, Staffordshire
Pottery*

Stevenson Brothers,
The Workshop, Ashford
Road, Bethersden,
Ashford, TN26 3AP
Tel: 01233 820363
Rocking Horses

Tenterden Bookshop,
60 High Street,
Tenterden, TN30 6AU
Tel: 01580 763005
Books

Variety Box, 16 Chapel
Place, Tunbridge Wells,
TN1 1YQ
Tel: 01892 531868
*Button Hooks, Goss &
Crested China, Fans,
Glass, Hairdressing &
Hat Pins, Sewing, Silver,
Tunbridge Ware*

The Warehouse,
29-30 Queens Gardens,
Worthington Street,
Dover, CT17 9AH
Tel: 01304 242006
Toys & Models

Wenderton Antiques,
Tel: 01227 720295
*(by appointment only)
Kitchenware*

Westerham House
Antiques, The Green,
Westerham, TN16 1AY
Tel: 01959 561622/562200
Collectables, Silver, Bronzes

Wooden Chair Antiques
Centre, Waterloo Road,
Cranbrook, TN12 0QG
Tel: 01580 713671
Collectables

Woodville Antiques,
The Street, Hamstreet,
Ashford, TN26 2HG
Tel: 01233 732981
Tools

Lancashire

Walter Aspinall Antiques,
Pendle Antique Centre,
Union Mill, Watt Street,
Sabden, BB7 9ED
Tel: 01282 778642
Collectables

British Heritage Telephones,
11 Rhodes Drive,
Unsworth, Bury, BL9 8NH
Tel: 0161 767 9259
Telephones

Roy W. Bunn Antiques,
34-36 Church Street,
Barnoldswick,
Colne, BB8 5UT
Tel: 01282 813703
*Ceramics, Staffordshire
Pottery*

A. T. Fletcher,
(Enthusiast & Collector)
Automobilia

Glasform Ltd,
123 Talbot Road,
Blackpool, FY1 3QY
Tel: 01253 695849
Glass

Roberts Antiques,
Tel: 01253 827798
Textiles, Ceramics

Tracks, PO Box 117,
Chorley, PR7 2QZ
Tel: 01257 269726
Rock & Pop Records

Leicestershire

Pamela Brooks,
Tel: 0116 230 2625
Textiles

Jessop Classic Photographica,
98 Scudamore Road,
Leicester, LE3 1TZ
Tel: 0116 232 0033
Cameras

Pooks Motor Bookshop,
Fowke Street,
Rothley, LE7 7PJ
Tel: 0116 237 6222
*Books, Automobilia,
Tins & Metal Signs*

Janice Williamson,
Tel/Fax: 0116 281 2926
Ceramics, Doulton

Lincolnshire

20th Century Frocks,
65 Steep Hill,
Lincoln, N1 1YN
Tel: 01522 545916
Textiles

Art Nouveau Originals,
Stamford Antiques Centre,
The Exchange Hall, Broad
Street, Stamford, PE9 1PX
Tel: 01780 62605
Art Nouveau

Junktion, The Old Railway
Station, New Bolingbroke,
Boston, PE22 7LB
Tel: 01205 480068
*Toys, Tin & Metal Signs,
Automobilia*

Legends Rocking Horses,
Yew Tree Farmhouse,
Holme Road, Kirton
Holme, Boston, PE20 1SY
Tel: 01205 79214
Toys, Rocking Horses

Janie Smithson Antiques,
Tel: 01754 810265
Kitchenware

Middlesex

Albert's Cigarette Card
Specialists,
113 London Road,
Twickenham, TW1 1EE
Tel: 0181 891 3067
Cigarette Cards

Joan & Bob Anderson,
Tel: 0181 572 4328
Pottery

Dorine Archer,
Tel: 01895 251246
Ceramic Figures Restoration

Hobday Toys,
44 High Street, Northwood,
HA6 2XY
Tel: 01923 820115
Toys

John Ives,
5 Normanhurst Drive,
Twickenham, TW1 1NA
Tel: 0181 892 6265
Reference Books

Vintage Pencils,
(Neil W. J. Davis)
Tel: 01895 824920
*Restoration of Fountain
Pens and Mechanical
Pencils*

Neil Wilcox,
113 Strawberry Vale,
Twickenham, TW1 4SJ
Tel: 0181 892 5858
Bottles

Norfolk

Roger Bradbury Antiques,
Church Street,
Coltishall, NR12 7DJ
Tel: 01603 737444
Oriental Porcelain

Cat Pottery,
1 Grammar School Road,
North Walsham, NR28 9JH
Tel: 01692 402962
Pottery

Trains & Olde Tyme Toys,
Aylsham Road,
Norwich, NR3 2AB
Tel: 01603 413585
Toys

Northamptonshire

Shelron, 9 Brackley Road,
Towcester, NN12 6DH
Tel: 01327 50242
Postcards, Collectables

Nottinghamshire

Catherine Barlow,
14 Windsor Road, Selston,
Nottingham, NG16 6JJ
Tel: 01773 860933
Ceramics

Stuart Barlow,
14 Windsor Road, Selston,
Nottingham, NG16 6JJ
Tel: 01733 860933
Toys

The Keyhole, Dragonwyck,
Far Back Lane, Farnsfield,
Newark, NG22 8JX
Tel: 01623 882590
Locks & Keys

Reflections of a Bygone Age,
15 Debdale Lane,
Keyworth, NG12 5HT
Tel: 01607 74079
Postcards

T. Vennett-Smith,
11 Nottingham Road,
Gotham, Nottingham,
NG11 0HE
Tel: 0115 983 0541
*Auctioneer, Ephemera,
Postcards, Sporting*

Oxfordshire

Dauphin Display Cabinet Co,
PO Box 602,
Oxford, OX44 9LU
Tel: 01865 343542
Display Stands

Manfred Schotten,
The Crypt Antiques,
109 High Street,
Burford, OX18 4RG
Tel: 01993 822302
Sporting

Teddy Bears, 99 High
Street, Witney, OX8 6LY
Tel: 01993 702616
Teddy Bears

Shropshire

Antiques on the Square,
2 Sandford Court,
Sandford Avenue,
Church Stretton, SY6 6DA
Tel: 01694 724111
Art Deco Ceramics

F. C. Manser & Son Ltd,
53-54 Wyle Cop,
Shrewsbury, SY1 1XJ
Tel: 01743 351120
*Collectables, Silver, Glass,
Textiles, Jewellery, Pottery,
Ceramics*

Mullock Madeley,
The Old Shippon,
Wall-under-Heywood, Nr
Church Stretton, SY6 7DS
Tel: 01694 771771/771772
Sporting Auctions

No 7 Antiques,
7 Nantwich Road, Woore,
Shropshire CW3 9SA
Tel: 01630 647118
Kitchenware

Teme Valley Antiques,
1 The Bull Ring,
Ludlow, SY8 1AD
Tel: 01584 874686
Ceramics, Silver

Somerset

Billiard Room Antiques,
The Old School,
Church Lane, Chilcompton,
Bath, BA3 4HP
Tel: 01761 232839
Billiard Collectables

The Gramophone Man,
North Street,
Wellington, TA21 8LT
Tel: 01823 661618
Radios

Heads n' Tails,
Bourne House, 41 Church
Street, Wiveliscombe,
Taunton, TA4 2LT
Tel: 01984 623097
Fax: 01984 624445
Taxidermy

London Cigarette Card Co,
West Street,
Somerton, TA11 6NB
Tel: 01458 273452
Cigarette Cards

Staffordshire

Brian Bates
Tel: 01782 680667
Amusement Machines

Gordon The 'Ole Bottleman,
25 Stapenhill Road,
Burton-on-Trent, DE15 9AE
Tel: 01283 567213
Bottles

Keystones, PO Box 387,
Stafford, ST16 3RX
Tel: 01785 256648
Ceramics

Peggy Davies Ceramics,
28 Liverpool Road,
Stoke-on-Trent, ST4 1VJ
Tel: 01782 848002
Ceramics

Trevor Russell,
Tel: 01889 562009
Fountain Pens

The Tackle Exchange, 95B
Trentham Road, Dresden,
Stoke-on-Trent, ST3 4EG
Tel: 01782 599858
Fishing

Suffolk

Crafers Antiques, The Hill,
Wickham Market, IP13 0QS
Tel: 01728 747347
*Ceramics, Staffordshire
Pottery, Sewing*

W. L. Hoad,
9 St Peter's Road, Kirkley,
Lowestoft, NR33 0LH
Tel: 01502 587758
Cigarette Cards

The Tartan Bow
Tel: 01379 783057
Kitchenalia, Garden Tools

Surrey

David Aldous-Cook, PO Box
413, Sutton, SM3 8SZ
Tel: 0181 642 4842
Reference Books

Childhood Memories,
The Farnham Antique
Centre, 27 South Street,
Farnham, GU9 7QU
Tel: 01252 724475
Dolls, Toys

Church Street Antiques,
10 Church Street,
Godalming, GU7 1EH
Tel: 01483 860894
*Art Deco Ceramics,
Commemorative*

Gasson Antiques, PO Box
11, Cranleigh, GU6 8YY
Tel: 01483 277476
Decorative Collectables

Gooday Gallery,
20 Richmond Hill,
Richmond, TW10 6QX
Tel: 0181 940 8652
Art Deco

New Ashgate Gallery,
Waggon Yard,
Farnham, GU9 7PS
Tel: 01252 713208
*Collectables, Ceramics,
Jewellery*

Nostalgia Amusements,
22 Greenwood Close,
Thames Ditton, KT7 0BG
Tel: 0181 398 2141
Jukeboxes

Richard Joseph Publishers,
Unit 2, Monk's Walk,
Farnham, GU9 8HT
Tel: 01252 734347
Directories

Succession,
18 Richmond Hill,
Richmond, TW10 6QX
Tel: 0181 940 6774
Art Nouveau

Alexis F. J. Turner,
The Workshop Gallery,
144a Bridge Road,
East Moseley, KT8 9HW
Tel: 0181 542 5926
*Taxidermy, Sporting,
Costume, Collectables*

Teresa Vanneck-Murray,
Vanneck House,
22 Richmond Hill,
Richmond-upon-Thames,
TW10 6QX
Tel: 0181 940 2035
*Staffordshire Pottery,
Commemoratives*

West Promotions,
PO Box 257,
Sutton, SM3 9WW
Tel: 0181 641 3224
Paper Money

Sussex

John & Mary Bartholomew,
The Mint Arcade, 71 The
Mint, Rye, TN31 7EW
Tel: 01797 225952
Postcards

Bears & Friends,
41 Meeting House Lane,
The Lanes,
Brighton, BN1 1HB
Tel: 01273 202940
Teddy Bears

Birdham Antiques,
The Old Bird & Ham,
Main Road, Birdham,
Chichester, PO20 7HS
Tel: 01243 51141
Metalware, Collectables

Bygones, Collectors Shop,
123 South Street,
Lancing, BN15 8AS
Tel: 01903 750051/763470
Collectables

C.A.R.S.
(Classic Automobilia &
Regalia Specialists),
4-4a Chapel Terrace Mews,
Kemp Town, Brighton,
BN2 1HU
Tel: 01273 601960

Children's Treasures,
17 George Street,
Hastings, TN34 3EG
Tel: 01424 444117/422758
Toys

Elite Designs,
Tel: 01424 434856
*Ephemera, Collectables,
Rock & Pop*

Tony Horsley
Tel: 01273 732163
Collectables, Ceramics

Clare Kinloch,
Tel: 01424 870364
Dolls

Libra Antiques,
81 London Road,
Hurst Green, Etchingham,
TN19 7PN
Tel: 01580 860569
Lighting

Limited Editions,
10 Old Printing House,
Tarrant Street, Arundel,
BN18 9DG
Tel: 01903 883950
Jewellery

Ann Lingard,
Ropewalk Antiques,
Rye, TN31 7NA
Tel: 01797 223486
Kitchenalia, Tiles, Pine

Sue Pearson,
13 Prince Albert Street,
Brighton, BN1 1HE
Tel: 01273 329247
Dolls, Teddy Bears

The Pianola Shop,
134 Islingword Road,
Brighton, BN2 2SH
Tel: 01273 608999
Pianos

Rokit Ltd,
23 Kensington Gardens,
Brighton, BN1 4AL
Tel: 01273 672053
Denim

Graham Webb,
59A Ship Street,
Brighton, BN1 1AE
Tel: 01273 321803
Musical

Witney and Airault,
Prinny's Gallery,
3 Meeting House Lane,
The Lanes,
Brighton, BN1 1HB
Tel: 01273 204554
Art Deco Ceramics

Tyne & Wear

Causey Antique Shop,
Gosforth, NE3 4DL
Collectables

H. & S. Collectables,
149 Salters Road, Gosforth,
Nr Newcastle-upon-Tyne,
NE3 1DU
Tel: 0191 284 6626
Collectables

Ian Sharp Antiques,
23 Front Street,
Tynemouth, NE30 4DX
Tel: 0191 2960656
Ceramics, Pottery

Warwickshire

Alien Enterprises,
Stratford Model Centre,
The Minories,
Stratford-upon-Avon,
CV37 6QW
Tel: 01789 299701
Television, Collectables

The Antique Shop,
30 Henley Street, Stratford-
upon-Avon, CV37 6QW
Tel: 01789 292485
Collectables Centre

Art Deco Ceramics,
Stratford Antique Centre,
Ely Street, Stratford-
upon-Avon, CV37 6LN
Tel: 01789 297496/299524
Art Deco Ceramics

Central Antique Arms &
Militaria, Smith Street
Antique Centre, 7 Smith
Street, Warwick, CV34 4JA
Tel: 01926 400554
Arms & Militaria

Tony Greenwood,
Warwick Antique Centre,
20-22 High Street,
Warwick, CV34 4AX
Tel: 01926 495704
Cameras

High Street Antiques,
11a High Street,
Alcester, B49 5AE
Tel: 01789 764009
*Glass, Brass, Postcards,
Pottery & Porcelain,
Art Deco*

Inglewood Antiques,
Ely Street Antique Centre,
Stratford-upon-Avon,
CV37 6LN
Tel: 01789 297496

Midlands Commemoratives,
The Old Cornmarket
Antique Centre, 70 Market
Place, Warwick, CV34 4SO
Tel: 01926 419119
Ceramics, Commemoratives

Midlands Goss, The Old
Cornmarket Antiques
Centre, 70 Market Place,
Warwick, CV34 4SO
Tel: 01926 419119
Goss & Crested China

Old Pine House,
16 Warwick Street,
Leamington Spa, CV32 5LL
Tel: 01926 470477
Collectables

Malcolm Russ-Welch,
59 Lime Avenue,
Leamington Spa, CV32 7DE
Tel: 01926 882026
Collectables

Tim's Spot, Ely Street
Antique Centre, Stratford-
upon-Avon, CV37 6LN
Tel: 01789 297496/204182
Glass, Ceramics

Time Machine,
198 Holbrook Lane,
Coventry, CV6 4DD
Tel: 01203 663557
Toys

James Wigington
Tel: 01789 261418
Fishing, Arms & Militaria

West Midlands

The Dog House,
309 Bloxwich Road,
Walsall, WS2 7BD
Tel: 01922 30829
Kitchenware, Collectables

March Medals,
113 Gravelly Hill North,
Erdington,
Birmingham B23 6BJ
Tel: 0121 384 4901
Militaria, Medals

Nostalgia Comics,
14-16 Smallbrook
Queensway, City Centre,
Birmingham, B5 4EN
Tel: 0121 643 0143
Comics

George Sawyer,
11 Frayne Avenue,
Kingswinford, DY6 9DU
Tel: 01384 273847
Postcards

Ken Smith Antiques Ltd,
171-175 Holliday Street,
Birmingham, B1 1SJ
Tel: 0121 633 4464
Collectables

Wiltshire

Robert Mullis, 55 Berkeley
Road, Wroughton,
Swindon, SN4 9BN
Tel: 01793 813583
Rocking Horses

North Wiltshire Exporters,
Farmhill House,
Brinkworth, SN15 5AJ
Tel: 01666 824133/510876
Collectables

David Wells, Salisbury
Antique & Collectors
Market, 37 Catherine
Street, Salisbury, SP1 2DH
Tel: 01425 476899
*Postcards, Toys,
Collectables*

Worcestershire

Michael Chapman,
Priorsleigh, Mill Lane,
Cleeve Prior, WR11 5JZ
Tel: 01789 773897/
0831 392542
Automobilia

Yorkshire

BBR, Elsecar Heritage
Centre, Wath Road,
Elsecar, Barnsley, S74 8HJ
Tel: 01226 745156
Auctioneer, Bottles

Camera House,
Oakworth Hall,
Colne Road, Oakworth,
BD22 7HZ
Tel: 01535 642333
Cameras

Cottage Antiques,
5 Ropergate End,
Pontefract
Tel: 01977 611146
*Pine, Pottery, Linen,
Kitchenalia*

Country Collector,
11-12 Birdgate,
Pickering, YO18 7AL
Tel: 01751 477481

Crested China Co,
The Station House,
Driffield, YO25 7PY
Tel: 01377 257042
Goss & Crested China

Echoes,
650a Halifax Road,
Eastwood,
Todmorden, OL14 6DW
Tel: 01706 817505
Textiles, Costume

G. M. Haley,
Hippins Farm
Blackshawhead,
Hebden Bridge,
HX7 7JG
Tel: 01422 842484
Toy Soldiers

John & Simon Haley,
89 Northgate,
Halifax, HX6 4NG
Tel: 01422 822148
Toys, Money Boxes

Muir Hewitt,
Halifax Antiques Centre,
Queens Road,
Queen's Road/Gibbet
Street, Halifax,
HX1 4LR
Tel: 01422 347377
Art Deco Ceramics

Holmfirth Antiques
(Ken Priestley)
Tel: 01484 686854
Gramophones

Old Copper Shop and
Post House Antiques,
69 & 75 Market Place,
South Cave, HU15 2AS
Tel: 01430 423988
Linen, Collectables

Shirley Tomlinson,
Halifax Antiques Centre,
Queens Road/Gibbet
Street, Halifax,
HX1 4LR
Tel: 01422 366657
*Linen & Lace,
Textiles & Costume*

Sigma Antiques,
Water Skellgate,
Ripon, HG4 1BH
Tel: 01765 603163
Art Deco, Boxes, Pottery

Andrew Spencer Bottomley,
The Coach House,
Thongsbridge,
Holmfirth, HD7 2TT
Tel: 01484 685234
Arms & Militaria

Windmill Antiques,
4 Montpellier Mews,
Montpellier Street,
Harrogate, HG1 2TJ
Tel: 01423 530502
*Copper, Brass, Boxes,
Rocking Horses, Dolls
Furniture*

Ireland

Cranks Antiques,
Powerscourt,
Townhouse Centre,
Dublin 2
*Pottery, Ceramics,
Collectables*

Michelina & George
Stacpoole, Main Street,
Adare, Co Limerick
Tel: 00 353 6139 6409
Pottery, Ceramics, Silver

Scotland

The Antique Shop,
69 St Mary Street,
Kirkcudbright, DG6 4DU
*Linen & Lace, Kitchenalia,
Collectables*

Chris Barge Antiques,
5 Southside Place,
Inverness, IV2 3JF
Tel: 01463 230128
Corkscrews

Laurance Black, 60 Thistle
Street, Edinburgh, EH3 6RA
Tel: 0131 220 3387
Tartan ware

Bow-Well Antiques,
103 West Bow,
Edinburgh, EH1 2JP
Tel: 0131 225 3335
*Gramophones, Scottish
Collectables, Pottery, Silver*

David Brown,
23 Claude Street, Larkhall,
Lanarkshire ML9 2BU
Tel: 01555 880333
Breweriana

Caithness Glass Ltd,
Inveralmond,
Perth, PH1 3TZ
Tel: 01738 37373
Glass, Paperweights

Collectables, Lein Road,
Kingston-on-Spey,
Morayshire IV32 7NW
Tel: 01343 870462
*Militaria, Jewellery,
Collectables*

Early Technology,
84 West Bow,
Edinburgh, EH1 2HH
Tel: 0131 226 1132
*Scientific & Medical
Instruments*

Edinburgh Coin Shop,
2 Polwarth Crescent,
Edinburgh, EH11 1HW
Tel: 0131 229 3007
Coins

David Gordon,
Now & Then,
7&9 Crosscauseway,
Edinburgh, EH8 9JW
Tel: 0131 668 2927/
226 2867
Tools, Telephones

Henderson,
5 North Methven Street,
Perth, PH1 5PN
Tel: 01738 624836
*Porcelain, Glass, Silver,
Jewellery, Coins, Medals,
Stamps*

Lochside Rocking Horses,
Lochside, Longhaven,
Peterhead, AB42 7PA
Tel: 01779 812277
Fax: 01779 812391
Rocking Horses

Rhod McEwan,
Glengarden, Ballater,
Aberdeenshire, AB35 5UB
Tel: 013397 55429
Golf Books

Oban Antiques,
35 Stevenson Street,
Oban, PA34 5NA
Tel: 01631 566203

Otterswick Antique
Telephones,
6 Lady Lawson Street,
Edinburgh, EH3 9DS
Tel: 0131 228 3690
Telephones

Stockbridge Antiques,
8 Deanhaugh Street,
Edinburgh,
EH4 1LY
Tel: 0131 332 1366
Dolls, Textiles

Timeless Tackle,
1 Blackwood Crescent,
Edinburgh, EH9 1QZ
Tel: 0131 667 1407
Fishing

Wales

Brindley John Ayers,
8 Bay View Drive,
Hakin, Milford Haven,
SA73 3RJ
Tel: 01646 698359
Fishing

APES Rocking Horses,
Ty Gwyn,
Llannefydd,
Denbigh LL16 5HB
Tel: 01745 540365
Rocking Horses

The Emporium,
92 St Teilo Street,
Pontarddulais,
Nr Swansea, SA4 1QH
Tel: 01792 885766
Brass, Cast Iron

Paul Gibbs Antiques,
25 Castle Street,
Conwy, Gwynedd,
LL32 8AY
Tel: 01492 593429
Pottery, Art Deco Ceramics

Howards Antiques,
10 Alexandra Road,
Aberystwyth,
Dyfed, SY23 1LE
Tel: 01970 624973
Pottery

Merlin's Antiques,
Market Precinct,
Carmarthen, SA31 1QY
Tel: 01267 237728
*Porcelain, Pottery, Glass,
Silver, Postcards*

Nostalgia Antiques,
1 Fidlas Road, Llanishen,
Cardiff, CF4 5LW
Tel: 01222 765122
Collectables

Teapot Museum & Shop,
25 Castle Street,
Conway, LL32 8AY
Tel: 01493 593429
*Teapots & Tea Related
Items*

Tortoiseshell Antiques,
Trebedw House, Henllan,
Nr Newcastle Emlyn,
SA44 5TN
Tel: 01559 370943
Ivory, Jewellery, Textiles

Watkins, Islwyn,
1 High Street, Knighton,
Powys, LD7 1AT
Tel: 01547 520145
Pottery

USA

Marilynn and Sheila Brass,
PO Box 380503,
Cambridge,
MA 02238-0503
Tel: 617 491 6064
Collectables

J's Collectables,
5827 Encinita Avenue,
Temple City, CA 91780
Tel: 001 (818) 451 0010
Disney

Postcards International,
Vintage Picture Postcards,
PO Box 2930, New Haven,
CT 06515-0030
Tel: 001 203 865 0814
Postcards

Roberts, Mike,
4416 Foxfire Way,
Fort Worth,
Texas 76133
Tel: 001 817 294 2133
Electric Fans

Jo Anne Welsh,
PO Box 222,
Riverdale, MD 20738
Tel: 001 301 779 6181
Chintz ware

DIRECTORY OF MARKETS & CENTRES

London

Alfies Antique Market,
13-25 Church Street,
NW8 8DT
Tel: 0171 723 6066

Angel Arcade,
116-118 Islington
High Street,
Camden Passage, N1 8EG

Antiquarius Antique
Market,
131/141 King's Road,
Chelsea, SW3 5ST

Antiques & Collectors
Corner, North Piazza,
Covent Garden, WC2E 8HB

Bermondsey Antiques
Warehouse,
173 Bermondsey Street,
SE1 3UW
Tel: 0171 407 2040/4250

Bond Street Antiques
Centre,
124 New Bond Street,
W1Y 9AE
Tel: 0171 351 5353

Chelsea Antique Market,
253 King's Road, SW3 5EL
Tel: 0171 352 1720

Chenil Galleries,
181-183 King's Road,
SW3 5EB

Corner Portobello Antiques
Supermarket,
Westbourne Grove, W11 2PS
Tel: 0171 727 2027

Cutler Street Antiques
Market,
Goulston Street,
Nr Aldgate End, E1 7TP

Dixons Antique Centre,
471 Upper Richmond Road
West, East Sheen,
SW14 7PU

Franklin's Camberwell
Antiques Market,
161 Camberwell Road,
SE5 0HB.
Tel: 0171 703 8089

Georgian Village Antiques
Market,
100 Wood Street,
Walthamstow, E17 3HX

Good Fairy Open Market,
100 Portobello Road,
W11 2QD
Tel: 0171 351 5950/221 8977

Grays Antique Market,
58 Davies Street, W1Y 1AR
Tel: 0171 629 7034

Grays Mews,
1-7 Davies Street, W1Y 1LL
Tel: 0171 629 7034

Grays Portobello,
138 Portobello Road,
W11 2DZ
Tel: 0171 221 3069

Greenwich Antiques
Market,
Greenwich High Road, SE10
Tel: 0171 237 1318

Hampstead Antique
Emporium,
12 Heath Street,
Hampstead, NW3 6TE

Kensington Antique Centre,
58-60 Kensington Church
Street, W8 4DB
Tel: 0171 376 0425

Mall Antiques Arcade,
359 Upper Street,
Islington, N1 0PD

Northcote Road Antiques,
155a Northcote Road,
Battersea,
SW11 6QB
Tel: 0171 228 6850

Old Crowther Market,
282 North End Road,
Fulham, SW6 1NH
Tel: 0171 610 3610

Peckham Indoor Market,
Rye Lane Bargain Centre,
48 Rye Lane,
Peckham, SE15 5BY
Tel: 0171 246 3639

Pierrepoint Arcade,
Camden Passage,
N1 8DU
Tel: 0171 359 0190

Rochefort Antique Gallery,
32/34 The Green,
Winchmore Hill,
N21 1AY

Roger's Antiques Gallery,
65 Portobello Road,
W11 2QB
Tel: 0171 351 5353

Steptoes Yard West Market,
52a Goldhawk Road,
W12 8DH
Tel: 0171 602 2699

World Famous Portobello
Market,
177 Portobello Road,
W11 2DY
Tel: 0171 221 4964

York Arcade,
80 Islington High Street,
N1 8EQ
Tel: 0171 833 2640

Avon

Bartlett Street Antique
Centre,
5-10 Bartlett Street,
Bath, BA1 2QZ
Tel: 01225 466689

Bristol Antique Market,
St Nicholas Markets,
The Exchange,
Corn Street,
Bristol, BS1 1HQ

Clifton Antiques Market,
26/28 The Mall, Clifton,
Bristol, BS8 4DS
Tel: 0117 974 1627

Great Western Antique
Centre,
Bartlett Street,
Bath, BA1 2QZ
Tel: 01225 424243

Bedfordshire

Dunstable Antique Centre,
38a West Street,
Dunstable, LU6 1TA
Tel: 01582 696953

Woburn Abbey Antiques
Centre,
Woburn Abbey,
MK43 0TP
Tel: 01525 290350

Berkshire

Hungerford Arcade,
26 High Street,
Hungerford, RG17 0NF
Tel: 01488 683701

Lodden Lily Antiques,
1 High Street,
Twyford, RG10 9AB
Tel: 01734 342161

Reading Emporium,
1a Merchant Place
(off Friar Street),
Reading, RG1 1DT
Tel: 01734 590290

Buckinghamshire

Amersham Antique
Collectors Centre,
20-22 Whielden Street,
Old Amersham,
HP7 0HT
Tel: 01494 431282

Antiques at Wendover,
The Old Post Office,
25 High Street,
Wendover,
HP22 6DU
Tel: 01296 625335

Bell Street Antiques
Centre,
20/22 Bell Street,
Princes Risborough,
HP27 0AD
Tel: 01844 43034

Olney Antiques Centre,
Rose Court,
off Market Square,
Olney, MK46 4BA
Tel: 01234 712172

Tingewick Antiques Centre,
Main Street,
Tingewick,
MK18 4NN
Tel: 01280 847922/848219

Winslow Antique Centre,
15 Market Square,
Winslow, MK18 3AB
Tel: 01296 714540/714055

Cambridgeshire

Collectors Market,
Dales Brewery,
Gwydir Street
(off Mill Road),
Cambridge CB1 2LJ

Fitzwilliam Antiques
Centre,
Fitzwilliam Street,
Peterborough, PE1 2R
Tel: 01733 65415

Willingham Antiques &
Collectors' Market,
25-29 Green Street,
Willingham,
CB4 5JA
Tel: 01954 260283

Channel Islands

Union Street Antique
Market,
8 Union Street, St Helier,
Jersey, JE2 3RF
Tel: 01534 73805/22475

Cheshire

Davenham Antique
Centre,
461 London Road,
Davenham,
Northwick, CW9 8NA
Tel: 01606 44350

Nantwich Antique Centre,
The Manor House,
7 Beam Street,
Nantwich, CW5 5LR
Tel: 01270 610615

Stancie Cutler Antique &
Collectors Fair,
Town Hall,
Sutton Coldfield, B73 6AB
Tel: 01270 624288

Cornwall

New Generation Antique
Market,
61/62 Chapel Street,
Penzance, TR18 4AE
Tel: 01736 63267

Waterfront Antique
Complex, 1st Floor,
4 Quay Street,
Falmouth, TR11 3HH
Tel: 01326 311491

Cumbria

Carlisle Antique & Craft
Centre,
Cecil Hall, Cecil Street,
Carlisle, CA1 1NT
Tel: 01228 21970

Derbyshire

Derby Antique Centre,
11 Friargate,
Derby, DE1 1BU
Tel: 01332 385002

Derby Antiques Market,
52-56 Curzon Street,
Derby, DE1 1LP

Glossop Antique Centre,
Brookfield,
Glossop, SK13 9JE
Tel: 01457 863904

Devon

Abingdon House Antiques,
136 High Street,
Honiton, EX14 8UP
Tel: 01404 42108

Barbican Antiques Centre,
82-84 Vauxhall Street,
Barbican,
Plymouth, PL4 0EX
Tel: 01752 266927

Barnes House Antiques
Centre,
11a West Row,
Wimborne Minster,
BH21 1LA
Tel: 01202 886275

Dorset

Antique Centre,
837-839 Christchurch Road,
East Boscombe,
Bournemouth,
BH7 6AR
Tel: 01202 421052

Bridport Antique Centre,
5 West Allington,
Bridport, DT6 5BJ
Tel: 01308 25885

Gold Hill Antiques &
Collectables,
3 Gold Hill Parade,
Gold Hill,
Shaftesbury,
SP7 8LY
Tel: 01747 54050

Sherborne Antique Centre,
Mattar Arcade,
17 Newlands,
Sherborne, DT9 3JG
Tel: 01935 813464

R A. Swift & Son,
St Andrews Hall,
4c Wolverton Road,
Bournemouth, BH7 6HT

Wimborne Antique Centre,
Newborough Road,
Wimborne, BH21 1RB
Tel: 01202 841251

Essex

Battlesbridge Antiques
Centre,
The Green,
Chelmsford Road,
Battlesbridge,
Wickford, SS11 7RF

Essex Antiques Centre,
Priory Street,
Colchester, CO1 2PY
Tel: 01206 871150

Grays Galleries Antiques
& Collectors Centre,
23 Lodge Lane,
Grays, RM17 5RY
Tel: 01375 374883

Townsford Mill Antiques
Centre,
The Causeway,
Halstead, CO9 1ET
Tel: 01787 474451

Trinity Antiques Centre,
7 Trinity Street,
Colchester, CO1 1JN
Tel: 01206 577775

Gloucestershire

Antiques Emporium,
The Old Chapel,
Long Street,
Tetbury, GL8 8AA
Tel: 01666 505281

Charlton Kings Antique
Centre,
199 London Road,
Charlton Kings,
Cheltenham, GL52 6HU
Tel: 01242 510672

Cheltenham Antique
Market,
54 Suffolk Road,
Cheltenham, GL50 2AQ
Tel: 01242 529812

Cirencester Antique Market,
Market Place,
Cirencester, GL7 2PY
Tel: 0171 262 5003 (Fri)

Cotswold Antiques Centre,
The Square,
Stow-on-the-Wold, GL54 1AB
Tel: 01451 31585

Gloucester Antiques Centre,
Severn Road,
Gloucester, GL1 2LE
Tel: 01452 529716

Painswick Antique Centre,
New Street,
Painswick, GL6 6XH
Tel: 01452 812431

Tolsey Antique Centre,
Tolsey Lane,
Tewkesbury, GL20 5AE
Tel: 01684 294091

Windsor House Antiques
Centre, High Street,
Moreton-in-Marsh,
GL56 0AH
Tel: 01608 650993

Greater Manchester

Antiques Gallery,
Royal Exchange Shopping
Centre, St Anne's Square,
Exchange Street, M2 7DB

Levenshulme Antiques
Hypermarket,
Levenshulme Town Hall,
965 Stockport Road,
Levenshulme, M9 3NP

Hampshire

Creightons Antique Centre,
23-25 Bell Street,
Romsey, SO51 8GY
Tel: 01794 522758

Folly Antiques Centre,
Folly Market,
College Street,
Petersfield, GU31 4AD
Tel: 01730 265937

Kingsley Barn Antique
Centre, Church Road,
Eversley, Nr Wokingham,
RG27 0PX
Tel: 01734 328518

Lymington Antiques Centre,
76 High Street,
Lymington, SO41 9AL
Tel: 01590 670934

Squirrel Collectors Centre,
9 New Street,
Basingstoke, RG21 1DE
Tel: 01256 464885

Hereford & Worcester

Antique Market,
6 Market Street,
Hay-on-Wye,
HR3 5AF
Tel: 01497 820175

Galleries Antiques Centre,
Pickwicks,
503 Evesham Road,
Crabbs Cross,
Redditch, B97 5JJ

Hereford Antique Centre,
128 Widemarsh Street,
Hereford, HR4 9HN
Tel: 01432 266242

Leominster Antiques
Market, 14 Broad Street,
Leominster, HR6 8BS
Tel: 01568 612189

Worcester Antiques Centre,
Reindeer Court,
Mealcheapen Street,
Worcester, WR1 4DF
Tel: 01905 610680 (Col)

Hertfordshire

Bushey Antiques Centre,
39 High Street,
Bushey, WD2 1BD
Tel: 0181 950 5040

By George Antique Centre,
23 George Street,
St Albans, AL3 4ES
Tel: 01727 853032

Humberside

New Pocklington Antiques
Centre,
26 George Street,
Pocklington, York,
YO4 2DQ
Tel: 01759 303032

Kent

Antiques Centre,
120 London Road,
Sevenoaks, TN13 1BA
Tel: 01732 452104

Beckenham Antique
Market,
Old Council Hall,
Bromley Road,
Beckenham, BR3 2JE
Tel: 0181 777 6300

Bromley Antique Market,
Widmore Road,
Bromley, BR1 1RL

Burgate Antiques Centre,
10 Burgate,
Canterbury, CT1 2HG
Tel: 01227 456500

Castle Antiques Centre,
1 London Road,
Westerham, TN16 1BB
Tel: 01959 562492

Cranbrook Antique Centre,
High Street,
Cranbrook, TN17 3DN
Tel: 01580 712173

Heirloom Antiques,
68 High Street,
Tenterden, TN30 6AU
Tel: 01580 765535

Hythe Antique Centre,
5 High Street,
Hythe, CT21 5AB
Tel: 01303 269043/269643

Malthouse Arcade,
Malthouse Hill,
Hythe, CT21 5BW
Tel: 01303 260103

Noah's Ark Antiques Centre,
5 King Street,
Sandwich, CT13 9BT
Tel: 01304 611144

Paraphernalia Antiques &
Collectors Centre,
171 Widmore Road,
Bromley, BR1 3BS
Tel: 0181 318 2997

Sandgate Antiques Centre,
61-63 High Street,
Sandgate, CT20 3AH
Tel: 01303 248987

Tenterden Antiques Centre,
66-66A High Street,
Tenterden, TN30 6AU
Tel: 01580 765655/765885

Thanet Antiques Trade
Centre,
45 Albert Street,
Ramsgate, CT11 9EX
Tel: 01843 597336

Tudor Cottage Antiques
Centre,
22-23 Shipbourne Road,
Tonbridge, TN10 3DN
Tel: 01732 351719

Tunbridge Wells Antique
Centre,
12 Union Square,
The Pantiles,
Tunbridge Wells, TN4 8HE
Tel: 01892 533708

Lancashire

Bolton Antiques Centre,
Premier Stores,
Central Street,
Bolton, BL1 2AB
Tel: 01204 362694

Bolton Antiques Centre,
Central Street,
Bolton, BL1 2AB
Tel: 01204 362694

Bygone Times,
Times House, Grove Mill,
The Green,
Eccleston, PR7 5PD

Darwen Antique Centre,
Provident Hall, The Green,
Darwen, BB3 1PW
Tel: 01254 760565

GB Antiques Centre,
Lancaster Leisure Park,
Wyresdale Road,
Lancaster, LA1 3LA
Tel: 01524 844734

Pendle Antique Centre,
Union Mill, Watt Street,
Sabden, BB7 9ED
Tel: 01282 776311

Preston Antique Centre,
The Mill, New Hall Lane,
Preston, PR1 5UH
Tel: 01772 794498

Leicestershire

Boulevard Antique Centre,
The Old Dairy,
Western Boulevard,
Leicester, LE3 5PT
Tel: 0116 254 1201

Oxford Street Antiques
Centre Ltd,
16-26 Oxford Street,
Leicester, LE1 5XU
Tel: 01533 553006

Lincolnshire

Aswell Street Antique
Centre, Louth, LN11 9HP
Tel: 01507 600366

Boston Antiques Centre,
12 West Street,
Boston, PE21 8QH
Tel: 01205 361510

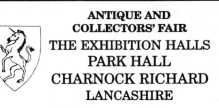

Eastgate Antiques Centre,
6 Eastgate,
Lincoln, LN2 1QA
Tel: 01522 544404

Hemswell Antiques
Centre,
Caenby Corner Estate,
Hemswell Cliff,
Gainsborough,
DN21 5TJ
Tel: 01427 668389

Irby Antique Centre,
Pinfold Lane,
Irby in the Marsh,
PE24 5AX
Tel: 01754 810943

Lincolnshire Antiques
Centre,
26 Bridge Street,
Horncastle, LN9 5HZ
Tel: 01507 527794

Portobellow Row Antiques
Centre,
93-95 High Street,
Boston, PE21 8TA
Tel: 01205 369456

Stamford Antiques Centre,
The Exchange Hall,
Broad Street,
Stamford, PE9 1PJ
Tel: 01780 62605

Sue's Collectables,
61 Victoria Road,
Mabelthorpe, LN12 2AF
Tel: 01507 472406

Merseyside

Hoylake Antique Centre,
128-130 Market Street,
Wirral, L47 3BX
Tel: 0151 632 4231

Middlesex

Calvers Collectables of
Ruislip, 156 High Street,
Ruislip, HA4 8LJ
Tel: 0181 561 4517

Hampton Village Antiques
Centre,
76 Station Road,
Hampton, TW12 2AX
Tel: 0181 979 5871

Jay's Antique Centre,
25/29 High Street,
Harefield, UB9 6BX
Tel: 01895 824738

Norfolk

Angel Antique Centre,
Pansthorn Farmhouse,
Redgrave Road,
South Lopham,
Nr Diss, IP22 2HL

Cloisters Antiques Fair,
St Andrew's & Blackfriars
Hall, St Andrew's Plain,
Norwich,
NR3 1AU
Tel: 01603 628477

Coltishall Antiques
Centre,
High Street,
Coltishall, NR12 7AA
Tel: 01603 738306

Fakenham Antique
Centre,
Old Congregational Chapel,
14 Norwich Road,
Fakenham, NR21 8AZ
Tel: 01328 862941

Gostling's Antique Centre,
13 Market Hill,
Diss, IP22 3JZ
Tel: 01379 650360

Old Granary Antique &
Collectors' Centre,
King Staithe Lane,
off Queen's Street,
King's Lynn, PE30 1LZ
Tel: 01553 775509

St Mary's Antique Centre,
Duke Street,
Norwich, NR3 3AF
Tel: 01603 612582

Wells Antique Centre,
The Old Mill,
Maryland, NR23 1LX
Tel: 01328 711433

Wymondham Antique
Centre, No. 1 Town Green,
Wymondham, NR18 0PN
Tel: 01953 604817

Northamptonshire

Antiques & Bric-a-Brac
Market,
Market Square,
Town Centre,
Wellingborough,
NN8 1AR
Tel: 01905 611321

Finedon Antiques Centre,
Church Street, Finedon,
Nr Wellingborough,
NN9 5NA
Tel: 01933 681260

Village Antique Market,
62 High Street,
Weedon, NN7 4QD
Tel: 01327 42015

Northumberland

Colmans of Hexham,
15 St Mary's Chare,
Hexham, NE46 1NQ
Tel: 01434 603811/2

Nottinghamshire

Castle Gate Antiques
Centre,
55 Castle Gate,
Newark, NG24 1BE
Tel: 01636 700076

Newark Antique
Warehouse,
Kelham Road,
Newark, NG24 1BU
Tel: 01636 74869

Newark Antiques Centre,
Regent House,
Lombard Street,
Newark, NG24 1XP
Tel: 01636 605504

Nottingham Antique
Centre,
British Rail Goods Yard,
London Road,
Nottingham, NG2 3AE
Tel: 0115 950 4504/5548

Top Hat Antiques Centre,
66-72 Derby Road,
Nottingham, NG1 5FD
Tel: 0115 941 9143

Oxfordshire

Antique & Collectors
Market,
Town Hall,
Thame, OX9 3DP
Tel: 01844 28205

Chipping Norton Antique
Centre,
Ivy House, Middle Row,
Chipping Norton,
OX7 5NH
Tel: 01608 644212

Cotswold Gateway Antique
Centre,
Cheltenham Road,
Burford Roundabout,
Burford, OX18 4JA
Tel: 01993 823678

Deddington Antique
Centre,
Laurel House, Bull Ring,
Market Square,
Deddington, OX15 0SE

Friday Street Antique
Centre,
2 & 4 Friday Street,
Henley-on-Thames,
RG9 1AH
Tel: 01491 574104

Goring Antique Centre,
16 High Street,
Goring-on-Thames,
RG8 9AR
Tel: 01491 873300

Henley Antique Centre,
Rotherfield Arcade,
2-4 Reading Road,
Henley-on-Thames,
RG9 1AG
Tel: 01491 411468

Lamb Arcade,
High Street,
Wallingford,
OX10 0BS
Tel: 01491 835166

Oxford Antiques Centre,
The Jam Factory,
27 Park End Street,
Oxford, OX1 1HU
Tel: 01865 251075

Oxford Antiques Market,
Gloucester Green,
Oxford, OX1 2DF
Tel: 01865 242216

Scotland

Bath Street Antique
Galleries,
203 Bath Street,
Glasgow, G2 4HG
Tel: 0141 248 4220

Corner House Antiques,
217 St Vincent Street,
Glasgow, G2 5QY
Tel: 0141 248 2560

King's Court Antiques
Centre & Market,
King Street,
Glasgow, G1 5RB
Tel: 0141 552 7854/7856

Past & Present,
46 Boyd Street,
Largs, KA30 8LE
Tel: 01475 675533

Victorian Village,
53 & 57 West Regent Street,
Glasgow, G2 2AE
Tel: 0141 332 0808

Shropshire

Cleobury Mortimer
Antique Centre,
Childe Road,
Cleobury Mortimer,
Nr Kidderminster,
DY14 8PA
Tel: 01299 270513

Ironbridge Antique Centre,
Dale End, Ironbridge,
Telford, TF8 7DW
Tel: 01952 433784

Pepper Lane Antique
Centre,
Pepper Lane,
Ludlow, SY8 1PX
Tel: 01584 876494

Shrewsbury Antique
Centre,
15 Princess House,
The Square,
Shrewsbury,
SY1 1JZ
Tel: 01743 247704

Shrewsbury Antique
Market,
Frankwell Quay
Warehouse,
Shrewsbury,
SY3 8LG
Tel: 01743 350916

St Leonard's Antiques
Centre,
Corve Street,
Ludlow, SY8 1DL
Tel: 01584 875573

Stretton Antiques Market,
36 Sandford Avenue,
Church Stretton,
SY6 6BH
Tel: 01694 723718

Telford Antique Centre,
High Street, Wellington,
Telford, TF1 1JW
Tel: 01952 256450

Welsh Bridge Antiques
Centre,
135 Frankwell,
Shrewsbury, SY3 8JX
Tel: 01743 248822

County Antiques Centre,
21/23 West Street,
Ilminster, TA19 9AA
Tel: 01460 54151

Dulverton Antique Centre,
Lower Town Hall,
10 Fore Street,
Dulverton, TA22 9EX
Tel: 01398 23522

Guildhall Antique Market,
The Guildhall, Fore Street,
Chard, TA20 1PP

Somerset

Taunton Silver Street
Antiques Centre,
27/29 Silver Street,
Taunton, TA1 3DH

Staffordshire

Antique Centre,
128 High Street,
Kinver, DY7 6HQ
Tel: 01384 877441

Barclay House Antiques,
14-16 Howard Place, Shelton,
Stoke-on-Trent, ST1 4NQ
Tel: 01782 274747

Rugeley Antique Centre,
161-3 Main Road,
Brereton,
Nr Rugeley, WS15 1DX
Tel: 01889 577166

Stoke-on-Trent Antique &
Collectors Centre,
The Potteries Antique
Centre,
271 Waterloo Road,
Cobridge, Stoke on Trent,
ST6 3HR
Tel: 01782 201455

Tudor of Lichfield Antique
Centre,
Lichfield House, Bore Street,
Lichfield, WS13 6LL
Tel: 01543 263951

Tutbury Mill Antiques,
6 Lower High Street,
Tutbury, Nr Burton-on-
Trent, DE13 9LU
Tel: 01283 815999

Suffolk

Debenham Antique
Centre,
The Forresters Hall,
High Street,
Debenham, IP14 6QH
Tel: 01728 860777

Old Town Hall Antiques
Centre,
High Street,
Needham Market, IP6 8AL
Tel: 01449 720773

Risby Barn Antique
Centre,
Risby, Bury St Edmunds,
IP28 6QU
Tel: 01284 811126

Waveney Antiques Centre,
Peddars Lane,
Beccles, NR34 9UE
Tel: 01502 716147

Surrey

Antiquarius Antique
Centre,
56 West Street,
Dorking, RH4 1BS
Tel: 01306 743398

Antiques Arcade,
22 Richmond Hill,
Richmond, TW10 6QX
Tel: 0181 940 2035

Antiques Arcade,
77 Bridge Road,
East Molesey, KT8 9HH
Tel: 0181 979 7954

Antiques Centre,
22 Haydon Place,
Corner of Martyr Road,
Guildford, GU1 4LL
Tel: 01483 67817

Antiques & Interiors,
64 Station Road East,
Oxted, RH8 0PG
Tel: 01883 712806

Cambridge Parade
Antiques,
229-231 Carshalton Road,
Carshalton, SM5 3PZ
Tel: 0181 643 0014

Dorking Antiques Centre,
17/18 West Street,
Dorking, RH4 1DD
Tel: 01306 740915

Duke's Yard Antique
Market,
1a Duke Street,
Richmond, TW9 1HP
Tel: 0181 332 1051

Farnham Antique Centre,
27 South Street,
Farnham, GU9 7QU
Tel: 01252 724475

Fern Cottage Antique
Centre,
28/30 High Street,
Thames Ditton, KT7 0RY
Tel: 0181 398 2281

Maltings Monthly Market,
Bridge Square,
Farnham, GU9 7QR
Tel: 01252 726234

Old Smithy Antique
Centre,
7 High Street,
Merstham, RH1 3BA
Tel: 01737 642306

Reigate Antiques Arcade,
57 High Street,
Reigate, RH2 9AE
Tel: 01737 222654

Surrey Antiques Centre,
10 Windsor Street,
Chertsey, KT16 8AS
Tel: 01932 563313

Victoria & Edward
Antiques Centre,
61 West Street,
Dorking, RH4 1BS
Tel: 01306 889645

Wood's Wharf Antiques
Bazaar,
56 High Street,
Haslemere, GU27 2LA
Tel: 01428 642125

Sussex

Antique Market,
Leaf Hall, Seaside,
Eastbourne,
BN22 7NH
Tel: 01323 27530

Antiques & Collectors
Market,
Old Orchard Building,
Old House, Adversane,
Nr Billingshurst,
RH14 9JJ
Tel: 01403 783594

Bexhill Antiques Centre,
Old Town,
Bexhill, TN40 2HA

Chateaubriand Antiques
Centre,
High Street,
Burwash, TN19 7ES
Tel: 01435 882535

Churchill Antiques Centre,
6 Station Street,
Lewes, BN7 2DA
Tel: 01273 474842

Cliffe Antiques Centre,
47 Cliffe High Street,
Lewes, BN7 2AN
Tel: 01273 473266

Cliffe Gallery Antique
Centre,
39 Cliffe High Street,
Lewes, BN7 2AN
Tel: 01273 471877

Collectors Market,
The Enterprise Centre,
Station Parade,
Eastbourne, BN21 1BE
Tel: 01323 32690

Copthorne Group
Antiques,
Copthorne Bank,
Crawley, RH10 3QX
Tel: 01342 712802

Courtyard Antiques
Market,
13, 15 & 17 High Street,
Seaford, BN25 1PE
Tel: 01323 892091

Eagle House Antiques
Market,
Market Square,
Midhurst, GU29 9NJ
Tel: 01730 812718

Foundry Lane Antiques
Centre,
15 Cliffe High Street,
Lewes, BN7 2AH
Tel: 01273 475361

George Street Antiques
Centre,
47 George Street,
Old Town,
Hastings, TN34 3EA
Tel: 01424 429339

Hastings Antique Centre,
59-61 Norman Road,
St Leonards-on-Sea,
TN38 0EG
Tel: 01424 428561

Horsebridge Antiques
Centre,
1 North Street,
Horsebridge,
Nr Hailsham, BN27 1DQ
Tel: 01323 844414

Kollect-O-Mania,
25 Trafalgar Street,
Brighton, BN1 4EQ
Tel: 01273 694229

Lewes Antique Centre,
20 Cliffe High Street,
Lewes, BN7 2AH
Tel: 01273 476148

Mamies Antiques Centre,
5 River Road,
Arundel, BN18 9DH
Tel: 01903 882012

Midhurst Antiques Market,
Knockhundred Row,
Midhurst, GU29 9DQ
Tel: 01730 814231

Mint Arcade,
71 The Mint,
Rye, TN31 7EW
Tel: 01797 225952

Newhaven Flea Market,
28 South Way,
Newhaven, BN9 9LA
Tel: 01273 517207/516065

Nineveh House Antiques,
Tarrant Street,
Arundel, BN18 9DG
Tel: 01903 884307

Old Town Hall Antique
Centre,
52 Ocklynge Road,
Eastbourne, BN21 1PR
Tel: 01323 416016

Petworth Antique Market,
East Street,
Petworth, GU28 0AB
Tel: 01798 342073

Pharoahs Antiques Centre,
28 South Street,
Eastbourne, BN21 4XB
Tel: 01323 38655

Seaford's Barn Collectors
Market & Studio Book Shop,
The Barn, Church Lane,
Seaford, BN25 1HJ
Tel: 01323 890010

Shirley Mostyns Antique Centre, 64 Brighton Road, Lancing, BN15 8ET
Tel: 01903 752961

Treasure House Antiques & Collectors Market, 31b High Street, Arundel, BN18 9AG
Tel: 01903 883101

Upstairs Downstairs Antique Centre, 29 Tarrant Street, Arundel, BN18 9DG
Tel: 01903 883749

Tyne & Wear

Blaydon Antique Centre, Bridge House, Bridge Street, Blaydon-on-Tyne, NE21 4JJ

Vine Lane Antique Centre, 17 Vine Lane, Newcastle-upon-Tyne, NE1 7PW
Tel: 0191 232 9832

Wales

Cardiff Antique Centre, 69-71 St Mary Street, Cardiff, CF1 1FA
Tel: 01222 30970

Jacobs Antique Centre, West Canal Wharf, Cardiff, CF1 5DB
Tel: 01222 390939

Offa's Dyke Antique Centre, 4 High Street, Knighton, Powys, LD7 1AT
Tel: 01547 528635

Pembroke Antique Centre, The Hall, Hamilton Terrace, Pembroke, SA71 4DE
Tel: 01646 687017

Second Chance Antiques & Collectables Centre, Ala Road, Pwllheli, Gwynedd, LL53 5BL
Tel: 01758 612210

Swansea Antique Centre, 21 Oxford Street, Swansea, SA1 3AQ
Tel: 01792 466854

Warwickshire

Antiques Centre, High Street, Bidford-on-Avon, Alcester, B49 5AE
Tel: 01789 773680

Antiques Etc, 22 Railway Terrace, Rugby, CV21 3LJ
Tel: 01789 773680

Barn Antiques Centre, Station Road, Long Marston, Nr Stratford-upon-Avon, CV37 8RB
Tel: 01789 721399

Dunchurch Antique Centre, 16/16a Daventry Road, Dunchurch, Nr Rugby, CV22 6NS
Tel: 01788 817147

Leamington Pine & Antiques Centre, 20 Regent Street, Leamington Spa, CV32 5EH
Tel: 01926 429679

Malthouse Antiques Centre 4 Market Place, Alcester, B49 5AE
Tel: 01789 764032

Meer Street Antiques Centre, Meer Street, Stratford upon Avon, CV37 6QB
Tel: 01789 297249

Old Cornmarket Antiques Centre, The, 70 Market Place, Warwick, CV34 4SD
Tel: 01926 419119

Smith Street Antique Centre, 7 Smith Street, Warwick, CV34 4JA
Tel: 01926 497864/400554

Spa Antiques Market, 4 Windsor Street, Leamington Spa, CV32 5EB
Tel: 01926 22927

Stratford Antiques Centre, 59-60 Ely Street, Stratford-upon-Avon, CV37 6LN
Tel: 01789 204180

Vintage Antique Centre, 36 Market Place, Warwick, CV34 4SH
Tel: 01926 491527

Warwick Antique Centre, 20-22 High Street, Warwick, CV34 4AX
Tel: 01926 495704

West Midlands

Birmingham Antique Centre, 141 Bromsgrove Street, Birmingham, B5 6RG
Tel: 0121 692 1414/622 2145

City of Birmingham Antique Market, St Martins Market, Edgbaston Street, Birmingham, B5 4QL
Tel: 0121 267 4636

Wiltshire

Walsall Antique Centre, Digbeth Arcade, Walsall, WS1 1RE

Antique & Collectors Market, 37 Catherine Street, Salisbury, SP1 2DH

Avon Bridge Antiques & Collectors Market, United Reform Church Hall, Fisherton Street, Salisbury, SP2 7RG

Marlborough Parade Antiques Centre, The Parade, Marlborough, SN8 1NE
Tel: 01672 515331

Micawber's, 53 Fisherton Street, Salisbury, SP2 7SU
Tel: 01722 337822

Salisbury Antiques Market, 37 Catherine Street, Salisbury, SP1 2DH
Tel: 01722 326033

Yorkshire

Ginnel Antique Centre, off Parliament Street, Harrogate, HG1 2RB
Tel: 01423 508857

Grove Collectors Centre, Grove Road, Harrogate, HG1 5EP
Tel: 01423 561680

Halifax Antiques Centre, Queens Road/Gibbet Street, Halifax, HX1 4LR
Tel: 01422 366657

Malton Antique Market, 2 Old Maltongate, Malton, YO17 0EG
Tel: 01653 692732

Memory Lane, 69 Wakefield Road, Sowerby Bridge, HX7 5EN
Tel: 01422 833223

Micklegate Antiques Market, 73 Micklegate, York, YO1 1LJ
Tel: 01904 644438

Montpelier Mews Antique Market, Montpelier Street, Harrogate, HG1 2TG
Tel: 01423 530484

West Park Antiques Pavilion, 20 West Park, Harrogate, HG1 1BJ
Tel: 01423 563658

York Antique Centre, 2 Lendal, York, YO1 2AA
Tel: 01904 641445

DIRECTORY OF COLLECTORS' CLUBS

This directory is in no way complete. If you wish to be included in next year's directory or if you have a change of address or telephone number, please inform us by November 1st, 1997. Entries will be repeated in subsequent editions unless we are requested otherwise.

Antiquarian Horological Society
New House, High Street, Ticehurst,
East Sussex TN5 7AL
Tel: 01580 200155

Antique Collectors' Club
5 Church Street, Woodbridge,
Suffolk IP12 1DS

Arms and Armour Society
Honorary Secretary Anthony Dove,
PO Box 10232, London SW19 9ZD

Association of Bottled Beer Collectors
Thurwood, 5 Springfield Close, Woodsetts,
Worksop, Notts S81 8QD Tel: 01909 562603

Association of Comic Enthusiasts: ACE!
8 Silverdale, Sydenham, London SE26 4SJJ

Avon Magpies Club
13 Coleridge Road, Paulsgrove, Portsmouth,
Hampshire PO6 4PB Tel: 01705 642393

Badge Collectors' Circle
3 Ellis Close, Quorn, Nr Loughborough,
Leicestershire LE12 8SH Tel: 01509 412094

British Art Medal Society
c/o Dept of Coins and Medals, The British
Museum, London WC1B 3DG
Tel: 0171 323 8170 Extn 8227

British Association of Sound Collections
National Sound Archive, 29 Exhibition Road,
London SW7 2AS
Tel: 0171 589 6603

British Beermat Collectors' Society
30 Carters Orchard, Quedgeley,
Glos GL2 6WB
Tel: 01452 721643

British Button Society
The Old Dairy, Newton, Kettering,
Northants NN14 1BW

British Compact Collectors' Society
PO Box 131, Woking, Surrey GU24 9YR

British Iron Collectors
87 Wellsway, Bath, Avon BA2 4RU
Tel: 01225 428068

British Matchbox Label and Booklet Society
Mr D. A. Alderton (Hon. Sec), 122 High Street,
Melbourn, Cambs SG8 6AL

British Model Soldier Society
22 Lynwood Road, Ealing, London W5 1JJ

British Numismatic Society
The Hunterian Museum, Glasgow University,
University Avenue, Glasgow, Scotland G12 8QQ

British Stickmakers' Guild
44a Eccles Road, Chapel-en-le-Frith,
Derbyshire SK12 6RG
Tel: 01298 815291

British Teddy Bear Association
PO Box 290, Brighton, Sussex BN2 1DR

British Telecom Heritage Group
Tamarisk, 2 Gig Lane, Heathand Reach,
Leyton Buzzard, Bedfordshire LU7 0BQ
Tel: 01525 237676

British Telecom Phonecard Collectors' Club
Camelford House, 87 Albert Embankment,
London SE1 7TS

British Watch & Clock Collectors' Association
5 Cathedral Lane, Truro, Cornwall TR1 2QS
Tel: 01872 41953

Buttonhook Society
2 Romney Place, Maidstone, Kent ME15 6LE

Calculators Collectors' Club
77 Welland Road, Tonbridge, Kent TN10 3TA

Cambridge Paperweight Circle
34 Huxley Road, Welling, Kent DA16 2EW
Tel: 0181 303 4663

Cartophilic Society of Great Britain
116 Hillview Road, Ensbury Park, Bournemouth,
Dorset BH10 5BJ

Charlotte Rhead (Newsletter)
c/o 49 Honeybourne Road, Halesowen,
West Midlands B63 3ET

Chintz Club of America
The Chintz Collector, PO Box 6126, Folsom,
CA 95763 USA Tel/Fax: 001 (916) 985 6762

**Cigarette Packet Collectors' Club
of Great Britain**
Nathan's Pipe Shop, 60 Hill Rise, Richmond,
Surrey TW10 6UA Tel: 0181 940 2404

**City of London Photograph and
Gramophone Society**
63 Vicarage Way, Colnbrook, Bucks S13 0JY

Clarice Cliff Collectors' Club
Fantasque House, Tennis Drive, The Park,
Nottingham, Notts NG7 1AE

Comic Enthusiasts' Society
80 Silverdale, Sydenham, London SE26 4SJ

Comics Journal
17 Hill Street, Colne, Lancashire BB8 0DH
Tel: 01282 865468

Commemorative Collectors' Society
Lumless House, Gainsborough Road, Winthorpe,
Nr Newark, Notts NG24 2NR
Tel: 01636 71377

Corgi Collector Club
PO Box 323, Swansea, Wales SA1 1BJ
Tel: 01792 476902

Costume Society
c/o The State Apartments,
Kensington Palace, London W8 4PX
Tel: 0171 937 9561

Crested Circle
42 Douglas Road, Tolworth, Surbiton,
Surrey KT6 7SA

Cricket Memorabilia Society
29 Highclere Road, Higher Crumpsall,
Gt Manchester M8 4WH Tel: 0161 740 3714

Crunch Club (Breakfast Cereal Collectables)
15 Hermitage Road, Parkstone, Poole,
Dorset BH14 0QG Tel: 01202 715854

Disney Enthusiasts' Club
Magical Moments & Memories, 31 Rowan Way,
Exwick, Exeter, Devon EX4 2DT
Tel & Fax: 01392 431653

Doll Club of Great Britain
16E Chalwyn Industrial Estate, St Clements
Road, Parkstone, Poole, Dorset BH15 3PE

Embroiderers' Guild
Apartment 41, Hampton Court Palace,
East Molesey, Surrey KT8 9AU
Tel: 0181 943 1229

English Playing Card Society
11 Pierrepont Street, Bath, Avon BA1 1LA
Tel: 01225 465218

Fan Circle International
Sec: Mrs Joan Milligan, 'Cronk-y-Voddy',
Rectory Road, Coltishall, Norwich,
Norfolk NR12 7HF

Flag Institute
10 Vicarage Road, Chester, Cheshire CH2 3HZ
Tel: 01244 351335

Friends of Blue
10 Sea View Road, Herne Bay, Kent CT6 6JQ

Friends of Broadfield House Glass Museum
Compton Drive, Kingswinford,
West Midlands DY6 9NS
Tel: 01384 273011

Furniture History Society
c/o Dr Brian Austen, 1 Mercedes Cottages,
St John's Road, Haywards Heath,
Sussex RH16 4EH
Tel: 01444 413845

Goss Collectors' Club
31a The Crescent, Stanley Common,
Derbyshire DE7 6GL
Tel: 0115 930 0441

Hat Pin Society of Great Britain
PO Box No 74, Bozeat, Northants NN29 7JH

Historical Model Railway Society
59 Woodberry Way, London E4 7DY

Honiton Pottery Collectors' Society
(Honiton & Crown Dorset Pottery), c/o Robin
Tinkler, 12 Beehive Lane, Great Baddow,
Chelmsford, Essex CM2 9SX
Tel: 01245 353477

Hornby Railway Collectors' Association
2 Ravensmore Road, Sherwood, Nottingham,
Notts NG5 2AH

Hurdy-Gurdy Society
The Old Mill, Duntish, Dorchester,
Dorset DT2 7DR

International Bank Note Society
43 Templars Crescent, London N3 3QR

International Bond and Share Society
Hobsley House, Frodesley, Shrewsbury,
Shropshire SY5 7HD

International Collectors' of Time Association
173 Coleherne Court, Redcliffe Gardens,
London SW5 0DX

**International Correspondence of
Corkscrew Addicts**
4201 Sunflower Drive, Mississauga,
Ontario L5L 2L4, Canada

King George VI Collectors' Society
(Affiliated to the Association of British
Philatelic Societies), 98 Albany, Manor Road,
Bournemouth, Dorset BH1 3EW
Tel: 01202 551515

Knife Rest Collectors' Club
Braughingbury, Braughing, Herts SG11 2RD
Tel: 01920 822654

Lace Guild
The Hollies, 53 Audnam, Stourbridge,
West Midlands DY8 4AE

Legend Lane Collectors' Club
Albion Mill, London Road, Macclesfield,
Cheshire SK11 7SQ Tel: 01625 665010

Matchbox International Collectors' Assoc
The Toy Museum, 13a Lower Bridge Street,
Chester, Cheshire CH1 1RS Tel: 01244 345297

Mauchline Ware Collectors' Club
Unit 37, Romsey Industrial Estate,
Greatbridge Rd, Romsey, Hampshire SO51 0HR

**Memories UK, Mabel Lucie Attwell
Collectors' Club**
63 Great Whyte, Ramsey, Nr Huntingdon,
Cambs PE17 1HL Tel: 01487 814753

Merrythought International Collectors' Club
Ironbridge, Telford, Shropshire TF8 7NJ
Tel: 01952 433116

Model Railway Club
Keen House, 4 Calshot Street, London N1 9DA

Musical Box Society of Great Britain
PO Box 299, Waterbeach, Cambs CB4 4PJ

National Horse Brass Society
12 Severndale, Droitwich Spa,
Hereford & Worcs WR9 8PD

New Baxter Society
c/o Museum of Reading, Blagrave Street,
Reading, Berkshire RG1 1QH

Old Bottle Club of Great Britain
2 Strafford Avenue, Elsecar, Nr Barnsley,
South Yorkshire S74 8AA
Tel: 01226 745156

**Ophthalmic Antiques International
Collectors' Club**
3 Moor Park Road, Northwood,
Middlesex HA6 2DL

Orders and Medals Research Society
123 Turnpike Link, Croydon, Surrey CR0 5NU

Oriental Ceramic Society
30b Torrington Square, London WC1E 7JL
Tel: 0171 636 7985

Pendelfin Family Circle
Cameron Mill, Howsin Street, Burnley,
Lancashire BB10 1PP Tel: 01282 32301

Pendelfin Family Circle
Shop 28, Grove Plaza, Stirling Highway,
Peppermint Grove, Australia 6011
Tel: 09 384 9999

Pendelfin Family Circle
Fazantenlaan 29, 2610 Antwerp, Belgium
Tel: 03 440 5668

Pendelfin Family Circle
1250 Terwillegar Avenue, Oshawa, Ontario,
Canada L1J 7A5 Tel: 0101 416 723 9940

Pendelfin Family Circle
Svebi AB, Box 143, S-562 02 Taberg, Sweden
Tel: 036 656 90

The Family Circle of Pendelfin
230 Spring Street NW, Suite 1238, Atlanta,
Georgia 30303, USA
Tel: Freephone US only 1-800 872 4876

Perfume Bottles Collectors' Club
Great Western Antiques Centre, Bartlett Street,
Bath, Avon BA1 2QZ Tel: 01225 837932/310388

Pewter Society
Hunters Lodge, Paddock Close,
St Mary's Platt, Sevenoaks, Kent TN15 8NN
Tel: 01732 883314

Photographic Collectors' Club of Gt Britain
5 Station Industrial Estate, Prudhoe,
Northumberland NE42 6NP

Poole Pottery Collectors' Club
Poole Pottery Ltd, The Quay, Poole,
Dorset BH15 1RF Tel: 01202 666200

Postcard Club of Great Britain
34 Harper House, St James's Crescent,
London SW9 7LW Tel: 0171 733 0720

Pot Lid Circle, Bucks Tel: 01753 886751

Quimper Association
Odin, Benbow Way, Cowley, Uxbridge,
Middlesex UB8 2HD

Railwayana Collectors' Journal
7 Ascot Road, Moseley, Birmingham, B13 9EN

Robert Harrop Designs Collectors' Club
Coalport House, Lamledge Lane, Shifnal,
Shropshire TF11 8SD Tel: 01952 462721

Royal Doulton International Collectors' Club
Minton House, London Road, Stoke-on-Trent,
Staffordshire ST4 7QD

Royal Numismatic Society
c/o Department of Coins and Medals,
The British Museum, London WC1B 3DG
Tel: 0171 636 1555 Extn 404

Royal Winton International Collectors' Club
Dancers End, Northall, Bedfordshire LU6 2EU
Tel: 01525 220272

Scientific Instrument Society
Dawes, PO Box 15, Pershore, Hereford & Worcs
WR10 2RD Tel: 01705 812104

Shelley Group
4 Fawley Road, Regents Park, Southampton,
Hants SO2 1LL

Silhouette Collectors' Club
Flat 5, 13 Brunswick Square, Hove,
Sussex BN3 1EH Tel: 01273 735760

Silver Spoon Club
Glenleigh Park, Sticker, St Austell,
Cornwall PL26 7JD Tel/Fax: 01726 65269

Silver Study Group
The Secretary, London Tel: 0181 202 0269

Susie Cooper Collectors' Group
PO Box 7436, London N12 7QF

SylvaC Collectors' Circle
174 Portsmouth Road, Horndean, Hants PO8 9HP
Tel: 01705 591725

Thimble Society of London
Shop 134, Grays Antique Market,
58 Davies Street, London W1Y 2LP
Tel: 0171 493 0560

Tool and Trades History Society
60 Swanley Lane, Swanley, Kent BR8 7JG
Tel: 01322 662271

Torquay Pottery Collectors' Society
Torre Abbey, Avenue Road, Torquay,
Devon TQ2 5JX

Train Collectors' Society
Lock Cottage, Station Foot Path,
Kings Langley, Hertfordshire WD4 8DZ

Transport Ticket Society
4 Gladridge Close, Earley, Reading, Berks RG6 7DL
Tel: 01734 579373

Trix Twin Railway Collectors' Association
6 Ribble Avenue, Oadby, Leicester, LE2 4NZ

UK Perfume Bottles Collectors' Club
PO Box 1936, Bath, Avon BA1 3SD
Tel & Fax: 01225 837932

Unofficial McDonalds Collectors' Newsletter
c/o Ian Smith, 14 Elkstone Rd, Chesterfield,
Derbyshire S40 4UT

USSR Collectors' Club
Bob & June Moore, PO Box 6, Virginia Water,
Surrey GU25 4YU Tel: 01344 843091

Victorian Military Society
Moore-Morris, 3 Franks Road, Guildford,
Surrey GU2 6NT Tel: 01483 60931

Vintage Model Yacht Group
8 Sherard Road, London SE9 6EP
Tel: 0181 850 6805

Wade Collectors' Club
14 Windsor Road, Selston, Notts NG16 6JJ
Tel: 01773 860933/0374 209963

Wedgwood Society of Great Britain
89 Andrewes House, The Barbican,
London EC2Y 8AY

**Wireless Preservation Society & CEM
National Wireless Museum**
52 West Hill Road, Ryde, Isle of Wight PO33 1LN
Tel: 01983 567665

Writing Equipment Society
Cartledge Cottage, Cartledge Lane,
Holmesfield, Derbyshire S18 5SB

INDEX TO ADVERTISERS

INDEX

Italic page numbers denote colour pages, **bold** numbers refer to information and pointer boxes

Key to Front Cover Illustrations

A. A Copeland Spode platter, dated '1912',
   12½in (32cm) wide. **£40–48** *TAC*
B. A Westminster China teapot, 1930s,
   9in (23cm) wide. **£32–40** *PC*
C. An EPNS toast rack, by Hukin & Heath, c1885,
   7in (18cm) long. **£450–500** *NCA*
D. *Meet the Saint,* Super Detective Library Series,
   1953, 7 x 5¼in (18 x 13cm). **£80–100** *CBP*
E. A Royal Winton Hazel pattern jug, 1930s,
   4in (10cm) high. **£90–100** *BEV*
F. A Selcol Beatles' Big 6 guitar, 1960s,
   30½in (77.5cm) long. **£250–300** *NTM*
G. A Carlton Ware fawn, advertising Babycham,
   1950s, 3½in (9cm) high. **£15–20** *BEV*
H. Chuck Berry and Bo Diddley, 'Chuck & Bo',
   EP, 1963. **£8–10** *ED*
I. An Art Deco cold-painted spelter dancer, 1930,
   10¾in (27cm) high. **£180–200** *DAF*
J. A pair of platform shoes, 1970s. **£38–45** *TCF*
K. A pair of Chinese hand-embroidered pyjamas,
   1940s. **£80–95** *TCF*
L. A Paddington Bear, 1960s, 20in (51cm) high.
   £40–48 *CMF*
M. An Arnold tinplate clockwork motorcycle,
   c1930, 4¾in (12cm) high. **£225–285** *OTS*
N. A Venini handkerchief vase, 1950s,
   8½in (21.5cm) high. **£400–450** *BEV*
O. An advertising show card, 1930s,
   32¾in (83cm) high. **£65–75** *P(B)*

MYSTERY OBJECTS – Do You Know What These Items Are?

An aluminium whistling saucepan,
1950s, 7½in (19cm) high.
£15–18 *WAB*

A bone and horn
snuff ladle, 19thC,
6½in (16.5cm) long.
£32–38 *WAB*

A tinplate cover for a car
headlight, used during the
blackout in WWII, 1940s,
8in (20.5cm) diam.
£10–15 *WAB*

A silver-plated adjustable
sauce bottle holder, 1930s,
3in (7.5cm) square.
£20–22 *WAB*

A mahogany napkin press,
c1820, 16in (40.5cm) wide.
£300–350 *COT*

GRAYS
ANTIQVE MARKET

With the fast moving stock of more than 200 professional dealers Grays
has been described as *"the best antique market in the world"*. Grays occupies
two air conditioned and splendid Edwardian buildings sitting
back to back **BY BOND STREET TUBE**

SOUTH MOLTON LANE LONDON W1Y 2LP
Tel 0171 629 7034   Fax 0171 493 9344   Mon-Fri 10-6

Own a majestic piece of Britain

£54.95

£84.95

£44.95

£54.95

£84.95

£54.95

£44.95